IN JOY AND
IN SORROW

IN JOY AND
IN SORROW

Women, Family, and Marriage in the Victorian South, 1830–1900

EDITED BY

CAROL BLESER

New York   Oxford
OXFORD UNIVERSITY PRESS
1991

Oxford University Press

Oxford   New York   Toronto
Delhi   Bombay   Calcutta   Madras   Karachi
Petaling Jaya   Singapore   Hong Kong   Tokyo
Nairobi   Dar es Salaam   Cape Town
Melbourne   Auckland

and associated companies in
Berlin   Ibadan

Copyright © 1991 by Carol Bleser

Published by Oxford University Press, Inc.,
200 Madison Avenue, New York, New York 10016

Library of Congress Cataloging-in-Publication Data
In joy and in sorrow: women, family, and marriage in the Victorian
South, 1830–1900 / [edited by] Carol Bleser.
p.   cm.   Papers of the Fort Hill Conference on Southern Culture,
held at Clemson University in the spring of 1989.
Includes bibliographical references.
ISBN 0-19-506047-4
1. Women—Southern States—History—19th century—Congresses.
2. Afro-American women—Southern States—History—19th century—
Congresses.   3. Family—Southern States—History—19th century—
Congresses.   4. Marriage—Southern States—History—19th century—
Congresses.   I. Bleser, Carol K. Rothrock.   II. Fort Hill
Conference on Southern Culture (1989: Clemson University)
HQ1438.A315   1991
305.4'0975'09043—dc20   90-34251

2 4 6 8 9 7 5 3 1

Printed in the United States of America
on acid-free paper

In memory of
Clinton Calhoun Lemon (1910–1989)
with admiration and affection

Contents

Preface

CAROL BLESER

THE DUST JACKET of this book bears a portrait of Anna Maria Calhoun Clemson, the favorite child of John C. Calhoun, one of the most important statesmen of the nation and of the South. On November 13, 1838, in the parlor of her family's home, Fort Hill, the twenty-one year old Anna Maria Calhoun of South Carolina married Thomas Green Clemson, a successful mining engineer from Pennsylvania and ten years her senior. In 1844, Clemson was appointed chargé d'affaires to Belgium by the secretary of state, his father-in-law. Anna Maria's portrait was painted in Brussels in 1848 by the Dutch artist Jacob Joseph Eeckhart when she was thirty-one years old. In Eeckart's painting, with her dark eyes, black hair, and pale skin, she looks very much the part of a fragile Victorian beauty—soft, pampered, and richly attired. As the private records clearly reveal, Anna Maria was much more than a sweet-faced young woman whose portrait hangs on the parlor wall at Fort Hill.

Anna Maria inherited more of John C. Calhoun's great intellectual talents than did any of his other children. As a teenager, she insisted on joining her father in Washington in order to make herself useful to him in his work. As a young wife in Belgium, she kept up a lively correspondence with her father, frequently detailing her spirited defense of slavery against the criticisms of the Belgians. However, like other women of her class, her time, and her place, Anna Maria wrestled most of her life not with problems of state but with her responsibilities and duties as a wife and mother.

On August 13, 1839, exactly nine months to the day after her wedding, she gave birth to a baby daughter. Her anxious father wrote that Anna Maria fell dangerously ill and recovered her strength only slowly. However, within three weeks her first-born child was dead, not an uncommon fate in that age of high infant mortality. By the time Anna Maria sat for her portrait, she had two living children, a son born in 1841 and named John Calhoun, for his illustrious maternal grandfather, and a daughter born in 1842 and named Floride, for her maternal grandmother. Three children had been born in four years. After several miscarriages, she delivered a fourth child in 1855, Cornelia, named for her handicapped sister Martha Cornelia. This daughter lived barely three years. A loving daughter, Anna Maria was heartsick to be in Brussels when her father's health deteriorated dramatically in 1849, and she grieved that she was not with him in Washington at the time of his death during the debates over the Compromise of 1850.

Life with Clemson must not have been easy. Moody and fretful, Clemson suffered periodically from depression, which led to stress, tension, and frequent family quarrels. Their marriage, however, survived not only the personal griefs, disappointments, and disputes but also the disasters and deprivations of the Civil War and its aftermath. It ended only after thirty-six years in 1875 with Anna Maria's death at Fort Hill at the age of sixty-eight. Clemson inherited Fort Hill and lived on there, a lonely old man (are there not any merry old men?) until his death in 1888 at the age of eighty, his wife and all his children having predeceased him.[1]

Fort Hill was the name of both the fourteen-hundred-acre plantation in the South Carolina upcountry and of the house which stood on it. Calhoun had come into possession of the plantation through his marriage to his second cousin, Floride Colhoun. Engaged in politics for almost all of his adult life (as a congressman, secretary of war, vice president of the United States, secretary of state, and several times as a United States senator), Calhoun needed the income from Fort Hill plantation to support his large family. From the time he became vice president of the United States in 1825, Calhoun, his wife Floride, and their family of seven children made Fort Hill their home. Compared to the elegant plantation homes of the low country near Charleston, the house itself is simple in style. Nevertheless, in upcountry South Carolina, Fort Hill, with its wide porches on two sides and its Greek-revival-style Doric pillars, must have impressed the many small farmers and townspeople who were Calhoun's neighbors. Family members continued to live in the house until Thomas Green Clemson's death.

In compliance with his wife's wishes, Clemson, on his death in 1888, gave to the state of South Carolina his father-in-law's former plantation for the founding of a "high seminary of learning," which grew to become Clemson University. The university now occupies the former Fort Hill plantation, with Fort Hill house presiding over the center of the campus (surely the most prominent historical family home to be found on a university campus anywhere in the United States). The triple coincidence of the university's centennial celebration, the one hundred and fiftieth anniversary of the wedding of Anna Maria Calhoun to Thomas Green Clemson, and the reawakening of an appreciation for the significance and importance of Fort Hill led to the concept of an event that would use Fort Hill as both a striking centerpiece and a thematic inspiration. Therefore, to commemorate the one hundredth anniversary of the university and the one hundred and fiftieth anniversary of the marriage of Anna Maria Calhoun to Thomas Green Clemson, Clemson University hosted a conference from April 9 to April 12, 1989, on "Women, Family, and Marriage in the Victorian South." A dazzling array of writers and scholars from across the country came to Clemson and presented original essays on Southern womanhood, family, and marriage over the whole spectrum of society—rich and poor, black and white, slave and free. The result of this landmark conference is this book, *In Joy and in Sorrow: Women, Family, and Marriage in the Victorian South, 1830–1900.*

The title, *In Joy and in Sorrow,* is taken from the matrimonial vows and reflects the lives of the people who inhabit this book—who intimately knew joy but who also were touched by sorrow. These essays give us a treasury of fascinating insights into those generations of Southern Victorians who had been born in the heyday of the Cotton Kingdom of the antebellum South or who had lived through the chaos of the Civil War and Reconstruction to the end of the century. This study looks at the private lives of individuals from the highest reaches of plantation society to the humblest of common folk, encompassing white and black, slave and free. It inquires into intimate family relationships and marriages, conventional and unconventional. It discusses frankly the subjects of incest, miscegenation, and insanity.

In Joy and in Sorrow is unified chronologically and thematically so that it does not read like a collection of separate articles written by a diverse group of scholars. This investigation of women, family, and marriage in the Victorian South has been edited into a continuous narrative, broken only by the last sentence of one chapter yielding unobtrusively to the first sentence of the next. The book opens with the study of a family in the last quarter of the eighteenth century, the Izard family of South Carolina, who were, according to the author, exemplars of the foundation upon which the edifice of elite Southern Victorian society was erected. Chronologically, the book advances through the nineteenth century observing the lives of planter elite women, their patriarchal husbands, their children, and the worlds of slaves, of free blacks, and of Confederate women. Chapters are included on the impact of the Civil War on a Southern marriage, on the lives of postwar sharecropper farm families, and on a gifted trio of Southern women writers. This last chapter provides insights into their creativity and into their critique of the Southern way of life. In one chapter, cookbooks, too, are proven important for what they can tell us about home life, housekeeping, and entertaining without slaves in the post-Civil War South. The book concludes with essays on a long-suffering

Southern wife and on the relationship of a Victorian father with his devoted son. Only two essays were added to the twelve original pieces of
work that were prepared for this volume—their presence, I thought,
added balance to the book and rounded out the story.

The special significance of *In Joy and in Sorrow* is that the contributors to
this volume have independently all dwelt upon the same theme. In my
view, the central underlying unifying theme of this outpouring of work by
the leading specialists in the field is not only that slavery crippled the lives
of slaves, free blacks, and the poorer whites before the Civil War, but also
that the institution of slavery damaged the lives of the husbands, wives, and
children of the Old South's planter elite, supposedly the principal beneficiaries of the peculiar institution. Moreover, what these essays convey emphatically is that the legacy of slavery continued to play havoc with the
institution of marriage and family life in the South long after the Civil War
had been fought and slavery had ended, keeping that region and its people
psychically isolated and socially regressive until well into the twentieth
century. Political and economic historians have always blamed the South's
lack of progress on its losing the war or on Reconstruction and its aftermath, but no one has seriously probed—as does this book—into the legacy
of slavery as the poison affecting Southern family life, doing damage to the
institution of marriage and wrecking the private lives of men and women,
especially the men, for generations. One writer stated that the white men
who people this book "are not a very admirable lot," and her only exception is a Northerner by birth. This book boldly explains why and helps us to
understand the great tragedy of the South, Old and New. This theme of the
impact of the legacy of slavery on the family, on marriage, and especially
on private individuals is of extreme importance, and hopefully, we will
never look at the South in the same way again.

In Joy and in Sorrow benefits from an impressive array of well-known
authors and a few talented newcomers (in order of their appearance):
Anne Firor Scott, C. Vann Woodward, Wylma Wates, Elizabeth Fox-
Genovese, Peter Bardaglio, Catherine Clinton, Eugene Genovese, James
Roark, Michael Johnson, Brenda Stevenson, a second appearance by Eu-
gene Genovese, in an after-dinner talk, Carol Bleser, Frederick Heath,
Alan Grubb, Bertram Wyatt-Brown, Jacqueline Jones, Virginia Burr, Sar-
ah Wiggins, and Drew Faust.

My greatest debt—an immense one—is to Dr. Robert C. Edwards, president emeritus of Clemson University who was the "angel" for the project
and without whose support neither the conference nor the book would
have become a reality.

It is my pleasure also to thank the many friends who contributed to the success of the Fort Hill Conference at Clemson University by appearing on the program, including Joseph Arbena, Jane Walker Herndon, Charles Joyner, Clemson University President Max Lennon, John Niven, Theodore Rosengarten, John Sproat, and Steven Stowe.

Many other persons at Clemson University gave of their time and expertise to make our work on the conference easier: Reba Brown, Deborah Dunning, Pamela De Fratus, Ina Durham, Debra Galloway, Charlotte Holmes, Elaine Holmes, N. Jane Hurt, Margaret Pridgen, Ann Russell, Linda Singleton, Rosemary Thomas, Flora Walker, and Sandra Woodward.

I am deeply grateful also for the advice and encouragement of the Fort Hill Committee—Harry Durham, Associate Vice President for Institutional Advancement, Ruth Lennon (wife of Max Lennon, president of Clemson University), and Alan Schaffer. Professor Schaffer, my colleague in the History Department, not only served on the Fort Hill Committee but also shared with me an all-consuming interest in the success of the event. My debt to him is extraordinarily large.

I wish to express great appreciation to Dr. Gary Ransdell, Vice President for Institutional Advancement at Clemson University, for his unwavering support and his generous expenditure of time and resources from start to finish in what became a very special collaboration.

It is a pleasure to acknowledge the kind asssistance of historian Jerome V. Reel, Jr., Vice Provost of Undergraduate Studies and chairman of the Clemson University Centennial Committee, who along with Provost W. David Maxwell endorsed and assisted in bringing both the centennial event and this book to fruition.

I wish to extend a personal note of thanks to two special people—Robert T. Barrett and Doreen Heimlich who rendered important assistance from the beginning of the planning of the conference to the final shaping of the manuscript for publication. Without their help, this book could not have appeared so expeditiously.

To Sheldon Meyer, my editor at Oxford University Press, I owe a great and long-lasting debt of gratitude. I consider myself privileged to work with him, and I thank him especially for assigning to me as my copy editor Scott Lenz, who imparted to the book his sharp editorial wisdom and a sense of professionalism rarely excelled. I am most grateful also to Karen Wolny, assistant editor, and Laura Brown, marketing director, for their continuing interest and expert help.

I am especially grateful to Robert A. Waller, dean of the College of Liberal Arts, for freeing up my time in the fall term 1989 to complete this book, and to David M. Nicholas, Jr., chairman of the Department of History, for his understanding during this time of pressure and deadlines.

I also wish to extend a personal note of thanks to Kathryn Lemon and her three children—Kaye, Mary, and Clinton. But finally, this book belongs to the late Clinton Calhoun Lemon. Neither the dedication of this book nor this brief acknowledgment adequately expresses the depth of our sorrow, or how much he shall be missed.

In conclusion, and on a more personal note, the dedication of my book, *Secret and Sacred,* published in 1988, read, "For Elizabeth and Gerald and those who come after." Caroline Johnson, the first "to come after," arrived on April 2, 1990, in the same week we were applying the finishing touches to *In Joy and in Sorrow.* Caroline begins a new generation of family relationships and brings us an abundance of joy as well. To her and the family go my love and appreciation.

Clemson, SC   C.B.
April 1990

Foreword

ANNE FIROR SCOTT

THIS RECORD of the lively Fort Hill Conference held at Clemson University on Southern womanhood, family, and marriage over the whole spectrum of society, rich and poor, black and white, provides the reader with plenty of food for thought. Such provender is always welcome in any field, old or new. As a historian of Southern women, I am especially interested in this volume, *In Joy and in Sorrow: Women, Family, and Marriage in the Victorian South, 1830–1900*, for its coverage of women—the study of whom is just now coming out of a long struggle for legitimacy and looking for new worlds to conquer.

In the writing of Southern history, there have been many ironies. How was it, for example, that a culture which claimed to admire and sometimes almost to revere women was for so long described by historians as if it contained only one sex? How was it that when the history of Southerners of African descent came, belatedly, to be written, it, too, encompassed principally men, despite the folk wisdom that black women had sustained the African-American family in its times of deepest trouble?

An observer in the 1930s who noticed these strange absences might have thought the first was about to be repaired when Julia Cherry Spruill published her magisterial study of Southern colonial women, based on virtually every extant document and foreshadowing some of the methods which would in time come to characterize the "new" social history.[1] But praise for Spruill came principally from Harvard University, where Arthur M. Schlesinger, Sr., had long been calling for more attention to women and to social history, and twenty-seven years after Spruill's book came out "women" merited two sentences and one footnote in the four-hundred-page authoritative historiographical volume, *Writing Southern History*.[2]

It was 1962 before an article appeared which presaged a steady stream of scholarship on Southern women—white, black, and native American.[3] By 1987, a fifty-page historiographical article could barely encompass a discussion of the work of the preceding twenty-five years.[4] For all the merit this scholarship has exhibited, however, it has not yet been much integrated into a vast body of Southern history in general, as a quick perusal of the other historiographical essays in *Interpreting Southern History* (1987) demonstrates. It is encouraging, therefore, to read these essays in which women are seen in the context of the family, of the law, of slavery, of literature. (There have, in the past, been studies, odd as it may seem, which appeared to define "family" as a man and his sons.) We may even begin to hope with the publication of this volume that the time is not far off when it will be impossible for anyone to write about almost any aspect of Southern history without attention to gender.

As for the second irony—the strange omission of women from African-American history—these essays (and a goodly number published elsewhere in the recent past) mark a decisive change. Black women may still be shadowy figures, but they are becoming less so all the time.[5]

The Fort Hill Conference marked a welcome change in other ways. "Southern women" historically considered have most often been white, most often members of the elite. Here we see the category "woman" broadened to include people from many segments of Southern society, including those long overlooked ones in the free black community. The women in these pages range from members of unassailably aristocratic eighteenth-century Charleston families to the anonymous black and white sharecroppers' wives of Jacqueline Jones's study. They range in time from the late colonial era to the twentieth century. Even when women appear in the wings rather than on center stage, they challenge us to think about them.

One of the potential virtues of conference papers is that studies prepared independently may turn out to throw light on one another, as indeed these essays do. Several of the essays of *In Joy and in Sorrow* provide data with which to test Elizabeth Fox-Genovese's hypothesis, presented here in her study of Sarah Gayle (and her recent book), that there is an "essentially Southern" female identity rooted in the family and that the nature of Southern society itself prevented women from developing an individual self-image. Reading Fox-Genovese's essay in conjunction with those about Virginia Clay by Carol Bleser and Frederick Heath, Gertrude Thomas by Virginia Burr, and Amelia Gayle Gorgas by Sarah Wiggins, one can ask whether each of them, Southern ladies all, "fashioned a mature identity that . . . [was] essentially Southern,"—and distinct from the prevailing identity of bourgeois women elsewhere? Virginia Clay and Gertrude Thomas make an interesting comparison since they shared so many characteristics: well-to-do families of origin, youthful marriages, economic disaster as a result of the war, husbands who fail them—even down to their late-life attachment to the suffrage cause. In cases so similar, if anywhere, we should be able to discern what is common to Southern women of their class and generation. Yet they discompose us by behaving so differently when their husbands turn out to be anything but the strong patriarchs of legend. And when we look for reasons for this difference, we notice that Virginia Tunstall (Clay) had been orphaned, while Gertrude Clanton was the child of a wise and very powerful father; Virginia Tunstall Clay had no children, Gertrude Clanton Thomas had more than she knew what to do with. Do these differences, attributable only to the contingencies of life, explain the fact that Clay, widowed, could think at first of no better way to cope than to marry a well-to-do older man, while Thomas, worse than widowed, set about earning the money necessary to keep her family afloat? And could we not find Northern bourgeois women who would match each of these two in her way of dealing with such challenges? Fox-Genovese's argument that women had no other source of identity than the family, that they did not (as she thinks Northern women were beginning to do) identify themselves as individuals, fits Gertrude Thomas: her family of origin and the family she created with her husband and children were vital to her sense of herself. Virginia Clay, however, is quite another matter. A headstrong, self-willed individual, she appears detached from any family—she had lost her family of origin, showed no special ties to the relatives who took her in, disliked her in-laws, and had no children. Like her friend Mary Chesnut, she exhibited a high level of self-absorption, perhaps in both cases exacerbated by childlessness in a society which expected every woman to do her duty in the child-bearing and child-raising line. Thomas particularly and Clay to some extent emerge as individuals in their work for woman suffrage. We might speculate that, while many Southern women (and many Northern ones) found their entire identity in the family, the difference between those who did and those who had begun to think of themselves as individuals was more a matter of life experience than of the region or the social relations of slavery.[6] Amelia Gayle Gorgas appears so indirectly (and so tantalizingly) in Wiggins's study of the Victorian patriarch that the reader can only speculate that if the Gorgas journal and papers were examined with her life as the focus, we would learn still more about the varieties of female identity in the generation that lived through the Civil War. In any event, to truly test the Fox-Genovese view, to find out whether the social relations of slavery made Southern women different, we would need to study identity formation in some matched pairs of Northern bourgeois women and comparable Southern women.

Before we leave Virginia Clay entirely, there is another point to be made. By Bleser and Heath's account, she was an unusually able, intelligent, charming human being, obviously a person of great potential. Socialization as a nineteenth-century lady made Virginia Clay an irresponsible, spendthrift butterfly—of no use to anyone except herself and from time to time (but not always) her husband. The waste of such talent from such causes could be multiplied a thousand times in that generation of women, Northern as well as Southern. In this matter, class was far more determining than region.

Regarding the essays by Michael Johnson and James Roark, Brenda Stevenson, and Jacqueline Jones, we find ourselves in quite a different world from that of the Thomases, Clays, Gayles, and their like. Here is the world of slaves, free blacks, and postwar poor farm families, black and white. Although Johnson and Roark take issue with Suzanne Lebsock's argument (in *The Free Women of Petersburg*) about the nature of free black women's experience, theirs is an interesting thesis: that free black men adopted an extreme patriarchal posture as a means of protecting their families from the dangers which beset all free blacks in the South. Occam's razor might suggest a simpler explanation: men will be patriarchs when they can and when women have no way to counter them. Lebsock's analysis showed that when the sex ratio left free black women on their own, they managed well within the constraints which white Petersburg placed on all free blacks. Whether the women viewed this coping behavior as a neces-sary evil or a positive good, we shall never know, but it is unlikely that they saw it as a positive good, given the evidence Evelyn Brooks has recently accumulated about the postwar struggles between women and men in the black Baptist church—they *sought* patriarchal oversight.[7]

Brenda Stevenson brings a new perspective to the long-recognized issue of slave family separation as she examines the phenomenon from the standpoint of slave women. Her notion that masters consciously encouraged the development of a matrifocal family, if true, would add one more paradox to a history that is full of paradoxes; for the last thing white slaveholders would have sought for themselves was a matrifocal family! She offers convincing evidence for a pattern of encouraged or even forced reproduction (an argument which is central also to Catherine Clinton's essay), and certainly the rapid increase in the black population does nothing to undermine this view. It may be worth noting that white Southerners also reproduced at rates higher than white women in the rest of the United States. Is it possible that white women, too, were positively encouraged to reproduce?[8]

Jacqueline Jones's essay focuses on the years after emancipation when so many Southerners, black and white, became tenant farmers of one kind or another. These rural poor people developed a family system of labor not much different, except for its lack of success, from that of pre-industrial farmers everywhere. Though her focus is not primarily on women but rather on the desperate struggles of families to make a living and a life within the economic and class constraints of the sharecropping system, she offers new and intriguing evidence that the women in these families were energetic in seeking ways to earn cash money to eke out an existence based on advances which could so rarely be paid up. Thus, she illuminates the life experience of that large group of Southern women who fell completely outside the range of the images and myths. Along with their counterparts who left farms to work in textile mills, Jones's picture of sharecroppers' wives reminds me of a poem I once recited in my Depression-Georgia youth. The subject was mountain women, but the substance would stand for all these women:

> Among the sullen peaks she stood at bay
> And paid life's hard account from her small store.
> Knowing the code of mountain wives she bore
> The burden of her days without a sigh;
> And sharp against the winter sky,
> I saw her drive her steers afield each day.
>
> Hers was the hand that sunk the furrows deep
> Across the rocky, grudging southern slope.
> At first, youth left her face, and later, hope. . . . [9]

Theirs is a world we need to understand since from it came so many of the people, now middle-aged or older, who are shaping the newest New South.

As those who heard these Fort Hill Conference papers and the discussion they engendered know and as careful readers will soon discover, almost every essay of *In Joy and in Sorrow*, no matter what its central focus, raises new questions about the history of Southern women. The measure of any conference is what comes next. Chances are that from this one a great deal will follow.

Introduction

C. VANN WOODWARD

THE FAMILY IS regarded in this work, *In Joy and in Sorrow: Women, Family, and Marriage in the Victorian South, 1830–1900*, not as a subject peripheral to main historical concerns but as one that belongs in the mainstream. As one of the contributors puts it, family is "a central metaphor for southern society as a whole." Family in this sense is an inclusive rather than an exclusive institution, one extending beyond the customary boundaries to embrace more than blood kin, common color, or those of equal status. It is treated in the following chapters not as an abstraction described in statistical and theoretical terms but rather in very concrete terms—personal examples, real people in all their diversity and eccentricity, rather than in categories, averages, mean, or median.

Familial relations of the intimate sort—between husband and wife, parents and children, and relations with in-laws, older generations, dependents, siblings, remote relations, permanent guests, house servants, slaves—are subjects historians have traditionally left to novelists, however much they may linger over love letters and revelation of scandal while scanning family papers for "important" data. They have finally had the sense to recognize the historical value of family records and the family as an institution subject to legitimate historical investigation and scholarly treatment.

The term "Victorian" in the general title, is to be understood as more than a chronological designation, or one taken to suggest conventional notions of propriety, authority, and prim conduct. "Victorian" South differed from Victorian England and Victorian New England. All doubtless had their seamier side, but rarely has that side, including incest, miscegenation, and insanity, been more frankly confronted than in these studies, aptly titled, *In Joy and in Sorrow*. And in few other cultures have appeared such varieties of women, family, and marriage—rich and poor, black and white, slave and free, plantation and urban. The designated limits of the period have been sensibly stretched at both ends to include background at the beginning and modern instances of various subjects.

For what Wylma Wates calls "the foundation upon which the edifice of Victorian society was erected" in the South, she takes us back to the Izard family in the eighteenth century and their life back and forth from England to South Carolina. This English-educated tribe of elite colonials was connected with another of the same sort, the Manigaults, when, in 1785, Margaret Izard married Gabriel Manigault, one of the richest men in America. Their families, in turn, formed marital attachments that made the Carolina aristocracy very much a family affair. When a widower took a bride who seemed unworthy of him, his sister philosophically wrote their mother comparing the union to a column of bricks in a marble edifice that had to be polished until it resembled the "fabric to which it is joined." That generation raised the children who, with their children, later became the Victorian elite of the South.

Unplanned and, I am sure, quite unanticipated, a common thread of tension also runs through many of these essays. This theme of tension takes several forms—tension between family loyalties, between ideal and reality, between conflicting family roles, and between racial and class pursuit of common family ideals. It is the main point of the essay on Sarah Gayle of Alabama by Elizabeth Fox-Genovese that "she belonged to a world that encouraged women to find their primary identities in the roles and relations of families." But women left one family to form another. Like many southern wives of her time, Sarah Gayle married as a mere girl and "remained psychologically bound to her family of origin and to her life as a cherished daughter." Tensions lingered between two sources of authority and two bonds of loyalty, mother and husband.

It is the contention of Eugene Genovese that "a slaveholder meant something special by 'family.' " As commonly used by this class "family" meant "household," and household included slaves. The often-used expression, "our family, white and black," usually dismissed as hypocritical apologetics, according to Genovese, "must be taken with deadly seriousness by those who would understand the political and social thought of the slaveholders." All members of the household, white and black, lived, of course, under the authority of a patriarchal master. It was assumed to be a benevolent despotism, but it was neither indiscriminate in its despotism nor in its benevolence. "After all," as Genovese says, "one does not readily put one's wife or children up for sale, no matter how financially embarrassed." Whatever reality was embodied in the "household" concept of family, the slave members must have been keenly aware of contradictions and tensions between their legal status and their family status.

The hierarchical nature of the household and the patriarchal authority of its head opened the way to the most outrageous contradiction of all. Patriarchal authority could be exploited criminally to give men sexual access to women and children in their family. Since the integrity of the family was the foundation of the southern social order and patriarchy was the ideal form of the family, this was an institution facing serious inner conflict. "The tension between the condemnation of incest and the commitment to patriarchy" is addressed by Peter Bardaglio, particularly in the way incest cases were handled by the judiciary of the southern courts. The courts reflected the tension between society's outrage against incest and the continued commitment to the patriarchal ideal by judicial ambivalence in such cases. While they roundly denounced incest as a crime against nature, courts were slow in actually prosecuting men for the crime. They shied away from criminal punishment when evidence of force and physical resistance was not clearly forthcoming, displayed basic mistrust in the victim's testimony, and placed a heavy burden of proof upon the plaintiff. The legal fiction of being an accomplice to incest permitted judges to condemn the crime while limiting convictions to the few undeniably guilty of deeds calling into question the legitimacy of patriarchal authority. Thus, they had it both ways—defenders of family integrity as well as patriarchal ideal.

The tensions that tore at the free Negro slaveholder are ably treated by James Roark and Michael Johnson, whose previous work on black slaveholders of South Carolina provides them rich background and whose close work in manuscript census returns breaks new ground. Among the quarter of a million southern free blacks in 1860, they find some twelve thousand slave owners with holdings near the average held by whites, a few with large holdings and many with small numbers. The black slaves of free blacks have usually been regarded by historians as members of their owner's family, bought and held for their protection. This study, however, finds that "few held family members in bondage" and that black owners bought and held slaves for much the same reasons that moved white owners. Moreover, they knew that their own freedom was "eggshell thin" and were fully aware of the tensions set up in white racial logic by the confusion of race and role, not only by blacks who were free but also by blacks who owned slaves. They were likely for these reasons to be all the more "sound" on the legitimacy of slavery. They saw their fate and their interest as quite distinct from that of their slaves and risked no reckless views or deeds. Their marriages took on an "exaggerated form of patriarchy" that distinguished them the more sharply from slave marriages, in which male authority was in short supply.

The shame, frustration, and distress of slave marriages and families are poignantly described by Brenda Stevenson. Indoctrinated with the marital and family ideals of their masters, slaves experienced constant "resentment, frustration and anger" over their inability to attain anything approximating these standards. Forced marriages, broken families, absent fathers, and orphaned children were some of the reasons for this frustration. Slave breeding is said to be "well documented," but it is admitted that the white women "bore more children than blacks." White-male sexual aggression toward slave women, married and unmarried, "created a great source of tension," perhaps the greatest of all these tensions so far as marriage and family integrity were concerned. Some offspring of such interracial unions professed shame for their white heritage; yet others boasted of it and considered themselves better than their black kin and posed as an elite in their families and communities. Some even succeeded in gaining status among blacks who resented the air of superiority. The black family emerged in the postbellum South threatened by forms of oppression "as well as internal tensions inherited from the previous era."

Womenfolk may appear rather more conspicuous in these accounts than their status in an oppressively patriarchal family system traditionally warrants. Professor Eugene Genovese, in a second appearance in this volume, comes forward with a justification for this seemingly disproportionate emphasis on the distaff side. In a revisionist argument, he attacks such familiar stereotypes as the simpering belle, the bepedestaled and brainless beauty, and the meek, obedient, and obliging spouse. As he sees the place women really occupied in the South's Victorian family, society, and politics, there can be no justification for the conventional equation that might be expressed as follows:

Slave : Master :: Wife : Husband

Not according to the record, says Genovese. There exists a "wholly untold story," he says, "of women who acted as trusted advisers and confidants to politicians, usually, but not always, their own husbands." He finds women shrewd, informed, and sophisticated in their political counsel. They could be moderate in a nurturing and feminine way, but they also proved stern and demanding champions of southern honor, who often stiffened the backbone of their menfolk. And they sometimes turned out to be more unyielding than men in their demand for an all-out struggle for the South's independence.

In their treatment of the married life of Clement and Virginia Clay of Alabama, Carol Bleser and Frederick Heath skillfully capture the tension between this husband and wife and picture Virginia as the stronger and sturdier of the two, especially after the Civil War when Clement became more and more ineffective. A woman of striking beauty, Virginia began her career as a belle surrounded by admirers at age fourteen and proved loath to give up the role after marriage, though she remained devoted to her husband. The authors compare her with her contemporary and friend, Mary Boykin Chesnut. Both remained childless, felt their deprivation keenly, and compensated by extending their belle role and becoming men dazzlers and manipulators. Chesnut conforms more to Genovese's image of female politician and manipulator, but Virginia Clay lived much longer—until she was ninety in fact—and served effectively during her widowhood as a leader of the women's suffrage movement.

An unusual and neglected subject is treated by exploiting as a source a branch of literature written almost exclusively by women, almost exclusively for them, and probably their most-bought and constantly used literature—cookbooks—by Alan Grubb. Plantation kitchens, like smokehouses and pantries, were often outbuildings unattached to the big house. By exploiting the cookbook, Grubb brings kitchen into home, and with it much transgustatory lore about husband-pleasing, child-parenting, and servant-handling. Beyond the kitchen, cookbooks turn out to be valuable sources about other household departments such as dining room, nursery, living room, and bedroom.

A fascinating study now in progress of a southern family is Bertram Wyatt-Brown's work on the American Percys from the eighteenth century to the present. His essay for this volume is not about family as institution but about the combination of creativity and depression that haunted the Percy family for more than two centuries. Here, the focus is upon three female members, all gifted writers in the nineteenth century—two sisters born Catherine Ann and Eleanor Percy Ware; and their niece, Sarah Ann Dorsey. Among them, they produced fifteen novels and several volumes of verse. The first American Percy to arrive on these shores was twice a bigamist, and he ended a suicide. Numerous suicides occurred among his descendants. The two sisters, Catherine and Eleanor, had their share of tragedy, what with a demented mother confined since their infancy and an intellectual and very wealthy father who left their care to others. Their literary subjects were tragic and romantic, their style gothic. They shared many tastes of their contemporary Edgar Allen Poe. Some of their writings were an implied critique of male dominance, some of them critical of slavery and plantation life, but "above all the Percy sisters," we learn, "believed in the code of honor." Their niece, Sarah Ann Dorsey, befriended Jefferson Davis in the postwar years and provided a house for him while he was writing *The Rise and Fall of the Confederate Government*.

As oppressive and poverty-ridden as the postwar system proved to be, it did provide gains in autonomy and integrity for the black family. As Jacqueline Jones points out, under the sharecropper system, which replaced gang labor, the black family, as well as the poor white family, became the workforce and labor unit—father, mother, and children. The new organization of labor necessitated a new measure of self-discipline, male status, parental authority, and family bonds of mutual interest, if nothing else. Subject to harassment and exclusion by caste and segregation, and often robbed of earnings by merchant and landlord, black sharecroppers were placed on the bottom rung of the economic ladder. Their vulnerability made them more easily manipulated and exploited, and for that reason, planters tended to prefer them to whites. While white croppers shared some of the evils of the cropper system, they had certain advantages from their caste status as whites. They moved more often and were more likely than blacks to be tenants rather than croppers. Both blacks and whites, however, were subject to close supervision by white landlords, and neither found the cropper's lot a happy one.

Two intrepid Victorians of the South, one a heroine and one a hero, are subjects of the last two contributions to *In Joy and in Sorrow*. A woman of indomitable fortitude, Gertrude Thomas of Georgia thoroughly earned the admiration that Virginia Burr's account of her inspires. Born in wealth and reared in a twenty-four-room mansion which, along with five plantations, belonged to her father, she started as "a true daughter of patriarchy and disciple of 'woman's sphere.' " She married Jefferson Thomas, bore him ten children, and saw him through the war, only to discover that in addition to losses suffered in the war, he had deceived her in managing her estate and left them in penniless poverty. He wound up an alcoholic who made a career of being a Confederate veteran and the oldest living Princeton graduate in Georgia. Their house burned to the ground, leaving them nothing but Gertrude's enormous journal, the main source for this study. Teaching for thirty-five dollars a month and peddling second-hand clothes in "years of miserable hand to mouth poverty," she raised and educated the children, one of whom finished medical school. She then realized some of her literary ambitions by publishing hundreds of articles and in 1899 entered politics as president of the Georgia Woman Suffrage Association.

In conclusion, in this study of the Victorian patriarchy, one patriarch receives a respectful salute in Sarah Wiggins's moving account of Josiah Gorgas. He earned his fame and his place in history as Confederate chief of ordnance, whose miracles of production and supply kept the South's struggle for independence going. It is not, however, as a military man but as a family man and father that he is treated here. Born in Pennsylvania, he identified completely with the South after he married Amelia Gayle of Alabama, daughter of Sarah Gayle, the subject of Fox-Genovese's essay in this volume. Between 1854 and 1864, Amelia and Josiah had six children, on whom their father lavished deep and nurturing affection. His ambition focused mainly on his oldest son Willie, whose backwardness in his studies and hopes for a military career were sources of despair and anguish for the father. In the postwar period, poverty and failure after years of wealth and success plunged Josiah into "despondency that was near suicidal," and his depression was deepened by the feeling that son Willie was "hopeless" and "terribly, shamefully backward." He nevertheless persisted in his affection and his emotional support for the struggling son until his death in 1883. Had he lived twenty years more, he would have seen the son's medical triumphs in Cuba and Panama make William Crawford Gorgas "even more famous than the father."

The papers comprising this volume, *In Joy and in Sorrow*, had their origin in the Fort Hill Conference on Southern Culture, organized by Carol Bleser and held at Clemson University in the Spring of 1989. The university grounds and house, Fort Hill, located on the broad acres of John C. Calhoun's plantation were bequeathed by his son-in-law and heir in 1888 to the state of South Carolina for the founding of a "high seminary of learning." Clemson University in celebrating its centennial year (1988–1989), wisely chose to honor its history by generously supporting its past. This conference, in part, celebrated the marriage of the daughter of John C. Calhoun, Anna Maria Calhoun, to Thomas Green Clemson in 1838. That marriage led to the founding of Clemson University and, in turn, led to the decision by the conference director that the subject be "Women, Family, and Marriage in the Victorian South." Leading scholars from across the country were invited to attend the conference and present their work. Most of the papers were read and discussed around the corner from Fort Hill, the simple but gracious plantation house that Calhoun made his home. Members of the conference were in and out of Fort Hill, which has been restored and furnished with many of the original Calhoun pieces that would have made its famous owner feel at home. A life-size oil painting of his wife Floride hangs in the dining room near the sideboard that is purported to be the gift of Henry Clay. The intellectual rigor of those present was brought forth in this historical setting and when combined with the old-fashioned hospitality of their hosts resulted in this significant contribution to southern social history.

More than one historian must have been inspired to wonder what the restless spirit of Calhoun would have made of current goings on. For one thing, the current issue of the student newspaper of the university carried on the front page a photograph of the recently chosen Miss Clemson. She was black. Perhaps quite as puzzling for the Sage of Fort Hill would have been the cool, dispassionate, and detached way in which these late twentieth-century scholars who visited his home could discuss matters that in his time were discussed with anything but coolness and detachment. The very mention of them then could bring men to their feet, with passion surging through their rhetoric and mayhem in their hearts. He had heard that passion on both sides and feared its consequences. He must have wondered whether any evocation or rehearsal of those issues could be complete or realistic without the component of passion that he remembered always accompanied them.

Perhaps it was some such reflection or felt need that prompted Catherine Clinton to explore the sexual exploitation of women under slavery and set forth her findings in the manner she did in her paper entitled "Southern Dishonor." If for these reasons she felt impelled to depart from the prevailing detachment of her colleagues at times, she did enrich their common theme of tension in pointing out the contradiction between the antebellum South's horror of racial mixing, amalgamation, and miscegenation and its occasional tolerance of owners begetting children on the women they owned. It was not this contribution, however, but the authenticity with which it was phrased in the very idiom, rhetoric, and style of his own period that would have riveted John C. Calhoun's attention. "These 'Christian slaveholders,' " we are told by Clinton—black, female, and northern slaveholders presumably excepted—were "self-serving, profit-mongering, sin-ridden monsters." The "monster" part of the characterization is repeated and supported by a quotation in comparable idiom from an abolitionist of the 1850s.

Any reader will have a greater understanding of the South of the past from *In Joy and in Sorrow: Women, Family, and Marriage in the Victorian South, 1830–1900*. It is not merely that the authors of these papers are the leading specialists in the field and have mined rich, primary, and often untouched sources, nor that they display unusual mastery of their craft, but also that they are often asking new questions and reporting their findings with engaging skill. Along with other recent signs, these essays portend another rebirth of scholarship and interest in the history of the South.

IN JOY AND
IN SORROW

1

Precursor to the Victorian Age: The Concept of Marriage and Family as Revealed in the Correspondence of the Izard Family of South Carolina

WYLMA WATES

"WRITING IS a delightful invention," Margaret Izard Manigault wrote in 1811, " . . . and the security which a little wafer affords to an intercourse of the most secret kind is a striking instance of the advantage of civilization. Is it not admirable that at the distance of thousands of miles we should be able to disclose with safety secrets of the utmost importance?"[1]

Margaret and the other members of the Izard family seemed to have a need to write to each other often and at regular intervals; they seemed to take pleasure in these personal exchanges. Letters were saved and re-read with enjoyment and passed on to the younger generation to be read for instruction and entertainment. Many of the family letters were brought together at one time by Margaret Izard Manigault's son Charles Izard Manigault and his sons.[2]

Margaret was the eldest child of Ralph and Alice DeLancey Izard of South Carolina. Her use of this "delightful invention" along with the rest of the family's correspondence with her and with each other, provides a wealth of information about the attitudes, ideas, and actions of this very remarkable family. They were a South Carolina family that, except for one of them, passed most of their lives elsewhere by choice. A family of plantation owners whose life-styles were supported by the plantation economy, they, for reasons of health or personal preference (with that single exception), chose to leave the management of their estates to others. The Southern context of their lives, in fact, is almost entirely absent from their writings, perhaps because in addition to living away from South Carolina for long periods of time, the regional self-consciousness and the convention of defending the institution of slavery emerged only fully in the 1830s, long after they had come of age. Although not the stereotyped antebellum Southern plantation family, they were the generation of South Carolinians that spanned the period of evolution from British colonial to American and, in a metaphor which they might have used themselves, laid the foundation upon which the edifice of Victorian society was erected.

Ralph Izard (1742–1804), was the fourth generation of his family in South Carolina. Left an orphan when he was only six years old, he was sent to England by his guardian for his education at Hackney and Trinity College, Cambridge. He inherited a large and productive estate in South Carolina which until the Revolution gave him a princely income of five thousand pounds sterling a year, with ten thousand pounds ready cash in his banker's hands.[3] On returning to South Carolina after an absence of about fifteen years, he found that growing up in England had not prepared him to live in the South. In 1764, he wrote to a friend, "the Climate of Carolina will not suffer me to take the management of my estate into my own hands. . . ."[4] For nearly twenty years, he was an absentee landlord rarely in South Carolina (and for ten of those years, not there at all).

On one of Ralph's trips to New York City, he met Alice DeLancey, whom he later married on May 1, 1767. Alice DeLancey's ancestry and family background matched his own. One of five daughters of Peter DeLancey and his wife Elizabeth Colden, Alice wrote of her own family after their political status had suffered from Loyalist leanings in the Revolution: "They have long been in the background. When I reflect on the situation of my family in my youth, it was with deep regret. I have seen nothing in America that equalled the consideration and respect my Uncles DeLancey enjoyed, particularly the eldest of them [James DeLancey, lieutenant governor of New York], who was esteemed and beloved by all ranks of people. . . . He died while he was Governor of New York. At that time the title of Governor exacted respectability as well as there as here. My Gd. Father, i.e. my Mother's father [Cadwalader Colden] succeeded him. So that in both parts of my family I had been accustomed to agreeable situations."[5]

Her family connections provided another dimension to the family correspondence. Although there are references to them in other letters, not many of the letters between Alice DeLancey Izard and her sisters have survived. Even more important was the entré into New York society provided by Alice's three married sisters and their families which made travel to the North and the family's eventual settlement there easier.

This well-connected young couple, Alice and Ralph Izard, spent their early married years moving between South Carolina and New York and then, in 1771, went to England, traveled about on the Continent, were caught by the American Revolution in England, and eventually made their way to France. Ralph was appointed minister to Tuscany by the Continental Congress, but the ministry was never accepted, and Izard remained in Paris—at loggerheads with Benjamin Franklin and allied to the Arthur Lee faction—until his return alone to America in 1781. His family followed in 1783, and they took up residence again in South Carolina until Izard's election to the United States Senate in 1789. After living first in New York and then in Philadelphia, Izard resigned his Senate seat in 1795 and returned with his family to South Carolina. He suffered a stroke in 1797 and until his death in 1804 lived with his family in the Izard mansion in Charleston on South Bay, making occasional visits to the family seat, The Elms, about seventeen miles from Charleston in St. James Goose Creek Parish.

John Adams, who knew the family well in Paris, described Alice DeLancey Izard as "a Lady of great beauty and fine accomplishments as well as perfect purity of conduct and character through life . . . , an excellent Domestic Consort . . . it was often jocularly said that she had given Mr. Izard a Son or Daughter in every great City in Europe."[6] It was a good story, but in spite of extensive travel on the Continent by Ralph and Alice Izard, only London and Paris qualify as birthplaces of Izard progeny. There were fourteen children in all, seven of whom lived to marry and have families of their own.[7] The marriages of three of them will be the focus of this study: Margaret, the eldest, born in 1768 and the first to marry; Anne, the ninth child, born in 1779 and the third daughter to marry; and Henry, the eldest son, born in 1771 and married twice. Through the marriages of these three representative family members, we will look at how they perceived marriage and what place it had in their lives and future happiness.[8]

That the parents' marriage was a happy one is borne out by the general tenor of their children's letters about them. Ralph's and Alice's few surviving letters to each other have nothing of the purely personal in them. The letters written by Ralph to Alice while he was at the center of the political scene are the letters of one equal to another—accounts of events are from a participant to one capable of understanding all the nuances of politics and public affairs. Some interesting tidbit would be followed by the cautionary phrase "this [is] entre nous."[9] Their exchange of letters when Alice set off alone with her children on the move back to South Carolina indicates a concerned and caring husband relying on his wife's judgment in handling emergencies—from sick children to impudent coachmen—and a wife's complete confidence in her ability to deal with them.[10]

Alice Izard's view of the role of women was in the tradition of separate spheres for men and women. If a woman's life was somewhat more limited in scope, it was definitely not an inferior one. She wrote her daughter in 1801:

> I have just finished reading the rights of Woman[11] to your Father i.e. as much of it as I could read, for I was often obliged to stop, & pass over, & frequently to cough & stammer &c&c. He is as much disgusted with the book as I am and calls the author a vulgar, impudent Hussy. Certainly our Sex will never be improved by following her precepts or example. It is not by being educated with Boys, or imitating the manners of Men that we shall become more worthy beings. The great author of Nature has stamped a different character on each sex, that character ought to be cultivated in a distinct manner to make each equally useful & equally amiable. The rank of a good woman in society leaves her little to complain of. She frequently guides where she does not govern, & acts like a guardian angel by preventing the effects of evil desires & strong passions & leading them to worthy pursuits. An author of merit remarks that many of the great events in life would never have taken place had not some men been married to some women. Their names are not brought forward but they enjoy the internal sense of their own abilities.[12]

This was the ideal she instilled in her daughters and inspired her sons to look for in their wives. There is every indication that Alice Izard knew her own worth—and knew how to make it felt.

Ralph Izard wrote from America to his wife just before her departure from Europe with the family in 1782, "Peggy is now arrived at such an age that I can not help being alarmed about her. I should be exceedingly unhappy if she were to form any attachment in Europe & I hope you take particular care to prevent it."[13] (There is no indication that any sort of attachment had been formed in Europe.) When Margaret returned to the Charleston she had left at the age of three, she was a polished Parisienne of fifteen. Within a few years, she had formed a most suitable attachment.

Gabriel Manigault was a well-to-do young Carolina planter who, like Margaret Izard, had received his education in England and on the Continent. He had studied at Lincoln's Inn in London for a time but never actually qualified as a lawyer. He was something of an amateur architect and designed several buildings in Charleston. He and his younger brother, Joseph, and two sisters, Anne (married to Thomas Middleton) and Henrietta or Harriett (later married to Nathaniel Heyward), had inherited the fortune of their grandfather, Gabriel Manigault, one of the richest men in America. In 1785, the eldest grandson was twenty-seven years old, the head of his family, and a gentleman of some standing in Charleston.

Their very diffident and circumspect courtship was chronicled in letters to young Margaret's cousin and good friend, Mary Stead, whom family tradition credits with being the maker of this match.[14] On February 24, 1785, Margaret began a letter, "I am now happy, I have done what is right. . . . I have told my Mama all. . . . She then gave me her opinion of

Mr. M., and it is exactly the same with my own & that you know very well."
In the very formal and correct etiquette of the day, adults were rarely
addressed by Christian names. Although there is no instance in surviving
letters of Margaret ever having called him Gabriel, there is also no indication of a lack of intimacy or feeling of inequality.

She continued in her letter the next morning, "And now my dearest
friend, my heart & my head are so full that I hardly know how to tell you
what I sat down on purpose to say. I believe the best way will be to put it
downright at first. Here then it is—Mr. M. has paid his addresses to me, &
made his declaration en formes. To tell you in what manner would be
utterly impossible & that you can easily conceive. . . . I believe two poor
people were never so much embarrassed as we were. He told me that it was
the first declaration of that nature that he had ever made—& I am sure it
was the first that ever was made to me. . . . All this is so new to me. . . .
One thing comforts me. It is as new to him, as it is to me. What shall I say
now when I am joked about him?"

When all the formalities had been observed—the formal consent of her
parents and the secret imparted to those entitled to know, Margaret Izard
could finally report, "Mr. M. is now like one of the family. He spends every
evening here. . . . His behavior is just as I should wish it to be. . . . No-
body but myself can perceive the attention he pays to me."

Both families, she confided to her friend Mary, were happy. Acceptance
by his family was important to her, and she boasted a little of the reaction
of Gabriel's uncle. "Old Mr. Wragg," she said, "is delighted with me. I am
not without my hopes of his thinking me one day worthy of his nephew."[15]
Although the parents first counseled a delay, since Margaret was only
seventeen years old, the wedding took place on May 1, 1785, her parents'
anniversary, a sentimental gesture that would be followed by others in the
family, who considered it a day of good omen.

Margaret and Gabriel were rarely apart, but an exchange of letters when
he had to make a short visit to his plantations early in their marriage
illustrates their relationship that endured for almost twenty-five years. She
had made him promise to write, and his first letter after leaving home
dutifully began, "You desire me, my dearest Peggy, to write to you. When I
look back upon the four hours which have passed since we parted, I really
do not recollect a single occurrence which has happened during that time,
excepting that I was in town, and am now in the country. . . ."[16]

Margaret received even this unloverlike letter with "more pleasure than I
thought myself capable of enjoying in your absence." Answering it the very
same day amidst family company, she wrote, "My Mother upon spying out
my letter just now asked who it was to & laughed a little when she heard.
Will you laugh too, my dearest Manigault when you find that I cannot live
without conversing with you some way or other?"[17] Their intimacy continued until Gabriel's sudden death in 1809. Because they were rarely apart,

few letters between them exist, but her letters to her mother and sisters reveal a happy and equal relationship with her "Mr. M."

The young Manigaults spent their early married years near Charleston, at Sullivan's Island, at his family's country place, The Oaks (he had allowed her to name it before their marriage), in St. James Goose Creek Parish; and at Accabee, another place nearer Charleston on the Ashley River. Ill health and the death of several children were the major causes of their leading the family exodus to the North, where they settled in the vicinity of Philadelphia, after the death of Ralph Izard, Sr., in 1804. Margaret, known to have been a very strong-minded woman, is credited by her son Charles with having been the chief instigator of the move.[18]

In 1798, Anne was the only grown-up daughter at home with her parents Ralph and Alice Izard. Her father, after his stroke in 1797, was an invalid more or less confined to the house in Charleston, and her mother's time was devoted to his care and to raising her youngest daughter Georgina, as well as her daughter Charlotte's children, Tom and Caroline. In a series of letters to her friend, Mrs. Elizabeth Farley Banister Shippen, Anne confided the details of her courtship. Anne's recently widowed friend had come South from Philadelphia with her invalid husband, Thomas Lee Shippen, who had died in Charleston in February 1798. Befriended by the Izards who had known the young Shippens in Philadelphia, Elizabeth Shippen, twice widowed, became a member of the family on her marriage to George Izard in 1803.

In Anne's letter of April 6, 1798, to Elizabeth was the cryptic reference, "With regard to the affair you mention, it is really pretty much in the same situation that it was when you left us, be assured that whenever anything is absolutely determined on you shall have it very soon."[19] Apparently, there were parental objections to "the situation," and Anne had some misgivings of her own, for later she wrote Elizabeth, ". . . the whole of this business at times appears to me like a Dream? . . . If I am not happy I shall have only myself to blame & this conviction makes me sometimes fear that I have done wrong. I never have let this confession pass my lips, nor ever have written it before. . . . I reasoned with myself after Mama last spoke to me. I asked myself if I thought I could be happy with him & as it really appeared that I could, I thought I acted right in accepting him. This I know, that the only objection that was made was his want of fortune, and I could not bear to think that that should influence me."[20]

Although his name never appeared, the object of her affections and indecision was William Allen Deas. His family's plantation, Thoroughgood, was near The Elms, in Saint James Goose Creek. He went to England for his education where he studied law at the Middle Temple. Later Deas returned to England to serve for several years as secretary to fellow South Carolinian Thomas Pinckney, the United States minister to Great

Britain. In 1798, he was representing St. James Goose Creek in the South Carolina House of Representatives.

Anne Izard soon reported that "the gentleman has prevailed with Mama to allow the ceremony to take place before he goes to Columbia. The awful day will be in the first week of November."[21] On October 25, 1798, she wrote, "Tomorrow week is the day fixed on which is to decide my fate for life. . . . I wish you were here my Dear Madam you would help me to support Myself & indeed I shall stand in need of support on the awful occasion. I don't know how it is, but altho' I am perfectly happy my spirits some times are low, it is the case I imagine with every thinking person in the same situation." She kept her letter open to describe "the awful occasion" at which, by the way, she "pronounced the awful Obey with an audible voice," and began her note, "It is Anne Deas now my dear Mrs. Shippen who addresses you. I am happy, he is all kindness, & my new Mother & Brothers all seem happy at having me in their family."[22]

Little of their personal relationship or of William Allen Deas's personality comes through in the letters. There was apparent pleasure in each other's company, for Margaret explained Anne's insistence on accompanying her husband to the country in 1804, "she thought he would be so uncomfortable & so lonesome, & that he would miss his little boy so much, to say nothing of herself that she determined to go. . . ."[23] There was shared enjoyment of their children and shared grief in the death of two of them. One who knew Deas later in Philadelphia described him as "of melancholy aspect. He had killed his uncle in a duel, which he engaged in to avenge an insult to his Father's honour, and never could get over the effects of it."[24] There must have been personal attractions, however, to cause Anne to prevail in her choice against family reservations. William Allen Deas would appear to have had all the right credentials, but the "want of fortune" would be the cause of much of their unhappiness. Although his brothers prospered, Deas was erratic, to say the least. After their marriage, he attempted a legal career several times without success, and his planting and business interests never seemed to prosper.

Anne's own health and the sickness and death of several children made life in South Carolina unhappy for her, and she shared her family's preference for the advantages and pleasures of life in a big city. Her brother George was perhaps very perceptive when he wrote from Philadelphia, "Mr. D. yet speaks of making an Establishment in these parts—it is probable however that he does so only to answer N. [Anne was known as Nancy to her family] who as I foresaw has been greatly disappointed at the Difference of her Importance in Society here and there, the Daughter of her Father and the wife of her Husband."[25] Her mother, remembering the earlier warnings about "the lack of fortune" and Anne's perseverance in her choice, wrote with frankness, "Her lot is a hard one but she brought it on herself."[26]

Henry Izard, the eldest son and after his father's death head of the family, was also the only one of his generation to live out his life in South Carolina. He had been left behind with his Grandmother DeLancey in New York when the family sailed to England in 1771, and he did not see his family again for ten years. Educated in the North while his father was serving in the Senate, Henry was sent home to Charleston in 1791 to study law with his father's old friend Edward Rutledge. After being admitted to the South Carolina bar, it was intended that Henry would then go to Europe for a year or two to complete his education.[27]

Within the year, Henry, in 1792, became engaged to Emma Philadelphia Middleton. She was the daughter of Arthur Middleton, a signer of the Declaration of Independence, and his wife, Mary Izard, a second cousin to Ralph. Ralph Izard wrote to Edward Rutledge, "I've had several conversations with my son on the subject of his attachment and am glad to find that his engagement is not of such a nature as to prevent his going to England & studying the law for two years. If his marriage could be postponed longer than that, it would be agreeable to me, because I do not see how he is even then to maintain a Family in the style of a Gentleman. . . . At a proper time nothing would be more agreeable to me than the connexion contemplated by my son."[28] Henry followed his father's plan. He attended the Inns of Court in London and had his Grand Tour, for, as noted earlier, he had been left behind when the family went to Europe before the American Revolution. On his return to Charleston in 1794, he and Emma Middleton were married, his father insisting that as Henry had kept his promise he not "defer his happiness" even the few months more until his father returned from Congress.[29] Henry never practiced law but settled down to the life of a planter.

As a daughter-in-law, Emma was soon absorbed into the Izard family. She was "our interesting and lovely Emma," "our sweet Emma," and "our amiable Emma," but her health was always a matter of concern. There was a desperate trip to England in the company of her mother in 1809 for a year or so—at a time when Henry's business affairs really demanded his presence in Carolina. Henry wrote to his sister Margaret about his plan to accompany his family and leave them in England under the care of Mrs. Middleton, "Nothing is in the way of our scheme but the obstinacy of Emma who like a little romantic of fifteen can't bear the idea of my leaving her for several months, & crossing the Atlantic twice without her."[30] After Emma's death four years later, Henry described their married life and the division of labors in their household, "I have been so completely in the habit of trusting to her care for all the little indoor accommodations of my life, that I am as ignorant as a schoolboy about the most common articles of necessity for my house. To my shame I have hardly ever given a thought to the practical education of my daughters. . . ."[31]

Although there had been no hint of trouble in earlier family letters and no complaints in his, one of the family wrote as Emma's death approached:

> I believe that which dimmed the lustre of her bright qualities was the want of a necessary tho' humble virtue called economy & attention to the minutiae of domestic arrangements. . . . She was not to blame, dear amiable woman, for she had never been accustomed to attend to anything in the domestic arrangements nor economy in anything. . . . Our Brother was certainly calculated for a most excellent domestic character, & had his home offered the comforts & amusements it was entitled to possess he never I firmly believe would have quitted it to make as he used to do a cure for ennui—& his dear little wife would have been spared many a bitter hour occasioned by jealousy. . . . I have wondered how it could happen that they who were both so charming & amiable & who most assuredly married for love could have lived so uncomfortably as they appeared to do.[32]

When Emma died on May 11, 1813, following childbirth, Henry was left with six motherless children to raise: one son, Walter, aged nine, and five daughters, aged fifteen years to one month old. The house at The Elms, which Henry had inherited as eldest son, had burned in 1807. Although he had begun to rebuild, his family was still living in the overseer's house when his widowed mother, Alice Izard moved South again, sacrificing her personal preference to her sense of family duty, in order to take over the supervision of her granddaughters' education. She had hardly settled in at The Elms, where the family planned to celebrate Christmas in 1813, when Henry began making frequent trips to Charleston. Claudia Smith's name began to appear in the family correspondence at about this time. She was the daughter of Thomas Loughton Smith, childhood friend of Ralph Izard, Sr., and the niece of William Loughton and Joseph Allen Smith, who had each married one of Henry's sisters. A reigning beauty in Charleston, Claudia had been one of the young ladies chosen to sit by President George Washington at the banquet in his honor in Charleston in 1791. Her mature charms apparently continued to attract, for by the latter part of April 1814, Henry reported to his mother that Claudia would soon be her daughter-in-law.

The family was shocked. Mrs. Alice Izard moderated her comments with, "Perhaps he could not have done better. . . . She is cheerful & good humored . . . and has besides a handsome independence which may help to put him at ease in his affairs. . . . I am persuaded that it was the interests of his children which made him think of marrying a person older than himself. He still is of an age to feel all the attraction of youth and beauty. She has had a full share of the latter & when I last saw her she looked extremely well."[33] Although the age difference loomed large in the minds of Henry's female relatives, Claudia's age is not a matter of public record. Her parents were married in 1763, and when her father died in 1773, she had three sisters—two older, and one younger.[34] In the 1850 census, she admitted to being seventy years old, which would indicate that she had been born seven years after her father's death![35]

On May 3, 1814, Henry wrote to his mother from Claudia's house in Charleston, "I last evening brought my little adventure to a close, & am now writing in a Room of which I am by courtesy of law, the Master."[36] Before this news reached Margaret in Philadelphia, she wrote, "My brother has probably by this time linked his fate to that of another—& that other composed of very different materials from those he has been accustomed to deal with. It is according to my view of things very much like a panel of bricks in a marble Edifice. Perhaps you may cover it over with a cement & polish it & make it in time resemble the previous fabric to which it is joined. It will delight me to find it is so. . . ."[37]

Alice DeLancey Izard replied immediately to her daughter Margaret, "I can not help thinking My Dear Child, that you must know more of the Lady's Character than I do, or you would not be so much hurt at the alliance as you are. . . . I do really believe her feelings are more congenial to your Bro. than those of his lovely first partner were. This lady enjoys excellent health, can take long walks without fatigue, relish a jest with great gout [taste], & is an excellent housekeeper & workwoman. All these qualities he has a great esteem for. The two last are very desirable & he has felt the want of them. . . . I think she runs full as great a risk as he does. She was independent, & was beloved by many friends & saw them often. Now she has a master, & a Husband not of the gentlest nature. He is very irritable, & if she does not manage him well at first, she will suffer greatly. . . . Think of the consequences which so frequently occur in this Country to single men, & think of the propensities of a certain gentleman. Let these teach you acquiescence in the present measure."[38] Although Claudia's fortune was not enough to help Henry escape financial disaster later, the marriage seemed to work out well. Perhaps Henry's choice was not as disinterested as his female relatives thought.

The experiences of these three family members—Margaret, Anne, and Henry—and the reactions of others in the family to them represent the concepts and attitudes of the Izard family towards the institution of marriage. There was the general assumption that marriage was the natural condition. All the children did marry; and in the case of the two sons whose wives died, remarried in short order. Single women had little place in society as the diffident and restrained courtships of Margaret and Anne illustrate. The amount of freedom permitted young ladies of good family and reputation was very limited. Part of the Izard family's scandalized reaction to the vivacious Claudia Smith as a desirable wife for Henry was no doubt based on her long and active career as an unmarried woman in society, for no hint of real scandal about her has survived. The respect for a married woman's position allowed her more freedom and latitude in society—not to the extent of immorality, however, for a woman's unsullied reputation was her most guarded asset. Mrs. Gabriel Manigault's salon could attract the male intelligentsia of Charleston and Philadelphia with no hint of impropriety, but Margaret Izard's courtship by Gabriel Manigault allowed very little enjoyment or fun by modern standards. The era of the "Southern belle" had not yet arrived.

Alice Izard's very forthright reasons for her son Henry's second marriage were as explicit as that very discreet grande dame ever committed to paper. She exhibited a very realistic appreciation of the situation of women of her day in admitting that Claudia ran as much risk to her happiness as Henry did to his by this marriage. Although recognizing the disadvantages of women in the society of their day, the women of this family circumvented rather than attacked them. In their letters, there is none of the rebellion against their fate that is found in the mid-nineteenth-century correspondence of many married women of their education and station in life.

Romantic love was the deciding factor in their choices of marriage partners. Both Margaret and Anne seemed to realize that their chances for future happiness depended upon their selection of a husband. Margaret was more confident in her choice and, until Gabriel Manigault's death in 1809, her marriage seems to have been a completely companionable and happy one. Anne agonized more over her choice and wondered "if I could be happy with him." Although experiencing much unhappiness later, she never admitted that she regretted having married William Allen Deas, having prevailed in her choice against apparent family opposition. Henry's first marriage to Emma Middleton in which romantic love had ruled his choice was apparently not always a comfortable one because of the incompatibility of the partners; a fact admitted by his family—but never by him—after Emma's death. Although one's future happiness was the ultimate goal, the chances of achieving it were only as sure then as they are now, or ever have been.

George Izard's wife—Elizabeth Farley Banister Shippen Izard—or "Mrs. George" as she appeared in the family letters, summed up the whole family's combined marital wisdom and experience in a letter to her son, William Shippen in 1816. He had gone South on a visit to Virginia and met a young lady there. His mother, originally from Virginia, wrote, "You say, you 'shall find it hard to relinquish the society of one of the best of girls, neither witty, handsome, nor rich.' Wit is assuredly not requisite in a wife, but without a comprehensive mind, I defy any man of understanding, and education to be happy (if happiness it can be termed) beyond the first moon of marriage. Beauty we have long known is not essential to happiness in the connubial state, but no one in his senses will deny that an agreeable exterior adds to the modicum of felicity bestowed upon us poor mortals. Riches or more properly writing—a competency—ought, in my poor way of thinking to belong to one side or the other. . . . I mean by a competency enough to live in the same sphere in which we have passed our previous lives. Take care, my Son, be cautious how you step. Recollect that this indescribable charm which you allude to may possibly be comprised in four little letters commencing with an l——. . . . Recollect that the individual whom you make your wife, is to be the mistress of your family, the Mother of your children, the companion of your life, the guardian of your honor. Now I have a great veneration for an amiable disposition, and a mild deportment, but I prize sound sense and a cultivated understanding a thousand times more. The reason why I objected to a Virginia wife was simply this, that I scarcely ever saw a gentlewoman from the Ancient Dominion that suited the Meridian of Philadelphia. Their Manners, habits, nay very ideas are different. I would not have you imagine that little Cupid's torch is to be forever burning, far from it my dear child, the heavy chains of Hymen soon put the little God of Love to flight and then wretched is the man who does not find his Wife, forbearing in her temper, affectionate in her manners, sensible in her conversation, neat in her person, and pious to her God. That you may meet with an individual of this description my dear William is the warm wish of your Mother. Your happiness is her first object. . . ."[39]

Happiness based on companionship and shared responsibilities for a successful marriage was the basis upon which the Izards founded their families. Anne wrote after the early death of her eldest son in 1813, "the little edifice of my happiness has lost its chief support & it will be long before these other little pillars can supply the place of that which is gone."[40] Margaret's use of the metaphor of the panel of bricks in a marble edifice in expressing her poor opinion of her brother Henry's choice of a second wife is another illustration of their concept that they were laying a foundation and building for the future. These were the concepts they instilled in their children who, in turn, with their children, would create and inhabit the Victorian world.

2

Family and Female Identity in the Antebellum South: Sarah Gayle and Her Family

ELIZABETH FOX-GENOVESE

IN MARCH OF 1820, Sarah Furman Haynsworth wrote to her granddaughter, Sarah Ann Haynsworth Gayle, to congratulate her on her marriage and to offer some advice. In particular, she advised her "not to take your maxims for the regulation of your conduct from the popular writing, such as are found in Romances and Plays, but from the unerring word of sacred truth, which abundantly and minutely instructs in the relative duties."[1] If her granddaughter would act with a "sincere and humble regard to divine instruction, and pray for that wisdom which is from above to illumine and direct you," she will surely achieve "such happiness as can be well expected in this imperfect World." We need, she insisted, associating herself with her granddaughter in the station of wife, a share of prudence "to retain the esteem and affections of our husbands," who should be treated "with at least as much good manners as other people." In return for "a meek, quiet, obliging, affectionate and virtuous conduct" women can count on retaining "the love and esteem of our husbands, when youth & beauty are fled." In contrast, a woman's "turbulent, ill natured, willful, disobliging" behavior can be guaranteed to "alienate and wean them from us."[2]

Sarah Haynsworth trusted her granddaughter to forgive her for "embarquing so much on this head," but "the subject is important, and you are dear to me." Above all, it would give her pleasure to know that her

15

granddaughter was happy.[3] In writing to mark her granddaughter's coming of age as a wife, Sarah Haynsworth was underscoring the ties that she believed bound successive generations of women of one family together and provided the necessary foundations for building a new family. She was also implicitly evoking the core aspects of a woman's identity as the member of interlocking families. Sarah Haynsworth's letter calls attention to the links between prescription and experience, between language and behavior, in female identity as she understood it. She takes for granted that Sarah Gayle would have read and been influenced by romances and plays but begs her to put them aside as she embarks upon her new married estate. She cogently reminds her that henceforth her happiness will, above all, depend upon the success with which she realizes her role as wife. A deep sense of family as the primary influence upon a woman's identity informs the advice that the grandmother felt obliged to tender to the new bride. Although Sarah Gayle's relations as daughter and granddaughter would continue to influence her identity, they would now lose priority to her relations as wife.

Sarah Haynsworth's advice to Sarah Gayle doubtless resembles the advice that innumerable other early nineteenth-century grandmothers would have offered at the time of a darling granddaughter's wedding. In truth, her professed values do not differ significantly from those which, according to Laurel Thatcher Ulrich, governed the lives of the women of northern New England during the late seventeenth and early eighteenth centuries. The words of Sarah Haynsworth, who had lived through the Revolution, also evoke the values of that republican motherhood which, as Linda Kerber has shown, took shape in its aftermath as an attempt to prescribe appropriate roles for women in the new world of male individualism.[4] There is, in short, nothing about Sarah Haynsworth's letter, considered abstractly rather than in context, to mark it as distinctively southern. But Sarah Gayle, in her attempt to follow the spirit of the letter during the fourteen years before her death, fashioned a mature identity that marked her understanding of its message as essentially southern.

Sarah Gayle had been born in Sumter County, South Carolina, in 1804. As an adult, she continued to treasure memories of her family's journey to Alabama Territory in 1810, still frontier country and not yet a state, although she also regretted the separation from her kin in South Carolina. Judge Wood Furman, the father of her grandmother, Sarah Furman Haynsworth, had signed the South Carolina "Declaration of Rights"; Richard Furman, her grandmother's brother, was the Baptist minister for whom Furman University was named. The parents of John Gayle, whom Sarah Haynsworth Gayle married in 1820, had also migrated from South Carolina to Alabama at the beginning of the nineteenth century. The Gayles, like the Furmans, the Haynsworths, and the kin of Sarah Gayle's mother, the Pringles, had actively supported the patriot side during the

Revolution. During Sarah Gayle's girlhood in Claiborne, in Monroe County, Alabama, her parents and the Gayles had become friends. In 1815, after graduation from South Carolina College, John Gayle, who had been born in 1792, read law with Judge Abner S. Lipscomb at St. Stephens, Alabama. In 1818, he joined his parents in Claiborne, where he established a law practice and met Sarah Haynsworth, whom he married a year later. The bride was a few months before her sixteenth birthday; the groom, twenty-eight.[5]

During the next few years, John Gayle pursued his law practice and began to make a career in Alabama politics. In 1818, President Monroe had appointed him to the first Council of the Alabama Territory; the year after, he had been elected solicitor of the Alabama circuit court; and in 1822, he was elected to the state legislature from Monroe County. Since the demands of law and politics kept John Gayle frequently away from home, he determined to settle in Greensboro, in Greene County, which provided a more central location and permitted him more time at home. After living there for a few years, John Gayle, in 1826, bought a house for his family and in 1828 resigned his judgeship so as to remain at home. The Greensboro in which Sarah Gayle lived as a young wife and mother bore the traces of its frontier status. Retaining a strong rural cast, it featured muddy roads and its share of disorderly residents. But by 1826, it could also claim a hotel, a tailor's shop, five stores, and a law office, as well as the possibility of attending Methodist, Baptist, and Presbyterian services. More important, it boasted a settled population, among whom Sarah Gayle found many women friends who provided companionship and assistance during John Gayle's frequent absences. Greensboro also provided John Gayle with a new political base from which he was elected to another term in the state legislature (during which he was chosen speaker of the House) and in 1831 to the governorship.[6]

By the time that John Gayle became governor, he and Sarah Gayle had been married eleven years and had four living children—Sarah, Matthew, Amelia, and Mary Reese. In 1832, they had a son, Richard, and in 1835 another daughter, Maria. Much of Sarah Gayle's life was given over to the bearing and rearing of her six children, although she always enjoyed considerable assistance from slaves. Hetty, Mary Ann, and especially Rose, all of whom had belonged to her parents, helped to supervise and care for the children, permitting Sarah Gayle the freedom to attend church, visit with her friends, and write her journals and letters.[7] In 1833, at the beginning of John Gayle's second term as governor, Sarah Gayle moved with the children to Tuscaloosa to meet the requirements of the new law that mandated the residence of the governor's wife in the capital. At the end of that term, she and the children returned to Greensboro to await what the Gayles expected would be a permanent move to Mobile. In the early summer of 1835, John Gayle left on a trip to investigate the possibilities of speculation in newly opened Indian lands in northern Alabama, and during his absence, Sarah Gayle died suddenly of tetanus following dental work. In many respects, her brief life of thirty-one years superficially resembled that of innumerable other American women, but in other essential ways, it differed significantly, as did her sense of her own identity.

At the heart of the experience that distinguished Sarah Gayle's life and identity from those of contemporary northeastern or Western European women lay the social relations of the slave society of the South. For as early as 1820, indeed earlier, Southerners were developing a worldview grounded in the life of rural households that remained centers of production as well as reproduction and that, for slaveholders like the Haynsworths and the Gayles, included slaves among household members. In attempting to explain this world and its values, as well as to rear children to perpetuate them, Southerners developed a distinct ideology of hierarchy and particularism that owed much to the heritage they shared with their northern counterparts, but also embodied significant differences. Southerners never remained immune to the influences of bourgeois culture, but in absorbing new currents of thought—from the celebration of republican motherhood and companionate marriage to the appreciation of Romanticism—they carefully selected and adapted them to fit their own circumstances.[8]

Among the various facets of this emerging southern worldview, the concept of womanhood and identity of women especially challenges the imagination. Bourgeois society, from which southern society was attempting to distinguish itself, remained notoriously conservative on the woman question. Scholars have carefully detailed the innumerable ways in which bourgeois women suffered continuing exclusion from the full benefits of individualism, lived under the dominance of men, and struggled against massive cultural odds to construct independent roles and identities for themselves. The early proponents of women's rights remained noteworthy exceptions and were frequently associated with a variety of radical political movements. Even among those who argued for enlarged roles and possibilities for women, many did so in the name of women's rights as women, combining their demands with an insistence upon women's special nature and domestic vocation. The case of female identity thus offers an especially arresting example of the complex ways in which antebellum Southerners were in but not of a larger capitalist world upon which their households depended but from which they sought to differentiate themselves. For even if practice remained conservative in the North as in the South, in the North capitalism and individualism were increasingly undermining conservative practice; whereas in the South, slavery was reinforcing and reshaping it.[9]

The concept of family—of women's relations to and places in families—illuminates the similarities and the differences. In practice and in imagination, the idea of family bound antebellum white Southerners together by providing a compelling representation of enduring and natural ties among individuals. Family figured as a central metaphor for southern society as a whole—for the personal and social relations through which individuals defined their identities and understood their lives. Women, especially, relied upon family membership to define their identities, for they normally did not have access to other, more abstract roles that would offer competing sources of identity. Men also emphasized family as an important source of identity, but they enjoyed other opportunities, notably as citizens but also through specialized occupations. Men's multiple identities underscored their special position as heads of families in which relations among members were not equal. Southerners, especially, relied upon the metaphor of family to cover a variety of relations, notably networks of kin, but also black slaves. Thus, the slaveholders' ubiquitous phrase "our family, white and black" emphasized the persistence of the metaphor of family as an appropriate representation for various social relations.

Family membership defined a southern woman's place in the world, as family roles articulated her deepest sense of herself in her immediate circle. There is every reason to believe that the pervasive sense of female self as predominantly a matter of family membership informed the lives of non-slaveholding as well as slaveholding rural women, but the direct evidence for their most intimate sense of themselves as women remains sparse.[10] Slaveholding women, who have left more direct evidence of their personal responses, certainly understood the female self as primarily the product of family relations. In this essential respect, the majority of slaveholding women differed from those bourgeois women who were beginning to define a sense of self in the abstract and to find ways of claiming for themselves the status of individual, and they even differed from those who were beginning to speak of women's public rights and responsibilities as women. In this respect, too, they were conforming to more traditional American and European notions of female identity as grounded in a web of relations, of which family membership was the most important.

Southern politicians, educators, and, especially, clergymen regularly reminded women of their primary responsibility to identify with their families. Religious and secular proslavery theorists alike forcefully insisted that all social relations—notably those of slavery—depended upon and were grounded in the natural and divinely sanctioned subordination of women to men.[11] But in so insisting, they very much resembled the proverbial lady who "doth protest too much." For, disclaimers notwithstanding, they were themselves unavoidably infected with the virus of a radical individualism that had been sweeping Western culture at least since the eighteenth century. Their cherished vision of hierarchy and particularism, of which women and slaves constituted the primary embodiments, thus contained a strong measure of defensiveness. They were not simply propounding an accepted view of the world as it was; they were attempting to construct a solid bulwark against a rising wave of disorderly social change.

Antebellum Southerners lived, and knew themselves to live, in a world that was increasingly challenging their most cherished values and social relations. In dangerous times, the family provided an especially attractive defense against the forces of change, not least because it apparently embodied human beings' most natural relations. As a metaphor, family privileged organic over contractual relations, community over individual self-interest, harmony over conflict, but the very notion of family, most dearly cherished by Southerners itself, owed a considerable debt to the cultural and ideological currents that most directly threatened their sense of a proper, hierarchical social order. When slaveholding women embraced the sense of themselves as preeminently members of families, they were frequently borrowing from a language or rhetoric of family that primarily derived from the emerging bourgeois discourse of domesticity, companionate marriage, and attentive motherhood.[12] But even as they selectively borrowed words and ideas, they were applying them to what they understood to be women's place in a modern slave society.

Sarah Gayle, like many others, albeit in her own way, continuously attempted to take stock of her own identity in relation to those whom she loved, with whom she lived, and in interaction with whom she forged her sense of self. The rich, if discontinuous, journal that she kept from 1827 until her death in 1835 provides striking, if incomplete, testimony to the ways in which she constructed and interpreted her self as the articulation of her place in interlocking families.[13] Perhaps most striking is that she addressed her most intimate recorded self-investigations to her children, especially her daughters. Marveling early in her first journal that so physically unattractive a woman as Miss Bates could be the friend of Mrs. Chambers, she reminds herself "that personal attractions are not indispensable to the forming of friendships" and explicitly enjoins her daughters, "I would have you my darling girls early impressed with the belief for it is a fact which experience will ultimately teach you."[14] Yet she could not entirely banish her regrets about the deterioration of her own looks or her fear that she might not continue to appear beautiful in the eyes of her husband. She worried about the example such superficial concerns might set for her daughters:

> But in acknowledging this weakness, I forget that you, my daughters may read these pages as the only means of learning the disposition of a parent who may have left you. Be it so—to you, I wish to be unveiled, that if I possess anything worthy to be adopted you may do it and if anything which out [sic] to be shunned it be a warning tho' you should say "it is *my mother's* frailty."[15]

If her words testify to the ways in which she understands her self in relation to her daughters and attempts to anchor her various feelings in her role as mother, they also betray her continuing preoccupation with death. At some time, be it sooner or later, she will exist only in the memories of those she has loved, notably her family. In reminding herself of her future identity as memory, Sarah Gayle draws upon her own devotion to those whom she has loved and who have died. Throughout her journal, she regularly returns to death—sometimes her own, sometimes that of another. For her sense of self depends heavily on continuity across generations and beyond the grave, on the ways in which she has internalized the love and examples of others, especially her parents. Recollecting her girlhood, she writes:

> so it is—my father, my mother, my idolizing mother—my friends, Amelia & Sara, my good tutor—all are buried—yet I am happy—the recollection of them has no bitterness in it—it only melts me, courses all that is good in my nature, makes me turn, with the more intense delight, to the good yet left, and with subdued hope to the moment, when those I possess and those I have lost will be secured to me, *forever & ever.*[16]

In such moments, Sarah Gayle expresses her confidence that she has indeed accepted the loss of those she loved by merging them in her own identity. She sees her identity as the product of her relations with others. She also takes seriously her responsibility for perpetuating the memories of those she has lost. Names, especially, signify continuities. She names her oldest son for her husband's father; her oldest daughter for herself, her mother, and her grandmother. Younger daughters receive the names of especially cherished friends; her younger son, that of her own father. She notes, after a visit, that Mrs. Erwin, like herself, "finds in 'auld lang syne' a sweet and inexhaustible theme."[17] But Mrs. Erwin's husband will not consent to her naming the new infant after her bosom friend Caroline Feemster. Sarah Gayle condemns his attitude as entirely ungenerous, for has he not brought his wife "away from her family & friends to a land of strangers, where she finds much to regret without any prospect of having it supplied"? Under such conditions, how can he deny her "the simple but to her inestimable privilege of perpetuating the names of those she loves in her own children"?[18] Every day of her life Sarah Gayle has reason to congratulate herself that Mr. Gayle has behaved so differently.

Concern with death frequently leads Sarah Gayle to worry about her children's futures and the likelihood of being reunited in heaven with all of those she has lost. Thus, she asks herself what will become of her "little flock": "Will they live, will I live, will their father the corner stone of our happiness?"[19] At least her baby who never breathed in this world is safe, "is now a child of Paradise." But what of her mother? "I should go mad, if I did not believe that she the excellent, the honorable, the true, the *all* that was good, had not received the reward."[20] And what of herself? Each confinement renews her fears about her own possible death. And what of her children if something happens to her? She is determined that they not have a stepmother, determined that they not be deprived of those maternal connections which alone can ensure the proper development of their characters.[21]

Past, present, and future imperceptibly merge in Sarah Gayle's developing identity. As she matures, the past in particular plays an increasingly important role in her sense of who she is. In 1828, at twenty-four, she reproaches herself for dwelling upon her outrage that the husband of one of her closest friends had remarried immediately after the friend's death. "I am very foolish to care anything for the matter, but I become more and more unwilling that any I used to know and with whom I used to be on terms of intimacy should be strangers now."[22] Her outrage suggests how easily she could project her fears about her own possible death into the death of her friend. From that perspective, she resents the husband who so quickly could forget his wife. Yet she also wishes to retain her personal relation with him, if only because they have known each other for so long. She admits that she values "old friends, old scenes everything I knew in early life, with something like romance."[23]

Even as she cherishes the memories of previous times, she insists that she is "willing to accept the pleasures proper to my time of life, or rather to the size of my family for I am but just twenty-four."[24] Perhaps no bliss could be compared to that she experienced when she was fifteen, but "now when my children are playing around me—and their father's head is on my knee, & his arms clasped in fondness around me—I look back to my days of girlish happiness as to a dream, sweet indeed, but which must not be compared to the quiet sober reality."[25]

The bliss of Sarah Gayle's fifteenth year, as she remembers it, consisted in watching the gallants of the country arrive at her father's house. She seems in this passage to be evoking the bliss of adolescence and of her brief life as a belle, which she no longer regrets exchanging for the more sober contentment of marriage and motherhood. Her own emerging identity as a mother leads her to reevaluate aspects of her youth, especially her feelings for her mother. Vowing to attend to her father's grave as a "mark of respect & affection," she admits that she has never so much as placed a rosebush beside her mother's grave. She has not been able to go to it, but she never thinks of it "without a gush of tenderness, more gratifying to her, if she knew it, a thousand thousand times more precious than the bloom of roses & the kissing of willow-boughs."[26] Each passing year makes her more conscious of the loss of her mother, whom she never valued as she should have. Now she recognizes her excellence and recognizes that "when she died I lost one who loved me with a more enduring, a more indulgent boundless affection, than any one else ever did or can more than almost any other mother ever cherished for a faulty child."[27]

At times, Sarah Gayle worries that although she loved her mother, she did not love her as her mother loved her. She now feels as if she "could never be happy again, because she went down to her grave without knowing, how was she to know, when I was ignorant myself?"[28] Now she knows how much gratitude and admiration her mother deserved and cherishes all memories of her, deprecating "as an evil every thing like forgetting her person, her manners, habits & high virtues."[29] And she delights to think that as soon as her daughters are old enough, she will describe her mother to them and encourage them to imitate her. At the same time, she is also probably thinking of how she hopes her daughters will love and remember their own mother.

She continues to cherish her mother as a standard for womanly excellence and, by implication, for her own identity. Finding herself unduly critical of Mrs. P.'s wearing a veil, which is really becoming to the features of fifteen but hardly those of fifty, she allows that she herself has doubtless been influenced by her mother's ideas. For her mother wore her raven hair parted on her forehead and nothing but a plain cap and bonnet. But then, nothing of her countenance should have been veiled. Her black eyes, which "expressed her true inborn nobleness" could "sparkle with indignation, with pleasure or with hope—but oh! how eloquently did their gentle glance speak to the heart of her child."[30] The fears that plague Sarah Gayle during her pregnancies, especially, lead her to think of her mother to whom she was wont to turn confidently with her complaints and unspeakable fears.

In Sarah Gayle's memory, her mother always counseled wisely, reproved mildly, and participated feelingly. There was no agony, she believes, that her mother would not gladly have borne for her. At the time, she barely noticed these "evidences of affection," but now "they rise upon my recollection & I think of them as they deserve."[31] Now she knows that her mother would have risked her life for her, could never have survived had anything happened to her. "I have wept bitter, bitter tears, when I recall'd the unkindness of my conduct towards her many times."[32] She does not think that she was "undutiful or rebellious," but her "temper was quick and did not well brook control." Her father's lessons, she now believes, pushed her toward "independence," and "too great carelessness for the opinions of others" made her "hardheaded."[33] But then, she reminds herself, she did love her mother, who especially had her entire confidence in matters of courtship and who preferred John Gayle for her daughter's husband. She recalls how devotedly she nursed her mother during her last illness and how, in recognition, her mother called her "my guardian angel."

The deep identification between mother and daughter in itself hardly marks slaveholding women as different from bourgeois women. To the contrary, psychologists, for whom bourgeois women constitute primary subjects, forcefully insist upon the importance of that identification for women's sense of self.[34] There are, nonetheless, reasons for which the identification would have been especially strong for antebellum southern women who, as girls, spent most of their time in their mothers' company and who could be expected to lead lives that closely replicated those of their mothers. Demographic patterns reinforced the special identification between southern mothers and daughters, for southern women, who continued to marry younger than their northern counterparts, would be close in age to their mothers and thus, to borrow Sarah Gayle's words, be their companions, friends, and sisters as well as their daughters.[35] Under these conditions, southern women like Sarah Gayle went to their marriages more as girls than as mature women, and they remained closely tied to their mothers. Sarah Gayle's journals suggest that she, at least, transferred many of her feelings for her mother directly to her husband, looking to him for a quasi-maternal love and understanding.

Sarah Gayle assuredly viewed her marriage as the foundation of her mature identity. By temporarily taking the perspective of the man who marries a young girl such as she had been, she finds a way of presenting her personal feelings as the general case. She writes that a man cannot but be happy when a lovely young woman gives her heart into his keeping and by her language and conduct says, "from this moment henceforth, I acknowledge none but you as my protector in the wide, wide world, upon no arm will I lean but yours, while buoyed up by prosperity; in adversity, no head but thine, shall be pillowed upon this bosom, while I whisper, that the vial of bitterness cannot be emptied, if thy sustaining love be spared to me."[36] At the wedding of a young friend, she thinks back on her own wedding. Her emotions overpower her as, significantly, she thinks in one breath of her husband, her father, her mother. As the ceremony progressed, she "was more and more sensible of the importance of the act which was then receiving an unchangeable seal. None but a wife could know what she wished."[37] The ceremony evoked powerful contradictory feelings, first tears and then an unaccountable fit of laughing. But when the bride left with her husband, there were tears again and "warm wishes rose for her, going, as she was, from the very bosom of her parents to the somewhat uncertain welcome of strangers."[38] The experience of others teaches Sarah Gayle that marriage in truth harbors dangers as well as joy and protection.

One Sunday, Mr. Hillhouse, the Presbyterian minister, "delivered a more touching sermon than I ever heard him pronounce. He told us he intended with the permission of the heads of the families to meet with them at their firesides and carry on there what might come less warmly & nearly from the pulpit."[39] She is sure he will not be excluded from theirs. She also thinks that she could "discover the domestic histories of those who were affected at various parts of the discourse." The woman who was sitting in front of her, for example, "shrunk as if from a probe, at the picture of the unhappiness of many who to observers are cheerful enough."[40] Sarah Gayle did not have to look far to discover the source of her grief. The husband who was sitting next to her was "a bloated victim of intemperance" whose character was "blackened by infidelities." Surely, Christian faith offered such a woman more than anything earth had to offer. Another woman, Mrs. Bell, almost suffocated with her emotions, and Sarah Gayle recalled that she had lying at home a beautiful daughter who had been suffering for two years with a fatal disease. Yet another, Mrs. Thurman, also attended to the sermon with particular care. Again, Sarah Gayle could understand the reason. "I had met *her* husband, staggering from the grog-shop to the home which should be approached alone by a man with sober & sacred and tender feeling. Is there a fate like hers?"[41] Surely, none could suffer more than the woman who "gave her destiny up to him, and far from shedding on it the light of his grateful affection, he forgets he has it in his keeping, while draining the bottle or seeking the vulgar amusement of the shuffleboard!" Such a betrayal of trust erodes a woman's very identity. "No wonder her cheeks have become pale and her appearance careless—what inducement has she to adorn her body, when the worm is gnawing within? None, None."[42]

Reading a set of lectures that acutely explored the relation between public and private virtue, Sarah Gayle thinks that the author "ably discourses on the pernicious effects of infidelity upon the public morals and the public good, while like most men the agony of the wife's outraged heart sinks into comparative insignificance!"[43] And what is a wife to do under such circumstances? She herself can form but the faintest idea of such misery, but what she can imagine is dreadful enough "—the bare supposition that Providence could make such a fate the punishment of my sins, would if followed up put me beside myself." The longer she is married:

> the more intense and single is my love for my husband and sometimes when he is gone & I am melancholy, I ask myself, can he still place first in his heart & his thoughts, the faded being who is changed in all but her feelings, who has nothing of youth of beauty of talent not even the poor charm of manner to fascinate?[44]

Happily, John Gayle's presence banishes such questions, which she believes wiser not to dwell on.

Some women defame the identity of wife and mother. When Mrs. Dann's two-day-old infant is reported to be dying, Sarah Gayle cannot but think that its death might be a blessing, if only by removing the evidence of the mother's shame. But she is surprised at Mrs. Dann's want of feeling, having expected her at least to show "the instinctive parental love in which even brutes seem her superior." Mrs. Dann also had a daughter of about five years who can be expected to follow in her mother's steps. Sarah Gayle knows that all of the women of that family are "of bad character," and Mrs. Dann herself "a young handsome & unblushing prostitute." The possible causes of such a career trouble Sarah Gayle who suspects that the first cause might indeed be slight, perhaps "an incautious word a light and unmeaning look—imprudence first placed the curse upon them—believing *all* lost, they became careless & callous—gave birth to unfortunate children

whose fathers dared not lay their hand upon them, and say 'it is mine.' "
She cannot imagine how such parents will be able to stand with "such
children before the Judgment seat of a holy God."[45] Beneath her moral
outrage lurks the conviction that mothers decisively shape the identities of
their daughters.

Sarah Gayle, drawing upon the example of her own mother, holds the
highest standards for women and takes strong exception to the behavior of
her sister-in-law Lucinda, who attempted to transact some matters of business, although Mr. Gayle had attempted to persuade her not to. But Lucinda's efforts, as was to be expected, availed nothing, for "no gentleman
would consent to transact business of importance with a lady whose husband was fully capable of attending to it himself." Lucinda should have
known that it "is a real misfortune for her thus to meddle in affairs to which
women are generally strangers, for it not only mortifies her friends, but
after she has failed leaves her to be laughed at." Sarah Gayle could love her
sister-in-law dearly if only she had more "straight forward honesty." But
Lucinda's failings should not be minimized for: "my dear children tho a few
good qualities may be liked you can never be respected & honored unless
you possess that high sense of honor which will lead you at all risks to speak
& act the true & the right."[46] In this example, she explicitly links her
standards of female honor to the acceptance of prescribed female roles.

By a clear train of association, these reflections on Lucinda's weakness of
character lead Sarah Gayle directly into a discussion of what she is doing
about her own children's education. She has started Matt with Mr. Hall but
fears that Matt, being small, will be overlooked among the larger boys.
Meanwhile, Mrs. Potts, whose school Sarah had been attending, has
moved to the upper end of the village, too far away for Sarah to walk.
Worse, on such a walk, Sarah "will be liable to hear, & see so much I would
be grieved for her to hear, that I would almost prefer her staying at home
and learning nothing."[47]

The very next day, Matt again reminds Sarah Gayle of her responsibilities as the educator of her children by asking her a series of difficult
questions, beginning with, "when was General Washington born?" then,
"when was God born?" and finally, "what is a sinner?" She replies that bad
men were sinners, "that all were sinners," and then names the sins of anger,
theft, lying. Matt protests, "But Mah you get angry, and that is sin, and the
sinner can't go to Heaven." She replies that she was sorry for it, and God
forgave her. But Matt insists, " 'you get mad again and keep getting so.' "[48]
At that point, she finds herself at a loss. Matt, undaunted, moves on to ask
if angels were sons of God. And what about the Devil? Matt persists with
his questions, all equally puzzling to her. And addressing him directly, she
writes of her hope that his spirit of inquiry would lead him, at a mature age,
to investigate these matters more thoroughly for himself.[49]

The burden of overseeing Matt's education plagues Sarah Gayle throughout her life, forcefully reminding her of the differences between male and female identity. She especially worries about his growing interest in guns. "I never saw a child so devoted to his gun, and I have many apprehensive moments lest he should do injury, perhaps a terrible one, to man or beast."[50] But should she take his gun from him? Would she not push him towards other, less innocent, amusements? Without his gun to occupy him, might he not take to the street or, worse, to the billiard room? There he might contract habits "of a nature to destroy his future usefulness and my happiness as a mother. A mere chance of accident is much preferable to such a fear."[51] In truth, she has only the most imperfect knowledge of the male vices that worry her, for she has always been sheltered from them. She is fully capable of appreciating and admiring Matt's masculinity, viewing him at the age of twelve on his return from one hunting expedition as a painter might have seen him: "His countenance flushed to the deepest red, his eyes flashing and sparkling, teeth white as ivory, his hair dishevelled but pushed back, shot bag hung around him, his gun in one hand, while he held the two 'coons upon his shoulder with the other."[52] But as he grows up, she increasingly views him as a man—as fundamentally different from herself. He thus evokes her deepest and contradictory feelings about men, who may be either women's protectors or their abusers.

For Sarah Gayle, the responsibilities of educating male and female children underscore different aspects of her own identity. Throughout her journal, she reveals a certain confidence in her dealings with her daughters. Here and there, doubts creep in and frustrations arise. Amelia proves willful and unmanageable, however bright and delightful. Sarah offers less reason for concern, consistently proving herself to be the most reliable and responsible of girls. But Matt poses entirely different problems, especially as he moves steadily toward such distinctly male interests as hunting and as he begins to make possibly undesirable companions outside of the household. On one frightful occasion, when a horse almost ran away with him and she was powerless to intervene, she was prompted to reflect on the implications of his danger and possible death. The experience led her to explore in her journal the difference in her feelings for him and her daughters:

> and if he had been kill'd happiness would not have visited my heart again. I love my daughters very dearly do I love them, and all that is amiable & good, intelligent & lovely would I have them, but all I possess of ambition, pride & the hope that steps over the threshold of home all such is centered in him, and if Death had crushed them, I should have mourned as Rachel.[53]

Obviously, such feelings could also plague bourgeois women who lived in a world that sought to bind women closely to a female sphere. Southern and bourgeois women alike lived with a steady stream of injunctions about their responsibilities as mothers. Both were heir to the ideology of motherhood that held women preeminently responsible for early childhood education.[54] But southern patterns of child rearing adapted a common prescriptive literature to a distinct reality in which southern mothers, especially slaveholding mothers, performed different tasks as mothers than their northeastern sisters. Rarely, for example, did southern women assume complete, or even primary, responsibility for the material care of their small children, including nursing. In this, as in so much else, all of their efforts were seconded or even superseded by the efforts of slave women.

Southern women of all classes were much less likely than northeastern women to send their children to school at an early age, if only because they lacked schools to send them to. Slaveholding women in particular would commonly assume primary responsibility not merely for the early training of their children's characters but also for their early formal instruction. In the case of daughters, especially as in Sarah Gayle's case in the semi-frontier conditions engendered by plantation slavery, they might continue that instruction for years or share it with a tutor. Only when it came time to send girls away to school would their fathers assume primary responsibility. Fathers might take over the education of boys much earlier, except in cases in which, like John Gayle's, they were often away from home and would not do so systematically. In any event, boys were commonly sent to such schools as were available at a younger age than girls.[55]

The ideals of southern women like Sarah Gayle for themselves as mothers, which lay at the core of their identities, had less to do with tasks than with a way of being in the world. Sarah Gayle intertwines her thoughts about her mother, her daughters, and herself with her basic thoughts about character, including religion. Even when concerned with the most abstract qualities of character that presumably applied to men as well as women, she commonly insists that for men these things are different. Even when she reproaches women with abstract failures of character, she ties those failures to their roles within families as mothers, wives, and daughters. Similarly, she expresses her continuing preoccupation with religion as an articulation of identity in relation to her family. Her feelings as a mother, especially, overcome her when she reflects on conversion and her hopes for her own children. Salvation, above all, promises the prospect of being permanently reunited with those she has loved, of reconstituting her household in heaven.[56]

The overlapping of family and household occurs in Sarah Gayle's self-representations when she writes of her slaves, who, although in significantly lesser ways than whites, also helped to anchor her identity as the member of interlocking families. In 1828, when she had been thinking about her parents, she notes that "Old Granny will soon close her earthly career." Granny was about eighty or ninety and "has been in my family since my mother's first marriage."[57] And she enjoins herself not to forget old Granddaddy who toward the end of his life loved to sit in the door and listen to her read the parts of the Bible that he most remembered. Their names, she reminds herself, were Roger and Nanny, although "the other appeleatives [*sic*] alone were used."[58]

Other slaves, notably Hampton and Hetty and even, on occasion, her favorite Mike, provoke angry outbursts for their recalcitrance in effecting her wishes.[59] But as soon as the heat of anger has passed, she forces herself to be honest. The fault lies as much with her as with them, if not more. Her mother had known how to manage servants properly—to exact obedience and to render justice. She does not and does no better with the children than with the servants. On a bad day, she notes that the children are troublesome, "but it is because my management is so faulty. When they misbehave my temper is terribly in my way, and I fail in attempts to reason, expostulate, entreat or command with necessary calmness."[60] Her difficulties with servants and children reinforce her sense of inadequacy. "Several of the negroes have been sick—all mending. My children are half-wild from their liberty."[61] Yet, however "perplexing" she finds the management of her children and however "lamentably deficient" she finds herself "in the art of governing them," she thanks "Heaven that I possess these to give my life some object and my body, mind and affections some employment, in my sort of widowhood."[62]

In wrestling with her own conflicting feelings and her frequent bouts of depression, Sarah Gayle attempts to cope with the "causes of disquiet peculiar to the mother and mistress of a family."[63] The phrase, "mother and mistress of a family," captures the essence of Sarah Gayle's mature identity, albeit one with which she continues to struggle, especially in John Gayle's absence. Loneliness and her own inadequacy continually threaten to engulf her spirits. "In spite of the size of my family," she writes, "many is the unpleasant moment, when such a feeling of loneliness and desolation comes over me, that I shut my eyes in hopelessness."[64] At the worst, she feels no disposition even to read or write. Thinking of the books she would like to read or the journal in which she would like to write, she sadly acknowledges that "I absolutely lack energy to send a servant for one, or to open the drawer, which has the other."[65] Time and again, her preoccupation with her own identity leads her back to her rearing of her children. "I fear I am lamentably deficient in that patient, calm firmness, without which a mother cannot properly manage her children."[66] Thus, she sees her personal identity as imperceptibly merging with her identity as a mother.

Worrying that her children "are far from improving as I desire" and alarmed at the "numerous rumors concerning the slaves," she nonetheless knows that the problem derives not from "what is *about* me," but from "the unsettled state of my mind and temper I am deeply sensible the error is in them, and in solitude and silence I make a thousand resolutions, quickly broken of amendment—they vanish before the first trial." And once again, she determines "to make a more vigorous effort for the sake of my children, I will."[67] In one moment of depression, she writes of her intense longing again to see old Sheldon (her father's place), to see in reality the scenes that remain so fresh in her memory. "What a creature of happiness and mirth I was then how young, how caressed, how worshiped by a father who was proud of me and a mother who lived in my life alone." Into that enchanted world and her young existence came "the revolution in my affections, the breaking up of old, and the forming of new and most ecstatic ties." Now she can only thank the "Fountain of Light . . . that this period of unmixed felicity has been mine, and that sometimes when I am wearied and lonely, and it may be *murmuring*, I may look back to it, and feel invigorated to pace on in the even and unvaried line of duty, which extends itself before me."[68]

Sarah Gayle's juxtaposition of the "unmixed felicity" of her youth and the "unvaried line of duty" of her present and future permits speculation that she harbored conflicting feelings about her adult situation as wife and mother. She indisputably had her bad moments and her flares of temper, but she never so much as hints that she did not love her husband. To the contrary, she repeatedly and convincingly writes of her deep and abiding love for him, implicitly associating him with her mother as her most important source of happiness and security. His long absences, nonetheless, left her in charge of children and servants whom she frequently found difficult to govern, thus confronting her with her own angers and limitations. Indeed, the presence of servants in her household and metaphoric family forced her, more than bourgeois women, to accept the austere, adult responsibilities of governance. But those responsibilities did not lead her, as some bourgeois women were being led by the logic of their society, beyond the home, much less to identify with an abstract identity as an individual. Instead, they forced her back upon her own identity as defined by her family membership. The evangelical virtues that she sporadically attempted to cultivate remained preeminently particular, not abstract, virtues—the virtues of her station, not those of the individual in general.

Like other women, in all times and places, Sarah Gayle frequently found the demands of adulthood trying and sought escape, if only in fantasy. Her quests to escape her burdens did not, however, lead her into overt rebellion against her situation. Doubtless, her frequent comments upon the unhappy marriages of others and the viciousness, brutality, and simple irresponsibility of some men can be read as covert protests against male privilege and its abuses. Similarly, her recurring lassitude and depression can be interpreted as an unconscious protest against what some part of her viewed as her crushing responsibilities. But we have no evidence that she saw her life that way. We do have evidence that she remained psychologically bound to her family of origin and to her own life as a cherished daughter. And in periods of depression, she would commonly turn to those memories, as other women have turned to other fantasies to ease distress. She also turned to those memories, much as her grandmother (whose letter must be read in its southern context) had recommended, as the foundation for a mature identity that she embraced. For like other southern women, she belonged to a world that encouraged women to find their primary identities in the roles and relations of families.

In 1859, Augusta Jane Evans published a novel, *Beulah*, in which she attempted to explore the implications of individualism for southern women. After a protracted exploration of her protagonist's progress toward philosophical skepticism, personal independence, and public authorship, she resolved the plot by having Beulah regain her faith, marry her guardian, and accept her ordained role as wife.[69] Although Evans does not especially dwell on southern social relations, notably slavery, the novel's conclusion forcefully endorses the superiority of southern over northern ways. Evans scrupulously exposes the ways in which the logic of bourgeois thought undermines family and religion. Her account of Beulah's travails appealed to many northern readers, for whom women's roles and identities remained a necessary bastion of conservatism, women's subordination to men the best protection against unacceptable egalitarianism. But Evans intended something more than a mere prescription for female duty. Beulah, in finally embracing her identity as a woman, was embracing a view of her identity as defined by southern society and articulated by its own peculiar family roles. And tellingly, in order to start Beulah on her misguided quest for independence, Evans represents her as an orphan. Only by her gradual ability to reclaim herself within the family relations specific to the slaveholding South could she consolidate her identity.

3

"An Outrage upon Nature": Incest and the Law in the Nineteenth-Century South

PETER BARDAGLIO

I

IN *ABSALOM, ABSALOM!*, William Faulkner explores the volatile mixture of patriarchy, incest, and racial tension that permeated family life in the Victorian South.[1] With the end of the war approaching in 1865, Charles Bon writes to Judith Sutpen that he intends to come back and marry her, even though they are both offspring of Thomas Sutpen. Bon tells Henry Sutpen, his half brother, about the letter, knowing that Henry will do everything in his power to prevent him from marrying his sister. Despite his fury at Bon, who is the product of Thomas Sutpen's first marriage to a Haitian woman, Henry feels a certain relief. In Faulkner's words:

> Henry said 'Thank God. Thank God,' not for the incest of course but because at last they were going to do something, at last he could be something even though that something was the irrevocable repudiation of the old heredity and training and the acceptance of eternal damnation.[2]

Henry, of course, kills Bon. As Faulkner's tale suggests, most white southerners preferred to settle kinfolk disputes and matters of sexual misconduct outside the legal system, viewing courts as a last resort. A staunch attachment to what Bertram Wyatt-Brown and others have termed "honor"—a constellation of ideas and values in which one's sense of self-worth rested on the degree of respect commanded from others in the community—persuaded southern whites that generally such affairs did not belong before the bench and should be handled without turning to the third party of the state. Honor thus placed a premium on personal rather than impersonal justice.[3]

This does not mean, as Charles Sydnor has pointed out, that southerners held the law in disrespect. The reputation for lawlessness stemmed mainly from the conviction that only the pursuit of personal vengeance could properly restore one's injured honor, and that state intervention was of little use in such circumstances—hence, the customs of brawling and disfigurement among backwoodsmen and dueling among planters. In this sense, Wilbur J. Cash's insistence on the extent to which the South's frontier character hindered the development of law and government in the region is well taken; clearly, the ethic of honor and deference to the law often clashed.[4]

It is within the context of this complex web of patriarchy, honor, and the law that the development of judicial policy regarding the prosecution of incest in the nineteenth-century South must be understood. As several historians have noted, the dynamics of family life in Victorian society had a distinctly incestuous character. The new emphasis placed on the cultivation of affection and sentiment among family members combined with great concern about the need to control sexuality produced profound strains in the household.[5] It should not be surprising, then, that the explosive nature of incest made its regulation a highly sensitive matter among Victorians, particularly in the South where the household was the foundation of the social order.[6]

Appellate opinions handed down in southern courts provide an especially valuable window on the anxiety and ambivalence generated by the issue of punishing incest. On the one hand, judges recognized that incest threatened the integrity of the family. A Texas jurist gave vent to these feelings when he proclaimed in 1882 that incest was "an outrage upon nature in its dearest and tenderest relations, as well as a crime against humanity itself." Incest, according to the Alabama Supreme Court, not only "contravenes the voice of nature" and "offends decency and morals" but it also "degrades the family."[7] Most important, incest among members of the nuclear family confused the roles and duties of individuals and eroded the stability of the household, thereby weakening its effectiveness as an institution of social control. To commit incest, consequently, was to fail grievously in meeting one's responsibilities both to the family and society at large. The Mississippi high court insisted in 1872 that incest was a transgression against "domestic virtues" and "the obligations of a citizen." Not to punish those who committed such crimes, said the same court in an earlier opinion, "would undermine the foundations of social order and good government."[8]

On the other hand, southern jurists wholeheartedly endorsed the patriarchal ideal of the household, even as they acknowledged that abuse of male power sometimes resulted in the practice of incest in certain families. As a

South Carolina judge stressed in 1858, "The obligation imposed on the husband to provide for their wants and protection, makes it necessary that he should exercise a power of control over all members of his household." The law, for this reason, "looking to the peace and happiness of families and to the best interests of society, places the husband and father at the head of the household."[9]

The tension between the condemnation of incest and the commitment to patriarchy shaped judicial behavior in cases that came before the state supreme courts in the South, leading to the expression of outrage against the occurrence of incest and to the conviction of those men who *clearly* used physical force in committing the crime. But, when evidence of force was unclear, judges shied away from imposing criminal punishment. By isolating those men who undeniably abused their power to gain sexual satisfaction from females in their family and treating them as deviants rather than locating the source of incestuous behavior in the hierarchical nature of the household itself, southern jurists helped to preserve the patriarchal ideal and minimize state intrusion in the private sphere.[10]

In the area of incest regulation, state legislatures rather than the courts took the lead in formulating policy, enacting legislation that restricted kin marriages and criminalized incest. Southern appellate judges left no doubt that they preferred to let legislators take the initiative in governing incestuous behavior. The firm adherence of the courts to the common law, which traditionally did not recognize incest as a crime and left its regulation to church authorities, made it almost certain that jurists would not impose incest prohibitions without legislative initiative.

While the new anti-incest statutes generally won judicial endorsement, southern courts placed a strict construction on this legislation and showed a high regard for the defendant's procedural rights in criminal trials involving incest prosecutions. Even when they had legislative authority to exact punishment from those who had violated incest bans, in other words, jurists approached the problem of controlling incest through state intervention warily. As we shall see, this wariness reflected the high value that the southern judiciary placed on family autonomy as well as an unstinting commitment throughout the nineteenth century to the notion of patriarchal authority.[11]

It is important to note that, in all likelihood, the majority of incest incidents did not come to the attention of local and state authorities in the South. Therefore, court records do not provide a reliable indication of the extent of incestuous behavior in southern society. In addition, because only a minority of cases concerning incest prosecutions reached state supreme courts, appellate opinions are not necessarily representative of the treatment of incest in the southern legal system. But the state supreme courts established guidelines for lower courts adjudicating incest cases. Moreover, appellate opinions, as well as the relevant statutory laws, provide important insights into the status of women and children, attitudes toward marriage and kinship, and the process by which public control was exerted over sexual behavior. As Wyatt-Brown has noted:

> The point is not to condemn the South for its sexual sins, particularly the wrongdoing that slaveholding so greatly encouraged. Enough has been said of those problems by others. Rather it is to ascertain how the issues of sexual misconduct were handled and what the means for their control reveal about the culture as a whole.[12]

Of all the varieties of sexual misconduct, incest has attracted probably the most widespread sanctions. Almost all human societies have prohibited sexual relations between persons who are closely related, and the banning of certain marriages has been nearly universal. Incest prohibitions developed in part to bolster the nuclear family and enable parents to socialize their offspring. The incest taboo also compels the young to look for mates outside the nuclear family. Such marriages create alliances between family groups, providing the basis for social order.[13]

Although most societies have frowned upon marriage and sexual relations between parent and child or brother and sister, the range of incest restrictions beyond the nuclear family has varied widely. Furthermore, not all societies have made incest, however it is defined, a criminal offense. Hence, the central issues for any analysis of the sanctions against incest are the extent of the prohibitions and the punishment exacted from those who violate them.[14]

II

The legal sanctions against incest in the nineteenth-century South had their roots in English canonical rules, which imposed numerous marital restrictions based on both consanguinity (relationship by blood) and affinity (relationship by marriage). Originally, canon law had banned marriages between persons connected in any degree whatsoever by consanguinity or affinity. Ecclesiastical courts could annul such unions, excommunicate offending individuals, and declare any offspring illegitimate, thus preventing them from inheriting property. Statutes passed during the reign of Henry VIII considerably reduced the number of prohibited relationships. Under these statutes, only unions that violated the sanctions in Leviticus against marrying nearer than first cousins were voidable by ecclesiastical courts. In 1563, Archbishop Parker of the Church of England drew up a table of degrees that incorporated the reduction in prohibitions, and the table provided the basis for most subsequent Anglo-American legislation on the topic.[15]

In the Anglican South, colonial statutes required that every parish display Parker's table. In contrast to New England Puritans, who strongly opposed first-cousin marriages, colonial southerners followed English tradition in their acceptance of such unions. Marriages in eighteenth-century Virginia were prohibited "within the Levitical degrees," and the children of such marriages were considered illegitimate. The Virginia General Court had the authority to separate offenders and to impose fines at its discretion. In South Carolina, a statute enacted in 1704 sought to prevent unions "not allowed by the Church of England" and "forbidden by the table of marriage." Those who married contrary to this act could be fined fifty pounds or imprisoned for twelve months, but civil authorities in the colony did not have the power to annul such marriages.[16]

Following the American Revolution, southern legal authorities maintained their relaxed attitude toward cousin marriages. Only Georgia prohibited first-cousin unions before the Civil War, and it lifted this ban in 1866.[17] In general, antebellum southern statutes outlawed matrimony between members of ascending and descending lines of a family, and between uncles and nieces or aunts and nephews.[18] Several states included illegitimate children and their relations, as well as half-blood kindred, in their marital restrictions.[19]

While state legislatures in the Old South generally agreed that kin marriages between first cousins and those more distantly related by blood needed little regulation, they found it more difficult to achieve a consensus on unions involving those related by affinity. Indeed, a significant disparity in attitudes toward such unions existed in the state laws. The majority of southern states did not allow one to contract matrimony with a daughter-in-law or son-in-law or with a stepparent, stepsibling, or stepgrandchild. Before mid-century, Virginia law went even further, prohibiting unions with an uncle's widow, a nephew's widow, a deceased wife's sister, and a brother's widow.[20] At the opposite pole, four states—Arkansas, Florida, North Carolina, and Louisiana—were entirely free during the antebellum years of any legal impediments to matrimony on account of affinity.[21]

Restrictions on marriages between close affines proceeded from the traditional religious conviction that the relations created by matrimony did not cease following the dissolution of marriage by death or divorce. From this perspective, marriage was less a personal matter involving the private emotions between two individuals than it was an event which brought together two families and promoted the ties between them. Rules prohibiting affinal marriages underscored the permanent status given in-laws, who were brought into what social scientists call "the intimate kin-group." Bans on unions between affines sought to protect the integrity of the family formed by the matrimonial contract and to minimize the threat to the family's unity. Thus in England, marriages with a deceased wife's sister and a brother's widow were frowned upon, for both of these individuals had been incorporated by marriage into the man's intimate kin-group to the extent that they were expected to be treated as consanguineous sisters.[22]

A reduction in the number of legal restrictions on affinal marriages took place in both the antebellum North and South.[23] As Michael Grossberg has noted, the loosening of prohibitions against unions between affines reflected a growing belief "that matrimony united two individuals, not two families." Once the original matrimonial contract ended, according to this line of reasoning, the surviving spouse was free to wed just about anyone, regardless of the marriage's impact on family unity and stability.[24] As an Arkansas judge declared in 1852:

> the relationship by affinity ceases with the dissolution of the marriage which produced it. Therefore though a man is by affinity brother to his wife's sister, yet upon the death of his wife, he may lawfully marry her sister.[25]

The paring down of bans on affinal marriages in the antebellum South suggests that the region was moving with the main currents of American social change as far as the selection of marriage partners was concerned. This evidence of southern legal change buttresses the recent findings of historians that personal preferences and affection—as opposed to family needs and prospects—played an increasingly significant role following the American Revolution in the choice of a mate in the South as well as the North. The gradual reduction of legal controls on persons related by affinity can be seen as part of the larger trend toward individualism and sentiment that was taking place in the new republic, a trend that allowed a person greater freedom to contract matrimony with whomever he or she wished.[26]

But one must be careful not to place too much emphasis on the loosening of restrictions regarding affinal marriage, for the fact of the matter is that on the eve of the Civil War, most southern states still prohibited unions between many affines. The most widely proscribed were those between a stepparent and stepchild, widower and daughter-in-law, and widow and son-in-law.[27] These and other limitations on affinal marriage combined with a generally tolerant attitude toward first-cousin unions to form a type of kinship which sociologist Bernard Farber has termed the "Biblical system." This system, predominant in much of the older South and New England, stemmed from the admonitions in Leviticus and English tradition. In contrast, according to Farber, a "Western American system" arose outside of these two regions which prohibited first-cousin unions but permitted marriage between any affines. Farber contends that the "Biblical system" of New England and the older South helped sustain a stable, family-oriented social hierarchy by incorporating in-laws into the intimate kin-group on a permanent basis and consolidating economic resources within the family. On the other hand, the "Western American system" encouraged the development of a more open society in the nineteenth century by facilitating marriages within a broad range of affines and outsiders, thus leading to a greater diffusion of family wealth.[28]

Undoubtedly, the widely accepted practice of first-cousin marriage in the South (except in the slave community, where, apparently, a taboo against unions between cousins prevailed) allowed whites to concentrate property within the family and keep the family name alive. Whether these were the main considerations prompting the arrangement of cousin marriages, however, is unclear. Surely, another important factor behind this southern marital custom was the social geography of plantation society. As Jane Turner Censer has observed, "kin formed a large part of the pool of possible mates" due to the extensive family ties in long-established communities or the social isolation of more sparsely settled areas. Therefore, it was not unexpected when cousins who had long known each other decided upon marriage.[29] In all likelihood, economic and social forces worked hand in hand to encourage such unions.

The antebellum evolution of legal rules concerning forbidden degrees of marriage in the South, then, revealed a continued preoccupation with viewing marriage as a way to build alliances between two families, to intensify kin-group solidarity, and to concentrate family property holdings. While personal preferences and sentimental love played a growing part in marital decisions, the laws regulating such decisions reflected the fact that matrimony was still a family and public concern. The primary aim of these laws before the Civil War was to encourage with a minimum of state intervention marriages that would sustain a highly stratified and close-knit society. Southern policymakers accomplished this in most states by permitting first-cousin marriages and continuing to prohibit unions between certain affines.

But in some states, fewer legal restraints were placed on those related by affinity. The lack of any controls whatsoever in Arkansas, Louisiana, Florida, and North Carolina stemmed from an emphasis on the rights of individuals. The developing law of prohibited degrees, in short, exhibited a fundamental tension between viewing marriage as a voluntary, contractual act and as an organic institution that provided the foundation of social order.

III

The development of legal rules regarding forbidden degrees of marriage furnished the framework for the criminalization of incest in the South and the rest of the country. Incest statutes in nineteenth-century America defined the crime generally as marriage or sexual relations between two parties related to each other within the prohibited degrees. In England, as mentioned at the outset, incest was not a crime at common law; ecclesiastical courts handled the offense until the passage of the Punishment of Incest Act in 1908. The criminalization of incest thus occurred in the United States long before it did in England, due perhaps to the separation of church and state in this country.[30]

By the mid-nineteenth century, most southern states had laws on the books making incest either a felony or high misdemeanor.[31] The main objective of the anti-incest legislation was to prohibit matrimony and inbreeding between near kin, not to protect women or children from sexual abuse. These laws, consequently, punished only intercourse and did not encompass other forms of sexual conduct. Furthermore, the punishments for those convicted of incest varied widely. Penalties during the antebellum period ranged from a maximum prison sentence of twelve months and a fine not exceeding one thousand dollars in Florida to life imprisonment in Louisiana. Several southern states also passed laws pronouncing incestuous marriages absolutely void from the outset or requiring the courts to declare such unions void upon conviction of the accused parties.[32] These statutes reversed the common-law tradition that made marriages within the forbidden degrees merely voidable rather than void, and therefore subject to challenge only in an ecclesiastical court.[33]

Of the criminal cases dealing with incest that reached the appellate level in the nineteenth-century South, the overwhelming majority involved prosecutions of incestuous sexual intercourse rather than marriage. Only five out of a total of forty-nine cases concerned charges against those who contracted matrimony within the prohibited degrees. The rest of the cases concerned charges of incestuous fornication or adultery, depending on the marital status of the defendant.[34] (See Appendix, pp. 261–63.)

By far the most common relationship between the parties in the forty-nine cases was that of father and daughter. As Table 3.1 shows, 39 percent of the state-supreme-courts' decisions involved the prosecution of father-daughter incest. In addition, 22 percent of the cases dealt with the prosecution of incest between stepfathers and stepdaughters, and 20 percent concerned uncle-niece incest. Over four-fifths of the incest cases that appeared in southern high courts during the nineteenth century, in other words, involved older men accused of carrying out incestuous relations with subor-

TABLE 3.1. Types of Incest Cases Before Southern High Courts, 1800–1900

Type of Incest	No. of Cases	Percentage
Father-Daughter	19	39%
Stepfather-Stepdaughter	11	22
Uncle-Niece	10	20
Brother- & Sister-in-law	4	8
First Cousin	2	4
Brother-Sister	2	4
Aunt-Nephew	1	2
Total	49	99*

*Percentages do not total 100 due to rounding.

dinate female relatives who were considerably younger. If these cases were
at all reflective of the kind of incest occurring in the population at large,
then incest in the South had clear patriarchal overtones. It can at least be
said with certainty that in the cases examined here, incest usually took
place in the context of an unequal distribution of power between the parties in terms of their age and position in the family.

In most southern states, the man only was punished for incestuous intercourse. Southern jurists did not consider incest a joint offense, so mutual
consent of the parties was not required for an incest conviction. As the
Alabama Supreme Court stated, "every element of the crime denounced in
our law may well exist against one party to the sexual act though the other
did not consent thereto."[35] In cases where force was used, for example, the
man might be guilty of incest and the woman innocent. Furthermore, in
such cases either rape or incest might be properly charged. The Texas
Supreme Court, in turning down an 1885 appeal by James Mercer, observed that:

> to make him guilty of incest, it was not necessary that his daughter should have
> consented to his carnal knowledge of her. She might be entirely innocent of
> any crime, and yet he might be guilty of rape or incest, or both, by having
> carnal knowledge of her.[36]

Because relatively few women were prosecuted for incest, almost all of
the appeals from convictions were submitted by male defendants. In fact,
only three out of forty-six individuals appealing incest convictions were
female.[37]

Since incest was a statutory rather than common-law crime, state supreme courts in the Old South usually construed the incest legislation
strictly according to its language. Especially in cases involving what might
be called "terminological incest"—that is, incest involving relatives outside
the conjugal family—the courts exercised their power to punish transgres-
sors with great caution. Rarely did the courts stray from a narrow interpretation of the relevant statutes.

The appellate court in antebellum South Carolina demonstrated such
prudence when regulating marriages within the forbidden degrees. In particular, the court shied away from assuming full ecclesiastical authority to
annul incestuous marriages without first gaining explicit legislative support
for such an enlargement of judicial power. *State v. Barefoot*, an 1845 bigamy case, reflected this reluctance. Scion Barefoot had married his mother's sister in 1838, and he married again seven years later, this time to a
Miss Elizabeth Odum. Indicted for bigamy, Barefoot came up with an
imaginative if flawed defense: he argued that his first marriage to his aunt
was void because of the consanguinity of the parties, and therefore he had
not committed bigamy when he married the second time. Barefoot's counsel held that if the nephew was "guilty of any thing, it is the crime of

incest." But the lower court believed otherwise, and it convicted Barefoot of bigamy.

In the appeal, Barefoot's attorney attempted to rouse the justices' presumed disgust with incest and thus persuade them that his client's first marriage had no validity. In the attorney's words:

> it is impossible that any enlightened system of jurisprudence can regard as valid contracts which do violence to the decencies of society, and which, if permitted by law, must so often degrade and debase the people of any country where they are allowed.[38]

Justice J. S. Richardson immediately grasped the thrust of Barefoot's defense: the nephew offered "to defend himself by insisting that the first marriage was intrinsically immoral and sinful, and therefore a nullity, in order to arrest the criminal consequences and legal punishment of bigamy." But Richardson pointed out that no legislation existed in South Carolina granting courts the power to annul marriages within the forbidden degrees. Hence, Richardson contended that he and his fellow judges could not intervene in Barefoot's union with his aunt, since at common law only church authorities could invalidate incestuous marriages. Although the South Carolina jurist recognized that "there may be deep feelings enlisted in this case," he strongly believed that the negative consequences of nullifying marriages and bastardizing children made it imperative for him to maintain his adherence to the common law on this matter. Richardson observed, however, that "it may well be deplored that a legislative Act has not been passed to reform the common law in this respect . . . and such incestuous marriages declared to be utterly null and void, if contracted after the statute."[39]

Despite Richardson's barely disguised call for action, the state legislature still had not pronounced incestuous marriages voidable thirteen years later when the South Carolina high court once again had to rule on the validity of such unions, this time in an estate dispute involving a marriage between an uncle and his niece. As before, the court refused to appropriate any ecclesiastical powers to annul incestuous unions until it had the statutory authority to do so. Once again, the appellate judges called on the state legislature to take corrective measures and authorize the court to nullify marriages "within the Levitical degrees." Without such statutory backing, the court refused to act. In its words, "It is far better to leave to the Legislature the appropriate duty of defining and prohibiting such evils rather than arm the Court of Chancery with ecclesiastical powers on a subject of great delicacy and pervading interest."[40]

These cases and others underscored the desire of most antebellum southern judges to leave the power to develop marriage rules in the hands of the state legislators.[41] This is not to say, however, that southern judges shrank from passing moral judgment on incestuous marriages; clearly, they disapproved. Moreover, when state legislatures invested the courts with the power to annul unions within the forbidden degrees and to punish the parties involved, appellate jurists in the South usually supported the exercise of this judicial power.[42]

The circumspective manner in which antebellum southern judges wielded their power to exact criminal punishment was apparent not only in cases of incestuous marriage but also in those involving sexual relations within the forbidden degrees. In *Ewell v. State* (1834), the Tennessee Supreme Court granted a new trial to Dabney Ewell, who had been convicted of carrying out a felonious sexual assault on his brother's daughter, not because there was a lack of evidence establishing incestuous intercourse between the parties but because no evidence was introduced during the trial proving where the offense was committed. Without proof of venue, the Tennessee judges felt compelled to reverse the judgment of the circuit court. Justice Peck, in his written opinion, underscored the unwavering adherence of the high court to the technicalities of the common law:

> I will not relax old and inflexible rules in the administration of the criminal law; there is no reason for it. Whenever we depart from the great landmarks which have been the guides for ages, we enter on a sea of uncertainty and hazard every thing.[43]

Despite such declarations, southern jurists occasionally refused to adhere to strict proceduralism. Judge Eugenius A. Nisbet of the Georgia Supreme Court issued the strongest call for a measure of judicial discretion regarding criminal procedure in incest cases. In an 1852 opinion, Nisbet rejected out of hand the argument that an indictment accusing George Cook of committing incestuous adultery with his daughter ought to be quashed on technical grounds, and the jurist vigorously supported the lower-court's decision to let the indictment stand:

> I have but little fear of judicial power in Georgia so aggrandizing itself, as to endanger any of the powers of other departments of the government; or to endanger the life and liberty of the citizen; or to deprive the Jury of their appropriate functions. The danger rather to be dreaded is making the Judges men of straw, and thus stripping the Courts of popular reverence and annihilating the popular estimate of the power and sanctity of the law. I am not, therefore, disposed to watch with great vigilance every act, phrase or sentiment, that may fall from the Court, with the hope of detecting an indiscretion, or fabricating an error. Surely some discretion ought to be allowed to able, pains-taking [sic], conscientious men, as to the *mere etiquette* of judicial procedure.[44]

Such an energetic endorsement of judicial discretion was a remarkable exception in the nineteenth-century South, however, and most judges insisted on the need for stringent adherence to the prescribed forms of criminal procedure, even if it sometimes led to the release of incest offenders.

In general, the impact of incestuous assault on women and children was only a secondary consideration, if that, in antebellum decisions. Sexual abuse appeared to disturb southern judges primarily because it undermined the family as an effective institution of social control. More specifically, sexual abuse exposed the coercion that underlay the exercise of patriarchal authority and, hence, threatened the legitimacy of this authority. As the Texas Supreme Court asserted in 1849, incest "was so shocking to the moral sense of every civilized being" because it reduced "man from his boastful superiority of a moral, rational being, to a level with the brutal creation." The Texas court proclaimed that only in the face of the "most indisputable proof" would it accept the possibility that such a crime had been "committed in this age and country." In the case before the Texas appellate judges, they found that there was not "the slightest legal proof, that our country has been degraded by the commission of so loathsome, so heartsickening an offence, in our midst," and they awarded a new trial to a man indicted for committing incest with his daughter.[45] This mixture of strong rhetoric and reluctance to prosecute patriarchs continued to mark incest cases after the Civil War.

IV

During the postwar period, the development of incest statutes in the South exhibited several notable characteristics. Alterations in the legal rules regarding forbidden degrees of marriage continued to reflect the antebellum tension between competing views of matrimony as private and contractual on the one hand, and as a public affair involving the preservation of the social order on the other. The emphasis on individualism and contractual rights could be seen in the unimpeded trend of southern states toward the relaxation of restrictions on affinal marriages. Mississippi in 1871, Virginia in 1873, and Georgia in 1875, for instance, lifted their bans on unions with an uncle's widow. At the same time, Virginia abolished its prohibition against marrying a nephew's widow.[46]

In contrast to this loosening of controls on affinal relationships, preoccupation with marriage as a source of social stability led to tighter regulation of consanguineous unions. Most important, Arkansas and Louisiana imposed bans on first-cousin marriages by the end of the century.[47] Other blood relations also fell within the forbidden degrees during the postwar period. Alabama legislators in 1867 extended their marital prohibitions to unions with the daughter of a half brother or half sister, and North Carolina lawmakers in 1883 included half-blood relatives in their list of restrictions. Furthermore, the Mississippi legislature in 1880 proscribed marriages between uncles and nieces for the first time, and in 1892 it saw fit to state explicitly that grandparents and grandchildren could not contract matrimony.[48]

It is not entirely clear why southern lawmakers moved in the late nineteenth century to enlarge the number of statutory prohibitions against unions between blood relatives at the same time that they were paring down the number of affinal restrictions. New concerns about the possibility of transmitting hereditary defects through marriage, concerns that also made themselves evident during this period in laws banning interracial marriages, accounted in part for the closer regulation of consanguineous unions. Legal commentators throughout the country began to cite such biological arguments with greater frequency after the middle of the nineteenth century to support their opposition to marriages between persons closely related by blood.[49] The Arkansas Supreme Court reflected these heightened fears in 1886 when it explained the aim of the new state ban on first-cousin unions:

> The intention of the legislature was to prohibit the intermarriage of persons nearly related by blood, partly no doubt, on account of the supposed evil consequences to body and mind resulting to the offspring of such marriages.[50]

Besides anxiety about inbreeding, a concern with preserving social order during the postwar era led to new criminal punishments for incest. In particular, lawmakers in North Carolina, South Carolina, and Virginia expanded their incest prohibitions, which before the war dealt only with marriage within the forbidden degrees, to include sexual intercourse between certain near kin.[51]

On balance, these statutory developments in the late nineteenth century created the potential for greater public intervention in southern domestic relations. But the ambivalent attitude of southern jurists toward criminal punishment as a means to regulate incestuous behavior placed significant limits on the extent of this intervention. Indeed, between 1865 and 1900, state courts in the South considered the appeals of thirty-seven individuals convicted of incest and granted new trials to eighteen of these defendants.

In part, the high rate of reversals stemmed from the unwillingness of appellate judges to break sharply with the antebellum argument that statutory provisions authorizing criminal penalties for the violation of incest bans were in derogation of the common law and thus should be narrowly construed. The strict constructionism of southern jurists after the Civil War led them to order new trials in several appeals from incest convictions. In *Johnson v. State* (1886), the Texas Supreme Court overturned the conviction of Robert Johnson, who had been indicted for sexual intercourse with his fifteen-year-old stepdaughter, Kinnie. The Texas justices did not dispute evidence that intercourse had occurred between these two individuals and that Johnson may have used force to gain his stepdaughter's compliance. But the judges pointed out that sexual relations between the girl and her stepfather did not take place until after her mother had died. Therefore, according to the court, Johnson could not be charged with incest because the relation of stepfather and stepdaughter, within the meaning of the statute, "had ceased to exist" following the termination of the marriage relation between Johnson and Kinnie's mother, even though the girl continued to live in Johnson's house. "Under the facts of the case, he may be guilty of fornication and of adultery and perhaps of rape," concluded the Texas jurists, "but not of incest."[52] Likewise, the Tennessee Supreme Court refused in 1898 to uphold the incest conviction of a man charged with impregnating his wife's sister because the sexual relationship had commenced after the wife had died. The court contended that the deceased wife's sister was no longer an affinal relative, and hence, sexual intercourse between them was not incestuous. In its words, "This is the literalism of the statute, and the spirit is not broader than the letter."[53]

Besides a continued propensity to interpret the incest laws strictly, southern high courts maintained a firm commitment to procedural formalism in criminal cases, often awarding new trials to defendants accused of incest on grounds that were quite technical in nature. As a Tennessee judge explained in 1891:

> no feeling of abhorrence respecting the crime should obscure the judgment or abate the vigilance of the Court to see that he has the fullest and fairest trial and chance to establish his innocence under the law, which in its best strictness is in its best purity.[54]

Appeals from incest convictions after the Civil War raised three major procedural issues: flaws in the indictment process, admissibility and sufficiency of evidence, and corroboration of female testimony. A systematic examination of the way in which southern courts handled these issues reveals the extent to which the judiciary sought to ensure the defendant's procedural safeguards in criminal trials. At the same time, such an analysis demonstrates the general lack of regard on the part of southern jurists for the victims of incest.

An almost unnerving insistence on procedural niceties was especially evident in the judicial response to flaws in the indictment process. The Mississippi Supreme Court reversed an incest conviction in 1891 because the word "feloniously" had been omitted from the indictment.[55] The Arkansas court exhibited a similar predisposition to quash incest indictments on the basis of technical defects. In an 1886 case, the court held that an indictment was insufficient because it accused the parties of incestuous fornication without making it clear that they were unmarried at the time of the alleged crime. Seven years later, an Arkansas father won his appeal from a conviction for copulation with his daughter on the grounds that the indictment charged him with incestuous adultery but did not state his marital status. "A particular description of the specific act which constitutes the crime of incest, when committed by parties within the prohibited degrees, as well as the status of the party charged" were necessary components for an adequate indictment, the Arkansas court decided, requiring adherence to this rule, "however technical it may seem."[56]

Expressing concern about the slightest imperfections in indictments, southern jurists throughout the nineteenth century commonly ordered new trials because of convictions based on faulty indictments, not just in incest cases but in other criminal cases as well. Even antebellum slaves convicted of felonies were able to take advantage of small mistakes in indictments to gain new trials. According to Daniel Flanigan, in his thorough study of criminal procedure in southern slave trials, the preoccupation with accurately drawn indictments stemmed from the belief that the accused had the right to know exactly what crime he or she had allegedly committed.[57] Certainly, judicial attention to the form of the indictment was called for when substantial flaws, such as seeking conviction for a nonexistent crime or a truly inadequate description of the offense, were involved.[58] As Flanigan notes, however, "This quite sensible requirement . . . when too rigidly applied resulted in numerous reversals and new trials because of minuscule drafting errors."[59]

Not only did southern jurists uphold a strict observance of the indictment process, they also adopted tough requirements for the admissibility and sufficiency of evidence. Although southern judges had demanded high standards of proof during the antebellum period, the increased number of incest appeals after the Civil War led to the development of more detailed evidential rules. In order to prosecute for the crime of incest, two main elements had to be established: the relationship of the parties and sexual intercourse between them. On the first issue, southern high courts argued that "the evidence should be clear and unequivocal as to the fact of the relationship." If the evidence fell short of this standard, the courts did not hesitate to overturn an incest conviction, because proof of the relationship was "absolutely essential to the establishment of the crime charged." In *McGrew v. State* (1883), for instance, Texas appellate jurists ordered a new trial for William McGrew, who was accused of incestuous intercourse with his stepdaughter, on the grounds that his legal marriage with the girl's mother had not been "proven affirmatively." At issue was whether the mother's original marriage had been legally terminated, either by divorce or death of the first husband, before she married McGrew. "If she was not his lawful wife," observed the court, "then the illicit connection of McGrew with her daughter by the previous marriage, however reprehensible in morals, would not constitute the crime of incest in law."[60]

While crucial for an incest prosecution, proof of relationship was usually not difficult to attain. Establishing the act of sexual intercourse was far more complex, and state supreme courts in the South grappled at length with this knotty legal problem. Generally, southern jurists agreed that in prosecutions for incest, evidence could be admitted relating to sexual acts between the parties at any time prior to the indictment charging incestuous

intercourse. When attempting to establish that the illicit relations continued, the prosecution also had the right to present proof of sexual intercourse following the act specifically under trial.[61] Nevertheless, since the
majority of incest offenses were committed within the privacy of the family
home, they remained difficult to prove. Often other family members were
the only witnesses, and they were frequently reluctant to testify. In most
jurisdictions, moreover, wives were prohibited by law from testifying
against their husbands in prosecutions for incest. The Texas Supreme Court
in 1882 granted Daniel Compton a new trial because his wife had testified
against him, claiming that Compton had engaged in sexual intercourse with
her fourteen-year-old daughter by a former marriage. The appellate court
in South Carolina took a less-restrictive approach, deciding that a wife
could act as a witness against her husband in an incest prosecution as long
as she was not compelled to disclose "any confidential communication"
during the marriage.[62] Restraints of any sort, however, on the testimony of
wives obviously made it more difficult to establish the occurrence of incestuous intercourse in the household.

Even more serious as an obstacle to the effective prosecution of incest
was the fact that in many cases the uncorroborated testimony of the female
party was not enough to bring about the conviction of the accused. Although southern courts usually did not prosecute the female party in incest
cases, they held that when she consented to incestuous intercourse, she was
an accomplice. In Florida, a conviction could be supported on the uncorroborated testimony of an accomplice, but this was not true in other southern states, where accomplice testimony required corroboration.[63]

To authorize an incest conviction on the testimony of an accomplice in
these states, corroborating evidence had to connect the accused with the
commission of the offense. According to the Georgia Supreme Court,
evidence which went "no further than merely to raise a grave suspicion that
the accused committed the crime in question" was insufficient. Hence, the
court contended, a young woman's pregnancy did not corroborate her
testimony against her stepfather to the extent that it warranted his conviction of incestuous adultery. But evidence that the stepfather had tried to
bribe the arresting sheriff and, when this proved unsuccessful, "exclaimed
that the thing would ruin him and his whole family" was adequate corroboration. Appellate courts elsewhere in the South laid down similar rules on
the extent of corroboration necessary to support the testimony of an accomplice to incest.[64]

Failure to instruct the jury on the law of accomplice testimony and the necessary corroboration was a reversible error, and in several late nineteenth-
century cases, defendants gained new trials on these grounds.[65] More important, though, the issue of accomplice testimony raised the questions of what
constituted consent on the part of the female party and at what point she
became an accomplice to incestuous intercourse. In *Mercer v. State* (1885),

the Texas Supreme Court defined an accomplice in the following terms: "If the witness, knowingly, voluntarily, and with the same intent which actuated the defendant, united with him in the commission of the crime against him, she was an accomplice." On the other hand:

> if in the commission of the incestuous act, she was the victim of force, threats, fraud or undue influence, so that she did not act voluntarily, and did not join in the commission of the act with the same intent which actuated the defendant, then she would not be an accomplice, and a conviction would stand even upon her uncorroborated testimony.[66]

These seem like fairly straightforward and sensible guidelines, yet in the very same case, the Texas court appeared to construe the phrase "force, threats, fraud or undue influence" in an extremely restrictive manner. According to the prosecution witness, her father "first forced her to submit to his unnatural desire when she was thirteen years old, and he continued to have sexual intercourse with her from that time until she was twenty years old." The father had impregnated her at that time, and when she was about four-and-one-half months advanced, she revealed the paternity of the child. The court did not believe that "this long continued incestuous intercourse" could have taken place without the consent of the witness, and it argued that she was an accomplice to the crime. The judges noted that she was "a stout, healthy girl" and yet offered "no resistance" during the last sexual encounter in which she became pregnant. But the woman said that she "did not cry out, nor did she make any great resistance, simply because she was afraid." And well she might be, for she had tried to resist her father's sexual advances two years earlier, and he had "whipped her severely with a board." In addition, following the final copulation, her father told her that "if she ever reported the occurrence to any one, he would beat her to death." Surely, this constituted threatening behavior and the exercise of "undue influence." Why the Texas judges did not think so is difficult to explain, but they obviously demonstrated enormous insensitivity to the woman's ordeal. Fortunately, in this instance, the jurists felt that enough corroborating evidence existed to uphold the father's conviction.[67]

In other cases, however, where the court considered the female party an accomplice and there was insufficient corroboration of her testimony, southern appellate justices overturned the incest convictions of male defendants. In an 1896 case, for example, Ada Coburn testified that her father coerced her into copulating with him, beginning when she was six years old. Despite this testimony, the Texas Supreme Court claimed that certain circumstances "were such to indicate that she was consenting." Specifically, the court asserted that "no objection or resistance was interposed when the least act of resistance or objection interposed by her would have prevented the acts of sexual intercourse." Since no corroborating evidence existed outside of the woman's testimony and because the lower court had failed to instruct the jury on the subject of accomplice testimony, the Texas high court reversed the father's conviction and ordered a new trial.[68] Apparently, unless there was evidence of actual physical resistance on the part of the female party, she was considered an accomplice to incest. Most southern judges gave little weight to the concept of psychological coercion in their determinations of whether a female had consented to incestuous intercourse. In *Taylor v. State* (1900), Maggie McGuire insisted that "she had never consented to the illicit intercourse" with her stepfather; "in each instance it occurred against her will, and . . . she was forced to submit to his lustful embraces." The Georgia Supreme Court, though, decided that "she in fact consented to it, so doing however with that reluctance and disinclination which would naturally be felt by any young girl in sustaining such relations with her mother's husband." Of course, by acknowledging that she was a "young girl," the court underscored the fact that she lacked the maturity and autonomy to make a real choice respecting sexual relations with her stepfather. It is hard to imagine circumstances under which sexual relations between these two parties would not have been abusive.[69]

Although appellate judges by and large discounted the significance of psychological coercion, not all of them were unaware of the subtler dynamics of incest. At least one southern jurist recognized that often incest was not consensual and that it often involved sexual relations based on power and inequality. According to Judge McKay, a member of the Georgia Supreme Court, "The unnatural crime . . . is generally the act of a man upon a woman, over whom, by the natural ties of kindred, he has almost complete control, and generally he alone is to blame." Unlike most of his colleagues, the Georgia jurist realized that there was "a *force* used, which, while it cannot be said to be that violence which constitutes rape, is yet of a character that is almost as overpowering."[70]

Given the central role of psychological coercion in the exercise of patriarchal authority, it is not surprising that southern judges largely accepted the legitimacy of its use.[71] For the most part, jurists assumed that absence of physical resistance to the male's sexual advances meant that the woman consented to incestuous intercourse and was thus an accomplice. The predisposition to classify women as accomplices, together with the rule in most jurisdictions prohibiting an incest conviction upon uncorroborated accomplice testimony, made it difficult to prosecute the crime because often there was no other witness to provide sufficient corroboration.[72]

Northern courts in the nineteenth century appeared to have devised a strikingly different approach to the prosecution of incest cases, especially regarding the issues of psychological coercion and corroboration of female testimony. Appellate jurists in the North more widely embraced the notion that incestuous assaults could take place even in the absence of physical force. In an 1895 case, the Wisconsin Supreme Court upheld the incest conviction of Ernest Porath, who engaged in sexual intercourse with his thirteen-year-old daughter while they were pitching hay in the family's barn. The Wisconsin judges noted that "her resistance was not as strenuous and effective as it might have been. . . . It does not necessarily follow in all such cases, that the female is to be regarded as an accomplice, and particularly in a case like the present, in view of the relation between the parties, and the coercive authority of her father over her." Likewise, the Michigan high court pointed out that James Burwell did not employ physical force in an assault on his daughter, and that she "yielded on account of threats and fear." As a result, the judges contended:

> Evidence tending to show that he had abused and beaten her before, that he was abusive to his wife and other children, and the language used on these occasions, were competent and important for the jury to consider in determining whether she yielded under those circumstances which under the law are the equivalent of force.

Northern jurists, in other words, more readily recognized that although a female party might not physically oppose the sexual advances of her father or stepfather, this did not automatically mean that she became an accomplice in the commission of the crime.[73]

Even when the woman or girl was considered an accomplice, many northern jurisdictions allowed incest convictions based on her uncorroborated testimony. According to the Vermont Supreme Court, the evaluation of such testimony was "always a question for the jury, who is to pass upon the credibility of the accomplice, as they must upon that of every other witness." In cases where the prosecution of incest rested upon the uncorroborated testimony of an accomplice, warned the Vermont appellate jurists, the court should always "advise great caution on the part of the jury in giving credit to it," but the jury should not be instructed, "as a matter of law, that the prisoner in such a case must be acquitted."[74]

Requiring corroboration of female testimony in circumstances that pitted one person's word against another indicated that southern courts had a basic mistrust of the victim's testimony. It also suggested that while appellate jurists in the nineteenth-century South roundly denounced incest as a crime against nature, they were ambivalent about actually prosecuting men for the crime. Much the same mistrust of female testimony and ambivalence about punishing men can be seen in the prosecution of rape. The emphasis on evidence of physical resistance to prove lack of consent and the careful consideration of the woman's prior sexual conduct in rape cases reflected a deep-seated belief in the notion of the seductress, an image that often cropped up in incest prosecutions as well.[75]

Judicial ambivalence in such cases stemmed in large part from a continued commitment to the patriarchal ideal. Rather than attacking the traditional family as an outmoded institution, southern jurists focused their criticisms on individual men whom they perceived as misusing their "natural" power to rule. In short, the judges did not mean to imply by their criticism of the particular males in these cases that patriarchal authority ought to be eliminated or transformed. On the contrary, they continued to assume that inequality and hierarchical control formed the very basis of the family and society.

In this context, the concept of being an accomplice to incest was a legal fiction that allowed judges to express their disapproval of incest while restricting convictions for the crime mainly to those indisputable instances of assault which exposed the coercion inherent in the exercise of patriarchal authority and which thus called into question its legitimacy. The criminalization of incest in this manner actually buttressed male dominance by isolating those patriarchs who used physical violence against female members of their family to gain sexual satisfaction, and labeling these men as "deviants." For those men who employed psychological coercion, apparently, the chances of successful conviction were far less. Despite the judicial rhetoric of outrage, then, the reality was that during the nineteenth century, the sexual access of men to women and children in their family remained largely unchallenged. In this sense, legal change led to the persistence rather than decline of patriarchy.

4

"Southern Dishonor": Flesh, Blood, Race, and Bondage

CATHERINE CLINTON

OVER A HALF CENTURY after the end of Emancipation, W.E.B. Du Bois wrote:

> I shall forgive the white South much in its final judgement day: I shall forgive its slavery, for slavery is a world-old habit; I shall forgive its fighting for a well–lost cause, and for remembering that struggle with tender tears; I shall forgive its so-called "pride of race," the passion of its hot blood, and even its dear, old, laughable strutting and posing; but one thing I shall never forgive, neither in this world nor the world to come: its wanton and continued and persistent insulting of the black womanhood which it sought and seeks to prostitute to its lust. I cannot forget that it is such Southern gentlemen into whose hands smug Northern hypocrites of today are seeking to place our women's eternal destiny. . . .

In his moving personal essay, "The Damnation of Women,"[1] Du Bois rages that the "crushing weight of slavery fell on black women." Du Bois decries the legacy of slavery which continues to oppress black women and the historical issues which have been too long neglected.

When we review slavery's interlocking systems of power, we often factor in gender, race, and class. However, sexuality is a central and significant element which must neither be ignored nor discounted. Flesh and blood were an explosive mix in the Old South. The impact of sexuality on family and antebellum culture seems reserved for authors of fiction rather than writers of history. But family ties within slavery were profoundly complex and deserve more than memory. Slavery itself remains a provocative topic.

As Toni Morrison warns: "There is not a place you or I can go, to think about or not think about, to summon the presences of, or recollect the absences of slaves; nothing that reminds us of the ones who made the journey and of those who did not make it. There is no suitable memorial, or plaque or wreath or wall or park or skyscraper lobby. There is no two-hundred-foot tower. There is no small bench by the road. There is not even a tree scored, an initial that I can visit or you can visit in Charleston or Savannah or New York or Providence or better still, on the banks of the Mississippi."[2] Morrison's Pulitzer-prize-winning work, *Beloved*, provides a tribute, a memorial, yet historians have their work cut out for them.

Kenneth Stampp's path-breaking study, *The Peculiar Institution* (1956), assaulted the previous century of scholarship—comfortable notions about paternalistic Southern planters and their racially inferior slaves. Thousands upon thousands of pages have followed—reassessing, refuting, refining, and refueling our passions on this controversial topic. The debate over slavery for the past quarter century has resulted in an increasingly knotted and fraying skein of data and theory, making slave studies a field of brilliant and at times brutal academic challenge.

Kenneth Stampp's vision of slavery may have been dramatically revised by the past quarter century of work, but I think his title ironically will stand the test of time. Perhaps the study of slavery as an economic system should be laid to rest for a time, for as those of us in agricultural history know, letting a field lie fallow for future harvesting can reap greater reward in the long run than continuing to heap on the fertilizer.

Slavery was a system of production, and its significance to the antebellum South remains undisputed. However, the fact that slavery fostered a distinctive system of *reproduction* in the plantation South during the first half of the nineteenth century merits more attention. Despite the explosion of work, both the sexual dynamics of slavery and the racial dynamic of sexuality remain relatively unexplored.

From the viewpoint of cotton planters at the turn of the nineteenth century, a legal fluke shut down the supply of imported slaves during a crucial period of economic expansion. Smuggling supplemented the system by adding approximately fifty thousand to the ranks of slavery, but this was not an effective measure. The problem was resolved by other means: slaveowners maximized their slave population by natural increase. The number of slaves grew at an annual rate of 2.5 percent per year for almost sixty years, a phenomenal rate for any population but especially impressive when compared with the net natural decreases of other slave populations in the hemisphere.

Therefore, the American South did create a "peculiar institution," even if scholars and slaveowners themselves did not grasp the dimensions of distinctiveness. Slavery, as Orlando Patterson persuaded in his monumental *Slavery and Social Death*, has been a persistent rather than peculiar system: "there is no region on earth that has not at some time harbored the institution. Probably there is no group of people whose ancestors were not at one time slaves or slaveholders."[3] As Peter Kolchin demonstrated in his prize-winning study, *Unfree Labor: American Slavery and Russian Serfdom*,[4] depriving members of the agricultural work force of the fruits of their own labor was a significant but not a peculiar development within rural societies worldwide.

However, slavery was not simply a system of labor extraction but a means of sexual and social control as well. As H. J. Nieboer argued in his path-breaking *Slavery as an Industrial System* (1910), deprivation of an individual's labor was not the most striking feature of slavery, but rather the deprivation of one's own *kin*. This point is echoed and brilliantly enhanced with Patterson's argument concerning "natal alienation." The destruction of bonds of kinship, exerting control over reproduction, the resultant distortion of family relations (among the owner class as well as the owned) perhaps contributed to American slavery's most peculiar feature. With the exception of a few British territories where the experiment was much shorter in duration, the American South was the only slave society where the labor force was not resupplied by imports. The "way of death" (as Joseph Miller has dubbed the slave trade) was replaced by a way of life in the Old South.

The question of slave breeding remains a subject of debate. U. B. Phillips's assertion in 1918 that there was "no shred of supporting evidence" is no longer convincing, like many of his claims. Frederic Bancroft demonstrated in 1931 that slaveowners put a high value on fertile women, and women were given incentives to become mothers. The agricultural historian Lewis C. Gray reported the rearing of slaves constituted an important element in the agricultural economy of the South. Since we have evidence that infant mortality among slaves was roughly 25 percent and we know that the slave population grew at 2.5 percent per year, we cannot assume, as scholars have suggested, that slaveowners merely let nature take its course.[5] The reproduction of the slave labor force was too vital for planters to leave such matters to the slaves themselves.

Evidence from the slave narratives suggests that "nature" was aided and abetted by planter intervention, and these interferences were unwelcome. Forced mating was not uncommon, and some slaves reported barbaric indignities, as Luisa Everett tells in the Works Progress Administration (WPA) interviews: "Marse Jim called me and Sam ter him and ordered Sam to pull off his shirt—that was all the McClain niggers wore—and he said to me: 'Now do you think you can stand this big nigger?' He had that old bull whip flug acrost his shoulder and Lawd, that man could hit so hard! So I jes said 'yassur, I guess so,' and tried to hide my face so I couldn't see Sam's nakedness, but he made me look at him anyhow. Well he told us what we must git busy and do in his presence, and we had to do it. After that we were considered man and wife." Barren women involved in monogamous relationships were encouraged and upon occasion required to find new sexual partners. Indeed, Luisa Everett reported, "me and Sam was a healthy pair and had fine, big babies, so I never had another man forced on me, thank God." Some ex-slaves even reported the use of "stockmen" or "breedin' niggers," as well as castration as a means of "improving" the slave population.[6]

All of these practices contributed to the slaveowners' sense of absolute power and reassured the planter hierarchy that precious resources would not be wasted. The maximization of slave reproduction was a strategy for the maintenance of the system as a whole as well as for the success of the individual planter. In Georgia during the Revolutionary era, the hunger for slaves was so great that records indicate slave mothers could not hope to keep their children beyond the age of six, when they might be sold off for profit.[7] An account in *The Savannah Georgian* in January 1856 reported: "We notice from reported Sales in various localities that Men, Women and children, generally brought in good prices—affording gratifying evidence that the times are not as hard as has been supposed. . . . In short, stock raising was never in a more flourishing condition." Similar reports in the *Wilmington Journal*—"Good breeders are at least *30 per cent* higher now (in the dull season of the year) than they were in January"—demonstrate the important role of breeding in slave economics.[8]

In most Western societies, patriarchy's tenacious hold exerted the legal rights of the alleged father over those of the biological mother. Children inherited names, property, and status through their fathers. Yet in slave societies and within many colonial contexts, the extension of the slaveowner's or conqueror's will superseded the natural father's, and a hierarchy of male power emerged. Within the slaveowner's world, the sexual supremacy of dominant males subsumed the interests of all women and the men of the subordinate nation, race, or class.

In colonial America, where this system rooted and flourished as the invading populations conquered and thrived, if slaveowners and slaves refrained from sexual contacts, men of property might insure the smooth transfer of wealth. But sexual trespass and illegitimate offspring were part of every society, and slaveowners felt the need of rigid regulation within their own fragile system. Thus, colonial America witnessed a legislative frenzy, an attempt to monitor sexual behavior, to institute the male will of the master class.

One of the first *statutes* tackling the issue of slavery in the British colonies dealt with this thorny question of interracial sex: in Virginia in 1662, the mulatto children of slaves followed the status of the mother, defying centuries of English tradition.[9] White males might stray, yet slave concubines and bastards could make no legal claim. Indeed, this law provided errant males with an *incentive* to prefer slave women as illicit partners. White women involved in these liaisons could expose male misconduct in the courts and sue for support of illegitimate offspring. Slave women had no such recourse.

The state of Virginia determined "fornication with a negro man or woman" was a crime which doubled the penalties for sexual trespass with a white.[10] These early laws clearly discriminated on the basis of gender and were directed as much at sexual control as they were at racial domination, mainly because the two systems were by necessity interlocking. The taboo status of interracial sex perhaps heightened its attractiveness among both races and genders, but the law evolved to satisfy the crisis only according to the needs of the white males intent upon social control.

The first wave of legislation did not reckon with the sexual defiance of white women. When laws established *partus sequitur ventrem* for slave women, colonial legislators did not intend for slave fathers to provide their children's freedom by impregnating free white females. White women were at a premium in the Southern colonies, and legislators panicked over their sexual misconduct. They were the cornerstone of the family and the foundation of colonial culture. By 1691, the Virginia assembly, alarmed about "abominable mixture and spurious issue," targeted those English women who dared to cross the color line: any woman who gave birth to a mulatto was fined heavily; if she could not pay, she was sentenced to five years of servitude, and the child was to be sold into servitude until the age of thirty.[11] Although most of this could be confined to questions of slave law or to laws against illicit sex, legislators expanded their language to embrace both persons of color (not just slaves) and marriage (not just fornication). In Maryland, white women who married slaves were forced to serve their husband's masters, and any children of these unions were required to serve as well until the age of thirty. In Virginia, racial intermarriage with free blacks was discouraged by banishing the white partner from the colony, and after 1705, a white person who dared to marry someone of color was incarcerated for six months.[12]

These early statutes and cases indicate that lawmakers recognized the dangers to their system when you "mixed flesh" into "mixed blood." Without rigid racial barriers and gender dictates, such sexual activity chipped away at white-male imperative. Slaveowners responded with laws on the one hand, and an elaborate code of sexual and racial etiquette on the other. They could not sexually segregate the races, but white men of property devised elaborate modifications of the system to transform any liabilities to their own advantage. Although timetables for these laws vary from state to state and each separate region provided its own distinctive subset, generally laws evolved that discouraged dramatically any interracial sexual liaisons between white women and black men and prevented white men from attempts at legitimating their sexual unions with African-American women—slave or free. Furthermore, the living testimonies, the mulattoes, were recognized as the flesh of their white parents, but denied the privilege of their blood. Only upon rare occasions did states recognize mulatto status.[13]

The frenzy over racial purity provides an ironic twist. As novelist James Baldwin once challenged a white: "It's not that you wouldn't want your daughter to marry me, you wouldn't want your wife's daughter to. . . ." Quite naturally, racial discrimination resulted in the phenomenon of "passing," and the possibility of "tainted" blood drove some white Southerners wild. In defense, white Southerners became obsessive about pedigree. Class membership drove many white slaveholders to search for impeccable family trees, tracing roots only to European origins. This paranoia could and did provide tragic consequences, as Kate Chopin poignantly chronicles in her short story "Desirée's Baby."

Within the antebellum South, the mixing of the races—"amalgamation"—was a "horror" and "sin" which compounded the sexual contacts between owners and owned. White politicians had long railed at this evil, and travelers regularly commented on the lightening of the slave population: Lucius Bierce's perception in 1822 was that "more than half the slave population are mixed with whites."[14] But this problem was labeled "miscegenation" in 1864 and emerged as a political as well as a social ill.[15] The intertwining of flesh and blood produced a wide spectrum of racially mixed populations, spawned living witnesses to the hypocrisy of the slaveholders' "Christian" system, and bred racial and sexual tensions which remain some portion of slavery's legacy today.

Southern honor, as Bertram Wyatt-Brown has argued with great eloquence, was woven into the fabric of antebellum white experience. Honor is defined, illuminated, and the discourse creatively explored in Wyatt-Brown's path-breaking study. Although Edward Ayers, Kenneth Greenberg, Wyatt-Brown, and others have examined critical aspects of this issue, I wish to examine aspects of "Southern dishonor" which highlight "slavery as it was" rather than the discourse on slavery.

First and foremost, I intend this term to be ironic as much as an homage to Wyatt-Brown's work. The "authenticity," "validity," or "sincerity" of the slaveowners' worldview seems relatively unscathed, despite repeated floggings in emerging African-American histories. These "Christian slaveholders," as the new literature labels (and I gather the current popularity of this phrasing is not to distinguish them from newly discovered Muslim or Jewish slaveholders), remained self-serving, profit-mongering, sin-ridden monsters as far as the majority of slave men and, especially, women were concerned. By using slave voices and African-American memory, we need to re-tint our lenses to review our slave past.

The systematic sexual exploitation of slaves was a crucial component of the system—not because, as sociobiologists suggest, the slaveowner's ability to turn his own flesh into capital was the purest form of natural selection theory, but rather because the political and social consequences of this activity were more significant than economic profits accrued.

Sexual domination, sexual coercion, and sexual violence were not rare violations of the compact between owner and owned. Counting up the number of rapes and beatings or the number of children resulting from assaults or coercive unions should secondarily concern us. Rather, we must be aware of the constant threat which threw a long shadow across planta- tion life and considerably clouds any portraits of the sunny South. Further, as Susan Brownmiller, Herbert Gutman, Deborah White, and Jacqueline Jones have all condemned, we do injustice to the story of slaves' struggles if we merely "seek totals." Nevertheless, the ample evidence amassed by Jones, White, and other scholars of African-American women to document the sexual exploitation of slave women further undermines those scholars who seek to minimize this aspect of slavery through neglect, rationaliza- tion, or even denial.

What were the practical results of this "peculiar" pattern within South- ern society? First and foremost, there was the disruption of the slave family and the creation of destructive elements which affected the lives of African- Americans;[16] second, the distortion of sexual and family mores for white Southern families; and third, a sharpening of sexual and racial ideology which provoked violence and created, at a minimum, the doubling rather than the reduction of sexual and racial inequalities.

White women who lost status when they cohabited with African-Ameri- cans were victims by today's standards, as well as perpetrators of Southern dishonor by those of their own day. Honor was wholly a male domain—a man's to bestow and a man's to withdraw.[17] Even if the occasional woman might exert influence that produced a definable difference, women as so- cially constructed persons remained imprisoned within secondary-status boundaries.

"Ladies" who compromised their reputations by sexual contact with slaves or free blacks dishonored kin. They would do irreputable harm to their own status and might ruin their entire family as well. Female virtue was a concern of brothers and uncles, nephews and cousins, as well as the powerful *pater familias*. But the male circle of kin was only part of the problem; because of the sexual double standard fostered within slave- owning society, white women's purity was a premium which all white males struggled to protect. Indeed, slurring a white woman's virtue was punish- able by law, and the court might set a price on a woman's reputation.[18] Furthermore, an assault upon a white woman, especially by an African- American, was tantamount to a full-scale attack upon social order—a blow directed at white males below the belt. Pollution of the symbol of cultural purity—a white woman's body—threatened white supremacy. This created a bond among white men and a form of social bondage for white women. This protection racket was a deeply embedded tenet of Southern honor.

A white woman's fall from grace was not just a failure for the individual but also, if she were sexually promiscuous with a black, an abomination which fouled the entire society. The fact that these liaisons continued despite the harshest prohibitions, indicates the depth of feelings—either feelings between individuals or responses to the temptations of taboo.

Associations stirred by taboos, particularly sexual taboos, might create "deviant" behavior, especially in those trapped within repressive bonds. Sexual discourse denied white women their most erotic components in antebellum slave society.[19] And this denial had very profound effects upon cultural perceptions. Freud reminds us that the meaning of the word "taboo" "diverges in two contrary directions. To us it means, on the one hand 'sacred,' 'consecrated,' and on the other 'uncanny,' 'dangerous,' 'forbidden,' 'unclean.' "[20] James Henry Hammond, a Southern slaveholder, in his confessional diaries, referred to the genitalia of his pubescent white nieces as "secret and sacred." The double edge to this sword was apparent in Hammond's case, as this dalliance proved irresistible and the cause of his political downfall. But what were the implications of taboo and interracial sex?

At the extreme, in those interracial sexual encounters where it was determined white women had been raped—with no prior sexual familiarity with blacks—Southern justice was unforgiving: execution or castration. But the courts recognized that some women within society had "yielded their claims to the protection of the law by their voluntary associations with those whom the law distinguishes as inferiors."[21]

Indeed, some innocent women were deemed guilty by association. In the case of a Mrs. Stevens of Virginia, although the jury convicted an accused free black of the attempted rape of Mrs. Stevens's daughter, because her mother "had long entertained negroes . . . and she would cheerfully submit to his [the accused's] embraces, as she had undoubtedly done before . . . ," the governor was petitioned to have mercy for the condemned. The all-white panel could not condemn this man to death without commenting that "the law was made to preserve the distinction which should exist between our two kinds of population, and to protect the whites in possession of their superiority."[22] The jury believed the evidence indicated that Stevens had abandoned this precious commodity along with her virtue.

In many cases where African-Americans were accused of rape, the sexual history of the white woman was introduced as a means to undermine the prosecution's claim. For example, the jury recommended mercy for twenty-seven of the sixty slaves sentenced to death for alleged rape or attempted rape of white women between 1789 and 1833 in Virginia, pleading that these white women had either "encouraged" or consented to sexual intercourse.[23] That nearly half the white women who testified against rapists and won their cases were subjected to the indignity of a jury's post-conviction condemnation is a strong indication of the paranoia interracial sex provoked. White women had to be above suspicion or reproach, or the full force of patriarchy pledged to "protect" them could turn against them. Despite the dangers, many white women defied the color line and paid dearly for defiance. And like black women, they might lose the court's recognition of their right to sexual consent.

Indeed, the national disgrace which surrounded these questions of white-women's rape by black rapists continued for the century following Emancipation precisely because of the hysteria over the question of interracial sex. Evidence, however slim, remains of white women choosing slaves or free blacks as sexual partners, even longtime lovers, from the earliest period of settlement.[24] Too often, our evidence is the "discovery" of these liaisons where a white woman was at risk of exposure—to her family, her neighbors, or even the courts. Yet, these rare examples provide us with telling clues. Joel Williamson reports the tale of a planter's wife in Orange County, North Carolina. After giving birth to a mulatto, the woman confessed that on the day of conception, fumes from a neighbor's still had put her in a stupor, and she had unwittingly submitted herself to a slave, thinking he was her husband.[25]

The penalty attached to violation of sexual taboos was so severe for white women that a "cry-rape" syndrome evolved. The tragic consequences of false confessions, mistaken trespasses, and the social hysteria of white vengeance provide a chronicle soaked in blood, a Southern landscape dotted with Billie Holiday's "strange fruit." Some feminist scholarship has challenged the view that the lynched men were the only victims.[26] Some fictional treatments of the topic, such as Harper Lee's *To Kill a Mockingbird*, have raised our consciousness considerably about the complexities of these issues.

White men suffered much less disadvantage from interracial liaisons. Even those publicly acknowledged, longstanding, and heir-producing relationships did not threaten the male tenets of Southern honor or the society as a whole, unless white men failed to abide by elaborate rules of conduct which evolved within slave society to regulate such matters peaceably. The unwritten rules of Southern etiquette were so convoluted, yet culturally embedded, that white Southerners themselves had difficulty sorting out correct conduct. In matters of sexual and racial etiquette, the public and private domain were delineated rigidly. A white woman discovered in an interracial sexual relationship would have to deny consent or suffer drastic consequences; this topic would not be one for polite society, and polite society would not tolerate any gossip about such matters. Gossip failed to stain males involved in interracial liaisons unless they flaunted or publicly acknowledged such conduct. Sanctions might be imposed but almost always within the family, not in the public sphere.

The sexual double standard reigned. For a white man to be exposed in such a connection was a different matter entirely from even a hint of a white woman's impropriety. Strict adherence to tenets of white superiority and racial discrimination could render a white man fully clothed, even if he were caught with his pants down.

W. E. B. Du Bois was particularly outraged at the charade of Southern chivalry:

> Down in such mire has the black motherhood of this race struggled,—starving its own wailing offspring to nurse to the world their swaggering masters; welding for its children chains which affronted even the moral sense of an unmoral world. Many a man and woman in the South have lived in wedlock as holy as Adam and Eve and brought forth their brown and golden children, but because the darker woman was helpless her chivalrous and whiter mate could cast her off at his pleasure and publicly sneer at the body he had privately blasphemed.[27]

Despite Southern discourse on the immorality of such connections, hypocrisy prevailed. The fact that Southern white males failed to live by the rules they imposed on others did not undermine social order, but those few men who tried to legitimize and "honor" these relationships rocked the very foundation of racial domination.

We have evidence that some planters were smitten by the African-American women with whom they became sexually involved, that they forgot the rules and tried to live outside the bounds of proper conduct. If this were the case, they might be ostracized by family and community, driven out, or forced to steal away—as Thomas Foster, Jr., did when he abandoned his Mississippi home in 1826 in the company of his beloved Susy, a slave his wife had tried to sell away.[28] Foster gave up his land, his status, and his legitimate white wife and children when he exiled himself for love (although in later years this concubine was sold off). Vice President Richard M. Johnson suffered public attacks during his political career, and his bachelor status made him particularly vulnerable. When Johnson contracted a series of relationships with free mulatto women, he followed a common pattern among young Southern men. But when he failed to marry, his conduct became suspect. Ironically, a white wife could shield a husband from reproach concerning his attachment to any "colored concubines." Johnson compounded his troubles by trying to introduce his mulatto daughters into society. When Democrats met in 1835 to select a presidential slate, Virginians—decrying the "spirit of Nat Turner"—walked out on Johnson's nomination. Although his running mate, Martin van Buren, went on to victory, this unflattering publicity crippled Johnson's political clout.[29]

White men risked dishonor if they were suspected of compromising their racial politics under the influence of sexual or blood ties with blacks. Slave-owning patriarchs and their wives constantly referred to "their families, black and white," with no hint of irony. The paternalism cultivated by plantation slavery was an alleged good to oppose the necessary evils fostered within the system. Yet these sexual liaisons provided for potentially dangerous results.

Sexual contact with slaves and concubinage, Southerners rationalized, were "pardonable" offenses which protected white female purity.[30] Others buttressed their arguments with claims of black women's lasciviousness and promiscuity. Evidence remains that planters could and did have long-standing affectionate relationships with black women; some might have begun in violence or coercion but evolved into permanent and perhaps even mutually satisfactory commitments.[31]

Permanent liaisons and those which became subjects of gossip were more often than not obstacles to white marital harmony. Not only "wronged" wives but also social and family pressures could force couples apart if illicit conduct became flagrant. Records are littered with wives delivering ultimatums to faithless husbands.[32] James Henry Hammond purchased a slave seamstress named Sally and her one-year-old daughter Louisa for $900 in 1839.[33] Hammond took Sally as his concubine, a situation his wife Catherine seems to have tolerated, although we have no evidence of her knowledge of the affair. However, we do know that his wife objected to Hammond's taking Sally's daughter Louisa (age twelve) as his concubine in 1850. Indeed, Catherine Hammond refused to return home for several years following her discovery of her husband's liaison with Louisa.

The greatest potential for danger was not a wife leaving home or a society turning its back on a man for his infidelity with a slave, but rather the explosive problem of mulatto offspring. White men faced their own children in the ranks of slavery, and the strains of the double standard are revealed in much of the documentation dealing with these children. Although Hammond was far from a typical planter, in a letter to his son Harry in 1856 concerning his slave offspring, he appears remarkably representative. Hammond confesses, "I cannot free these people and send them North. It would be cruelty to them. Nor would I like that any but my own blood should own as Slaves my own blood or Louisa. I leave them to your charge, believing that you will best appreciate and most independently carry out my wishes in regard to them. Do not let Louisa or any of my children or possible children be slaves of Strangers. Slavery *in the family* will be their happiest earthly condition. . . ."[34] So, many planters contented themselves with clauses in wills to provide for their slave heirs.

Bachelors without legitimate children had the easiest time passing on their property, and their wills testify to the frequency of these cases. In one case, the document demurs: "Testator was a bachelor . . . treated all the negroes with like humanity. . . . Among the negroes . . . were a family of mulattoes to which testator, for reasons not necessary be repeated, had a strong affection."[35] But at times brothers or other white heirs would challenge the wishes of a dead relation.[36] Some benefactors tried to insure that wills would not be broken—for example, when a Mr. Carter provided that his heirs would only inherit the bulk of his property if they freed seven certain "negro kids and three yellow boys."[37] Despite careful provisions, many mulatto offspring received harsh treatment, even, if not *especially*, at the hands of white half-siblings. Henry Grimké gave specific instructions in his will that his sons (Archibald, Francis, and John) by his mulatto slave maid Nancy be generously dealt with by his white heir Montague. However, the concubine and her children were neither emancipated nor properly cared for by Grimké's heir. When the two older slave boys turned ten, Montague took them from their mother and forced them into service as house slaves. One brother was sold away into the Confederate army. After the war, the two brothers were picked up by the Union army. Although they were later rescued by their aunts, Angelina and Sarah Grimké, their vagabond and careworn adolescence was not what their father had planned for them.[38] It was perhaps particularly foolish that a father would expect generosity from half brothers who viewed these siblings both as rivals as well as a means of increasing a portion of the estate. Attempts at keeping illegitimate, racially mixed offspring "within the family" proved dangerous in many cases, despite patriarchal dictates.

Other fathers did not suggest that mulatto bastards remain under the family roof, as Hammond had instructed. Some wished to repay faithful concubines and these "natural children" by settling them where they might be free. Liberia was an uncommon but logical solution. One slaveowner requested that at the expense of his estate "Louisa (mulatto) and her [three] children, Louisa (light negro) and her [two] children, Sue and her son, . . . Cecilia and her daughter" all be sent to Liberia. His weakness was not for African-Americans in general, as he went on to instruct "sell any of my slaves except those specially named."[39] Ohio appears a more frequently designated destination for offspring emancipated in wills.[40] The popularity of this method was so successful that one angry Mississippian proclaimed: "The State of Ohio . . . [is] afflicted with a *negro-mania*. . . ."[41]

But heirs were not always willing to follow the spirit of the will. When Mr. Bailey wanted his concubine Adeline manumitted in 1861 and instructed his estate to donate twenty thousand dollars for the care and education of his son Talbot, his heirs balked. They were able to argue successfully that slaves could not own property, and so Talbot's inheritance vanished.[42] In another case in Mississippi in 1856, the heirs of Mr. Carter filed petition. Mr. Barksdale had been given a slave woman and child as payment for raising Harriet (aged twelve years, born of the house-woman Fanny) "as a free white person, and in no way to be treated as a slave . . . to be fed from his table, in his house; to sleep in his house, and be clothed from the store, both fine and common." Carter had tried to avoid lawsuits: "should any of Carter's heirs attempt to enslave Harriet, it shall in no wise affect this deed for . . . Jane and William. . . ." Despite Carter's very clear wishes, the court decreed *all* slaves should be sold. The language of the judge is especially instructive: "No court certainly would lend its aid to enforce rights predicated upon immorality of the grossest and most dangerous kind—dangerous because the example of a negro, or mulatto, brought up in the . . . style specified . . . would necessarily exert a most baleful influence upon the surrounding negro population."[43]

Significantly, our rare clues as to these illicit bonds and illegitimate offspring are most often extracted from legal documents. We discover the legal complexities of bonds of blood. For example, Mr. Dupree shot and killed Mr. Smith when he caught Smith skulking behind one of his slave cabins—indeed, the cabin where his concubine Clara lived. Smith had threatened Dupree's life, and so Dupree claimed self-defense, but his only witnesses were his mulatto offspring: "defendant offered three witnesses, aged nine, eleven, and thirteen years . . . the children of the woman Clara; and proposed to prove by them, that . . . the killing was done in self defense. . . ." But his defense was foiled when "the solicitor then stated that these boys . . . were not competent witnesses . . . the children were produced and appeared to be white. . . . [Witnesses] testified that Clara was the mother of the . . . children by the defendant, a white man; . . . that her mother . . . Anastasia . . . was a dark griffe. . . . [traces pedigree] . . . that these colored women were always free, and owned slaves and other property; and that they were treated as husbands and wives under the Spanish laws. . . ." Dupree was reduced in this case, not to defending his innocence but to trying to demonstrate the "whiteness" of his mixed-blood heirs. Although his conviction of manslaughter was reversed, the court still ruled that "the children of Clara were incompetent witnesses."[44] Whether or not Dupree believed in his children's whiteness, his case shows the tricks racial ideology could and did play upon men involved in these interracial liaisons.

But finally, we need to explore the ways in which the system fostered indifference to inhumanity and, upon occasion, turned a blind eye toward subsequent brutalities. As one abolitionist raged, how could slaveholders tolerate these cruelties "when Woman shrieks under the Lash, when Woman's affections are outraged, when Woman is torn from Husband and Child, when Woman is crushed and Polluted by lawless and domineering lust, when Woman is transformed into a beast."[45] And slave women were not the only ones affected by this dehumanization, as slaveowners' wives could and did fall victim and also victimize. Bestial acts are too often revealed in the WPA interviews, as an ex-slave recalled, "one white lady that lived near us at McBean slipped in a colored gal's room and cut her baby's head clean off 'cause it belonged to her husband. He beat her 'bout it and started to kill her, but she begged so I reckon he got to feelin' sorry for her. But he kept goin' with the colored gal and they had more chillun."[46] Such reports illuminate with chilling effect Southern dishonor's most tragic effects.

The most stark and unvarnished portrait is necessary to counter the whitewash historians continue to offer on this critical issue. Some of the most brilliant and insightful work of the 1970s was riddled with romantic denials and ridiculous rationalizations, not from the mouths of slaveowners but from the pens of scholars. I do not believe, as one scholar dismissed, that "slavery was a sexual fantasy." My work focuses on what I call the sexual realities too few are willing to consider.

Hazel Carby, in her *Reconstructing Womanhood*, persuasively proclaims that African-American women's narratives reveal the brutality of their treatment by owners in order to emphasize their resistance to victimization. By focusing on this aspect of the system, we do not perpetuate the image of slave women as victims but rather allow their voices, their experiences, to emerge despite the weight of evidence amassed to deny their sufferings. Silence on the subject of rape, as feminist scholarship has proven, perpetuates male domination. Repeated avoidance further perpetuates the racism and sexism these systems of exploitation nurtured. As I have warned before, slavery bred strong and sturdy monsters.

Under the law, white males who subjected female slaves of adult age to sexual violation were not charged with rape. This denied slave women the right to consent to sexual relations—just as the law denied, for example, female children this legal empowerment. But in cases of sexual congress between female children and adult males, the state punished men—charging them with rape in such cases. If a white male did assault a slave woman, the woman's owner might charge the man with assault and battery, but the woman had no legal recourse. The injury sustained was defined legally as that of the woman's owner—she was denied her humanity, her body, and her will. The reality of sexual violation was transformed into the fantasy of property rights. Despite the lack of consent, records demonstrate African-American women's struggle against sexual assault was fierce. Published slave narratives provide us with compelling evidence, especially in Harriet Jacobs's *Incidents in the Life of a Slave Girl*.[47] In John Thompson's account of his life, he depicts his sister's plight:

> One day, during his wife's absence on a visit to her friends, being, as he thought, a good opportunity, [her master] tried to force my sister to submit to his wishes. This she defeated by a resistance so obstinate that he, becoming enraged, ordered two of his men to take her to a barn, where he generally whipped his slaves; there to strip off her clothes and whip her, which was done, until the blood stood in puddles under her feet.[48]

Thompson's sister was repeatedly beaten and, at her mistress's prodding, she finally confessed her dilemma. Her master's wife collapsed, took to her bed, and died without intervening. Alexander Crummell and scores of other ex-slaves testified to this brutal aspect of slavery.[49] Southern dishonor weighed heavily against a slave woman's ability to protect her person against such odds.

It is no surprise that concubines are so rarely revealed in the private papers of the planter class.[50] We have too few clues as to the meanings and motivations of relationships revealed in legal records—nevertheless, divorce records, court disputes over inheritance, and dozens of other public documents attest to the widespread practice of concubinage. Preliminary research indicates a serious challenge to the conventional wisdom of current slave scholarship.[51] These relationships were not rare aberrations, but a built-in subculture within the slaveowner's world.

According to Mark Tushnet, tracing a history of sexual violation, when law and custom denied slave women could be raped, will take more ambitious and dogged research.[52] When a male slave raped a slave child in 1859, the court ruled that statutes concerning sex crimes "did not explicitly include slaves and common law did not cover slave crime."[53] The lawyer for the accused stated the prevailing view:

> The crime of rape does not exist in the State between African slaves. Our laws recognize no marital rights as between slaves; their sexual intercourse is left to be regulated by their owners. The regulations of law, as to the white race, on the subject of sexual intercourse, do not and cannot, for obvious reasons, apply to slaves; their intercourse is promiscuous, and the violation of a female slave by a male slave would be a mere assault and battery.[54]

However, rape and its consequences appear in court records. In a capital case in Mississippi in 1859:

> The prisoner introduced as a witness in his behalf a slave named Charlotte, who stated that she was the wife of the prisoner, and [also belonged to Fondren. . . . about nine or ten o'clock in the morning. . . . Coleman had forced her (witness) to submit to sexual intercourse with him; and that she had communicated that fact to the prisoner before the killing.][55]

We have black family histories to document these savage violations of black women.[56] We have oral histories to document these coercive liaisons: Ella Baker's acknowledgement that her great-grandfather was the master on her great-grandmother's plantation.[57] Scholars are pushing back the boundaries of our knowledge of sexual exploitation with oral history, as in Susan Tucker's splendid study, *Telling Memories Among Southern Women*.[58]

We have recently completed studies by new scholars—Peter Bardaglio's dissertation on miscegenation and incest in his "Families, Sex and the Law: The Legal Transformation of the Nineteenth-Century Southern Household," and Adele Logan Alexander's fascinating work on her ancestor in "Ambiguous Lives: Free Women of Color in Rural Georgia, 1787–1789." Also, dissertations are in progress by Kent A. Leslie at Emory University, who is working on free women of color; Leslie Schwalm of the University of Wisconsin, working on slave women and emancipation; and Martha Hodes of Princeton University, who is exploring interracial sex during the antebellum era. These accounts promise insight into questions of sexuality and race. We will profit from Melton McLaurin's manuscript in progress on the life of a slave concubine Celia, who in Missouri in 1855 murdered her master-tormentor; she was tried, convicted, sentenced to die, and finally hung on the gallows after appeals and an escape failed to win Celia her freedom.

And with each passing year, new work in literary theory, scholarship on African-American women writers (especially Jean Fagan Yellin's forthcoming biography of Harriet Jacobs), and new work by black women writers themselves add to our appreciation of the slave past and its legacy for race and gender relations today. This fresh and important burst of energy injects scholarship on race relations with needed vitality.

Yet, too much of "Southern dishonor" remains cloaked in mystery. We have little evidence of what happened to those mulatto children who were unacknowledged—those "of my own blood" who did not remain "within the family." Frederick Law Olmsted quoted a Louisiana planter who proclaimed, "There is not a likely-looking black girl in this State that is not the concubine of a white man. There is not an old plantation in which the grandchildren of the owner are not whipped in the field by his overseer."[59] And although Olmsted was a Yankee and a considerably biased observer, a justice on Georgia's high court gave similar testimony: "Which of us has not narrowly escaped petting one of the pretty little mulattoes belonging to our neighbors as one of the family?"[60]

A key phrase in the above passage is the justice's assertion of these mulattoes as "belonging to our neighbors." Mary Boykin Chesnut provides insight, as she does on so many significant issues: "Any lady is ready to tell you who is the father of all the mulatto children in everybody's household but her own. Those, she seems to think, drop from the clouds."[61] As V. S. Naipaul's new volume on the South indicates, this self-delusion continues unabated. One South Carolinian explained to Naipaul that "there had been little mixing of the races. The planters thought it demeaning to have relations with slave women."[62]

Southern honor's propaganda denies the fact of sexual exploitation by slaveowners and once exploitation is discovered claims it was rare. When evidence piles up, the "blame the victim" syndrome and the "blame the neighbor" strategy are trotted out. White antebellum Southerners struggled to escape blame, and their descendants often remain defensive.

These patterns of exploitation can no longer be viewed as Southern dishonor, but should be viewed within the context of national disgrace.[63] The South alone cannot bear the burden for the perpetuation of the patterns of racial and sexual exploitation which flourish throughout the country long after slavery's demise, despite the South's distinctive culture which in the past nurtured crippling racial and sexual stereotypes.

The regional differentials are clear. Southern honor provided a bulwark for maintaining white male supremacy. Slaveowners, especially, wanted to stave off encroachments by Northern pollutants—elements which might emasculate the planter class or undermine white virility and sexual primacy. The encroachments of Northern middle-class values frightened slaveowners. They militarized, closed ranks, and prepared for the worst. And I propose that we make sure the worst is yet to come: that Southern honor be dethroned and that antebellum Southern dishonor take its rightful place at center stage.

5

"Our Family, White and Black": Family and Household in the Southern Slaveholders' World View

EUGENE GENOVESE

THE EXPRESSION "our family, white and black" appeared in the South in early colonial times and became ubiquitous during the nineteenth century. Recurring constantly in the slaveholders' private diaries, family letters, and conversations, it cannot be dismissed as a propaganda response to the critics of slavery or as mere ideological rationalization. The slaveholders assimilated that special sense of family to their self-esteem, their sense of who they were as individuals and as a people, their sense of moral worth, their sense of honor. The claim that slavery created an extended, biracial family or, more accurately, an enlarged household, contained a large dose of rationalization and self-serving cant, but it also contributed to a broadly held critique of the reigning transatlantic theories of property, government, and social order and to emerging alternate theories with portentous political implications.

After the Civil War, the highly respected and politically influential Reverend Benjamin Morgan Palmer published a book on the family that summed up views that had become gospel in the South well before secession. He began by describing the family "as the original society from which the State emerges, and the Church, and every other association known amongst men." The family, he added, provides the materials for the construction of all secular and religious institutions.[1]

At the core of these materials lay the authority of the father: "In this little empire the parent is supreme, and no appeal can lie to a higher tribunal, except the divine. The power to enforce is as complete as the authority is absolute. It is a government under which the subjects are helpless." Palmer held the family to be "the model state" and simply "a device for the propagation and maintenance of the species, . . . a strongly compacted government," which naturally expands into a tribe and ultimately a nation under a "strictly patriarchal" administration.[2] Lest the point be missed, the irrepressible Palmer declared: "Under every government, the sovereignty must rest in some recognized head; there must be a last tribunal, beyond which no appeal can lie." In the family, the fundamental unit on which state and church rest, the power of God, "attaches to the husband and father."[3]

The implicit link between the father or male head of household and the slave echoes a dominant theme of the proslavery ideology—that slavery was "ordained of God" and had its roots in God's prior assignment of power to men over women. The scriptural defense of slavery held pride of place in proslavery ideology, as Calhoun and most secular proslavery theorists cheerfully acknowledged. And according to Scripture, the subjugation of women to men preceded the subjugation of slaves to masters which merely extended the principle of social and political hierarchy.[4]

The Reverend Joseph R. Wilson spoke, if anything, more forcefully than most in a sermon delivered in Augusta, Georgia, in 1861 and widely distributed as a pamphlet. He noted that God "has included slavery as an organizing element in that family order which lies at the very foundation of Church and State." He argued that since all families, like all societies, require menial services, servitude is inherent in the human condition—an argument that transcended considerations of race. "Everywhere," he explained, "such *service* ought to be as universal as such higher and tender relations: that no household is perfect under the gospel which does not contain all the grades of authority and obedience, from that of husband and wife, down through that of father and son, to that of master and servant."[5] Or as expressed by the Reverend H. N. McTyeire, Methodist minister in Greensboro, Alabama, "Every Southern plantation is *imperium in imperio.*"[6]

Southern proslavery theorists did not merely assert that the family provided the cornerstone of society—an assertion to which many bourgeois theorists might readily have assented, even as they struggled uncomfortably to shift the focus to the nuclear family and, beyond it, to the individual. Southern theorists extended the God-ordained family of natural kin to include dependent laborers. That is, despite superficial similarities, they reversed the direction taken by even the most conservative of bourgeois theorists. They thereby rejected the doctrine of individual autonomy and equality and, instead, advocated a doctrine of social stratification and interdependence with justice and equity but without any concession to the doctrine of equality.

The Reverend George W. Armstrong, Presbyterian pastor in Norfolk, Virginia, elaborated the argument in his book *Theology of Christian Experience* (1858). Man was made for society, he began, and the family constitutes society's basic unit. "Of all the unreal visions," he continued, "which 'the foolish heart, darkened' has conjured up, none is more unreal than the vision of man standing by and for himself. Of all the foolish imaginations which man has dignified with the name of philosophy, none is more foolish than that such an independence is necessary to a righteous responsibility."[7] Armstrong walked a straight line between his book on theology and his book *The Christian Doctrine of Slavery*, in which he envisioned the family-based Christian slavery of the South as the ultimate solution to the class warfare that was wracking the capitalist countries and threatening Western civilization with disaster.[8] The Reverend Frederick A. Ross, Presbyterian pastor in Huntsville, Alabama, who like Armstrong and many others viewed slavery as the natural condition of most laborers regardless of race, added that God gave man only such rights as were compatible with government. "He first established the family; hence all other rule is merely the family expanded. The *good* of the family limited the *rights* of every member."[9]

This view, so sharply at variance with the bourgeois theory that dominated the North, Great Britain, and much of Western Europe, corresponded to the material reality of southern slavery—to its social relations and political economy. In New England and elsewhere, early industrialization undermined the productive nature of the household, as the celebrated example of the Lowell girls makes clear. By drawing the surplus labor of the family away from the home, industrialization separated members of the family away from the production of the farm in a process that would not run its course until a large majority of the population had undergone proletarianization. Where the process was resisted and slowed down, as in much of the Northwest as well as the South, family farms retained their household character and, up to a point, rendered northern farmers and southern nonslaveholding yeomen similar.

In essential respects, the plantations and the small rural slaveholdings shared the same household features, which were distinguished by the role of production and reproduction. And, again up to a point, they shared those features with family farms throughout the United States, but with radically different implications in North and South. A shortage of free agricultural laborers plagued both regions, though the South much more so than the North. But in the South, farmers could aspire to break out of the economic limits imposed by the dependence upon family labor by earning enough money to buy a slave or two.[10]

The similarity between northern and southern farms therefore went only so far. In the North, the shortage of landless agricultural laborers placed severe constraints upon the expansion of commodity production and en-

couraged a strong bias toward self-sufficiency as well as toward mechaniza-
tion. When farmers did enter the market, as they generally strove to do,
they were able to sell off the surplus of the very food crops that constituted
the basis of their self-sufficiency. In the end, the accumulation of substantial wealth depended primarily upon land speculation and investment in
nonagricultural pursuits. Thus, the emerging wealthy classes and the rural
proletariat were steadily separated from household production, and the
household itself became a separate sphere oriented toward consumption
rather than production.

In the South, family farmers could only enter the market by assuming the
higher level of risk attached to the raising of crops other than foodstuffs,
and they could do so to a significant extent only by expanding the labor
force—the "family" itself—to include slaves. The absorption of slave labor
into the household thereby deepened and broadened the productive nature
of the household—a process reinforced by the retardation of urbanization.
In consequence, the road to wealth in the South lay through the expansion
of slaveholdings and the integration of slaves into households that served
primarily as centers of consumption. The ideology of household and family
grew naturally from the political economy of slavery and rendered the
expression "our family, white and black" an authentic, if deeply flawed,
projection of an essential social reality.

Southern proslavery thought diverged from the bourgeois ideology of the
family in two principal ways. First, it embraced the laboring class, or the
largest section of it, as part of the household, which it identified with the
family itself. This divergence from the bourgeois norm included laborers
within the master's household at the very moment at which the employers
of free labor were excluding them and making a moral virtue of the exclusion. The slaveholders' doctrine of "property in man" constituted the direct
antithesis of the bourgeois doctrine of property in oneself and one's labor-
power, which proved the ideological rock of the capitalist system.

Second, the slaveholders' ideology diverged from the bourgeois in a
more subtle way. For although both rooted authority in the male head of
household and although both tempered their formulations over time to
concede a widening swath to the human rights of women, children, and
other dependents, the slaveholders conceded a good deal less. In so doing,
they sought ways to uphold the principle of legitimate authority in the
household and the polity at a time in which, as they repeatedly noted with
alarm, the marketplace ideology was plunging bourgeois thought and action in the North and in Europe toward a radical egalitarianism that was
slowly eroding the family itself.

For the slaveholders, "family" meant "household," and household implied slaves, or "servants," as they preferred to call them. "I am much
gratified by the sincerity of your expression," Andrew P. Butler of South
Carolina wrote Waddy Thompson. "Out of one's own family there is not

much real fixedness."[11] Any bourgeois, any worker, any peasant might have uttered those words, but a slaveholder meant something special by "family." The difference appeared in the diary of another South Carolinian, James H. Hammond, an unfaithful husband, a less than supportive father, a lecherous uncle, and a demanding and often harsh slave master. "I have not a Christian's hopes nor feelings," he lamented in his customary way. "The comforts of Religion are wholly wanting to me. . . . I love my family, and they love me. It is my only earthly tie. It embraces my slaves, and there to me the world ends. All beyond is blank."[12]

John Randolph of Roanoke would have understood. A staunch defender of southern rights, including and especially property rights, he nonetheless had grave doubts about slavery and freed his own in his will. Yet toward the end of his life, he told his fellow delegates to Virginia's constitutional convention:

> I do contend that necessity is one principal instrument of all the good man enjoys. The happiness of the connubial union itself depends greatly on necessity; and when you touch this, you touch the arch, the keystone of the arch, on which the happiness and well being of society is founded.

> Look at the relation of master and slave (that opprobrium in the opinion of some gentlemen to all civilized society and all free Government). Sir, there are few situations in life where friendships are so strong and so lasting are formed as in that very relation. The slave knows that he is bound indissolubly, and must from necessity remain always under his control. The master knows that he is to maintain and provide for his slave so long as he is in his possession. And each party accommodates himself to the situation.[13]

In this idyllic picture, the father and his authority remained central. Congressman Lawrence Keitt of South Carolina spoke bluntly in 1857: "In its very beginning slavery flowed from the absolute authority of the father. . . ."[14] And a year later, J. P. Holcombe pithily summed up the common attitude in an address to the Virginia State Agricultural Society. Speaking of the southern slave, he announced, "Indeed, he scarcely labours under any personal disability to which we may not find a counterpart in those which attach to those incompetent classes—the minor, the lunatic, and the married woman."[15]

Southern alarm over the erosion of the traditional family in the North accompanied a growing sense that the family, to survive and prosper as the basis of a good society, had to absorb all who labored for it. In 1835, the Episcopalian Reverend George W. Freeman of Christ Church, Raleigh, North Carolina, won the praise of Bishop Levi Silliman Ives, among many others, for his sermon on the "Rights and Duties of Slaveholders." Freeman began by dating slavery from God's curse upon the progeny of Adam and Eve and his injunction to mankind to labor for its sustenance:

Though this sentence was passed upon mankind generally, it was not to be expected that its effects would continue for any length of time to be felt by all alike. There would, of necessity, very soon arise an inequality among men. The father, as the head of the family, would of course direct and command the labours of his children; and as the number of these increased, and the operations of the household became, in consequence, extended, his time would be more and more occupied in planning and superintending the labours of the rest, until, in the process of time, he would find it essential to the welfare of the whole, that he should *withdraw entirely from manual toil*, and devote himself exclusively to the cares and labours of a different kind. . . . The wants of the idle and improvident would, after a while, constrain them to enter the service of the more industrious and prudent; the incapable and the weak would naturally become dependent on the intelligent and strong; and a regard to the common safety, if no other causes, would ultimately lead to something like the *enslaving* of the lawless and violent.[16]

In 1860, another Episcopalian, the Reverend William O. Prentiss, delivered a Fast-day sermon in Charleston in which he unleashed a veritable diatribe against the North for permitting the steady dissolution of the family and especially for undermining the power of the father. New England Puritanism, he argued, led logically to Unitarianism and on to heterodoxy and infidelity:

Surely and rapidly, it overthrows the discipline of the parent and the authority of the husband. Children are urged to obedience on the sole ground of the parent's superior wisdom, not because the parent exercises an authority divinely delegated—When the wisdom of parental rule is no longer appreciated and acknowledged by the child, he assumes to himself the government of his own actions, or listens to the moral suasion of another more competent than his natural adviser, to direct him to the conduct of his affairs.[17]

The Yankee wife obeys her husband not out of solemn, divinely commanded duty but because he is convincing. No wonder, Prentiss thundered, that divorce is increasing at an alarming rate in the North. In such a society, the family unravels.

The slaveholders, or at least the better educated among them, knew ancient history and classical literature, almost as well as they knew the Bible, and they understood much better than most recent historians that "patriarchy" is an ambiguous and misleading term. Too often, it becomes a catchword for male supremacy, in which case all historical periods and social systems are collapsed under a single and ahistorical rubric. Male supremacy may indeed have characterized most social systems throughout history, but male supremacy has taken many forms and with widely differing consequences for women as well as men. To collapse them under a single rubric is to destroy all possibility of understanding historical change and the specific attributes of discrete social systems.

The slaveholders did sometimes invoke the term "patriarchy" promiscuously to describe their slave system, but the ablest of them did so with considerable care. They did not often make the mistake of applying it to bourgeois and other social systems, the male-supremacist nature of which they duly noted. Rather, they drew attention to two types of patriarchy in the ancient world, rejecting one and embracing the other. The patriarchy they embraced was that of Abraham and the regime of the ancient Israelites, which they usually referred to as "the Hebrew Theocracy." The slaveholders understood the biblically described patriarchy as operating according to God's law, the Mosaic Code, and as guaranteeing the human rights of women, children, and slaves. The patriarch, the male head of the house, held vast but not absolute power since he himself remained bound to the higher law of God.

The great patriarch Abraham emerged as their model slaveholder, and ancient Israel emerged as the prototype of the regime to which they aspired and toward which they insisted their social system was tending. Abraham's authority depended entirely on his exercising it according to the Word of God, as John Fletcher argued in his widely acclaimed and immensely influential *Studies on Slavery.* "Scholars will concede the fact that 'his household' is a term by which his slaves are particularly included, over whom his government was extended, and without its proper maintenance, the covenant so far on his part would be broken." For, he added, God intended slavery to provide good government to the slaves and to protect their interests. The master has the duty to make all his dependents keep the ways of the Lord.[18]

The abolitionists fired back that they saw no relation between Abraham and the southern slaveholders. Implausibly, they claimed that Abraham ruled a household of free men rather than slaves and denied that ancient Israel was a slaveholding society at all.[19] More strongly, they argued that Abraham's relations with his servants, whatever their legal status, set high standards for humanity. The Reverend Frederick A. Ross returned their taunts during the debates in the New School Presbyterian Church. "Do you tell me that Abraham, by divine authority, made these servants part of his family, social and religious? Very good. But still he regarded them as his slaves. . . . Every Southern planter is not more truly a slaveholder than Abraham."[20]

As a corollary, the southern theorists rejected and denounced the early Roman patriarchy, which empowered the patriarch—the husband, father, master—with absolute control of his dependents. The Reverend George Armstrong, for example, minced no words in condemning the pure patriarchy of the Romans as an abomination. The head of the household, he noted, had absolute power of life and death over his wife, children, dependents, and slaves and presided as a tyrant. Armstrong was, to be sure, engaging in a bit of a special pleading, for he noted that Jesus did not declare the family sinful because of these excesses; rather, he sanctified the family and preached reformation—much as he refused to condemn slavery despite its particularly harsh quality in Roman times. The spread of Christianity, according to the interpretation Armstrong advanced along with numerous other southern divines and classical scholars, influenced heads of households to accept limits to their power and to respect the rights of their dependents and influenced the state to promulgate a much more humane legal code.[21]

Writing about the same time, Reverend Thornton Stringfellow, a Baptist, joined his Presbyterian colleague in denouncing the Romans for reducing the slave to mere property, to the status of a thing, and credited the teachings of Paul and Peter for the slowly developing limitations on the power of the master. He assailed the abolitionists for falsely identifying southern theory and practice with those of the pre-Christian Romans, and then, with a fine sense of irony, he cited the skeptical Edward Gibbon's account of the softening effects of Christianity on ancient practice. Stringfellow, with an eye on the harsher features of the southern slave codes, thereupon put Christianity's seal of approval on the transfer of a portion of the master's power to the magistrates.[22]

Although southern theorists credited Christianity with introducing human practices into the exercise of domestic and political power, they knew that they could stretch the case for moral suasion only so far. Indeed, they welcomed the challenge in the spirit of John Randolph's remarks on the role of necessity in human affairs, for it provided an opportunity to defend slavery frankly as an economic as well as a social system. "Fallen man," observed the Reverend Benjamin Morgan Palmer, "cannot be trusted with absolute power; and the checks against abuse are interposed by Infinite Wisdom, just where they can be operative and most safe." Within the family, narrowly defined, love and affection guided by Christian morality check abuses, he argues, and he proceeded to spin out some interesting theories on the nature of the marital tie and the different natural traits of men and women.[23]

Parental control of children required sterner medicine, a discussion of which helped Palmer to ease toward the even knottier problem of the master-slave relation. He began by insisting that society rested on the subordination of men to their distinct and allotted spheres in life. "The first lesson to be taught," he wrote, "is the necessity of obedience. . . . If men are to acquire mastery over themselves, they must be put at first under the pressure of a despotism. No milder form of authority will achieve the end in view."[24] Thus, Palmer had no need to flinch from the description of the slave plantation, indeed of the family itself, as a despotism, albeit a benevolent one.

Palmer defended slavery as a moral and benevolent relation. As with the nuclear family, so with the household. It has a moral basis and, by its very nature, encourages mutual affection and Christian kindness. "Neither the husband nor the father," he wrote, "is simply a ruler. In these higher relations, he is immeasurably more; and even in the lowest relation, the rule is softened by a sentiment of sympathy and kindness. . . . Conversely, too, the obedience of the ruled is the homage paid, not so much to authority, which is the outward body, as to love, which is the indwelling and actuating soul."[25]

The source of the mutual love had to be the master-slave relation itself. For the master, the problem seemed easily resolved since he had a direct, pecuniary interest in the slave's well-being, comfort, and good cheer. And such interest, Palmer assured one and all, constitutes "the most universal and controlling of all of the motives which influence human conduct."[26] Palmer saw no special problems for the slave since his own interests were served by his master, who protected and succored him. Apparently, Palmer did not consider that, not having willingly consented to the arrangement, the slave might prove ungrateful and less than appreciative and loving.

However extravagant the claims of Palmer and his fellow slaveholders to describe the master-slave relation as paternalistic or the slaveholding household as patriarchal, it does not imply that either was inherently kind, loving, and benevolent. It implies only that each rested on the assumption of mutual duties, responsibilities, and privileges appropriate to an organic rather than a market society. Paternalism, like the nuclear family itself, has often been accompanied by meanness, oppression, exploitation, and even flagrant cruelty. A slaveholding paternalism must rest on the daily threat and periodic actuality of violence—must rest on command of the whip. The paternalistic household, especially if not so large as to exclude genuine intimacy between master and field slaves, may well have generated the softening attitudes celebrated by proslavery ideologues, but countervailing pressures simultaneously asserted themselves, not the least of which was the pressure of the market to maximize returns in an export-oriented economy of commodity production.[27]

Ideologically, the slaveholders had to identify paternalism with kindness and benevolence, especially in their polemics against the abolitionists, and, perhaps even more important, they did internalize the identification and thereby did provide solid resistance to any lingering doubts about the moral and Christian nature of their conduct. George McDuffie expressed their attitude as briefly and as well as anyone: "The government of our slaves is strictly patriarchal, and produces those mutual feelings of kindness which result from a constant interchange of good offices, and which can only exist in a system of domestic patriarchal slavery."[28] A planter in Mississippi revealed the meaning and limits of this paternalism, or patriarchalism as McDuffie chose to call it, in an article for the *Southern Cultivator*, in which he strongly advocated plantation hospitals and improved medical attention for the slaves. Whether the slave "lives or whether he dies," he wrote, "we have the satisfaction that *we have done what we could—we have discharged our duty*."[29]

This notion that the plantation constituted a household that embraced a "family, white and black" reverberated through the public as well as private sphere, most notably in the published advice on plantation management that filled the agricultural journals. Thus in 1843, M. W. Phillips, a prominent planter and agricultural reformer in Mississippi with a reputation for hard driving, explained his concerns in an article in the *South-Western Farmer*. He expressed a sincere desire to contribute to the welfare of his neighbors in the most extended and Christian signification of the term— "especially when it cannot detract from the interest of our immediate household." A decade later, "Foby," wrote in the *Southern Cultivator*, "All living on the plantation, whether colored or not, are members of the same family and to be treated as such." All, he continued, have duties, responsibilities, and rights, and the prosperity of all depends upon the cohesion of the whole. He nonetheless added, "The servants are distinctly informed that they have to work and obey my laws, or suffer the penalty."[30]

The assimilation of slaves to the household had a twofold aspect. Generally, it projected a theory of labor relations and counterposed the duties and responsibilities of slaveholding to the irresponsibility and callousness of the marketplace, which reduces labor-power to a mere commodity and forces the laborer to suffer or even starve on his own. This doctrine assumed a large measure of incapacity in all laboring classes; the assimilation of black slaves to southern households assumed either a genetically or culturally determined racial inferiority. Hence, even politically moderate southerners who may have harbored doubts about slavery and certainly did not want to break up the Union over it cried out against emancipation schemes on the grounds that the blacks could never take care of themselves if thrown into the competition of free society. They argued as strongly as the militant proslavery ideologues that all workers were at risk in free-labor markets and that blacks would have no chance at all. And they stung their critics by reminding them that emancipated blacks would be met with intense racial hostility if they tried to move North to find work.

The Episcopal Bishop Otey of Tennessee, who remained a unionist until the final hour, wrote a northern clergyman in 1861: "The party that elected Mr. Lincoln proclaimed uncompromising hostility to the institution of slavery—an institution which existed here and had done so from its beginning, in its patriarchal character. We feel ourselves under the most solemn obligations to take care of, and provide for, these people who cannot provide for themselves. Nearly every Free-soil State has prohibited them from settling in their territory. Where are they to go?"[31]

John Hughes, Roman Catholic bishop of New York, spoke in similar accents: "Where are they to go gentlemen abolitionists? You would have destroyed the relations between them and their masters. . . . You could not expect their masters to still provide them with food, clothing, and medicines and medical attention. Whose business will it be to see to all this?" And during the War, the Roman Catholic Bishop Elder of Mississippi cried out in despair that the occupying Union troops were making clear the intention of their government to cut the slaves off from the protection of their masters in full expectation that they would die out as a race.[32]

These clergymen were picking up an old refrain. James H. Hammond, hardly a sentimentalist, wrung his hands over the possible fate of his slave mistress and mulatto children. To free them and send them North would, he felt sure, be an act of wanton cruelty. He pleaded with his son, "Do not let Louisa or any of my children or possible children be slaves of Strangers. Slavery *in the family* will be their happiest earthly condition."[33]

The most obvious and burning contradiction in the ideology of the southern household lay in the sale of slaves. "Our family, white and black" had its reality, but a grimly qualified reality it was. After all, one does not readily put one's wife or children up for sale, no matter how financially embarrassed. The abolitionists tormented the slaveholders on this question and received replies that were at best weak and at worst dishonest. The slaveholders could not easily repel the sneer of Ben Wade, the fiery radical Republican from Ohio, when he rose in the Senate to respond to the pleas of George Badger of North Carolina that slaveholders be allowed to take their dear old mammies into the territories—the dear old mammies who had suckled them and whom they loved and cherished. Wade wryly replied, "We have not the least objection and would place no obstacle to the Senator's migrating to Kansas and taking his old 'Mammy' along with him. We only insist that he shall not be empowered to *sell* her after taking her there."[34]

Occasionally, southerners vehemently denied, in the face of overwhelming evidence, that slave families were broken up at all or at least insisted that they personally had never witnessed such a thing. Most admitted the evil and tried to explain it away. Were not, some asked, northern families often forced to separate as children moved west to earn a living? More readily, they insisted that wives and husbands and parents and children would not be separated except for "fault," that is, unless one of the parties proved to be a troublemaker. And those slaves they ranked as necessary and proper for the social order and well-being of the household and the larger family.[35] The crudest apologists fell back on the palpably racist argument that blacks invested little affection in each other and quickly got over the sense of loss. That argument, while sometimes heard, does not seem to have played well among the slaveholders, whose private papers and public testimonials reveal a widespread recognition of its falsehood.

The primary argument rested upon economic exigencies. What could the most humane of masters do when pressed by creditors? No one defended the separation of husbands and wives, but, surely, it would be better to sell off a young slave or two rather than risk foreclosure and the breakup of the entire household and its "plantation family." The argument was worse than none at all, for it damned the slave system by forgiving the sinner while throwing the sin into bold relief. Harriet Beecher Stowe, among others, rammed it down the slaveholders' throats, and their outcries against *Uncle Tom's Cabin* leave no doubt that they choked on it.

The most dangerous challenge to the image of the slaveholding household as a mutually advantageous set of family relations came from within their own ranks—from a man who may well rank as the Old South's greatest jurist and whose commitment to slavery could hardly be doubted. In 1831, Thomas Ruffin, chief justice of the North Carolina State Supreme Court, handed down a chilling decision in the case of *State v. Mann*, in which he led the court in ruling that the crime of battery against one's slave could not be sustained at law.

Ruffin bluntly rejected the analogy between the parent-child or even the master-apprentice relation and the master-slave relation: "There is no likeness between the cases. They are in opposition to each other, and there is an impassable gulf between them. The difference is that which exists between freedom and slavery—and a greater cannot be imagined." Ruffin noted that the discipline, however severe, was attendant upon the parent-child or master-apprentice to the privileges and responsibilities of freedom, whereas "with slavery . . . the end is the profit of the master, his security and the public safety." He then characterized the position of the slave as starkly as any abolitionist could have: "The slave is doomed in his own person and his posterity to live without knowledge and without capacity to make anything his own, and to toil that another may reap the fruits. What moral considerations shall be addressed to such a being to convince him what it is impossible but the most stupid must feel and know can never be true—that he is there to labor upon a principle of natural duty or for the sake of his own personal happiness?" The requisite service, he added, can only be expected from one who has no will of his own, who surrenders his will to that of another. "Such obedience is the consequence only of uncontrolled authority of the body. There is nothing else which can produce the effect. The power of the master must be absolute to render the submission of the slave perfect. . . . This discipline belongs to the state of slavery. . . . It is inherent in the relation of master and slave."[36]

Thomas Ruffin admitted that as a man, rather than a duty-bound jurist, he recoiled at the doctrine and the possible abuses it opened the way to. But as Mark Tushnet has convincingly argued, he felt the need to draw a hard line between the business aspects of slavery, which the courts should adjudicate as market relations, and the human aspects, which the courts felt compelled to return to the jurisdiction of the master.[37] Ruffin did not dwell upon the theoretical implications of an important qualification to his stern doctrine—that the power of the master could, in fact, be abridged by statutory law. Most notably, the state legislatures abridged the master's power by treating the willful killing of a slave as murder. In fact, Ruffin, in two drafts of the decision but not in the decision itself, hinted broadly that the legislature of North Carolina might do well to curb further the master's power. Despite his argument that the courts must uphold the absolute authority of the master, he added a pregnant qualification in the "Rough Draft" of his decision. On the question of whether a master could be charged with battery against his slave, he noted, "This Court disclaims the power to lay down such a rule, or to enforce it, without it be first prescribed by the Legislature." And in the "Second Draft" he wrote, "While therefore Slavery exists among us or until it shall seem fit for the Legislature to interpose express enactments to the contrary, it shall be the imperative duty of the Judges to refrain from laying down any rule, which can diminish that dominion of the Master, which is necessary to enforce the obedience and exact the services of the Slave accorded by our law to the owner."[38]

Ruffin, ordinarily a good logician, did not explain how the legislature could dare to do such a thing if, indeed, the power of the master and its attendant discipline had to be rendered absolute in order to secure the submission of the slave—how the legislature, in good conscience, could presume to interfere with the master's absolute power if, as alleged, it was inherent in and necessary to the very existence of the slave system. He did, however, piously express relief that the steady improvement in the character of masters and slaves and the growing public concern for the well-being of the slaves were rendering the system increasingly humane and rendering abuses ever more rare.

If Ruffin was troubled by the implications of his judicial decision, so were his colleagues. Shortly after the ruling in *State v. Mann*, Ruffin's kinsman, Judge William Brockenbaugh of the Virginia Court of Appeals, sought his counsel on slave cases while reminding him that English villeinage provided a strong analogy and set of precedents for southern slavery. "The master," wrote Brockenbaugh, "stands to him [the slave] not only in the relation of Owner, but in the relation which each member of a political society bears to every other member." The master, he concluded, is charged with the defense of his slave "as much as a father is with the defense of his child."[39]

Ruffin's personal behavior as a slave master left no doubt about his attitude toward paternalistic responsibility. "I have a negro girl about 12 or 13 years of age," the Episcopalian Ruffin wrote the Baptist Reverend John Holt, "who is extremely low with consumption, and indeed is expected daily to die. She is very desirous to be baptized, and, of course, I am anxious that she should be and feel it to be my duty to procure for her that sacrament, if I can."[40] Somehow, Ruffin's certainty that the slaves could never feel themselves part of the plantation household seems to have wavered. He may have meant only that the master's moral duty as a Christian

obtained, whatever the attitude of the slave and whatever the power regis-
tered at law.

Yet much more appears to have been at issue. If Ruffin meant to preach
and practice Christian behavior toward slaves while standing by his judgment that the slaves could not be expected to reciprocate—that only the
whip could serve—he did not do a good job of it. Or if he changed his mind
in the years after *State v. Mann*, he never admitted to it. A year after the
illness and presumed death of his slave girl, he delivered an address before
the State Agricultural Society of North Carolina in which he reviewed these
issues for his fellow slaveholders:

> The interest of the owner is not the only security to the slave for humane
> treatment; there is a stronger tie between them. Often born on the same
> plantation, and bred together, they have a perfect knowledge of each other,
> and a mutual attachment. Protection and provision are the offices of the
> master, and in return the slave yields devotion and obedience and fidelity of
> service; so that they seldom part but from necessity. The comfort, cheerful-
> ness, and happiness of the slave should be, and generally is, the study of the
> master; and every Christian master rejoices over the soul of his slave saved, as
> of a brother, and allows of his attendance on the ministry of God's word and
> sacraments, in any church of his choice in his vicinity.[41]

Those abolitionists and others who did not know slavery, Ruffin maintained, were committing the grave error of attributing to the master the
absolute authority claimed by a despotic prince. Such a prince, he argued,
stands in a radically different relation to his people: "He knows them not,
nor loves them. He sympathizes with none of them but their positions and
feelings are in constant hostility." In contrast, Ruffin defended authority in
"domestic life" —the slaveholding household—as naturally, although not
necessarily, "considerate, mild, easy to be entreated." The relation, he continued, "tends to an elevation in sentiment in the superior, which generates a
humane tenderness for those in power." Only when the slave disputes and
resists the master's authority does a conflict arise. Contrary to the opinion he
voiced in *State v. Mann*, Ruffin did not view such challenges as normal or
natural, for he professed to believe that unless provoked by outsiders, the
slaves "will seldom give occasion in that way for rigor." He thereupon asked,
"Why should this propitious state of things be changed?"[42] In the end, Ruffin
himself could not sustain the hard doctrine he had forcefully laid down in
State v. Mann.

The southern divines, whose scriptural arguments provided the cornerstone of the proslavery ideology, could not swallow Ruffin's legal reasoning
and much preferred the kind of reasoning he offered to the State Agricultural Society. They did not reject the argument from profit. To the contrary, as students of political economy, which many of them were, they
insisted that all forms of labor, not only slave labor, yielded the economic

surplus necessary to sustain a ruling class and, through it, civilization itself. But for that very reason they insisted that domestic slavery provided the most humane and moral of all forms of labor control.[43] And in this view, they were joined by the outstanding legal scholar Thomas R. R. Cobb of Georgia, a devout Presbyterian who combined the arguments for the divine sanction and historical ubiquity of slavery with the argument for the inevitability of some form of slavery in all civilized societies.[44]

Divine sanction implied the absorption of the slave into the household as a member of the master's family. The divines, therefore, viewed slaves, especially racially backward black slaves, as analogous to children. Many of them, nevertheless, refused to declare blacks to be perpetual children, and they held open the possibility of their eventual elevation to a higher status as serfs or formally free but personally dependent laborers. Even those who held to the theory of the perpetuity of the existing form of slavery insisted upon slaves' rights as members of the household and expressed hopes the laws would be softened to protect slave families, promote slave literacy, and punish cruel masters.

The divines joined leading secular theorists in seeking to make slavery conform to the biblical model and to the standard set by Abraham. In so doing, they thrust the theory of the patriarchal household into the polity and undergirded their campaign for state rights and the imposition of limits on federal power. According to Augustus Baldwin Longstreet, a Methodist minister, jurist, college president, and celebrated writer, John C. Calhoun regarded the patriarchal Hebrew Theocracy as the most perfect government the world had yet experienced and as the model toward which the South should aspire. "There," he quoted Calhoun as saying, "each tribe had its place on the march and in the camp, each managed its own concerns in its own way, neither interfered, in the slightest degree, with the private affairs of another, nor did any of them in any matters save such were of equal interest to all, but unmanageable by them as distinct and independent communities."[45] Calhoun's link between the patriarchal family, community order, and local rights found many echoes. Thus, Colonel B. F. Hunt, probably provoked by Louis Kossuth's attempt to embroil the United States in Central European affairs, lashed out in Charleston in 1854:

No one can manage his neighbor's household as will he to whom it belongs. The attempt is unmitigated vanity and self-conceit, and its end is mischief. It is a spirit that would lead us into crusades to liberate the serfs of Russia, to restore her nationality to Poland, to heal the wounds of bleeding Hungary, to avenge the wrongs which bear down the genius of Ireland, to succor the wretches who toil in dreary mines and waste away in the crowded factories of England, and even essay the act of gallantry in restoring the beautiful victims of Turkish grossness and open the well-guarded door of the harem; and, in the meantime, the North and the South, the East and the West, would become

diverted . . . and all our present greatness and internal prosperity would vanish like a fitful dream.[46]

Hunt wanted no such "madness."

Henry Hughes of Mississippi also invoked the Hebrew Theocracy as the
model for the God-ordained social system of the South: "The system mis-
called slavery is warranteeism, economically, and Ebionism religiously."[47]
Two decades earlier, the Reverend James Smylie urged his fellow Missis-
sippians not to be provoked by "the anti-Christian doctrines" of the abolitionists but to strive to perfect Christian benevolence toward their slaves.
We must, he intoned, follow the example of Abraham: "Let us, as masters,
not be hindered from rendering to our slaves that which is just and equal.
They are 'our households.' "[48] With the onset of secession, a newspaper in
Alabama proclaimed, "Looming up from the golden portals of the east, the
sun throws his broad beams upon the landscapes of the very Eden of the
South—the Palestine of a new Republic." And a newspaper in Georgia
added, "We will in a half century show to the world such a people and such
a Government as has not existed since the days of Theocracy."[49]

Notwithstanding the usual quotient of pretension and blather, the force
and resonance of the intertwined themes of divine sanction, patriarchalism,
and slavery exhibited impressive political power, as may be gleaned from
the comment of Alexander Campbell, leader of the Disciples of Christ (the
"Campbellites"), who opposed slavery while agreeing that it was not sinful:
"The South has said much on the patriarchal character of this institution. It
was indeed in Abraham's time a very happy institution; and it is to be
hoped that it will yet become so in the South."[50]

Alexander Campbell, like other Protestants, had to notice the contradictions between the organicism of slave society, which rested on the master-
slave relation rather than the buying and selling of labor-power (abstract
labor divorced from the person of the laborer), and the nuclear-family-
based individualism of bourgeois society and of Protestantism itself. And
the Roman Catholics rarely lost a chance to exacerbate their discomfiture.
Southern Catholics, supported by the Vatican, also denied the sinfulness of
slavery, but they had long recognized the Protestant origins of an individualism that logically ought to have excluded slavery. Writing after the War, the
harshly anti-Protestant Father J. J. O'Connell of South Carolina enjoyed
himself immensely by taunting those southern Protestants who wanted the
right of private judgment and the rest of the Reformation's doctrines and
yet also wanted a patriarchal social order and a Christian slave society. "It
is," he wrote, "only under Catholic governments, where the Church can
regulate the relative duties between the servant and the master, that slavery
can exist as a Christian institution, and the human being protected against
the injustices and passions of the owner, likewise every other member of
society."[51]

The leading Protestant divines, preferring to see their difficulties as creative tension rather than dilemma, distanced themselves from the implication of Ruffin's judicial doctrine. But in assimilating slaves to the household and its family and by relating slavery, household, and family to the governance of the state, they exposed themselves to another of the abolitionists' more formidable counterattacks. With some other proslavery theorists, the divines found themselves driven to deny, against the intent and letter of the law and against all evidence and common sense, that slaveholders actually claimed property in man. They asserted that the slaveholders held property only in their slaves' labor and services, not in their person. They were by no means unanimous in making this assertion. Some did join George Fitzhugh and other secular theorists in openly defending the right to property in man. The Reverend Joseph R. Wilson, for example, in his sermon on "The Mutual Relation of Masters and Slaves," insisted that slavery refers "to a man who is in the permanent and legal bondage to another: this other having in him and his labor the strictest rights of *property*."[52]

John Fletcher embraced the doctrine of property in man in a more nuanced way. Although a northern-born, long-time resident of the South and not a clergyman, his command of Hebrew, Greek, Arabic, and other languages and his close biblical scholarship impressed the divines, a number of whom praised his work highly. He accepted the doctrine of property in man but rejected the bourgeois theory of absolute property. "Qualifiedly, we are the property of the great family of man, and are under obligations of duty to all; more pressingly, to the national community of which we compose a part, and so on down to the distinct family of which we are a member." Slaves, he wrote, cannot be treated as mere brutes, and, for that matter, morally, even animals cannot be abused at will. All property is held as a trust, he added in a manner that echoed Henry Hughes of Mississippi, whose own theories foreshadowed the idea of a corporate state. "Man," continued Fletcher, "has no right to live independent of his fellow man; consequently, his rights must be determined and bounded by the general welfare." Fletcher then cleverly turned the bourgeois argument for absolute property in one's own person against itself by observing that if a man has absolute property in himself, he must surely have the right to alienate that property.[53]

While professing the utmost respect for John Fletcher, many of the South's intellectually outstanding divines wanted no part of that conclusion and shied away from the premise, advancing instead the bizarre theory that slaveholders held property only in labor and services. No less a figure than James Henley Thornwell, widely and properly regarded as the intellectual giant of the southern churches, led the way by ridiculing the notion that slavery gave the master property in his slaves' bodies, to say nothing of their souls. With apparent anger, but protesting too much, he maintained that strict control of that labor and that service was alone at stake.[54]

Thornwell and the Presbyterian entourage he led were joined by the luminaries of the other denominations. The Baptist Reverend Thornton Stringfellow, author of an especially influential and widely read proslavery tract, distinguished sharply between Roman law, which he denounced for reducing the slave to the status of a mere thing, and the southern, which recognized the slave's humanity and rights. "The property in slavery in the United States is their *service or labor*. . . ." But a few pages on, he assimilated the slave himself to property while considerably qualifying and easing the import of the assimilation. God proclaimed on Sinai, he recalled, that we shall not covet our neighbor's house, wife, man or maid servant, ox, horse, or anything else that is his. Stringfellow concluded, "Here is the patriarchal catalogue of property, having God for its author, the wife among the rest."[55]

Among the Methodists, William Smith, president of Randolph-Macon College, who had led the floor fight for the southern forces at the national conference of 1844, which split that church, presented the same view in a way that illuminated a variety of deep concerns as well as polemical strategies:

> Domestic slavery is an instance in which the order or state of thing constituting the system itself, is made part of the family relation. The head of the family is the *master*, and the slave is subject, as to the use of time and labor, to the control of the master, as the other members of the family. Domestic slavery, therefore, is one of the forms of the *general* system of slavery. The system has existed under various forms. The ancient system of villeinage in England, of serfdom in Russia, peon system of Mexico, as well as the domestic slavery in the United States, are all examples of slavery proper.[56]

In short, Smith joined Thornwell and a growing number of southern divines in upholding the extreme doctrine that slavery, in some form, was the God-ordained, morally sanctioned, historically ubiquitous, and socially necessary and proper role assigned to the laboring classes of all climes and races. Only one step was required to place him in the camp of those who, like Fitzhugh and Thornwell, predicted the demise of the free-labor system and the worldwide restoration of slavery. Smith, notwithstanding a good deal of fudging, took that step in his criticism of the free-labor system. Thornwell, Palmer, Armstrong, Ross, and a host of divines did little or no fudging and proclaimed the southern social system the world's best and the wave of the future.

The Reverend Robert L. Dabney, heir to Thornwell's mantle as the South's leading theologian, deftly related the southern view of the family to the defense of slavery and rejection of capitalism. All civilized societies, he wrote, tend to depress the conditions of labor, and under the market system of free-labor societies, that tendency leads to the immiscibility of labor and threatens a Malthusian population crisis. Only slavery creates a floor beneath which the living standards of the laboring classes cannot sink, and that floor is established precisely by the household structure and its family relations. For the laborers can only be safe when they are absorbed into a master's household and become part of his family.[57]

The expression, "our family, white and black," so easily dismissed as moonlight-and-magnolias apologetics, thus must be taken with deadly seriousness by those who would understand the political and social thought of the slaveholders. For notwithstanding its ideological rationalizations, its gaping contradictions, and its dose of hypocrisy, it lay at the core of the slaveholders' world view and sense of themselves as good and moral men who walked in the ways of the Lord. The slaveholders took up an age-old notion—that the family constitutes the basic unit of society—stripped it of the bourgeois sleight of hand that would make the family a virtual surrogate for the individual, and forged it into a neo-Aristotelian doctrine of the interdependence of human beings. On that firm theoretical basis, they proceeded to launch their counterrevolution against the rationalism of the Enlightenment and its radical, egalitarian, and democratic doctrines and to defend hierarchy, inequality, and authority in political and social life. That they ended with one or another version of the doctrine of "slavery in the abstract"—of the natural and proper subordination of the laboring classes to personal lordship—should come as no surprise. For their special interpretation of the place of the household and family in human affairs had deep roots in their social relations and political economy, which steadily led them toward the formation of a world view appropriate to the triumph of the slaveholding world order they were struggling to create.

6

Strategies of Survival:
Free Negro Families
and the Problem of Slavery

MICHAEL P. JOHNSON AND JAMES L. ROARK

"GENEALOGICAL TREES did not flourish among slaves," Frederick Douglass announced on the first page of his classic autobiography. Families withered in the slave quarters, Douglass believed, because the slave system ruthlessly dismantled slave families, root and branch. His conviction stemmed from his painful experience as a virtual orphan. Because his mother was hired out and lived several miles away, he rarely saw her. His only recollections of her were "of a few hasty visits made in the night on foot, after the daily tasks were over, and when she was under the necessity of returning in time to respond to the driver's call to the field in the early morning." Douglass apparently believed that his father was almost certainly a white man, probably his mother's master. But he realized that a free father was a worthless taproot for a slave family tree. "Slavery had no recognition of fathers," he declared. "That the mother was a slave was enough for its deadly purpose. By its law the child followed the condition of its mother. The father might be a freeman and the child a slave. The father might be a white man, glorying in the purity of his Anglo-Saxon blood, and the child ranked with the blackest slaves." Douglass concluded that the institution of slavery "had no interest in preserving any of the ties that bind families together. . . ."[1]

Historians have discovered elaborately branched genealogical trees among slaves. The discoveries have shown that many slaves lived in family units and that they understood and respected their family relationships. But the impressive achievement of slave wives and husbands, mothers and fathers, who found ways to shelter families and nurture kinship within the quarters, does not contradict Douglass's claim that slavery was an assault on the slave family. Slavery offered the family no economic foundation, little social sanction, and not a shred of legal security. Without the traditional buttresses that supported free families, the slave family depended entirely on the will of the master. With a mere word, a master could blast and scatter any slave family. That cabins in the slave quarters provided little security for the families that dwelled within them was brutally obvious to slaves.[2] It was no less apparent to the South's free people of color.

Freedom meant many things to free people of color, none more important than the ability to found, endow, and defend their families. Although poor free Negroes and slaves both experienced wretched living conditions, their shared poverty hardly rendered the question of status meaningless. Free Negroes enjoyed legal protection for their contracts, including marriages. Unlike slaves, they could protect their marriages against arbitrary disruption. No slave enjoyed legal protection for contracts of any sort. Above all, as free people, Negroes could pass on their precious heritage of freedom to their children. Freedom—like slavery—was a matter of ancestry. Free Negro mothers bore children who were free, no matter the status of the father.[3]

Despite the sharp legal distinction between the privileges of freedom and the debilities of slavery, the overwhelming preponderance of Negroes who were slaves threatened the liberties of the tiny fraction of free people who were Negroes. The freedom of free people of color was eggshell-thin, and its fragility caused them constant concern. Their ability to defend their families was subject to crushing pressure from the hostile climate for freedom created by the antebellum environment friendly to slavery.

In the South by 1860, a quarter of a million free Negroes lived surrounded by nearly four million Negroes who were slaves. Moreover, free Negroes suffered from the common white assumption that they were neither necessary nor legitimate members of southern society. Negroes in the North also confronted whites who doubted their desirability, but all of the North's quarter of a million Negroes were free. Although northern free Negroes struggled to expand the limited meaning of their freedom, they did not risk freedom's abolition, for the survival of their free status was guaranteed by state laws against slavery. Nothing better illustrates the significance of this context of freedom than the vigorous public antislavery activity of many northern Afro-Americans. They identified with the plight of slaves and did what they could to bring slavery down.[4] In the South, free people of color had no floor under their freedom; they had to find their footing in the quicksand of slavery. In his seminal book, *Roll, Jordan, Roll*, Eugene D. Genovese suggested that free people of color in the South acted "like Negroes first and free men second."[5] We read the admittedly limited evidence differently. To us, it suggests that in the South, free people of color acted like free men and women first and Negroes second. The problem of slavery made the Mason-Dixon line divide the nation's free Afro-Americans as decisively as it did whites.

Free Afro-Americans in the South were engaged in a desperate struggle for survival as a free people. In several state studies, in a handful of family histories and biographies, and in Ira Berlin's landmark synthesis and re-interpretation, historians have documented the white South's harsh repression of free Negroes. Together, these studies emphasize the precariousness and vulnerability of free status.[6] They underscore the truth of C. L. R. James's observation that "in a slave society the mere possession of personal freedom is a valuable privilege."[7]

Slavery made the proper social policy toward free people of color a major issue for southern whites. Whites had a divided mind about free Negroes. First, some feared that racial loyalty might lead free Afro-Americans to oppose slavery and perhaps even to lead slave insurrections. This fear inclined whites to separate free Negroes as much as possible from associations with slaves, minimizing the possibility of the free Negroes identifying with the slaves' miseries. Second, most whites despised free people of color (except perhaps the few they knew personally and re-spected) because of the presumed inferiority of their race. This attitude led whites to push free Negroes toward the status of slaves. Both tendencies were manifest in antebellum legislation, but the inclination to collapse the distance between free Negroes and slaves, to degrade the status of Negroes who were free, prevailed.[8]

Consequently, the small but significant trend in favor of freedom for Afro-Americans at the turn of the nineteenth century proved short-lived. State after state restricted, then almost entirely prohibited, manumission. In the antebellum period, the trend ran toward slavery, and in each decade the pace accelerated.

In the lower South, the proportion of the Afro-American population that was free dropped to 1.5 percent by 1860, less than half that of 1830. Free people of color stood on a tiny borderland between slavery and freedom, bounded on one side by over 98 percent of Afro-Americans who were slaves and on the other by all white people, who outnumbered free people of color ninety-nine to one.[9] The existence of more than 250,000 free Negroes made it difficult to squeeze southern society into the rigid categories of whites' racial logic. In 1851, however, proslavery theorist George Fitzhugh rehearsed one solution. "Humanity, self-interest, [and] consistency," he declared, "all require that we should enslave the free negro."[10]

Absolute insistence on racial subordination and the pervasive assumption of racial inferiority edged free Negroes toward slave status, giving them what a modern observer might think were ample reasons to sympathize and identify with those in bondage. Thousands did just that, especially with slaves who were members of their families. But for every free Negro who conspired with slaves to undermine slavery, many more saw their fate as separate and distinct from that of slaves. Risks of cooperating in an attempt at insurrection were so great as to be suicidal. A less dramatic but much more important hazard for free people of color was association with slaves in their daily lives in any way that raised white suspicions. Such behavior could bring down on free Afro-Americans all the repressive power of white society. Thus, most free Negroes put what distance they could between themselves and slaves.

Free Negroes could not hope to establish autonomy in the antebellum South. The laws that regulated their lives put a premium on their relationship with whites. Laws made them a conspicuous caste and held their white neighbors responsible for monitoring and judging their behavior.[11] Whites could be brutal to those who failed to live up to the law and unstated white expectations. But local whites could also support and defend those free Afro-Americans whom they knew on a personal, face-to-face basis and whom they deemed worthy. Several states—through a guardianship system—made freedom contingent on having a personal relationship with a reputable white man.[12] Without white acceptance, people of color could not obtain white patronage, protection, or security. With white acceptance, they gained all the security and opportunity the antebellum South offered Negroes who were free.

With everything hinging on white perceptions, it was imperative that free Negroes gain a reputation for respectability. Whites had clear expectations of correct behavior, habits, and demeanor, and most free Negroes attempted to order their lives accordingly. They sought to persuade their white neighbors that they were honest, sober, pious, respectful, and hardworking members of the community. Above all, they sought to convince whites that they were safe on the fundamental issue of slavery.

Many free Negroes were unable to put much distance between themselves and bondsmen. Often scattered sparsely over the rural South, with no economic stake and few hopes of getting one, they mingled with slaves. They did so, however, at the risk of their special status. For those who had accumulated a little property, or hoped to, association with slaves offered risks they were not prepared to take. These Afro-Americans were able to distance themselves from slaves because, despite all the ways the law assimilated them to near-slave status, the law gave them, as free people, invaluable protection to their life, liberty, and property.

One might suppose that the right to marry legally would have caused free Negroes to rush to the altar. According to Suzanne Lebsock's recent interpretation, however, free women of color avoided matrimony whenever possible. As evidence, she offers census data that show that more than half of the free Negro households in antebellum Petersburg, Virginia, were headed by women. By choosing to remain single, she argues, free women of color avoided oppressive marriages and protected their legal rights to their persons and property. By avoiding husbands, they were in some respects Petersburg's "most autonomous women." She defines autonomy as "freedom from day-to-day domination by black men." Not only did free black women not marry black men, they engaged in "open antagonism" with them. Antagonism, she concludes, was better than "routine, abject submission."[13]

We suspect that free Negro women (and men) looked out upon a social landscape quite different from the one Lebsock imagines. To begin with, the sexual imbalance in Petersburg (and other southern cities) assured that a high percentage of free women of color would remain legally unmarried. Eligible marriage partners were in short-supply. Free women of color could not marry white men, and in Petersburg they outnumbered free Negro men ten to seven. (In Charleston, the ratio was ten to six.) The majority of free Negro women who headed households in Petersburg had children living with them. Thus, while they did not have legal husbands, they had men. Some were widows of free Negro men, others concubines of white men, but most were probably the wives of slaves, whom they could not legally marry. A slave man may have seen the attraction of a free Negro wife. Although he could not become free and his marriage had no legal standing, his children would be free. But Petersburg's free women of color, who were the poorest of the city's poor, could not afford to buy their slave husbands, and even if they could, after 1806 they could not free them and have them remain in Virginia.[14] The failure of many free women of color to marry legally was less likely a proud badge of personal independence, as Lebsock suggests, than it was an example of the power of white society to deny free Negroes what they wanted most—independent and secure families. Rather than avoiding legal marriages, many free women of color simply were unable to attain them.

It is possible, although Lebsock does not argue it, that free Negro women who married free Negro men often encountered an exaggerated form of patriarchy. Patriarchy was the dominant model of family relationships in the antebellum South, of course, but free Negro families had good reason to strengthen power at the center.[15] Interior family relationships were partly dictated by the need to protect family members from an intrusive, dangerous white society. Certainly patriarchy was magnified in the household of free-Negro cotton-gin-maker and planter William Ellison of Stateburg, South Carolina. Ellison was obsessed with preserving the freedom of his family, and he never relaxed his grip. Ellison family members were compelled to act within a framework of familial obligation, as if the best way to confront the family's vulnerability was solidarity. Unity meant acceptance of the patriarch's leadership. As best we can tell, the other Ellisons identified their welfare as individuals with that of the family as a whole. Their familial subordination was almost certainly related to an appreciation of the corrosive reality of white society just outside the family's front door.[16]

Even the prospect of a domineering black patriarch was probably not enough to frighten off an eligible free woman of color. Certainly, it is difficult to imagine a free Negro woman deciding against marriage in order to retain her "autonomy." To suggest as much is to misconstrue the free black world, to mistake political struggle as gender conflict. In Lebsock's Petersburg, the battle of the sexes replaces the struggle to remain a free people. Everywhere else in the South, and probably in Petersburg, too, black husbands did not pose the principal threat to free women of color; instead, white society jeopardized free status itself. Seen through the eyes of free Negro women, independence may not have looked so positive. Autonomy was impossible for free Negroes, and independence was dangerous, especially if one were female, black, and desperately poor. The free Negro community was not much of a safety net. It was too thin, too scattered, too internally divided, too poor, and ultimately too vulnerable itself to white power to offer much security to a solitary individual. Elizabeth Fox-Genovese recently argued that elite white women generally viewed the domination of the plantation patriarch as legitimate and protective, not unnatural and oppressive.[17] Although in vastly different situations, free Negro women had reason to view black patriarchs similarly.

Lebsock's imagined world of antebellum free-black marriage patterns runs counter to postbellum experience, when freed women and men eagerly sought legal marriage. It also contradicts antebellum experience wherever the sex ratios permitted free Negroes to marry one another. Contrary to Lebsock, it appears that free women of color chose legal marriage whenever possible. In 1860, two-thirds of the free Negro households in South Carolina outside the city of Charleston were headed by men. Almost three out of four of these men lived with their wives, and more than eight out of ten of these couples had co-residing children.[18] Despite the potential for domination by husbands, free Negro women in the countryside chose free Negro husbands. And despite heavy odds, these husbands and wives succeeded in maintaining and protecting their families. Kinship and marriage offered free women of color a vital form of protection and support.

Second to freedom to marry and establish a family was the free Negro's right to chose an occupation and to own property. This freedom was far from perfect. The economy put free Negroes at the mercy of local whites for patronage and employment. Most remained extremely poor. Nevertheless, through hard work, endurance, self-denial, and constant improvisation, they achieved enough economic security to maintain freedom and to sustain their families.

Some even achieved prosperity. Southerners regarded wealth as a mark of merit, and free Negroes realized it was a powerful tool in gaining respect in the white community. Nothing was more likely to inspire whites' admiration than owning slaves. Individuals at the top of the free-Negro economic structure often diverted a large fraction of their wealth to the purchase of slaves. No other investment promised such handsome returns—both economically and socially. No other act put as much distance between a free Afro-American and slave status.

The anomaly of Afro-Americans owning other Afro-Americans in the antebellum South has attracted the attention of historians but has stimulated little research. Until very recently, scholars generally accepted the conclusions Carter G. Woodson reached in 1924 in his pioneering study of free Negro slaveholders. While recognizing that free Negroes sometimes held slaves for other reasons, Woodson argued that most of those who owned slaves possessed family members or others they held for benevolent purposes.[19] As recently as 1982, for example, James Oakes declared that "the evidence is overwhelming that the vast majority of black slaveholders were free men who purchased members of their families or who acted out of benevolence." He cites two kinds of evidence: petitions by black masters asking state legislatures to exempt them from laws barring manumission and statistics about the size of free Negroes' slaveholdings. "That free black masters were usually the owners of their families," Oakes declares, "explains why their average slaveholding was only slightly more than three bondsmen."[20] Slightly more than three slaves was almost precisely the number owned by the typical white master. Few would conclude from those numbers that whites owned family members or held slaves for philanthropic reasons.

There can be no doubt that some free Negroes owned members of their families.[21] After states prohibited manumission, it was difficult to free a slave unless the freed person left the state. Some free Negroes, like John Berry Meachum of St. Louis and Jane Minor of Petersburg, bought slaves expressly to free them.[22] But evidence is gradually accumulating in the form of biography and autobiography, diary and memoir, of free Negro slaveholders who held slaves for other reasons, reasons made intelligible by the South's peculiar social order.

William Johnson, familiar as the "barber of Natchez," owned slaves who were not family members, slaves he employed in his barbering business and on his plantation. Andrew Durnford traveled as far as Virginia to purchase slaves for his Louisiana sugar plantation.[23] In 1847, Durnford's white friend and benefactor John McDonogh asked for Durnford's opinion of McDonogh's practice of allowing slaves to work to obtain their freedom. Durnford responded that the practice was one "a man will not be forced into except he has a natural disposition to benevolence. World men will not work on the plan." Durnford counted himself as one of the "world men," one who understood, as he said, "Self interest is too strongly rooted in the bosom of all that breathes the American atmosphere. Self interest is à la mode."[24] In South Carolina, former slave William Ellison behaved in the same mode; he bought slave men to employ in his cotton-gin business at almost the same time as he purchased his wife and daughter. By the time Ellison died in 1861, he owned sixty-three slaves. During his forty-one years as a slaveholder, he never freed a single slave, other than his wife and daughter.[25] James Thomas, a free Negro in Tennessee, recounted that "it seemed a great surprise to many people coming from the north to learn that one Negro owned another. I said to many, why not. The Negro has to work for somebody. Why not for a black man as well as a white man."[26]

Revealing as it is, this biographical evidence may be unrepresentative of most free Afro-American slaveholders. However, suggestion that it tells us a good deal about other free Negro masters comes from the neglected slaveholding data found in the manuscript census schedules. Three kinds of evidence—regional differences between the upper and lower South, rates of growth of free Negro slaveholding when there were the fewest restrictions on manumission, and detailed information about the age and sex of slaves owned by free Negro masters—all strongly suggest that the growth of slaveholding among free Afro-Americans did not occur because masters owned members of their own families.

Analysis of Woodson's data makes clear that free Afro-American slaveholders were not rare. In the South in 1830, they numbered over 3,600. They composed 2 percent of the South's free Negro population, or about one free Afro-American family in ten. On the average, a free Negro master held three slaves. Together, free Negroes owned more than 12,300 slaves. (see Tables 6.1 and 6.2).[27] Compared to whites, however, free Negro masters owned just a tiny fraction of the slave population. In 1830, of every one thousand slaves, free Afro-American masters owned only six.

Two significant differences existed in the slaveholding patterns of free Negroes between the upper and lower South. First, free Negro masters were twice as common in the lower South. In the upper South, approximately one free Afro-American family in twelve owned slaves, compared to about one family in six in the lower South. Second, free Afro-American slaveholders in the lower South possessed an average of twice as many slaves as their counterparts in the border states. The mean number of slaves owned by upper-South free Negroes was two, while those in the lower South held four. Four times as many free Negro masters in the lower South owned six or more slaves; ten times as many owned ten or more slaves.

These regional patterns call into question the assumption that, in general, free Afro-American masters held slaves for philanthropic reasons. If the slaves owned by free Negro masters were typically family members, why would upper-South masters own only half as many family members as their lower-South counterparts?

Perhaps free Negro masters in the lower South held more family mem-

TABLE 6.1. Free Afro-American Slaveholders in the South, 1830

	Number of:			Percentage of Slaveholders Owning:			
	Masters	Slaves	Mean	1	2–3	4–5	6 or more
Upper South							
Delaware	9	21	2.3	56%	22%	11%	11%
D.C.	120	227	1.9	67	18	10	6
Kentucky	120	271	2.3	46	36	12	7
Maryland	653	1,575	2.4	51	31	10	7
Tennessee	68	159	2.3	65	24	15	6
Virginia	950	2,235	2.4	54	30	10	6
Total	1,920	4,488	2.3	54%	30%	10%	6%
Lower South							
Alabama	48	197	4.1	42%	27%	13%	19%
Florida	13	92	6.3	31	38	8	38
Georgia	61	207	3.4	30	39	10	21
Louisiana	921	3,908	4.2	31	32	19	17
Mississippi	17	74	4.4	35	24	24	18
North Carolina	192	624	3.3	48	28	15	9
South Carolina	459	2,781	6.1	22	25	14	39
Total	1,711	7,883	4.6	31%	30%	16%	23%
South							
Total	3,631	12,371	3.4	43%	30%	13%	14%

Note: This table omits four free Afro-American slaveholders in Missouri and one in Arkansas.

Source: Woodson, comp. and ed., *Free Negro Owners of Slaves in the United States in 1830* (reprinted, New York: Negro Universities Press, 1968), 1–42.

bers as slaves because state laws prohibited or severely restricted manumission. If most free Negro masters held family members whom they could not free without violating the law, then states with restrictive manumission laws should have had a much higher proportion of free Negro slaveholders than other states in their region.[28] A Virginia law of 1806, for example, required newly freed slaves to leave the state, a strong incentive for a free Negro who purchased a family member to hold that person as a slave.[29] Yet the proportion of free Negroes in Virginia who were slaveholders was lower than in Kentucky, where manumission was not similarly impeded. In the upper South, no obvious correlation existed between free Negro slaveholding and restrictions on manumission. The lower South also fails to exhibit the expected correlation. All the states except Louisiana had significant restrictions on manumission. Yet Louisiana had about the same fraction of free Negro slaveholders as South Carolina, where manumission was prohibited. These patterns are not easy to explain if, in general, the slaves owned by Afro-Americans were family members whom they held for benevolent purposes.[30]

Further evidence of the motive for slaveholding comes from the number of free Negro slaveholders in the South during the decades following the American Revolution, when the fewest restrictions existed on manumission. Manuscript census data from the states of Maryland, Virginia, North Carolina, and South Carolina reveal that while record numbers of slaves were becoming free, record numbers of free Negroes were acquiring slaves. (see Tables 6.3 and 6.4).[31] In the 1790s, the number of free Negro slaveholders grew by 89 percent and increased the following decade by an additional 35 percent. But it was particularly in the twenty years between 1810 and 1830 that free Afro-American slaveholding mushroomed. In those two decades, free Negro slaveholders in the South grew by 273 percent, a growth rate four times greater than the growth rate of the southern free Afro-American population. In the same years, the number of slaves owned by free people of color skyrocketed by 353 percent. An extraordinary number of the free Afro-American population exercised their freedom by purchasing slaves.

TABLE 6.2. Free Afro-American Slaveholders in the South, 1830

	As Percentage of:		*Percentage of State's:*	
	Total Free Negro Population	*Total Free Negro Families*	*Slaves Owned by Negroes*	*Total Free Population Made of Free Negroes*
Upper South				
Delaware	0.1%	0.5%	0.6%	21.6%
D.C.	2.0	10.0	3.7	18.2
Kentucky	2.4	12.0	0.2	0.9
Maryland	1.2	6.0	1.5	15.4
Tennessee	1.5	7.5	0.1	0.8
Virginia	2.0	10.0	0.5	8.2
Total	1.5%	7.5%	0.5%	6.3%
Lower South				
Alabama	3.1%	15.5%	0.2%	0.8%
Florida	1.5	7.5	0.6	4.4
Georgia	2.5	12.5	0.1	0.8
Louisiana	5.5	27.5	3.6	15.7
Mississippi	3.3	16.5	0.1	0.7
North Carolina	1.0	5.0	0.3	4.0
South Carolina	5.8	29.0	0.9	3.0
Total	3.4%	17.0%	1.1%	3.4%
South				
Total	2.0%	10.0%	0.6%	5.1%

Note: The average size of free Afro-American families is estimated to be 5.

Source: Woodson, *Free Negro Owners of Slaves in the United States in 1830,* pp. 1–42.

TABLE 6.3. Free Afro-American Slaveholders, 1790–1810

	Number of Slaveholders	Number of Slaves	Mean Slaves	As Percentage of:	
				All FPC	All Slaves
Maryland					
1790	60	158	2.6	0.7%	0.2%
1800	189	541	2.9	1.0	0.5
1810	168	464	2.8	0.5	0.4
North Carolina					
1790	27	72	2.7	0.5%	0.1%
1800	64	198	3.1	0.9	0.1
1810	68	259	3.8	0.7	0.2
South Carolina					
1790	55	151	2.8	3.1%	0.1%
1800	44	251	5.7	1.4	0.2
1810	32	240	7.5	0.7	0.1
Virginia					
1810	444	1,041	2.4	0.1%	0.2%
South, Estimated					
1790	324	875	2.7	1.0%	0.1%
1800	612	2,020	3.3	1.0	0.3
1810	974	2,728	2.8	0.9	0.2

Note: The estimates for the South were derived from the aggregate figures for the three states in 1790 and 1800 and the four states in 1810.

Source: Manuscript schedules of the 1790, 1800, and 1810 censuses.

Although there were many fewer free Negro masters than white slave-holders, the growth rate of free Afro-American slaveholders far out-stripped that of white masters. In the sixty years between 1790 and 1850, the number of slaveholding families in the nation increased by 262 per-cent.[32] In the forty years between 1790 and 1830, the number of free Negro slaveholders increased 1,000 percent, four times faster than the growth rate of the southern free Negro population. It is certainly true that between 1790 and 1830 hundreds of free Afro-Americans purchased their family members and freed them. If similar benevolent motives account for the slaves owned by hundreds of other free Afro-Americans in the same period, why did these individuals not express their benevolence by freeing their slave family members?

Detailed information about the age and sex of slaves owned by free Negro masters in South Carolina in 1820 also suggests that the phenomenal growth of slaveholding among free Afro-Americans did not occur because masters owned members of their immediate families. Between 1810 and 1820, the number of free Afro-American slaveholders in South Carolina grew almost sevenfold, from 32 to 218. The number of slaves they owned increased fourfold, from 240 to 1,061. Slaveowners made up about one out of every seven free Negro families in the state. While the data must be interpreted cautiously since the census gives just the name of the head of household and ages are specified within broad categories, only fourteen (6 percent) of these free Negro masters appear to have owned either their spouses or their children; they owned a total of twenty-seven slaves, just 3 percent of all slaves held by free Afro-Americans.

The vast majority (two-thirds) of South Carolina's free Negro masters lived in households that contained a free Negro man and woman whose ages were similar enough for them to be plausibly considered husband and wife. Eight out of ten of these masters also had free children. If any of the 701 slaves owned by these masters were family members, it is difficult to explain why they were held in bondage while their parents or siblings were free. More likely, these slaves were neither spouses nor children of their owners.

The remaining third of free Afro-American slaveholders in South Carolina are more likely candidates for owning family members since their households did not contain a free Negro man and woman who can be assumed to be husband and wife. If these masters did indeed own family members as slaves, we would expect a free Negro man to own a slave woman (his wife) and slave children (since the children inherited the status

TABLE 6.4. Free Afro-American Slaveholders, 1790–1810

		Percentage Owning:			
	1	*2–3*	*4–5*	*6 or more slaves*	*(N)*
Maryland					
1790	55%	23%	15%	7%	(56)
1800	40	32	18	10	(189)
1810	52	27	14	8	(168)
North Carolina					
1790	41%	37%	7%	15%	(27)
1800	47	34	6	13	(64)
1810	41	24	16	19	(68)
South Carolina					
1790	44%	36%	9%	11%	(55)
1800	32	32	11	25	(44)
1810	19	25	19	38	(32)
Virginia					
1810	50%	32%	12%	6%	(444)

Source: Manuscript schedules of the 1790, 1800, and 1810 censuses.

of the mother), but not a slave man or free children. Likewise, we would expect a free Afro-American woman to own a slave man (her husband) and free children, but not a slave woman or slave children. On the whole, the census data contradict these expectations.

Of the fourteen free Negro men who owned slaves and did not reside with a free Negro woman, only three appear to have owned a slave wife. Two of these men lived alone with their slave women; one owned a slave woman and a child. The other eleven free Negro men (79 percent) owned slaves who do not appear to have been spouses. Seven of these men owned both slave women and slave men who could plausibly be considered married to each other; three others owned only slave men; the other owned only a child.

Of the sixty-five free Negro women who owned slaves but did not reside with a free Negro man, just eleven (17 percent) appear to have owned their husband. These women owned a slave man but not a slave woman. Eight of these women had either no children or only free children (as we would expect), and three women owned one or more slave children. The other fifty-four free Afro-American mistresses do not appear to have owned either their husbands or their children. Twenty-five owned adult slaves of both sexes who can plausibly be considered married to each other. Twenty-five others owned only slave women and children. Four owned just slave children. Of all the slaves owned by these free Negro mistresses, only 7 percent appear to have been family members (see Table 6.5).[33]

It is possible, of course, that all the slaves of all these masters were more distant kinfolk than husbands, wives, and children. The census data simply do not provide definitive information. However, if they were members of the masters' extended families, it is still difficult to understand why they were held as slaves since the law to prohibit manumission in South Carolina did not pass until several months after the census was taken in 1820. Unless the forces at work in South Carolina were vastly different from those

TABLE 6.5. Free Afro-American Slaveholders in South Carolina, 1820

	Households of Free Negro Adults of Opposite Sex	Households of Free Negro Women Without Men	Households of Free Negro Men Without Women
Number	139	65	14
Number of Slaves	701	318	42
Percentage Owning One or More:			
Slave Man and Woman	45%	38%	50%
Slave Woman but No Man	33	38	21
Slave Man but No Woman	17	17	21
Slave Child Only	7	6	7

Source: Manuscript schedules of the 1820 census of South Carolina.

elsewhere in the South, these findings indicate that few free Negro masters held family members in bondage.[34]

Instead, it appears that free Afro-American masters owned slaves as part of a general strategy to secure their own freedom and to separate themselves and their family members from slaves. The magnet of economic self-interest—even of greedy accumulation—probably attracted free Negro masters as much as most people. But as free people of color in a slave society, they had compelling reasons to respond to the attraction. Poverty could snare anyone, white or black, but slavery was reserved only for those who were not white. Wealth, especially in slaves, provided an economic foundation for their freedom. More important, by showing that they did not hesitate to own, use, and exploit slave labor, the free Afro-American masters demonstrated their social and political reliability. Whites could see that the primary loyalty of black masters was not to slaves with whom they happened to share racial ancestry but to security and self-advancement within the existing social order. Despite all they could do for themselves, free people of color could not defend their freedom alone. Slaveholding provided the families of black masters a kind of social and economic insurance, a shield against the full force of white repression.

Accommodation to whites and separation from blacks was not an acceptable strategy to every free person of color. But most took the world as they found it and sought to wring from it whatever they could. They submitted to what they could not change and then made every effort within society's restraints. Their world offered precious few assurances, and accommodation was as much a necessity for them as for slaves. In the past two decades, we have learned to understand slaves in the context of their world, not ours. We are not as quick as we once were to scan antebellum plantations for rebels and Sambos, for heroes and traitors, to cast men and women engaged in a life-long struggle for survival into roles that seem appropriate to us in the late twentieth century.

Free Negroes—living in a society that at bottom wished all Negroes slaves and that had the power to make wishes reality— were locked in their own battle for survival, as individual families and as free people. As they struggled to defend their families and to avoid slipping backwards into bondage, some became participants in an oppressive regime and helped to perpetuate it. But behind what appears to be outright capitulation to white society and assimilation of white values often lay a kind of resistance, resistance to the white notion that they did not deserve to be free. In a peculiar way, then, Carter G. Woodson was correct. Free Negro slaveholding was compelled by family considerations. Most of their slaves were not family members, as Woodson argued, but they were, black masters hoped, the means by which family members could remain free.

Free Negro slaveholding is the most visible demonstration of the power of the Mason-Dixon line to divide the country's Afro-American population. Prosperous free Negroes in the South—whose counterparts in the North were most likely to strike out against slavery—were those most likely to distance themselves from slaves, even to the point of becoming masters. The southern social order drove wedges between Afro-Americans who were free and those who were not. Willis Augustus Hodges, a free man of color in Virginia who eventually fled North, argued that it was white policy "to keep up disunion between them [free Negroes] and their bond brethren," and he concluded sadly in 1849 that it "has to a great extent been successful."[35]

However, free Negroes were not just slavishly mimicking white practices. They were not free Sambos. They behaved deliberately according to their judgment of the demands of a slave society. They distanced themselves from slaves, attached themselves to prominent whites, molded family life to defend against white assault, and even owned slaves—all as strategies of personal and family survival. And after 1865, when opportunities presented themselves, members of the antebellum free Negro elite were not slow to take advantage of them. A small incident that occurred in Charleston, as the new age of freedom was being born, suggests the tensions that tore at old slaveholding families as they experienced the transition to a society without slaves.

Two brothers, Frank and John Lee, were members of a prominent free Negro family that had resided in Charleston since before the American Revolution. Their grandfather and their father were long-standing members of the elite, mulatto-only Brown Fellowship Society. In 1863, Frank was drafted into Confederate service as a laborer; he soon deserted, was apprehended, and then was saved from execution by a friendly white physician who claimed that Frank was his slave. Frank subsequently enlisted in the Confederate army and served for the duration of the war. His brother John took a different route. In 1863, John swam across Charleston Bay to the federal fleet that lay off the coast, where he enlisted in the Union army. Two years later, he was among the soldiers who marched into Charleston and, among other acts unthinkable in 1860, scrawled above the mantel in the office of the Charleston *Mercury*, "Wendell Phillips for President in 1868, Frederick Douglass for Vice President."[36]

7

Distress and Discord in Virginia Slave Families, 1830–1860

BRENDA STEVENSON

THE FAMILY WAS an institution that was by all measures vitally important to every faction of the population of antebellum Virginia, white and black, slave and free. Moreover, the family was important to these various groups of Southerners for quite similar reasons. They believed that a positive family life was necessary to both individual and group survival—emotional, physical, cultural, economic, and social. For many, its existence implied an assurance of comfort in a world that more often than not proved to be harsh, unpredictable, and violent. Regardless of one's racial or cultural identity, political status, social class, or religious beliefs, "family" was an ideal and a reality that antebellum Southerners prodigiously sought and fought to protect. Family was for them the most natural of institutions, and within its confines the most fundamental human events—birth, life, marriage, and death—took on a legitimacy that guaranteed one's humanity and immortality. The family institutions that antebellum Southerners erected provided organization and structure to their lives and resources.[1]

Yet, for many residents of pre–Civil War Virginia, the opportunity to live, act, and take comfort within the physical and emotional boundaries of one's family were privileges that were often elusive, if not impossible to obtain. No group of early nineteenth-century Virginians found it more difficult to create and maintain stable marriages and families than did slaves. This essay is an examination of Virginia slave families during the latter half of the antebellum era. Of primary concern are the problems that adult slaves encountered within their families, particularly as marital partners and parents.

103

Blacks suffered greatly from the constant pressures attendant to living and working within a slave society. Ideologies of race differences and hierarchy were so popular that few whites, even those who did not benefit directly from the slave system, could conceive of any roles for blacks in their communities other than as exploited, dehumanized workers—and producers of workers. As members of a numerical minority defined by racial difference, they were the targets of profound sociocultural, political, and economic oppression that was meant to create and maintain the financial success and social prestige of elite whites in antebellum society. Moreover, white Virginians tried to impose their authority on every aspect of slave life, including the family in order to fulfill their need to control the labor of their human chattel. It was not unusual for slave masters to choose their slaves' marital partners, to separate those couples they had united, to force extramarital sexual partners on them, and even to sell off their children when it became economically advantageous, promoted discipline in the quarters, or helped to secure their own authority.

The negative implications of such actions for slaves who were trying to maintain functional family groups were, of course, substantial. An acutely detrimental phenomenon was the forced outmigration of slaves from Virginia in the antebellum period to other parts of the South as part of the lucrative domestic slave trade. This mandatory and often indiscriminate exodus which separated husband from wife, and mother from child, stripped many slaves of the kin- and community-based networks that they had managed to construct over generations of residence in Virginia. Slave owners sold and shipped literally hundreds of thousands of slave men, women, and children representing all age groups with various family and marriage commitments out of the state. Richard Sutch conservatively estimates that during the decade from 1850 to 1860 alone, slaveholders and traders exported almost sixty-eight thousand Virginia slaves to the lower South and Southwest.[2] More often than not, masters sold their slaves without regard to family groups or marital status. Even those slaveholders who wanted to keep slave families united had little control over their future unity once the slave family was purchased by someone else. Donald Sweig's survey of the marital histories of slaves in northern Virginia, for example, indicates that as many as 74 percent of those exported left the state without accompanying family members.[3] Moreover, one can reasonably surmise that since most of the slaves exported were between twenty and forty-nine years old,[4] many of them were spouses and parents at the time of their departure. Regional studies substantiate this generalization. When Jo Ann Manfra and Robert Dykstra reviewed a survey of late antebellum slave marriages in southern Virginia, for example, they found that at least one-third of those couples who separated did so as a result of slaveholder demands.[5] Manfra and Dykstra's analysis also documents that mandatory division was the predominant reason young married slave couples separated.[6] Separated slave couples and the breakup of families also produced orphans. The disruption of family ties and its consequences (such as orphaned childern) were especially serious problems for Virginia bondsmen and women during the latter half of the antebellum period.

Other information descriptive of Virginia slave life in the last decades before the Civil War also documents these phenomena. When one considers the recollections of ex-slaves, many of which record the personal histories of the last generation of slave children, adolescents, and young adults, the scope of these problems is obvious. Charles Perdue, Thomas Barden, and Robert Phillips provide the largest collection of published Virginia slave narratives in *Weevils in the Wheat: Interviews of Virginia Ex-Slaves* (1976). Of the 142 autobiographical statements found in this compilation, 87 include both impressionistic and detailed statistical information that ex-slaves provided about their parents. Among this group of former slaves, fully 18 percent suggested that neither their mothers nor their fathers contributed significantly to their rearing.[7] While some of these children lived with other kin, such as grandparents and aunts, others were less fortunate. The details they offer of their lives elucidates the painful consequences of orphan status in a society where individual slave survival was almost synonymous with family and community support. Consider the personal history of Armaci Adams, a slave born at the very end of the antebellum era who suffered parental loss.

"I was bawn in Gates County, North Carolina but I ain't stayed down dere long," Adams began her account of her life. The ex-slave inferred in her statement that as an infant she lived with both of her parents in a domestic unit that was similar in structure and function to a nuclear family. Isaac Hunter, "an ole Methodist preacher," owned Armaci and her parents. When she was only three years old, two catastrophic events drastically changed Armaci's family situation and tore her away from the nurturing world of her parents' home forever: in the same year that her mother died of an unspecified cause, Isaac Hunter decided to sell most of his other slaves South. Among the first group to leave was Armaci's father. The Reverend Mr. and Mrs. Hunter then moved their much-reduced agricultural unit, including Armaci, to a farm in Huntersville, Virginia. Instead of placing the child in a slave home for rearing, however, the Hunters kept Armaci in their house and raised her themselves. Within a few months, Armaci had suffered the loss of both of her parents and most of her slave community.[8]

In addition to having to cope with what must have been a tremendous sense of loss, displacement, and abandonment, the young child found herself in the precarious position of having to rely solely on her white owners for care and guidance. Unfortunately, it was not a situation that Armaci or her new caretakers appreciated or adjusted to well. The Hunters never developed a close or affectionate attachment to their small ward. They obviously doubted that Armaci, a young child growing up during the era of a civil war that might well mean an end to slavery, would ever be worth the minimal material support they supplied her. At one point, their uneasiness about gaining a financial return on their investment even prompted them to try to sell her. Yet, they were unable to do so because the potential buyer thought her physically handicapped—much of Armaci's body was covered with extensive burn scars that she received while trying to cook her food in a fireplace without adult supervision. "De . . . man wouldn' buy me 'cause he 'fraid I won' be no good on account o' de burn scars," she explained.[9]

When the Civil War ended, the Hunters refused to free Armaci. By that time, she had become an important domestic laborer in their household and the only one of their slaves who remained with them. Armaci was only seven years old at war's end and did not know that she was free. Her master and mistress continued to hold and treat her as a slave for six more years. They even conspired to discourage her father's attempts to find and to take the young girl home with him. Skillfully employing well-honed techniques of psychological and physical intimidation, they were able to gain and maintain control of Armaci. They developed an emotional hold over her even though they treated her harshly. (Years later Adams did not hesitate to characterize both Mr. and Mrs. Hunter as "hell cats," yet it was difficult for her to leave them.[10])

Without the presence of her own black family or fictive kin, Armaci became the kind of slave Mr. and Mrs. Hunter wanted. She was passive, submissive, and hardworking. Acting out of a profound belief that she had no other alternative, Armaci met the Hunters' demands for hard work, accepted their meager material aid, and submitted to the beatings that she received from them for any mistake or misunderstanding. Over the years, her emotional dependency became acute. For example, when her father arrived at the Hunters' home some time after the end of the war to take Armaci back to his new family, Armaci was confused as to whether or not she should leave and eventually was convinced to stay with her owners. Mrs. Hunter told the child stories about her stepmother, and Armaci was afraid to leave with her father. Mrs. Hunter's lies apparently held more credibility for the frightened Armaci than her father's obvious desire to have her reunited with his family. She understandably feared life away from the small plantation which had defined her worldview for most of her life. "When paw come ter git me," she noted, "dey wouldn' let 'im see me so he went on 'way." It was not until she was a young adolescent that Armaci realized that she was "free" and finally was able to break the bonds she had with Mr. and Mrs. Hunter.[11]

Slave kin groups and communities on large holdings ideally provided alternate means for slaves to exchange and share emotional and economic support with loved ones in spite of the potentially destructive power of the owners to separate slave families. Regardless of the many

Virginia slave family groups that had some characteristics of a nuclear structure, extended and stepfamilies persisted in slave communities as innovative sources of socialization, social intercourse, material aid, and cultural expression.

Within the arena of the slave community, child rearing was a shared responsibility. In the absence of a parent, other nuclear and extended family members and sometimes fictive kin took on the major responsibility of rearing children. Adult female siblings or maternal female kin were the first choices as surrogate primary care-givers. When Robert Bruce constructed a list of slaves located on his plantation in Charlotte County, Virginia, during the late 1830s, he noted that three maternal grandmothers served as the primary care-givers of small children whose mothers were either dead or had been sold away.[12] Hannah Valentine, a domestic servant to Governor David Campbell of Abingdon, Virginia, took on the care and rearing of her grandchildren when her daughter, Eliza, accompanied the governor's family to Richmond. Writing to her in 1838, the surrogate mother noted reassuringly: "Your Children are all . . . doing very well and have never suffered from sickness one moment since you Left here. [T]hey talk some Little about you but do not appear to miss you a great deal."[13]

The importance of any one person's particular contribution to the rearing of children within slave families was determined by a number of variables. Generally, physical proximity to the child, the closeness of the consanguinal tie, and gender implied one's responsibility in this familial matter. Another important variable was the size of the slave child's nuclear and extended family. Slave children who were members of large families and slave communities, for example, were surrounded by a number of kin who could serve as child rearers. Other considerations which affected this decision were the age of possible care-givers and the status of these nurturers' physical and mental health, the other domestic responsibilities of these potential rearers, and, relatedly, their willingness to accept the responsibility of helping to raise the youngsters. Ideally, adult slave kin and friends fully embraced these additional commitments of time, energy, and material resources if it were necessary to do so. Yet, there certainly were some slaves who were reluctant to cooperate. The opinions of other family members and the larger slave community also helped to assess how child-rearing tasks were to be distributed. Slave owners, however, *ultimately* decided who would assume such responsibilities, and slaves, in general, had to act accordingly.

Slave masters insisted on the importance of the slave mother in the slave family, particularly in regard to child rearing. In so doing, they helped to sustain both African and European cultural traditions that slaves drew upon when deciding how to order their social world. Accordingly, slave mothers took on the most significant long-term obligations of child care. Virginia slave owners promoted matrifocal and matrilocal families among their slaves in several ways.[14] First, a Virginia law dated 1662 stipulated that black children take the status of their mothers.[15] This legal association between slave mother and child reinforced, within the slaveholder's perception of an ordered domestic world, the cultural dictates of their society concerning gender differentiated responsibility. Masters believed that slave mothers, like white women, had a natural bond with their children and that therefore it was their responsibility—more so than that of slave fathers—to care for their offspring. Consequently, young slave children routinely lived with their mothers or female maternal kin, thus establishing the matrilocality of slave families. Moreover, masters compiling lists of their human property routinely identified the female parent of slave children but only sometimes indicated paternity. Also, when prompted to sell a group of slaves which might include parents and their children, owners sometimes tried to sell a mother with her small children as a single unit but rarely afforded slave fathers this same consideration.

At the same time that slaveholders promoted a strong bond between slave mothers and their children, they denied to slave fathers their paternal rights of ownership and authority, as well as denying them their right to contribute to the material support of their offspring. Undoubtedly, slave masters felt that if it became necessary for them to challenge the power that slave parents had in the lives of their children, it would be much easier to do so if the parent with whom the child most readily identified as an authority figure was a female rather than a male. Slaveholders' insistence on the importance of the slave mother by identifying her as the head of the slave family and primary care-giver of the children, along with the derivation of the slave child's status from that of the mother, firmly established the matrifocality of most slave families. Thus, while slave fathers had a significant presence in the consciousness of their children, mothers obviously were much more physically and psychologically present in the children's lives.

A review of the slave narratives can elucidate further these issues of slave family structure and membership. If one considers the sample Perdue provides in his compilation, it is clear that the large majority of Virginia ex-slaves identified their mothers as the primary providers of care and socialization during their childhood. Significantly, 82 percent spoke of the physical presence of their mothers during most of their childhood years, while only 42 percent recalled continuous contact with their fathers. Moreover, fully one-third of those who did make mention of the presence of their fathers during their childhood indicated that these men did not live with them but only visited on their days off.[16]

The absence of slave fathers was not a problem which was restricted to the latter part of the antebellum period. Since the colonial period, young male slaves were the primary targets of intrastate and interstate trading in Virginia. As such, their arbitrary removal from wives and children always was a source of difficulty plaguing slave families. Of course, the numbers of young male slaves exported increased over time. Their continual decline on some farms and plantations in Virginia meant a decrease in the number of slave families with both parents present. (Significantly, only 42 percent of the ex-slaves interviewed as part of the Virginia Federal Writers' Project suggested in their autobiographical accounts that they had close physical contact with both of their parents.)[17] Moreover, the removal of adult male slaves from their Virginia kin networks robbed even slave families that were matrifocal, since they, too, had benefited significantly from material and emotional resources that fathers, husbands, and other male relatives who lived close by routinely provided. Many Virginia slave children born in the last decades before the Civil War, therefore, grew up without fathers or black male role models and nurturers, while women bore and reared children without the comfort and support of their husbands or other male kin.

Virginia Bell, an ex-slave from Louisiana, recalled her parents' personal histories: "Both of them was from Virginny, but from diff'rent places, and was brought to Louisiana by nigger traders and sold to Massa Lewis. I know my pappy was lots older than my mother and he had a wife and five chillun back in Virginny and had been sold away from them out there. . . . I don' know what become of his family back in Virginny, 'cause when he was freed he stayed with us."[18] Katie Blackwell Johnson was a Virginia ex-slave who never had the privilege of living with her father. As an adult, Johnson recalled very little about her male parent. "I only remember seeing him once," she stated. "He was stretched on the floor. He took me in his arms and I went to sleep. My mother said he was a great gambler and he never came to see us without a jug of liquor."[19]

Although many of the ex-slaves interviewed obviously knew and lived with their mothers, some slaves also grew up without their mothers. This was particularly so for the last generations of Virginia slaves who were born and reared between 1830 and 1860 when masters increasingly were selling women to traders who took them out of the state. Information descriptive of the slave exports from the state documents this activity. Richard Sutch estimates that by 1850, slaveholders were selling equal numbers of adult women and men and actually more adolescent and young adult females than males within those broad age cohorts.[20] Because the average age at first birth for Virginia slave women was between nineteen and twenty years,[21] large numbers exported were probably young mothers, many of whom were forced to leave without their young. Liza McCoy recalled that her Aunt Charlotte, a slave who lived in Matthews County, "was sold to Georgia away from her baby when de chile wont no more three months."[22] Ex-slave Fannie Berry included in her autobiographical account of life in late antebellum Virginia a tragic scene of slave mothers separated from their infants. She described the incident in part as:

Dar was a great crying and carrying on 'mongst the slaves who had been sold. Two or three of dem gals had young babies taking with 'em. Poor little things. As soon as dey got on de train dis ol' new master had de train stopped an' made dem poor gal mothers take babies off and laid dem precious things on de groun' and left dem behind to live or die. . . . [the] master who bought de mothers didn't want gals to be bothered wid dese chillun 'cause he had his cottonfields fer new slaves to work.[23]

Berry went on to explain the fate of the abandoned infants that "some po' white man would take dem an' raise dem up as his slaves and make 'em work on his plantation and if he wanted to, would sell 'em."[24]

Unfortunately, the socialization of slave youth was a difficult task for slaves regardless of the composition of their individual families. Slave child rearers faced obstacles to success that most whites did not. The most important deterrent was a legal one which had negative implications for all aspects of the relationship between rearer and child. Simply, slave parents were not the legal guardians of their children—white owners were. Moreover, since slaveholders were quite willing to share their authority with persons other than slave kin, particularly nurses, overseers, drivers, and other whites residing on their property, slave family members had many threats to their influence over the lives of their youngsters. Slave children were confronted with a variety of authority figures, white and black, each with his or her own priorities, demands, and contributions to their upbringing. These youths had to learn to assess the power and value of each of these adults as well as to appease their demands, often simultaneously.

Slave kin and white owners held the most important positions of power in the lives of slave children. Yet, as the balance of power was both a delicate and complex phenomenon that could shift quite suddenly, slave kin had to work diligently to retain some control in the face of unsolicited interference from others. White owners balked at attempts by slave kin to gain control over the lives or allegiances of black children in opposition to their authority as masters. They understood that such challenges to their authority showed that their slaves did not accept their assigned inferior status and were teaching their slave children to resist as well. Masters met such trials with extreme hostility and often open brutality. Also, since most antebellum Virginia slaveholders were white and male and most slave child care-givers were bondswomen; masters, especially, were incensed at the notion that their authority and power might be questioned by someone they viewed as three times their inferior—that is, black, female, and slave. A slave mother's successful defiance of an owner's authority would have meant a weakening of the control that the slaveholder hoped to exert over his other slaves—a situation few Virginia masters would tolerate.[25]

Matilda Carter was an ex-slave who lived on a farm near Newport News. She recalled that her master, John Wynder, even refused to allow his wife to interfere with his command over his slaves. "My sister Sally was a favorite of my mistress," Carter noted. "She didn' have to wuk in de fields. She ain't had nottin' to do 'ceptin play wid de chillun all day. But de Marser he try to make lil sis wuk. So my mistress she jes' hide her when she think Marser goin git her." Wynder was determined to end his wife's attempts to undermine his decision-making power with regard to his property. He remedied the situation by selling his wife's favored slave to the Deep South. "Mother never did get over dis ack of sellin' her baby to dem slave drivers down New Orleans," Carter concluded.[26]

Caroline Hunter's recollections about her life as a child with her slave mother and three brothers on a small farm near Suffolk, Virginia, at the end of the antebellum era include a telling example of the frustration that slave kin felt in response to the intrusion of white authority in the lives of their children. The scene she describes also suggests important questions about the slave child's general perception of black adult authority:

> During slavery it seemed lak yo' chillun b'long to ev'ybody but you. Many a day my ole mama has stood by an' watched massa beat her chillun 'till dey bled an' she couldn' open her mouf. Dey didn' only beat us, but dey useta strap my mama to a bench or box an' beat her wid a wooden paddle while she was naked.[27]

Stripped naked and beaten before her daughter, other family members, and the slave community, Caroline Hunter's mother must have known that such an example of her obvious helplessness in the face of slaveholder power would jeopardize her authority within her own domestic sphere—authority that she needed in order to rear Caroline and her other children. Nevertheless, the owner's demonstration of control did not destroy the bond between child and parent or the respect that Caroline had for her mother. On the contrary, the experience seemed to have deepened the young girl's appreciation for her mother's plight and helped to further instill in the daughter a profound hatred for their cruel owner. Yet, these expressions of white dominion and control that slave youth repeatedly witnessed had some impact on the ways in which slaves differentially identified and related to white and black authority.

Ex-slave Nancy Williams of Yanceville, Virginia, recounted an experience which demonstrates the influence that owners could have on a slave child's perspective of parental authority. Williams explained that as a young child, she was a favorite of her master who, consequently, did not beat her and frowned on the strict disciplinary policy of her parents. Her parents probably believed that their master was spoiling Nancy and resented his intrusion in their domestic affairs. It was clear to slave parents that children reared in such a manner eventually would face harsh confrontations with whites and also risk alienation from their slave peers. As such, slave child rearers like the Williams's had to fight a war of wits with their owners to gain the necessary authority to properly socialize their own children.

Not surprisingly, slave children did not always cooperate with their parents' efforts. Nancy Williams sometimes tried to manipulate her master's "benevolence" in order to avoid the stinging punishments that her parents often inflicted. The ex-slave recalled that on one such occasion, she had refused to do a task that her mother had assigned her. Nancy was fleeing from her parent and the inevitable beating she was to receive when she decided that the best place to hide was between her owner's legs. Nancy, mindful of her master's fondness for her, knew that her mother would not whip her in his presence. "I run up de stairs rit 'tween marsa's legs," Williams remembered, "an ask him for 10 [cents]. She couldn't ketch me den." Mrs. Williams, however, was not about to let her child get away with this obvious act of disrespect or her original offense. Years later, the errant daughter noted her mother's eventual triumph: "[W]hen she did [catch me,] she beat de debil outa me."[28]

One can expect that with the decline of the viability of the extended slave family and the nonrelated surrogate kin network in the wake of increased exportation of slaves, the overall socialization of many slave youth suffered. One must also concede, however, that even under optimum conditions for success, slave kin rarely were able to rear children that were not affected to some degree by the actions and ideologies of whites who held so much power over their physical, psychological, and intellectual developments. Obviously, slaves sometimes internalized prevalent racist views which created tension within their families and communities. Color stratification was a problem which posed particularly negative consequences for those slaves touched by it, because of the explosive issues of force, sex, female purity, and marital sanctity that it evoked. Color consciousness and stratification among blacks resulted from a combination of factors, such as a consistently high rate of miscegenation and, relatedly, a large biracial population among slaves and free blacks, as well as the popularity of racist ideologies concerning race difference and hierarchy and their practical application in antebellum Virginia society.

Much of the interracial sexual activity that resulted in the state's biracial population involved white-male coercion and rape of black females. Consequently, the children born of these assaults were potent symbols of the immense power that whites held over the most intimate spheres of black life. They were a constant reminder to their mothers and her kin of their powerlessness in the face of white male domination and violence. "My mama said that in dem times a nigger 'oman couldn't help herself," May Satterfield recalled, "fo she had to do what de marster say. . . . she had to go."[29] Consequently, the presence of racially mixed children in homes of slaves sometimes engendered feelings of shame, humiliation, and anger.

Slave families and communities usually attached an even deeper stigma to those children conceived as a result of the voluntary sexual relations between black women and white men. Although slaves were very empathetic to those women who were the victims of coercion, they often ostracized slave women who openly consorted with white men. Many bondswomen and men viewed these concubines as promiscuous and disloyal. Their children shared, to a certain extent, the dishonor of their mothers.

It is not surprising, therefore, that many racially mixed children felt shame and confusion about their white parentage. Patience Richardson Avery, for example, immediately rejected the notion that Thomas Hatcher, Jr., a white resident of some prominence in Chesterfield County, was her father. When her mother first introduced Mr. Hatcher to their small daughter, Patience remembered that she screamed: "I ain't got no father; . . . He no father o' mine! He white!"[30] Although she was only a few years old at the time, Patience profoundly understood the sociopolitical distinction between "black" and "white" and was horrified that she might be related to a white man. So, too, were some of her kin. Their rejection of Patience because of her racially mixed heritage caused her a great deal of physical and emotional pain as she grew older. Moreover, her account of her extended-family's response remains as an important illustration of the kinds of conflict miscegenation brought to slave families. It also demonstrates the failures of some extended families to fully embrace those persons who were born outside of the nuclear core.

Forced to live with a maternal uncle (Robert Richardson) and his wife and children after the death of both her mother and maternal grandmother, Patience Richardson was the victim of discrimination and ill-treatment at her uncle's home. Mrs. Richardson's attitude toward the girl was especially cruel. She not only assigned Patience excessively heavy work loads and blamed her for things beyond her control but also viciously beat her when displeased with her performance or overall behavior. The manner in which the aunt chose to discipline Patience is clearly indicative of her disdain for the child. Also, Mrs. Richardson's beatings acutely resembled the type of punishment that slaveholders inflicted on blacks in their attempts to humiliate and "break" them. Surely her intent was similar to that of a slave master. "Ev'ry time dat ole 'oman would whip me she would strip me nacked an' cut me wid a strip 'till I was whelped all over, an' de blood blister was everywhere," Mrs. Avery remembered. "I couldn' walk, neither set down," she added.[31]

Patience Avery emphatically believed that the lack of consideration and harsh beatings her aunt gave her were due to her white paternity. Obviously, Mrs. Richardson resented Patience's parentage and presence in her home. Recalling the time when she lived with her uncle's family, the ex-slave noted: "Four years I stayed wid a mean 'oman, an' she was de meanes' . . . 'oman I ever saw. Mean an' cruel. You see, I was treated cruelly 'cause I was dis white man's chile."[32] Eventually, Patience sought refuge from Mrs. Richardson's violent beatings and verbal assaults with a neighboring white farmer and his wife who provided the girl with minimal material support for her domestic labor. Rejected and brutalized by her black kin, Patience Avery ironically found greater acceptance in the homes of those whites toward whom she initially felt so much hostility.

Mothers and other family members were sensitive to the kinds of teasing, insults, and rough treatment that their mulatto children might receive at the hands of blacks and whites. They often lied to them about their paternity or taught them to avoid the issue when questioned about it. "Who's yo' pappy?" was the question that slaves often asked Candis Goodwin, the illegitimate daughter of a neighboring slave owner and a slave woman. Goodwin often quipped back at those teasing her: "Tuckey buzzard lay me an' de sun hatch me," but she secretly knew her "pappy" was "Massa Williams."[33]

Despite the obvious hostility with which many slaves responded to miscegenation, the reaction in the slave quarters to racially mixed children often was a complex and contradictory one. While many felt uneasy with the presence of these children and a few openly rejected them, unresolved feelings of black inferiority caused some to treat racially mixed and generally light-skinned children as superior to their darker peers. Many slaves also respected the operative class system in antebellum Southern society. The combination of color and class stratification caused some slaves to afford the mulatto offspring of elite whites a particularly elevated status. Biracial slaves sometimes also held themselves aloof from other blacks. Consider the personal history and behavior of Ary, an octoroon woman who came to work for the missionaries at Craney Island, Virginia, in 1863.

Ary was the proud daughter of a Virginia planter and a mulatto house servant. By young adulthood, she had become the concubine of her young master, who also was her first cousin. She eventually bore him a child who died during the Civil War. Convinced that she was the favorite child of her wealthy father and that her young master's feelings of affection were genuine, Ary believed that she was superior to her darker peers. While on Craney Island, she often boasted of her elite white parentage and insisted that she was better than the other "contraband."[34] Remembering her lover's pronouncement that she was to have nothing to do with "colored men" because they "weren't good enough" for her, Ary was determined not to associate too closely with any blacks. Yet even before she had told her story, her physical appearance, especially her long, straight hair, had gained the octoroon a measure of status even among those "contraband" who resented her air of superiority.[35]

Certainly, many male and female slaves viewed African-Americans with light skin and eye color, straight hair and noses, and thin lips as exceedingly attractive. When the mulatto Candis Goodwin was a young woman living on the Eastern Shore, she was considered "de purties" girl in the area.[36] Virginia Haynes Shepherd of Churchland was the daughter of a domestic slave and a white doctor. Although she was embarrassed when asked about her paternity, Mrs. Shepherd was quite forthcoming with her impressions of black feminine beauty. Describing one slave woman of local acclaim, Shepherd noted: "Diana was a black beauty if there ever was one. She had this thin silk skin, a sharp nose, thin lips, a perfect set of white teeth and beautiful long coal-black hair."[37]

Thus, while Patience Avery and other mulattoes were uncomfortable with an ancestry that was partially white, other racially mixed African-Americans, like Ary, were proud of it, considered themselves superior to other blacks, and believed they were the elite within their families and their communities. Many blacks must have accepted these notions of entitlement that some light-skinned slaves promoted—few racially mixed slaves could have afforded to prolong such pretensions of superiority otherwise.

Of course, other problems related to the flaws in the antebellum South also haunted the families of bondsmen and women. Reared in a society that was extremely violent, even by standards of the nineteenth century, slaves sometimes also chose brutal force as a means of control of their families and among their peers. (Recall the description of the beatings that Patricia Avery stated her Aunt Richardson gave her.) Privy to some of these events, whites from the South and North did not hesitate to comment on what they perceived as violent behavior that some slave child rearers exhibited when they punished their children.

Indeed, the stories regarding widespread violence of slaves toward each other were prevalent enough to warrant discussions of this issue in nineteenth-century guides outlining appropriate measures of treatment and control of slave property. Authors writing on the subject of slave management, on the one hand, routinely advised masters to carefully scrutinize the domestic relations of their slaves in order to prevent physical abuse within the quarters.[38] Slaves, on the other hand, drew on both West African and European cultural dictates concerning the issue of corporal punishment. Most believed that, "a few licks now and then, does em good," and whippings in response to numerous offenses were an important part of their children's socialization.[39]

The violence and brutality that whites imposed on their slaves undoubtedly influenced the ways in which bondsmen and bondswomen treated their own children and other dependents. The ability to beat someone, to hold that kind of physical control over another human, was a sadistic expression of power that blacks learned repeatedly from their interaction with and observation of white authority figures. This expression of control was meant to impress children with their parents' ability to command some power over their offspring's behavior. Also, adult slave kin wanted to demonstrate to whites, who often tried to usurp or demean slave parental authority, that they claimed a right to control and chastise their own children regardless of the legal guardianship that white owners possessed.

Perhaps it was this demonstration of black slave power within their own domestic sphere rather than the concern for the actual physical pain the children endured that really offended whites.

As "contraband of war," for example, Virginia slaves who took refuge behind Union lines and went to reside in the federal army and freedmen aid-society camps quickly claimed their freedom which they, in part, defined as a right to make vital decisions regarding their own children. It is obvious that they were no more receptive to the judgments that Northern teachers and missionaries made about their methods of child discipline and rearing than they were of their former owners' "interference." One Northern white teacher of the "contraband" in Virginia's southern coastal area wrote in 1864, "we have our sympathies called out, almost every day, for the innocent children who are harshly beaten by their willful enemies[,] their harsh mamas. . . . close by us lives a black woman who lashes her little boy with a rawhide. We have remonstrated repeatedly, but she 'Reckons I shall beat my boy just as much as I please'; . . . and she does beat him till his cries wring the anguish from our hearts."[40]

Ex-slave Nancy Williams recalled that both of her parents gave her severe beatings when they thought that her behavior warranted it. Williams's mother sometimes feared that her husband was too harsh when he punished the mischievous girl. Nancy remembered one incident in which her father became particularly incensed with one of her pranks. After her father detected that she had stolen money from him and had then tried to disguise her crime with a lie, he exploded. Placing her in an old guano bag, Williams hung his daughter up on a rack in the meat house and began to "smoke" her. He hoped that this type of torture would induce the child to tell the truth. Instead, the odor and smoke from the burnt tobacco along with her physical discomfort made Nancy "drunk." Angered even more by his failure to get her to confess, Mr. Williams then dumped the disoriented child onto the floor and began to beat her "somepin awful," all the while demanding that she recant her lie. The combination of pain, fear, and the smoke caused Nancy to faint briefly. When she regained consciousness, she fled her father's whipping, calling on members of her family and community to intervene.[41]

Certainly, the severity of the physical abuse that Nancy Williams's father inflicted on his child was probably unusual among slaves. Most ex-slaves recalling relationships with their parents spoke of receiving much more moderate discipline. One must not discount, however, the tremendous emotional stress under which adult slaves lived that definitely affected their relationships with each other, sometimes even to the point of gross maltreatment. Yet, one must also note that while Nancy's father's response was undoubtedly severe, he thought that his actions, regardless of their obvious harshness, would help his daughter to become a more responsible adult. Moreover, Mr. Williams believed that it was his duty and right as a Christian father to insure that he reared his children with strong moral character, and therefore, he felt that he had acted appropriately. "Father said he'd rather die an' go to hell an' burn den to live agin in heaven roun' Christ robe an' leave a passel o' tongue tied niggers to steal," Nancy Williams explained.[42] Still, Mr. Williams's behavior on that occasion indicated that he sometimes could lose control and that his anger and frustration could expose his family to acts which would hurt and humiliate as much as teach and protect.

Abuse in slave families was not limited to children alone. Spousal ill-treatment was another serious problem. Relationships between husbands and wives suffered from slaveholders' usurpation of control in slave marriages even more profoundly than those relationships between parents and children. Verbal and physical abuse among married partners were sometimes responses to complex issues of discord within slave marriages. This prevalence of mistreatment among some antebellum blacks toward their spouses prompted one ex-slave to comment that "some good masters would punish slaves who mistreated womenfolk and some didn't."[43]

Unfounded in Virginia law, slave marriages were tenuous relationships in which couples struggled to survive among the immense and divisive pressures of slave life. Slaveholders had the final say as to which slaves would marry and whom they could marry and when and, therefore, exercised immense dominion over this most intimate of decisions affecting adult slaves. Because they controlled vital aspects of slave marriage, owners' actions often meant the success or failure of these relationships.

Concerned with economic and logistic issues that slaves were not privy to, masters sometimes imposed marriage partners on slaves whom the individual bondswoman or man might not have chosen if given the opportunity to decide otherwise. Charles Grandy, an ex-slave from Norfolk recalled that on the farm where he resided:

> Marsa used to sometimes pick our wives fo' us. If he didn't have on his place enough women for the men, he would wait on de side of de road till a big wagon loaded with slaves come by. Den Marsa would stop de ole nigger-trader and buy you a woman. Wasn't no use tryin' to pick one, cause Marsa wasn't gonna pay but so much for her. All he wanted was a young healthy one who looked like she could have children, whether she was purty or ugly as sin.[44]

Although Grandy spoke specifically of the lack of choice male slaves had in acquiring wives, it is evident from his description of the process that the women involved—young women recently sold away from families and perhaps husbands—had absolutely no choice in the matter whatsoever. Apparently, the sexist perspectives of many male owners persuaded them to be more solicitous of the desires of male slaves in the matter than those of female slaves. Ex-slave Katie Blackwell Johnson explained that the slave women she knew "had no choice in the matter as to whom they would marry. If a man saw a girl he liked he would ask his master's permission to ask the master of the girl for her. If his master consented and her master consented, then they came together."[45] The emotional and sexual exploitation of some women slaves forced to marry men whom they did not love undoubtedly increased their resentment toward their masters and their husbands, which then sparked marital discord. Likewise, those males forced to marry women they did not know or even think physically appealing hindered the development of a loving, respectful marital relationship.

On some rare occasions, the preferential treatment that white male owners allowed bondsmen with regard to their choice of marriage partners (along with other salient variables such as the depletion of the young male slave population in some areas and an emphasis on slave breeding) contributed to polygamous marital relations among slaves. Israel Massie of Emporia, Virginia, noted that he knew of a few male slaves who were each married to several women simultaneously. Usually, these wives lived on different farms, yet Massie also recalled a polygamous marital situation where the husband and his wives lived on the same plantation. "When Tom died dar wuz Ginny, Sarah, Nancy, an' Patience," the Reverend Mr. Massie explained. "All four dar at de grave crying over dat one man. Do ya kno' chile, dem women never fou't, fuss, an' quarrel over dem men folks? Dey seemed to understood each other."[46]

Massie's description of polygamous marriages among Virginia slaves provides important documentation of the existence of alternative and, perhaps, competitive marriage forms in Virginia at the end of the antebellum era. ("Competitive" because it is obvious that many slaves embraced monogamy rather than polygamy as the appropriate manner to orient their marriages.) Given the paucity of information regarding the persistence of polygamy as a viable form of marital organization, however, it is difficult to discern whether it existed throughout the era or emerged as a response to slaveholder-engineered breeding schemes. Yet, the cooperation of the women married to the slave Tom that Massie describes suggests that there were sociocultural and, perhaps, historical bases for the continual manifestation of polygamy among slaves.

Clearly, the marital forms and relationships of slaves were related in part to their owners' desires to increase their slave holdings. Many antebellum Virginia slaveholders insisted that their slaves exercise their procreative powers to the fullest extent and encouraged various forms of marriage or sociosexual bonding between male and female slaves to insure high rates of birth. Slave breeding in Virginia is well documented through child-to-woman ratios, the personal papers of owners, and the testimonies of slaves. As one ex-slave noted: "The masters were very careful about a good breedin' woman. If she had five or six children she was rarely sold."[47] A comparison of white and slave child-to-woman ratios from the period 1820 to 1860 as an indicator of fertility, for example, documents that slave women began having children at an earlier age than white females, although Anglo-American women eventually did bear more children than black slave women. An analysis of several slave lists from Virginia, which include information descriptive of the age at first birth of slave mothers, further substantiates these findings. The average age at first birth for Virginia slaves was approximately twenty years. White women, on the other hand, began to have children later, at about twenty-two.[48] Moreover, while white child-to-woman ratios for both the considered age cohorts 0–14 years (child):15–49 years (mother) and 0–9 years:10–49 years declined over the antebellum era, child-to-woman ratios for slave women considered in the cohorts 0–14 years (child):15–49 years (mother) increased noticeably during the same time period.[49] This evidence along with a review of the changes in demographic patterns among slaves over time documents that slave breeding was, in some cases, an important priority among Virginia slaveowners. (See Tables A and B, pp. 296–97.)

The slave register of William Bolling and his heirs of Goochland County, Virginia, for example, offers just such information for analysis.[50] William Bolling's register is a particularly valuable document because of the long time period it details (1752 to 1860) and the numbers of mothers whose children's birth dates were recorded. The Bolling list includes 103 mothers who had 493 children (an additional six were reported as stillborn) born to them during this 108-year period. Careful scrutiny of this document indicates that although the age at the mother's first birth did not change significantly, the time between the live births of slave children declined significantly. For the period 1800 to 1820, for example, the average time between slave births on the Bolling plantations was about thirty-three months. By the decade beginning in 1850, however, slave mothers were giving birth to a live child approximately every twenty-two months. In other words, the average time between live births had decreased by one-third from 1820 to 1860.

While the information is less conclusive regarding the change in the average number of live children these women bore, it is clear that women in the last years of the antebellum era were having more children than those in the earlier decades. Within the ten-year period from 1850 to 1860 alone, the slave mothers on the Bolling plantations bore an average of four live children. Significantly, this figure conservatively represents only one-half of the childbearing years of these mothers. When one analyzes the numbers of children that Bolling slave women had during the period 1820 to 1850 (which represents a more complete childbearing cycle), an average of five live births is calculated. Clearly, those slave women who were beginning to bear children at the end of the antebellum era demonstrated a greater potential for natural increase than those of earlier generations. That this demographic change came at a time when slave marriages and families were so threatened by substantial exportations of adult slaves of childbearing age speaks to the resolve of owners to encourage procreation among their slaves. In order to promote the rapid birth of slave children, slave masters not only offered material incentives and may have threatened those slaves who refused to cooperate, but they also usurped the slaves' decision as to whether or not to participate in monogamous marital relationships. Thus, some slaveholders forced slave women and men to have several sexual partners outside of their marriage. Elige Davisson of Richmond, for example, stated that he was married once before he became free, but his owner still brought "some more women to see" him. Davisson insisted that his master would not let him have "just one woman" but mandated that the young male slave have sexual relations with several other female slaves so that they would bear children.[51] Such demands to participate in their owner's breeding schemes brought a great deal of pain and anger to the individual slaves and to the couples involved.

Undoubtedly, slave marriages varied in terms of quality, length, and ideals even in the most supportive environment. Most slaves wanted long-standing, loving, affectionate, monogamous relationships with their spouses. Yet, they could not expect that their partners would be able to protect them from some of the most violent and abusive aspects of slave life. Most could only hope that their spouses would understand the lack of choices they had with regard to labor, attention to domestic responsibilities, and to their relationships with whites. The inability of slave wives and husbands to actualize their ideals of gender differentiated behavior, even those which were obviously unrealistic given their positions as slaves, often was the source of marital discord.

Slave women with "abroad marriages" usually had no alternative but to take on the role of the central authority figure within their immediate families, especially as child rearers, while their husbands lived on separate plantations. In doing so, however, they challenged Western tradition concerning gender specific behavior and power in nineteenth-century households that slaves often respected. Consequently, matrifocal families were common among late antebellum Virginia slaves but were not always acceptable to the couples who comprised them. Since many slave women and men hoped to function in their families according to the proposed ideal of the larger Southern society, their inability to do so engendered resentment, frustration, and anger.

Thomas Harper, for example, a slave blacksmith in Alexandria, Virginia, decided to escape to Canada because he was not allowed to support his family. It was, he explained too "hard to see them in want and abused when he was not at liberty to aid or protect them."[52] Another Virginia slave confessed that he traded stolen goods in order to provide material support for his wife and children. "There were, in our vicinity," he noted, "plenty of 'poor white folks,' as we contemptuously called them, whom we cordially despised, but with whom we carried on a regular traffic at our master's expense."[53] Dangerfield Newby became so frustrated in his attempts to secure his family's freedom that he helped plan and execute the raid of John Brown on Harpers Ferry in 1859. His need to offer his wife and children the security of freedom was enhanced by his wife's constant appeal. "I want you to buy me as soon as possible," she wrote to him in August 1859. "I want you to buy me as soon as possible, for if you do not get me somebody else will. . . . Do all you can for me, which I have no doubt you will," she begged.[54] The blacksmith's desire to "protect" and "support" his family as well as Mr. and Mrs. Newby's feelings about his duty to provide the security of freedom to his family suggest that some slaves held ideals of manhood also popular in some European and African cultures.

Slave husbands sometimes imposed nearly impossible ideals of womanhood on their wives as well. Some were reluctant to commit themselves to women who did not meet their standards of beauty. Charles Grandy stated that slave men resented slaveholders who chose wives for them that were "ugly" instead of "purty." Ralph, a slave from Richmond, commented that when he first met his future wife (a free black), he thought that she "was one of the most beautiful of women." According to the Richmond bondsman, her beauty was one of the principal reasons that he "soon became madly in love."[55] Of course, no one wanted to marry someone as "ugly as sin," and certainly many slave women were physically attractive. Nevertheless, their harsh work routines, nutritionally deficient diets, poor material support, and limited access to medical attention robbed many slave women of their vitality and beauty when they were still young. Moreover, white men often reserved the most attractive slave women for themselves, refusing to let them marry slaves, or violated slave marriages whenever they chose to do so. Not surprisingly, ideals concerning female purity and marital chastity presented extreme challenges to slave couples.

The instances of white male sexual aggression toward married slave women created a great deal of tension and discord in the marital relationships of slaves. Although slave husbands theoretically understood the inability of their wives to protect themselves against the sexual overtures and attacks of white men, they resented and were angered by such occurrences. Their reactions were in response equally to their own sense of powerlessness to defend their wives and to a recognition of the physical and psychological pain their spouses experienced. When slave husbands did intervene, they suffered harsh retaliation—severe beatings, sometimes permanent separation from their family, or even murder. Many probably felt, as did Charles Grandy, who spoke of the murder of a male slave who tried to protect his wife from the advances of their overseer, that a "Nigger ain't got no chance."[56]

Consequently, some slave husbands targeted their helpless wives to be the recipients of their frustration, pain, guilt, and rage rather than the white men who attacked them. Regardless of whom the slaves struck out at, however, their responses had little effect on modifying the behavior of those white men who raped female slaves. "Marsters an' overseers use to make slaves dat wuz wid deir husbands git up, [and] do as they say," Israel Massie noted. "Send husbands out on de farm, milkin' cows or cuttin' wood. Den he gits in bed wid slave himself. Some women would fight an tussel. Others would be 'umble—feared of dat beatin.' What we saw, couldn't do nothing 'bout it. . . . My blood is bilin' now [at the] thoughts of dem times. Ef dey told dey husbands he wuz powerless."[57]

Many slave women were ashamed that they had been victimized by their white masters and were afraid of the consequences for themselves, their families, and the children they might have conceived. They tried to conceal the sexual assault from their husbands. "When babies came," Massie went on to explain, "dey [white fathers] ain't exknowledge 'em. Treat dat baby like 'tothers—nuthing to him. Mother feard to tell 'cause she know'd what she'd git. Dat wuz de concealed part."[58] Some slave wives went to great lengths to keep the truth from their husbands, claiming that mulatto children actually belonged to their spouses. "Ole man, . . . stop stedin' [studying] so much foolishness," responded one frightened slave wife when her husband noted that their youngest child was very physically distinct from their other children.[59] She was able to end her husband's open suspicions by constructing a story, but few could hide the obvious.

Faced with such overwhelming problems, some slave couples responded in ways that further augmented the destruction of their marriages and families. Alcoholism, domestic violence, jealousy, and adultery were internal problems which sometimes plagued these relationships. More than a few slave couples voluntarily separated. Manfra and Dykstra's review of a survey of late antebellum slave couples who resided in the south of Virginia, for example, indicates that of those marriages terminated before general emancipation, 10.1 percent ended as a result of mutual consent and another 10.8 percent because of the desertion of a spouse.[60]

Given the degradation of monogamous marriage relations among slaves, it is not surprising that some slaves had limited respect for the institution. Ralph (mentioned earlier) noted that when he first met his future wife, he realized that she was married and a mother but persisted in his pursuit of her. Explaining his behavior, he noted:

And how can the slave be expected to observe the marriage vows? In most cases they make none—plight no troth—have a sort of understanding that their agreement shall continue until one or both choose to form some other tie. And even if wishing to continue faithful unto death, they know their master deems their vows null and void, if he chooses to separate them; and he often does without scruple, by selling one or both. When their superiors disregard their slaves' obligations, the slaves will think lightly of them, too; and this utter contempt of the whites for the sacredness of marriage amongst slaves has done more to demoralize and brutalize the slave than all the personal wrongs he suffers. . . . The *sentiment* that should exist in marriage is excluded or crushed by the necessity of their condition; and the tie becomes a mere *liaison*, founded upon the instinct of the brute.[61]

Perhaps Ralph's impressively erudite critique of slave marriages derived principally from his attempt to justify his own adulterous actions. Yet, his analysis of the marital commitment between slaves is suggestive of the demoralizing effect that slavery must have had on some couples. Ralph did not hesitate to ignore the bounds of propriety when he sought and succeeded in winning another man's wife as his own. "For a good while," the slave noted, "she might be said to have two husbands: but finally her first husband went . . . and Sally became my acknowledged wife."[62]

Most slaves certainly respected the institution and believed that to interfere with the relations between a husband and a wife was wrong. Even Ralph felt that he was morally wrong in so doing. His inevitable guilt regarding the matter surfaced several years later. Trying to comprehend the reason for his wife's untimely death, the mourning slave concluded that he "deserved to lose her" because of the immoral way he had won her—"a just retribution and requital of her first husband's wrongs."[63]

The forced separation of slave couples, of course, had the most devastating impact on slave marriages. Large numbers of loving commitments ended in this manner. When slaveholders separated husbands and wives by long distances, it was almost impossible for these couples to retain close ties to one another. The difficulty was a result of the emotional and sociosexual needs of adult slaves as well as of the insistence of their owners that they remain sexually active and thus naturally reproductive. Some masters expected these separated couples to form new relationships as soon as possible. Many did eventually remarry, but the pain and sense of loss that they felt must have been a source of continual anguish for them and their children, who had to adjust to the authority of stepparents and to their inclusion in stepfamilies.

When one Virginia "contraband" woman found her first husband in a refugee camp in 1864, she testified that the two, "threw [them]selves into each others arms and cried." The husband as well as the woman, however, had remarried since their forced separation. While his new wife looked on the touching scene of reunion with obvious jealousy, the older wife was disturbed for other reasons. Although she described her present husband as "very kind" and she was determined not to leave him, she had to admit that she could not be happy after seeing her first husband. The thought of the source of their permanent separation still angered and frustrated her, even though she claimed she was pleased with her present spouse. "White folk's got a heap to answer for the way they've done to colored folks! So much they wont never *pray* it away!" she concluded in disgust.[64]

The voice of this one ex-slave in condemning of those slaveholders who purposefully destroyed slave marriages and families is no doubt representative of the voices of many who were similarly hurt. Their personal testimonies as well as the plantation records of their owners document the destruction that came to many Virginia slave families during the last decades of the antebellum era. Involuntary separation and the dispersal of husbands and wives from the rest of their families, sexual abuse, material deprivation, and forced marriages were some of the tremendous problems faced by slave families. Domestic violence, color stratification, spousal abandonment, and adultery were some of the manifestations of the internal strife within black slave families and marriages which were caused in large measure by their oppressive living conditions.

Late antebellum Southern society was indeed a harsh environment within which slaves tried to establish and maintain successful marriages and families. Many were able to do so, yet others failed in their efforts to sustain viable slave marriages and kin networks. The lives of Virginia slaves were too precarious to guarantee the complete and the constant success of any social institution, including marriage and the family. Consequently, the slave family emerged in the postbellum South as a viable but battered institution, threatened by new forms of economic and social oppression as well as the internal strife inherited from the previous era.

8

Toward a Kinder and Gentler America: The Southern Lady in the Greening of the Politics of the Old South

EUGENE D. GENOVESE

ACCORDING TO ONE STRAIN OF radical-feminist thought, which—thank God—has not gone unchallenged in the feminist movement, we should raise women to political power in order to promote world peace, international personhood, and a more humane and loving environment. For it would seem that women, unlike men, are naturally peace-loving, nurturing, mild-tempered, moderate, kind, and humane. Yet I must confess to a certain uneasiness when I reflect upon some of the historical figures I most admire, or at least respect: Elizabeth the First of England, who crushed Spanish naval power abroad and ground the face of the poor at home; Isabela of Spain, who was not perceived as a nurturing mother by the Muslims of Spain or the Indians of America; Catherine of Russia, who drowned tens of thousands of rebellious peasants in their own blood; Maria Theresa of Austria, about whom the Tsar of Russia said in response to the tears she shed at the partition of Poland, "She weeps, she weeps, but she takes her share." And problems arise upon consideration of the wonderfully pacific and nurturing policies pursued by such recent heroines as Indira Ghandi, Golda Meir, Cory Aquino, Benazir Bhutto, Margaret Thatcher, and our own beloved Jean Kirkpatrick. I confess, too, to some querulousness when I recall the history of the socialist communist move-

125

ments. For while yielding to no one in admiration for the great ladies of the left, I am not sure that a motherly instinct for nurturing has exactly been their strongest suit. It has, after all, often been remarked that when the German Social Democrats abandoned their principles in 1914, the intransigent Rosa Luxemburg and Clara Zetkin may well have been the last real men left in the party. But my personal favorite remains Anna Pauker, the battle-hardened revolutionary who became foreign minister of Rumania after World War II. According to party gossip, she was the only foreign communist whose telephone calls Stalin would take any time of day or night. As is well known, Comrade Stalin loved nurturing women, and Anna Pauker displayed her own nurturing qualities by her complicity in Stalin's execution of her husband.

I do not wish to be thought to be hostile to the demand that we raise women to political power. Not at all. I merely suggest that there may be better reasons for doing so than the expectation of a more compassionate, loving, humane regime. Personally, I am convinced that their elevation would result in immeasurably greater administrative efficiency, social stability, and political firmness—all of which we should welcome. I would therefore do everything in my power to persuade you to support my wife, should she run for president of the United States. She would make a great president. True, certain constitutional difficulties might arise when she appointed herself director of the FBI and CIA and secretary of defense. But I ask you to take my word for it. The drug problem, which the male wimps in Washington find intractable, would be solved with dispatch; law and order would return to the streets of our cities, and the planes would fly on time. In fairness, I must file a caveat: the Nervous Nellies of the American Civil Liberties Union might not approve of all her methods. Then, too, you may have to pay higher taxes to finance the labor camps. But I have no doubt that if we could bring the people of the Old South back to life, they would approve of her regime. Certainly, the ladies would offer their resolute and enthusiastic support.

These probably perverse reflections bring to mind those admirable ladies, whose world-renowned meekness, mildness, moderation, and self-denial led them to defer to their lords and masters on all questions, and most notably on all political questions.

We are, nonetheless, compelled to face certain ambiguities, certain inconsistencies, and certain anomalies. Southern men, protesting too much, never ceased to assure us that a woman's place was in the home, that their own ladies had no interest in politics, and that all southerners, male and female, agreed upon the unsuitability, incompetence, and, indeed, the light-headedness of the ladies in all such matters. Alas, those same men, in a thousand-and-one ways, demonstrated in word and deed that they believed no such thing. More precisely, they no doubt did believe that a woman's place was in the home and out of politics, but they also knew that a great many of their very own ladies followed politics closely, cared passionately, and found an assortment of ways to influence, not to say torment, their fathers, husbands, and brothers on political questions. All of which might not have mattered much were it not that the discernible influence of the ladies came down hard on the side of proslavery and political extremism—a largely unnoticed trifle.

Women loomed large in the proslavery ideology of the Old South. Suffice it to note that proslavery rested, above all, on biblical sanction, and that one proslavery spokesman after another spelled out the central point: the justification of black slavery derived from the general justification of slavery, regardless of race, as ordained of God, and slavery and all class stratification derived from the prior divine command that women submit to men—racial subordination derived from class subordination, which derived from gender subordination. For the mouth of the Lord hath spoken it.

The Reverend Benjamin Morgan Palmer summed up the virtually unanimous neo-Aristotelian and flatly anti-individualistic attitude by declaring the family the cornerstone of both church and state and by insisting that the father and husband must reign supreme, with no appeal from his judgments except to God. And the southern idea of family included dependent laborers—not merely kin—as captured in the oft-repeated expression, "My family, white and black." The Reverend Frederick A. Ross explained, "The slave stands in relation to his master precisely as the wife stands in relation to her husband."[1]

All across the South, leading educators, ministers, and politicians used similar words to justify women's exclusion from politics and public life. And all across the South, the women gave formal assent to their own alleged political incapacity. Yet paradoxically, everyone knew that the southern ladies followed political events closely, debated them hotly, and often battered their men on the issues. The personal papers of the slaveholding families leave no room for doubt. Among other curiosities is evidence that the men knew and accepted it. Thus, the men often read the political newspapers, speeches, and political pamphlets aloud to the family circle, and the women read them aloud to each other and to the men.

Consider Anna Maria Calhoun's relation to her father, the great John C. Calhoun. As a teenager, she adamantly insisted upon joining him in Washington to make herself useful to his work. He responded in a manner that, along with much else, belies his reputation as a cast-iron man devoid of a capacity for tenderness and sensitivity to others: "You say you are anxious to know what is going on in the political world, as you have no opportunity to learn passing events in your secluded section. I am not one of those who think your sex ought to have nothing to do with politics. They have as much interest in the good condition of their country as the other sex, and tho' it would be unbecoming of them to take an active part in political struggles, their own opinion, when enlightened, cannot fail to have a great and salutary effect."[2]

The spirit manifested in Calhoun's letter to his gifted daughter reverberated throughout the southern states, both in its generosity and respect for female intelligence, and in its determination to keep women out of practical politics and public controversy. As a strong and broadly mounted counterpoint, a great many men manifested the determination but not the generosity. Some men argued, much as women like Louisa McCord did, that the physical weakness of women condemned them to subservience despite their intellectual parity. Others denied the intellectual parity, although almost all agreed on women's moral superiority or at least their especially important and discrete moral qualities. Henry Hughes of Mississippi, normally a bright fellow, captured the attitude of those who saw what they regarded as a particularly debilitating combination of female physical and intellectual inferiority, although even he celebrated their superior moral virtues. In 1856, Hughes, a bachelor, lectured in New Orleans on women in society to a mercifully small audience. "A baby is better fitting a woman than an oration. She is intended for home duties, labors and responsibilities. Her physical characteristics prove this. Fat makes beauty and orders repose; women are fatter than men, and their fat settles their status. It is not natural for women to be politicians and strong-minded; political women are social excrescences. Nature has settled woman's social status. They have not physical power to be anything other than home folk."[3]

John Randolph of Roanoke had set the tone during the congressional debate over statehood for Missouri. Randolph vigorously objected to the presence of many women who had crowded the galleries and even the floor: "Mr. Speaker, what pray are all these women doing here, so out of place in this arena? Sir, they had much better be at home attending to their knitting." Randolph's attitude toward women may be gleaned from a letter to a friend in Charlotte County, Virginia: "I am well aware that ladies are as delicate as they are charming creatures, and that, in our intercourse with them, we must strain the truth as far as possible. . . . brought up from their earliest infancy to disguise their sentiments (for a woman would be a monster who did not practice this disguise) it is their privilege to be insincere, and we should despise [them], and justly too, if they had that manly frankness, which constitutes the ornament of our character, and the very reverse of theirs."[4]

Now, flagrant denigration of women did not appear often in the South, probably no more often than in the North. But James H. Hammond, a prominent South Carolina planter and politician, as might be expected, proved a particular sinner. He categorized women in the privacy of his diary as "mostly fools and savages and not to be called either civilized or thinking or reasonable Beings." And even he could get misty-eyed when paying tribute to the exemplary character of his wife, mother, and mother-in-law.[5]

Thirty years after Randolph's outburst in Congress, David Outlaw, Whig congressman from Bertie County, North Carolina, and, it would appear, a good family man, read Randolph's speech and reflected upon it in a letter to his wife. He began by deploring the crowds of women who choked the Capitol each day, many dressed at the height of fashion and bent on flirtations. He dissociated himself from "the length and breadth" of Randolph's words but admitted some degree of sympathy. David Outlaw wrote his wife Emily Outlaw that "ladies had no business to be present where men contended for victory & empire any more than they had to be in a military camp because things frequently occur there which are unfit for them to hear."[6] During the 1840s and 1850s, David wrote many letters from Washington to his wife, whose intelligence he obviously regarded highly. His letters included a steady stream of news that kept her well informed about political affairs. Yet like so many others in a similar position, he could not resist filing an occasional, formulaic self-rebuke: "I have written more politics this morning than usual—it is not I know a very interesting subject especially to you."[7] In fact, we may be certain that he knew no such thing.

Or among a host of others, consider the family correspondence of John A. Quitman of Mississippi. In 1828, in the early days of his political career, he sprinkled his letters to his wife with political news. Yet he, too, filed the usual self-rebuke. Writing from Jackson, where he was serving in the state legislature, he declared, "I scarcely know what to say to you in my letters. Matters of legislation will not, I know, interest you, and nothing else is worthy of notice." His self-rebuke led to no reformation, for, if anything, his reports on legislation and political matters became more and more detailed as time went on. It is obvious that Eliza Quitman expected and enjoyed the political intelligence from Jackson.[8] In later years, Quitman wrote his daughters, Louisa and Antonia, in much the same vein, and they responded by encouraging and reinforcing his political extremism, especially when he was under fire from unionists and other enemies. Everywhere in the South, the politicians replicated the performance of Outlaw and Quitman: Howell and Thomas Cobb in Georgia, Willie P. Mangum in North Carolina, J. Marion Sims in Alabama, almost anyone in South Carolina.[9] They all kept their wives and daughters closely informed about politics, showed considerable respect for their responses, and ended their letters by apologizing for having bothered the little ladies with such boring stuff, which they knew was of no interest to them.

From all across the South—and this is a wholly untold story—we find evidence of women who acted as trusted advisers and confidantes to politicians, usually, but not always, their own husbands (for example, Mrs. Robert Tyler in Virginia, Augusta Jane Evans in Alabama, Mrs. John Reagan in Texas, and Mrs. George Towns in Georgia). According to a normally reliable witness, Judge Richard Clark of Georgia, the number of such cases was in fact much larger than anyone wanted to admit publicly.[10]

The men squirmed over the contradictions in their stance and on one issue after another made themselves ridiculous without bothering to notice. Let us settle for one example of where their squeamishness could lead. The *Magnolia*, an impressive magazine published in Savannah in 1842, assailed those who disparaged the female intellect and came out for female education. Women must be educated, the editors insisted, so that they could make themselves the mothers of great men. "We believe," they wrote, "that they are able to comprehend political topics, even when they are not at liberty to discuss them."[11]

That the politically influential women generally held moderate views may be doubted. Many, like Miss Evans and Mrs. Reagan, were militants. Significantly, little protest was heard about the political activity of South Carolina's Maria Henrietta Pinckney, who did yeoman work for the nullifiers. Her little book, *The Quintessence of Long Speeches, Arranged as a Political Catechism*, offered a notably effective summary of the nullifiers' political creed and was widely hailed for doing so. Not content with a literary intervention, she joined Governor Hamilton in importing a cargo of sugar in a deliberate attempt to provoke a challenge to the hated sugar tariff.[12] And what could the devotees of female nurturing, pacifism, and humane proclivities make of Elise Bragg, wife of the ill-starred Confederate General Braxton Bragg. Like Mary Boykin Chesnut and some other ladies, she considered herself a formidable military strategist and tactician, and she had the advantage of being married to a man who, to his great misfortune, followed her impetuous advice more often than not. Her "warm-hearted" and "humane" temperament came through with special force in a letter in which she expressed her admiration for the troops from Louisiana and Mississippi and her contempt for those from Tennessee: "Dear husband, please *do not* trust the Tennessee troops. Put the Tennesseans where your batteries can *fire* upon them if they attempt to run. Lead them into action yourself and *shame* them into fighting."[13] During the secession crisis and the war, southerners from Virginia to Texas commented on the political influence of the ladies, which, they said, heavily bolstered the extremists. During earlier decades, British and other travelers had noticed the same spirit. Mrs. Basil Hall remarked after a dinner party at Judge DeSaussure's in Columbia, "I had as tough an argument with some of the ladies over slavery as ever Basil had on any subject with the gentlemen." Fredrika Bremer, among others, found the women "more irritable and violent than their men on political questions."[14] During the war, the widespread proslavery radicalism and Negrophobia of the southern women broke over the head of a beleaguered Jefferson Davis, when he made his forlorn plea to recruit blacks into the Confederate army. Catherine Devereux Edmonston raged at the very idea of black troops, but especially at the promise of freedom for slave recruits. "Can one credit it?" she cried, "that that silly Congress should consume their time and our money in a grave discussion over the best means to destroy the country is a depth of folly too deep for me to fathom." She then went to the heart of the ideological impasse: "We give up a principle when we offer emancipation as a reward or boon, for we have hitherto contended that slavery was Cuffee's normal condition, the very best position he could occupy. . . ."[15]

In evaluating the "humanizing" and "softening" effect of the southern ladies on politics, a few words on their role in the grand sport of dueling might prove suggestive. According to received wisdom, which on balance may be sound, women disapproved of dueling, even if they rarely, if ever, tried to stop it. The exceptions, nonetheless, proved legion and instructive, as the famous advice Andrew Jackson got from his mother testifies: "Never lie, nor take what is not your own, nor sue anybody for slander or assault and battery. *Always settle them cases yourself!*" Periodically, ladies pushed their gentlemen into duels in defense of honor—their own, their lady's, their family's. In a particularly charming incident (for which Tallahassee, Florida, and Milledgeville, Georgia, both claim provenance), the sister of Willis Allston established herself as a legend. When her brother Augustus died in a duel at the hands of General Leigh Reed, she extracted the bullet, remolded it, and sent it to her other brother, Willis, with instructions to do his duty. Returning east from Texas, he did his duty—shooting and, for good measure, stabbing Reed to death.[16]

Then there was the high-spirited lady in Mississippi whose husband received a challenge in 1838 and suggested that he thought he would decline. "Accept it sir, for I would rather be a widow of a brave man than the wife of a coward."[17] Elsewhere, a gentleman who had agreed to act as a second visited the opponent, who had fallen ill, to find out whether he would be able to keep the engagement. The opponent's wife replied for him: "If he is not there, I will take his place!"[18]

On a variety of occasions ladies demanded that their gentlemen avenge real or imagined slights for them. In the 1840s, according to the report of a shocked Matilda Houstoun, who had just arrived in New Orleans, an Englishman killed a young man in a duel. "The quarrel," Mrs. Houstoun explained, "originated in the St. Louis ballroom, and was caused by the willful and vindictive spirit of a young lady, who protested that the Englishman had insulted *her* by placing his partner above her in the dance, and that she *would have satisfaction*."[19] In Sunbury, in the Georgia low country, the village belle, a notorious flirt, teased and encouraged two army officers simultaneously. Not surprisingly, the men quarreled, and a duel ensued. One went down with a severe wound and died in agony of gangrene a few weeks later. But I am happy to report that, for some reason, the winner thereupon lost interest in her.[20]

Mary Blount Pettigrew found some cause for mirth in such wonderful doings. "Look here, dear fellow," she wrote her brother, a student at the University of North Carolina, "you seem terribly smitten with a certain Smeadsite [student at St. Mary's school]. I hope you & John will never duel on her account, especially before she has decided which shall be killed."[21]

There can be no doubt that many women—a majority for all we shall ever know—did hold moderate views, support the Union, and cry out for peace. From the earliest days of the Republic to secession, large numbers of politically moderate women filled their diaries and letters with prayers for restraint and sectional accord, although they remained emphatically proslavery.

Examples could be cited and multiplied, but to little effect. For although the ladies could stiffen the resolve of their unionist male kin, they could not moderate the views of their extremist kin. As nurturing, pacific, timid creatures, they only acted as expected when they took moderate stands on politics. Since they were acting true to form, they could be patted on the head and reminded that men, not women, had to make the hard decisions for militant action and, if necessary, for war. The extremist women found themselves in a different position, and for the same reason, if with a twist. If they, as nurturing, pacific, timid creatures could take no more Yankee insolence and assaults on southern honor, what man could argue? Whether they spoke up, as they frequently did, or conveyed their opinions through the kind of withering silence in which they excelled, they could, in effect, question the courage and honor—the very manhood—of those of their men who showed the slightest wavering.

Southern ladies had a long history of stiffening the backbone of their men during sectional crises, and southern gentlemen had to quail when confronted with an outburst from one of their ladies like that fired off by Georgia King to her brother Tip. Writing from Milledgeville, Georgia, where the state legislature was meeting, she exploded, "All the women are RIGHT—but it is strange to say, there are MANY MEN quite willing to be ruled by the Yankee and the nigger!—I suppose you see that New York has passed the law for UNIVERSAL SUFFRAGE—ALL the niggers!"[22] Or consider the position of the sixteen-year-old son of Senator Louis Wigfall of Texas. We may doubt that he wished to dissociate himself from his parents' fire-eating politics or that he would have hesitated to join the Confederate army when Texas seceded. But even if he had had other inclinations, they would surely have dissolved in the face of the militant stance affected by his younger sister, Louly, who rushed to congratulate him for his manly determination to stand up for the rights of the South. Louly, who was at school in Boston, wrote home that she hoped "our brave men will fight till every drop of blood is shed before they submit to the rule of Black Republicans."[23] And then there was the young man under pressure to join the Confederate army on the eve of his marriage to a Charleston belle. She delicately expressed herself to a gentleman who had teasingly asked if she would not like to keep him home for a little while, "If he had not promptly volunteered for the defense of our state, he could never have entered this house; and, indeed, he could not have had access to any parlor in the city again. No woman of Carolina would for a moment tolerate a coward."[24] Whatever the young man's inclinations, he does not appear to have had much to think about.

In Georgia, John B. Lamar, brother-in-law of the old unionist Howell Cobb, received a letter from his niece. The ten-year-old Mary Ann Lamar Cobb expected war and announced that she herself would fight if she could. "I think if Southern men have any bravery in them," she wrote, "they will fight, and I think if they do fight they will gain the victory, for the right is on their side."[25]

Ten years earlier, during the struggle over the Compromise of 1850, Mary Jones, of the politically moderate C. C. Jones family, lashed out at Daniel Webster in a letter to her husband: "He does not mean to open our veins and bleed us to death by abolishing the Fugitive Slave Bill; but by confining us and our property to the original limits he will put his hand around our necks and strangle us to death. This seems to my mind to be his present position with regard to the rights of the South."[26] During the turbulent years that followed, the extremists found it increasingly easy to mobilize women in support of their various campaigns. The outpourings of support for Preston Brooks after he savagely caned Charles Sumner on the Senate floor provides a striking case in point. From all across the South, the ladies sent Brooks congratulations. In Charleston, in 1860, at the fateful convention that split the Democratic party, the ladies opened their homes to the radical southern delegates and to those who could be won over. Meanwhile, the Douglasites baked in sweltering, overcrowded hotels and faced the ire of the ladies at the convention hall, where they packed the galleries and applauded the intransigents. And if the female gossip mill may be credited, when Douglas did get the nomination in Baltimore, the wives of the radical senators successfully prevailed upon Mrs. Benjamin Fitzpatrick of Alabama to persuade her husband to decline the proffered vice-presidential nomination.[27]

When the South seceded, northern threats of war met scorn and defiance. "Do they think then," wrote the indignant Susan Cornwall of Georgia, "that we are as degraded as our slaves, to be whipped into obedience at the command of our self-styled masters?" Kate S. Carney uttered a "Hurrah for Tennessee" upon hearing of its refusal to acquiesce in Lincoln's call for troops, and she added, "If she will now secede, I will no longer be ashamed of her." A few weeks later, she applauded "the men of Tennessee for turning out so bravely in defense of their homes."[28]

Did the southern ladies deserve their reputation for political extremism? Did, in fact, the extremists outnumber the moderates? Probably we shall never know. But the numbers do not matter, and as for intensity of feeling, those who want action generally speak with greater intensity than those who do not. The prevalent notions of southern honor and aggressive masculinity positioned the extremist women to pressure their men in a way and to an extent their moderate sisters never could. If we eschew the luxury of historical hindsight, a strong, politically plausible case could be made for both secessionist and unionist responses to the fearful crises of the 1850s, and many women as well as men chose one side or the other bravely and intelligently, even if many others took the path of least resistance or acted mindlessly. We would do well to honor those women who did their best to resist the passions of the moment, who eschewed extremism, who worked and prayed for peace and the Union. But there is no reason to withhold respect from those who read the signs of the terrible times differently and who, according to their own lights, opted for an all-out struggle in defense of everything they held dear—those women who held their men's feet to the fire and demanded that they act in accordance with professed principles and standards of honor.

Henry Hughes may well have been right in insisting that women tend to fat and that the southern ladies naturally became pleasantly and beautifully fat. I would not know. What I do know is that, when it came to politics, fatheads they were not.

John C. Calhoun (1782–1850), American statesman and owner of Fort Hill. Portrait painted by George P. A. Healy in 1845. (*Courtesy of Clemson University, Clemson, S.C.*)

Fort Hill, home of John C. Calhoun and later the home of Anna Maria Calhoun Clemson and her husband Thomas Green Clemson. (*Courtesy of Clemson University, Clemson, S.C.*)

Parlor at Fort Hill. The marriage of Anna Maria Calhoun to Thomas Green Clemson took place in this room on November 13, 1838. Portraits of Anna Maria and Thomas Green Clemson are depicted in this photograph. (*Courtesy of Clemson University, Clemson, S.C.*)

Anna Maria Calhoun Clemson and her two children, Floride and John Calhoun Clemson, c. 1850. (*Courtesy of Clemson University, Clemson, S.C.*)

Mr. and Mrs. Ralph Izard (Alice Delancey) painted in Rome in 1775. Oil on canvas by John Singleton Copley. (*Courtesy of the Museum of Fine Arts, Boston, Mass.*)

Mrs. Gabriel Manigault (Margaret Izard). Oil on canvas by Gilbert Stuart, 1794. (*Courtesy of the Albright-Knox Art Gallery, Buffalo, N.Y.*)

Gabriel Manigault. Oil on canvas by Gilbert Stuart, 1794. (*Courtesy of the Albright-Knox Art Gallery, Buffalo, N.Y.*)

Lithograph by Nathaniel Currier, 1860s. This print captures the ideal of the benevolent patriarch. (*Courtesy of the Library of Congress*)

"Human Flesh at Auction." Drawing by Vanicen-Snyder. From *The Suppressed Book About Slavery,* published by the United States Congress, 1864. (*Courtesy of Mars Hill College Special Collections, Mars Hill, N.C.*)

"Sold to Go South." Drawing by Vanicen-Snyder. From *The Suppressed Book About Slavery,* published by the United States Congress, 1864. (*Courtesy of Mars Hill College Special Collections, Mars Hill, N.C.*)

Virginia Tunstall Clay, c. 1850, wife of Clement C. Clay, Jr. From *A Belle of the Fifties: Memoirs of Mrs. Clay of Alabama* (1905).

Virginia T. Clay (1825–1915) in the 1860s. From the C. C. Clay Papers. (*Courtesy of the William R. Perkins Library, Duke University, Durham, N.C.*)

Portrait of Clement C. Clay, Jr., in the 1850s as a United States senator (1853–1861). (*Courtesy of the Alabama Department of Archives and History, Montgomery, Ala.*)

Jefferson Davis (left) and Clement C. Clay, Jr. (right) after release from Fortress
Monroe, c. 1867. (*Courtesy of William R. Perkins Library, Duke University, Durham, N.C.*)

Portrait of Sarah Anne Ellis Dorsey (1829–1879), author of *Agnes Graham* and other novels, befriended Jefferson Davis after the Civil War. (*Courtesy of "Beauvoir," the Jefferson Davis Shrine, Biloxi, Miss.*)

Virginia T. Clay in later life. From the C. C. Clay Papers. (*Courtesy of William R. Perkins Library, Duke University, Durham, N.C.*)

From *Old Virginia Recipes,* by Ann E. Pretlow. Illustration by Rhoda C. Chase.

"Marcellus" the cook in *The Blue Grass Cook Book* (1904), by Minnie C. Fox.

"Love in a Cottage," frontispiece, *The Dixie Cook Book* (1882), by Estelle Woods Wilcox.

Sharecroppers at Beech Island, S.C., in the 1890s. (*Courtesy of the South Caroliniana Library of the University of South Carolina*)

Portrait of Ella Gertrude Clanton Thomas (1834–1907). "Second Day" wedding dress following her marriage to J. Jefferson Thomas, December 16, 1852. (*Privately owned by Michael F. Despeaux*)

Portrait of Jefferson Thomas (1831–1916), c. late 1850s. (*Privately owned by Michael F. Despeaux*)

Captain James Jefferson Thomas, class of 1851 at Princeton University, riding into Atlanta on his sorrel pony "Dixie Will Go" to welcome President Hibben of Princeton to the State of Georgia, c. 1916. (*From the* Princeton Alumni Weekly, *April 1916*)

Josiah Gorgas (1818–1883) as
captain, U.S.A., c. 1853.
(*Courtesy of the Gorgas
Home, the University of Alabama, Tuscaloosa, Ala.*)

Josiah Gorgas as colonel, C.S.A. (*Courtesy
of William Stanley Hoole Special Collections,
the University of Alabama, Tuscaloosa, Ala.*)

William Crawford Gorgas (1854–1920), son
of Josiah Gorgas, as first lieutenant, U.S.A.,
1883, the year of his father's death. (*Courtesy of William Stanley Hoole Special Collections, the University of Alabama, Tuscaloosa,
Ala.*)

9

The Clays of Alabama: The Impact of the Civil War on a Southern Marriage

CAROL BLESER AND FREDERICK M. HEATH

ALTHOUGH THE SOUTHERN BELLE is frequently depicted in popular novels of the Old South, she is harder to find in the actual historical records. Nevertheless, authentic belles did exist in the nineteenth-century Victorian South, and they were sought after by men, both young and old, who expected them to be pretty, unmarried, affluent, charming, fashionable, and flirtatious. In addition, the classic Southern belle was expected to have rudimentary skills at a musical instrument, the French language, and the art of flattering conversation. Playing this dependent and ornamental role not only trained women to manipulate men, important in a patriarchal society, but also had immediate practical compensations because an accomplished player could hope to marry a man of wealth and social position. While the goal for a belle was to marry for love, marry they did in any case, for, rightly or wrongly, they believed that marriage would provide them with social rank, material benefits, freedom, and companionship and, thus, was far more desirable than remaining single.

Once married, the belle usually disappeared from the social scene. The burdens of bearing children in rapid succession, of caring for a husband, and of managing a household left them little time to amuse either themselves or others. As Scarlett O'Hara put it, "Married women never have any fun." A few married women, however, never stopped behaving as if they were still belles. They continued to flirt, to pose at the center of groups of competing males, and to spark the devotion of prestigious men. These wives, including the famous diarist Mary Boykin Chesnut, were often free from the responsibilities that occupied most married women. Having no children and usually no home of her own to manage, Chesnut, in part, collected admirers in order to escape from boredom and to wield influence over the men around her, many of whom she considered inferior to herself.[1]

Similar on the surface in many ways to Mary Boykin Chesnut was Virginia Tunstall Clay. Both women dazzled men. Virginia's 1843 marriage to Clement Claiborne Clay united her with a husband whose political prominence gave her opportunities to seek attention from men of importance. Their childlessness and his failure to provide her with a home of her own freed Virginia from the responsibilities borne by most wives. Virginia Clay, ambitious, self-centered, energetic, attractive, and sociable, attempted for over twenty years to be a married belle, a role through which she enjoyed some of the delights of her single days and achieved both recognition and influence. The Civil War, however, which altered so many lives in so many ways, brought changes which enabled Virginia to apply her talents to purposes other than merely pleasing men.

Virginia Tunstall was born on January 16, 1825, in Nash County, North Carolina. Her mother, Ann Arrington Tunstall, died before Virginia was one year old, and her father left his daughter to be raised by relatives, of which there were more than enough. Her mother had twenty half-brothers and half-sisters.[2] Sometime before she turned eight, Virginia went to live with her aunt and uncle Mary Ann and Henry Collier in Tuscaloosa, Alabama. There she grew up, living at times with the Colliers and at other times with her mother's half-brother Alfred Battle and his wife, Millicent, both families being among Tuscaloosa's elite. Collier became a state judge in 1828, a member of the state supreme court in 1836, and its chief justice the following year. Alfred Battle, a merchant, was one of the town's wealthiest citizens. Both uncles owned sizable homes in town, plantations, and large numbers of slaves.[3] Virginia's aunts and uncles took good care of her, but she was always somewhat of a guest in their homes and, of necessity, learned the importance of being adaptable and congenial—traits that later served her well. Her father, Dr. Payton Randolph Tunstall, seldom visited her. Little is known of him except that he apparently mismanaged his personal finances.[4] Nevertheless, her other relatives had enough money and social position so that Virginia could aspire to be a belle. She attended the Female Academy in Nashville, Tennessee, where young women of her class studied arithmetic, composition, and geography and learned to play musical instruments, to draw, and to do needlework in the school's "Ornamental Department." Virginia, although only fourteen when she graduated from the academy in 1840, was already receiving a great deal of attention from male admirers.[5]

Her father, on one of his rare appearances, took her to Mobile, where he escorted her to a play and a ball, bought her a peach silk dress, and introduced her to Octavia Le Vert, whom Virginia and others would remember as one of America's most sophisticated women and famous belles. Virginia wrote in her memoir that in "those few charmed days, I saw, if not clearly at least prophetically, what . . . beauty and joy life might hold for me."[6]

In December 1842, Virginia, staying with the Colliers in Tuscaloosa, then the state capital, attended a round of parties marking the opening of the legislative session. At these gatherings she often saw Clement Claiborne Clay, a new member of the Alabama legislature and an old family friend. Clay, then twenty-six years old, was the son of Clement Comer Clay, one of the most prominent men in the state. Clement Comer had moved in 1811 from Tennessee to Huntsville, Alabama, which was the center of a fertile region in the bend of the Tennessee River ideal for growing cotton, and which would be home to Clay and his sons for the rest of their lives. Within a month of Alabama's statehood in December 1819, Clement Comer, only thirty years old and a planter-lawyer, became the first chief justice of the state supreme court. He also served three terms in the national House of Representatives from 1829 to 1835, was governor from 1835 to 1837, and was a United States senator from 1837 to 1841. In that year, he resigned from the Senate to return to Alabama to look after his personal estate. Clay owned two plantations, which included over 2,700 acres and at least seventy-one slaves, and he had a flourishing law practice and a fine home in Huntsville. Part of his financial success had come through his marriage in 1815 at the age of twenty-five to sixteen-year-old Susanna Claiborne Withers, the daughter of John Withers, a prosperous planter. Clement Comer and Susanna had three children, Clement Claiborne, John Withers, and Hugh Lawson. Both parents expected a great deal of their sons, especially of their eldest son, Clement, born December 13, 1816.[7]

In January 1833, when Clement Claiborne Clay was sixteen years old, he entered the University of Alabama, graduating a year and a half later. While still an undergraduate, young Clay decided that he wanted to study mathematics at Harvard. His father, however, insisted that he study law at the University of Virginia. After father and son visited Charlottesville, the son described the dormitories as "uncomfortable and unhealthy" and the students as "wild" and "harum-scarum." Clement became ill, law school was postponed, and he served as secretary to his father when the latter was the governor of Alabama. After two years as his father's aide, Clay acceded to his parent's wishes and entered the University of Virginia, earning a law degree in 1839, while his father was in the United States Senate. Returning to Huntsville, Clay worked as a junior partner in his father's law firm, helped manage the family's plantations, and wrote editorials for a newspaper controlled by his father. The elder Clay returned from Washington in 1841, apparently dissatisfied with his son's management of the family properties. The younger Clay was elected to the Alabama legislature in the fall of 1842, but this did not result in his escaping from paternal domination. Soon after he arrived at the state capital, his father followed him to Tuscaloosa and moved into an adjoining room.[8]

By the time of his father's arrival, however, Clement and Virginia were already in love. He sent her candy, books, and romantic verses. Clay confessed to being "a *small* poet," but he claimed to be a "great lover." By the end of December, Clement had persuaded Virginia to marry him.[9] She, in turn, found his appearance "striking and pleasing" and his features "classic in their beauty." Their courtship lasted less than two months, a briefer time than most couples took to arrive at such a binding decision. Virginia was eighteen years old when she wed Clement.[10] Although she had many beaus and was not likely to become a spinster, she was eager to marry Clement for she loved him, had no permanent home, and was tired of being passed from relative to relative. Moreover, he was an excellent prospect for any ambitious belle.

At twenty-six, Clement had reached the average age of marriage for men of his class.[11] He wrote his father that he had fallen in love with "a lady of as tender a heart, as sensible a head, and as noble a spirit, as any one I ever knew." Nor did he overlook that Virginia owned "enough property to support her[self] comfortably," and that numbered among her relatives were "some of the most wealthy & respectable persons of this place." Moreover, Clement thought he "ought to get married," for a wife would make him "a better man and a more useful citizen." He wrote, "I want some anchor to give me greater stability of character. I want some incentive to an exercise of economy in my time & money. . . . I want, in brief, something more to live for—some constant & abiding sense of responsibility in the world." Even though by the 1840s it was no longer necessary for a son to request formal permission of his parents before becoming engaged, Clement Clay, still dependent on his family financially and emotionally, asked for their approval. There was no family opposition.[12]

The wedding took place in Tuscaloosa on February 1, 1843, at the spacious, columned home of her uncle Judge Henry Collier. The realities of timing, social acceptability, and material prospects—as well as romantic love—lay behind the courtship and the marriage which had followed it so quickly. Clement and Virginia had known each other for some time. Governor Clay had appointed Virginia's uncle Henry Collier to the state supreme court when Clement had been his father's secretary. Moreover, a marriage between Clay's son and Collier's niece might advance the political fortunes of both families. Virginia and Clement could look forward to a bright future.[13]

Clay, as noted, had been confident that marriage would make him a happier and more responsible person. During the early years of their union, he filled his letters to Virginia with lengthy declarations of what she and their relationship had done for him. Clement, like most nineteenth-century men, believed that the presence of a woman in his life would soften the harsher aspects of his male behavior. When he thought of his wife, Clement claimed, "I forgive my enemies, I am sensitive as a child to acts of kindness, & compassionate as a woman toward the unfortunate, & grateful as such a sinner can be for the protection & care of Providence." He even admitted his dependence on his wife who "has almost supreme power over me & leads me about, whither she will, by the silken cord of love."[14]

Nevertheless, before their marriage Clement had revealed to his mother that he knew "one objection to herself—it is that she is a belle!" Also, in a letter to Virginia written two weeks before their marriage, Clay told her, "You love admiration quite to a sin & sometimes pay much too dearly for it." Marriage and maturity, Clement hoped, would cure her of her need to play the belle. That was not to be the case. Afterwards, Clement began to worry that Virginia's refusal to abandon the role of a belle might hurt his reputation. "You are so pretty & fascinating," he told her, "that I fear some fine-looking fellow will forget you are a married woman & make love to you. Beware of the follies of yr. sex. I know you love me too much to say or do willingly anything improper or unbecoming my wife; but yr. haste and vivacity may betray you into seeming errors." She must not forget that "yr. future is made—you are not beau-catching."[15]

Two weeks after their marriage, Clement took Virginia to Huntsville to live with his parents. Few of Virginia's letters of the early years of their marriage are extant, but it is clear that life under the eyes of the elder Clays could not have been very pleasant or satisfying for Virginia. Her mother-in-law, Susanna Clay, allegedly, was demanding, overly sensitive, and critical of others, especially of her daughter-in-law, whom she considered a social butterfly. Virginia had little to occupy her time except paying and receiving calls, doing needlework, gardening, practicing the piano, and seeking out whatever entertainment Huntsville could offer a wife with time on her hands. She did accompany Clement to Tuscaloosa in 1844 while he attended the legislative session. "The winter promises to be very gay," Virginia wrote enthusiastically to her mother-in-law. "[T]o be in the parlour you might imagine me Miss T. again!!"[16]

The Clays, to their disappointment, remained childless. Most of their contemporaries thought that wives without children were incomplete. Mary Boykin Chesnut referred to herself as "a childless wretch" and noted that "South Carolina as a rule does not think it necessary for women to have any existence outside of their pantries or nurseries. If they have not children, let them nurse the walls." Clement may have feared that in the eyes of the world their lack of children might seem to reflect a conspicuous flaw in his manhood. Nevertheless, he tried to cheer his wife when comments about their not having children undermined her normally good humor. On one occasion when she was off visiting relatives, he imagined "that they are rigging you about yr. *imputed wants* & our *connubial poverty* & bragging of some people's 'thumping luck & fat babies.' " There is no indication, however, that the childlessness of their marriage caused any major strain between them.[17]

More stressful to the Clays was their perception that Clement's political career was languishing; also, the reality that they were still financially dependent upon his parents was of great concern. Huntsville's voters did send Clement back to the state legislature in 1844 and again in 1845, and in 1846 the legislature chose him to be the judge of the newly established Madison County Court at Huntsville, but the salaries from these offices were inadequate to support the life-style envisaged by the Clays. They also received small sums from the rental of ten slaves that Virginia had owned since before her marriage, from the rental of an office building Clement owned on the Huntsville public square, and from the fees of his law practice. In 1846, Clay estimated his annual income to be $2,500. Then thirty years old, Clement, who had suffered since his teens with feelings of low self-esteem, wrote to his father and apologized for having "achieved so little to the credit of myself or family or to the substantial welfare of my spiritual or temporal interests."[18] Self-reliance and self-confidence had eluded him despite his marriage and what appeared to be a promising career.

As his letter revealed, Clement needed to do something to seek his independence and to escape from what he called the "squalls & storms" in his parents' home. In early 1847, Clement bought a house on three and one-half acres one block from his father's residence. In December 1851, they sold the place for $7,000, more than twice what they had paid for it, and moved back into his father's home.[19] Following the sale of their house (probably against his wife's wishes), Virginia persuaded Clement that she needed to take a holiday in the North to escape the tensions of living once again under her in-laws' roof and to seek a medical opinion for why she could not become pregnant after nine years of marriage. Clement, not able to leave his law practice, sent Lawson, his youngest brother, who had yet to establish himself in a profession, as Virginia's escort, an arrangement which caused some local gossip. Lawson and Virginia spent most of their time at the Orange, New Jersey, Mountain Water Cure, one of the many hydropathic spas which flourished at the time. There, a German physician diagnosed her condition as a displaced womb and prescribed hydro-therapeutic baths and douches. Virginia wrote her husband, "I never can leave Dr. W. till a new woman. If he fails, I shall die, or at *least try to, for my life shall no longer burden you or me.*"[20]

When Clement received this letter, he was distraught. It is apparent from their correspondence that throughout the first decade of their marriage, he was frequently depressed with most aspects of his life except his relationship with Virginia and had relied upon her to pull him out of recurring dark moods. Now, he rose to the occasion: "The whole secret of yr. unhappiness is the want of children. . . . It is the greatest grief to me, because you know that I take my full share of the cause of this want." He, too, yearned for children, he confessed, but insisted that he was determined not to give way to "paralyzing grief" and to "be thankful for what I have rather than thankless because I have not all I want." If he could live without children, so must she.[21]

Clement's optimism proved temporary. Soon he wrote Virginia: "I am making scarcely anything by the law [and] your property is too small to support us. . . . I own nothing of value compared with yr. happiness and contentment. I wd. give everything up & commence life with nothing but my poor talents & faithfulness, if I could ensure yr. contentment." She answered: "I have been away from you too long, & I know it, & shall come home as quickly as possible. If there is any real cause for despondency, I do not give way as you do, & you miss the usual counter-balance. . . . I wish we had more money, but we might have less."[22]

In the fall of 1853, Virginia and Clement's prospects brightened. Clement was nominated for Congress, and although he lost to the Whig candidate, W.R.W. Cobb, his political sacrifice for the Democratic party helped turn around his own fortunes. Three months after his defeat by Cobb, he won the endorsement from the Democratic caucus to the United States Senate. The Alabama legislature followed suit and elected him to the Senate by a vote of eighty-five to forty-three.[23] Two weeks after his victory, the Clays set out for Washington. In the nation's capital, Clement anticipated following in his father's footsteps, and at the same time, he hoped to become independent of his parents. Virginia, as a United States senator's wife, looked forward to entering into a society much more sophisticated than that of either Huntsville or Tuscaloosa. Moreover, after ten years of marriage, Virginia was seven months pregnant. Motherhood might give her a sense of place in Southern society, and fatherhood could signal Clement's long-sought-after release from self-doubt.

In mid-January 1854, however, Virginia gave birth to a daughter, stillborn. One wonders why she made the difficult journey from Alabama to Washington in her advanced state of pregnancy. She seldom thereafter mentioned the death of their daughter, although she wrote a favorite cousin, "I, poor mortal, would give all else on earth to be a mother."[24] Clearly, that must not have been the case, since Virginia undertook a trip which was recognized as potentially hazardous for one so far advanced in pregnancy. Virginia never became pregnant again.

Washington, however, offered Virginia many distractions. During the congressional sessions, since they lived in boarding houses or small hotels, Virginia was free to spend her days paying and returning calls, gossiping with friends, and planning for the receptions, balls, and trips to the theater which filled many of their evenings. Although nearly twenty-nine years old and married for over ten years when she arrived in the nation's capital, Virginia, in her reminiscences of these Washington years, referred to herself as "a belle of the fifties." While away from Washington on shopping sprees in Philadelphia and New York or on trips to visit relatives or to stop at health resorts, Virginia continued her search for admirers. At one spa, she thought she was "such a belle I was almost ashamed of it," she confessed to Clement.[25]

Frank Carpenter, a well-known news reporter, described Virginia as one of the most brilliant women "and the finest conversation[al]ist he had ever met of either sex." Virginia seems not only to have been skilled at making conversation but also to have taken a natural interest in what others said. One Alabaman considered her "an eloquent listener." Noted also for her wit, Virginia played the part of Aunt Ruthy Partington at a lavish costume ball given in April 1858 by Senator and Mrs. Gwin of California. Aunt Ruthy, a fictional character created by the humorist Benjamin Shillaber, was famous for her rustic quips and malapropisms. Virginia, dressed against type in a plain black dress and black apron, displayed a cleverness that made her the hit of the evening. Her barbs tweaked not only President James Buchanan and Senator William Henry Seward but even the wife of the British ambassador, whom she addressed as "honey" and of whom she asked if Queen Victoria had recovered from her latest "encroachment." She was the star of the evening.[26]

Virginia Clay's sparkling personality also led men to fall a little in love with her. The man she most cared for, however, other than her husband, was her cousin Tom Tunstall. When teenagers, Tom had given Virginia her "first kiss of love." After Clement had become a senator, he helped Tunstall obtain a position as United States consul to Cádiz. After Tom had left for Spain, Virginia wrote him: "Would to Heaven I cd. clasp my arms around your neck and burying my head in yr. fragrant hair, whisper in yr. ear how much I love you, how much pride & solicitude I feel for you, and how much dearer than almost all the rest of the world you are to my heart." It was a very intimate sounding letter, even by the effusively romantic standards of the day. But Clement demonstrated no jealousy toward Tunstall or his wife's other admirers. He no longer warned her, as he had in the early years of their marriage, of the supposed dangers to his reputation that male admiration of her might bring him.[27] The confidence Senator Clay had gained by his recent political successes enabled him to accept his wife's flirtations. He became proud of her continuing ability to attract attention.

Clay, although no longer worried about rivals, still fretted about money. Virginia's extravagance had long been a problem. Once, before she married, she had within ten months bought fifty-two pairs of shoes. While shopping in New York in 1854, Virginia wrote to Clement that she and her cousin Evelyn Collier were short of cash after purchasing twenty new dresses. She added that if they did not reduce their spending and if his salary were not increased, they would go bankrupt, but she did not suggest that she had any responsibility for curbing their expenditures. Nevertheless, despite her overspending and his fretting over finances, the Clays were far happier and much better off financially than they had been in Huntsville.[28]

Clement, like Virginia, won some fame in Washington, though he never ranked among the leading politicians of his day. Senator Clay, having considerable ability as an orator, used this talent to defend the South and its institutions by supporting the Kansas-Nebraska Act and the Lecompton Constitution and by attacking "Black Republicanism," particularly two of its leading representatives, John P. Hale of New Hampshire and Charles Sumner of Massachusetts. In 1857, the Clays returned to Alabama in time to campaign for his reelection to the Senate. Clement won easily following the withdrawal of his chief opponent, Governor John A. Winston.[29]

The sectional antagonisms, especially over the institution of slavery, which were clearly visible at the time of their arrival in Washington, increased with the passing of the decade. Virginia, not very interested in political issues unless they were entwined with social relationships, reacted to the crisis by refusing to socialize with Northerners, except with those who sympathized with the South. She bragged to her father-in-law that she and Clement would have nothing to do with "free-soilers, black Republicans & Bloomers." On the other hand, she recalled in her memoirs that Southerners expressed shock when she danced with Anson Burlingame, a Republican from Massachusetts who once challenged the South Carolinian Preston Brooks to a duel. Virginia could not pass up the opportunity to glide across the floor with a handsome man, even if he were a Yankee. Only once in her memoirs did Virginia Clay comment upon the institution of slavery and that was during the Civil War. She recalled an interracial church service held at Redcliffe at James Henry Hammond's plantation chapel. Clay described the scene "as the little company of white people, the flower of centuries of civilization, among hundreds of blacks . . . peaceful, contented, respectful and comprehending the worship of God." She wondered on that day if abolitionists "could they look upon that scene, fail to admit the blessing American 'slavery' had brought to the savage black men, thus, within a few generations at most, become at home in a condition of civilization."[30]

As the tensions between the North and South accelerated over slavery, Clement's health, never robust, deteriorated. In the spring of 1860, asthmatic seizures forced him to leave the Senate even before the session ended. For many years, respiratory infections and a persistent cough had bothered Clay, but, seemingly, the stress generated by an impending civil war triggered these new attacks. The best medical experts of the day recommended a change of scene, and for almost a year, Clement and Virginia moved from place to place seeking relief from his asthma. He improved sufficiently to return to Washington in early January 1861. They arrived just in time for Clay to resign his Senate seat following the secession of Alabama. A relapse of asthma followed; the Clays returned home to Huntsville, where Clement gradually regained his health. By October 1861, he was well enough to travel to Montgomery to campaign for his election to the Confederate Senate. Clay won, and the way now seemed open for their return to prominence—this time in Richmond.[31]

Virginia and Clement reached the Confederate capital in February 1862. In April, they received word that federal troops had occupied Huntsville. Officials arrested and briefly detained Clay's seventy-three-year-old father and confiscated livestock and provisions. Some slaves ran away. On August 31, 1862, the Union army withdrew from the town, and Clement, concerned about his family's condition, came home with Virginia in early October and stayed for several months before returning to Richmond at the end of the year. Federal troops reappeared in Huntsville in July 1863, and this second federal occupation prevented the Clays from visiting Huntsville until after the war. For almost all of 1863, Virginia stayed with relatives in North Carolina and Georgia, chiefly in Macon at the family home of her sister-in-law Celeste Clay. Virginia wrote frequently to Clement, urging him to let her and Celeste join him and Lawson, Celeste's husband, at the capital.[32]

Clement was eager to have his wife with him and knew that she would enjoy the social whirl in Richmond, but crowded quarters, expensive living conditions, and rumors of a possible Northern raid made him wonder if it were not better for her to remain in Georgia. Although Clay did not tell Virginia directly that she could not come, his letters continued to stress the adverse wartime conditions in Richmond. Virginia quickly tired of what she viewed as a manipulative game. "If you . . . *prefer* we shd. remain here," she insisted, "just *say so* as you shd. to grown up sensible people, & not be any more attempting to beguile or deceive us, like silly children into yr. wishes." Finally, he wrote her, "You can come on when you please," but she found this answer unsatisfactory. "At last you say we can come on & we, woman like, having gained our point, respectfully decline! . . . Women of our caliber must be wooed in more enthusiastic words I assure [you]." Clay must eventually have extended a satisfactory invitation, because Virginia and Celeste arrived in Richmond for a brief visit in late April 1863.[33]

Before Virginia left Macon, Clement mailed her one hundred dollars, "all the money I have. Do economize," he pleaded, "as we have nothing that we can rely on now, but my salary, & that is only for 11 months more." Her reply was vintage Virginia: "I am much obliged for the money, also the advice, but fear the *latter* will not do me nearly so much good as the former. However, I will *try*, but you know my blood."[34] Now as at other times during their marriage, she revealed few, if any, feelings of guilt over spending more money than Clement thought they could afford.

In 1862 and 1863, Virginia Clay spent only a few weeks in Richmond, but she was with Clement from early January to mid-February 1864, during the winter session of the legislature. During this visit, she refused to let the high costs and other problems of living in the wartime Confederate capital prevent her from enjoying one final fling. The organizers of a production of Sheridan's *The Rivals* asked Virginia to play the part of Mrs. Malaprop, the character who was the model for Aunt Ruthy Partington's unwitting and hilarious misstatements. Despite the multitude of troubles now facing the South, many of the beleagured Confederacy's elite came to see the comedy. Mary Boykin Chesnut, a member of the audience, wrote that Virginia's performance "was beyond our wildest hopes." "The back, even," Mrs. Chesnut gushed, "of Mrs. Clay's head was eloquent."[35]

Virginia's appearance as Mrs. Malaprop was her last hurrah as the wife of a powerful officeholder. Clement had already begun a political decline that would eventually end their hopes of prominence and wealth and permanently rearrange the balance of strength within their marriage. Clay was a lame-duck senator during the early 1864 session; in November 1863, the members of the Alabama legislature had elected Richard Wilde Walker to take his place. When Clay's term in Congress ended in mid-February, he and Virginia lost their only source of income, and they could expect no funds from his financially pressed father in occupied Huntsville. President Davis soon offered the former senator several positions, the most attractive of which was as a member of a commission to forward the Confederate cause in Canada. After a sentimental parting with Virginia, Clay ran the federal blockade and reached Halifax in the middle of May by way of Bermuda. He and the other members of the delegation talked of peace with numerous Northerners including Horace Greeley and former Attorney General Jeremiah Black, on the one hand, while, on the other hand, they concocted a grandiose and impracticable scheme to separate the Midwest from the East. This foundered as did other such plots. None of these efforts had any discernable impact on the outcome of the war; nor were these months a happy time for Clement. He quarreled with other members of the delegation, and one of his associates described him as a "peevish invalid." The eight-month Canadian adventure was the sad final chapter of his political career.[36]

Life within the shrinking Confederate lines was equally disturbing for Virginia. She first took refuge in Petersburg; then when the enemy army came close, she fled again to Georgia and to Celeste's family. Most of Virginia's letters to Canada never reached Clement. In one that did, she asked him to bring home for herself and their female relatives a long list of items including four French corsets, two dozen pairs of gloves, some books on the latest fashions, and an assortment of dresses, bonnets, handkerchiefs, and furs.[37] Her continuing extravagances were totally unrealistic at a time when so many others were making major sacrifices.

During the war, Virginia Clay not only failed to feel guilty over her improvidence but also usually avoided caring for wounded soldiers, rolling bandages, or knitting socks for the troops, activities that occupied the time of many women of her class. As Celeste Clay conceded to Clement, "Sister, & myself, deserve *no* credit for *any thing*. We have done *as little* for our country as any other two worthless women I know." Virginia made no such confession.[38]

In late December 1864, Clay began the slow journey home from Canada. Husband and wife were reunited at Macon in February 1865. Caught up in the turmoil of the last days of the Confederacy, the Clays were almost constantly on the move for the next three months. In May, they were near Lagrange, Georgia, when someone at the railroad station handed Virginia a newspaper which contained a copy of a proclamation offering sizable rewards for the capture of Jefferson Davis along with Clay and other members of the Canadian delegation and accusing them of conspiring with the assassins of Abraham Lincoln. Clement, confident that he was innocent of the charge, decided to surrender and turned himself over to a federal general in Macon. Guards took Clay, accompanied by Virginia and by fellow-prisoner President Davis and his family, to Fortress Monroe, Virginia. There, troops imprisoned Clay and Davis. Virginia, as she parted from Clement, gave him a Bible with a message inscribed on the flyleaf: "With tearful eyes & aching heart, I commend you, *my own precious noble, idolized husband* to the care & keeping of Almighty God."[39]

Clay remained a prisoner for almost eleven months. The government charged him with general treason, authorizing raids from Canada, conspiring with Lincoln's assassins, and with carrying out germ warfare by sending infected clothing across the border. Evidence for the last two accusations, of which Clement was almost certainly innocent, came primarily from the testimony of several individuals who eventually admitted that they had lied. At first, however, government officials believed him guilty of all the charges.[40]

While Clement was in Fortress Monroe, his wife worried about his health. Beginning in January 1866, Clement's asthma recurred, and prison doctors gave him "heavy doses of opium," a drug nineteenth-century physicians prescribed for numerous diseases and chronic conditions including asthma. Clay also suffered in prison from nervous dyspepsia and depression. He confessed to Virginia, "I am quite worn out & of very little value to you or anybody. You would probably be better off without me." Only his awareness of the love of his wife and his parents for him kept Clement from the final depths of despair. He told Virginia, "I'll try to live to see you," but "if you & they cared less for me & were less dependent on me for happiness, it would be better for us all."[41]

Virginia slowly made her way back from Fortress Monroe to Huntsville, harassed along the way by federal agents who searched her baggage in an attempt to discover incriminating papers. Life in Huntsville was even more unpleasant for Virginia than before the war. The people of the town were deeply divided between those who had supported the Confederacy and those who had worked with the federal army during its occupation. Slaves were free, but new labor agreements had not yet emerged. Clement Comer and Susanna were old, sick, discouraged, and in debt. Withers, the second son, was back from the war but could not earn a living for his wife, Mary, and their six children. Lawson had gone to Georgia to Celeste's family to try to become a planter. When Virginia urged Lawson to return to Huntsville to help care for his ailing father, he refused.[42]

With her husband incarcerated and immersed in melancholia and his father and brothers paralyzed by their own problems, Virginia undertook a letter-writing campaign to free Clement. When her initial efforts brought no results, she resolved to go to Washington. A contact there had written Virginia, "Tis said that the President likes the opportunity of granting personal favors direct to the parties on their own application . . . and that the ladies never fail with him." A president who reportedly could be swayed by feminine charms was a challenge too tempting for her to pass up. In November 1865, she borrowed one hundred dollars and enough silk from a local merchant for a new dress and took the train to Washington.[43]

Virginia wrote several letters to Andrew Johnson in which she sought to obtain the release of her husband by flattering the president and by pointing out to him that both her husband and her father-in-law were in ill health. She also called on Johnson at the White House where, she recalled, she and her female friends begged for Clement's release. On one occasion, she encountered Benjamin F. Perry, the provisional governor of South Carolina after the war, who wrote to his wife: "I met Ms. Senator Clay of Alabama at the White House and spent an hour with her whilst waiting to see the President. . . . She is one of the most intellectual women I ever met, a noble lady, a devoted wife. She seemed pleased when I introduced myself to her and told me all her history and troubles and trials." He continued, "we took seats in one corner of the room and had quite a tête à tête for one hour. She is with all very fine looking. The President gave her a package and she smiled as if her whole soul was radiant with joy. I hope it was the release of her noble husband."[44] Clay, however, was not released until two months later. Virginia claimed in her reminiscences that during one late evening visit to the White House, she had become so angry at the president's excuses and delays that she had threatened to remain until he complied with her demand. Her display of temper supposedly brought about the president's capitulation, and the next morning, April 18, 1866, the authorities freed Clement. The details of Virginia's account of her final confrontation with President Johnson must be viewed with some suspicion.

Nevertheless, Johnson's practice of humbling proud Southerners but ultimately granting their individual requests for pardons and Virginia's ability to get what she wanted from men probably worked in tandem to bring about Clement's liberation. Virginia and her husband both believed that *she* had rescued him.[45]

Following Clement's release, the Clays returned to Huntsville. Susanna Clay had already died on January 2, 1866. Clement Comer Clay did not long survive his wife, dying on September 6, 1866, four months after a reunion with his eldest son. Clement Claiborne, acting as his father's executor, sold several of the estate's most valuable assets, including his parents' Huntsville home. Cash from the sale of the house, which brought $10,600 and from other transactions went to pay Clement Comer's debts which totaled over $30,000. It would be six years before Virginia and Clement gained clear title from his father's estate to 1,420 acres of land located about twenty miles east of Huntsville near the village of Gurley.[46]

Like other members of the Southern elite, the Clays, especially Clement, found it extremely difficult to cope in the postwar years. Following the sale of the old family home, Clement and Virginia moved in 1868 to a small house on the farm called "Clay Lodge" and then, later on, to a nearby cottage which Virginia named "Wildwood." Clement took up farming. They raised cotton, corn, oats, peas, along with other grains and vegetables, chickens, cattle, and hogs. The sale of cotton and grain brought in some cash. Clay tried at different times several systems of farm management, including renting parts of his land, sharecropping, and using hired laborers. None of these arrangements proved profitable. His attempts to establish a shingle business and a sawmill on the farm and to mine soapstone also came to nothing. Although the income from the farm and from the rental of a Huntsville office building they owned kept the Clays minimally supported, they were forced to sell other assets to pay off some longstanding debts. Among their creditors was William W. Corcoran, a Washington banker and friend from the 1850s, who had lent Virginia $1,000. Corcoran finally gave up hope of repayment and returned Virginia's note.[47] The Clays' troubled and complicated finances dominated their final years together.

Clay, seeking to improve their economic situation, accepted a position in 1871 as the chief Alabama agent for the Life Insurance Association of America and spent much of the next two years traveling throughout the state attempting to sell policies and to recruit and supervise other agents. Clement discovered that old friends whom he considered prospective buyers welcomed him cordially into their homes and offices but were not interested in purchasing life insurance. He disliked traveling and being away from Virginia, and after two years, he resigned.[48]

Before their financial burdens and the responsibility of running the farm overtook them, they had taken several trips together. Virginia also went to

New York in July 1868 to attend the Democratic convention and to Washington in November 1868 to apply to friends for a loan. There, a letter from Clement arrived stressing their lack of funds. Virginia responded that he had saddened her soul, and she threatened to come home without even trying to borrow money. "Reserve yr. gloomy views of mankind & life for my ears not my eyes," she insisted. "When I see . . . luxurious homes . . . & trousseaus from Paris, & think of my lot, my home & my one black silk dress, I do not need in addition one word from you or any other one to realize my situation."[49] Although Virginia was quite aware that their fortunes had dropped, she had not accepted fully his pessimistic view of their future.

Clement was fifty-seven years old in 1873 when he left the insurance business and returned to the farm. Unable to escape from debt and often ill, Clay became more and more depressed and dependent on Virginia. "I can't understand or conceive," he woefully confided to his wife, "how some persons endure debt—it is worse than asthma, even to me. It robs life of all its enjoyments, makes death appear as a friend in need." He confessed on another occasion that "the cares & responsibilities of my present life, my short comings & long sinnings," had caused him to lose "all self-confidence & courage, as well as hope & faith." These and other doleful laments naturally troubled Virginia, as did her husband's frequent illnesses. Also, she had cause to worry about his drinking, which apparently had become a major problem following the war. Her letters to him are filled with pleas and admonitions to avoid all intoxicating beverages. He admitted in his letters to her that his slips had caused them both much pain, and he assured her that he was, as he once put it, "dry as a powder horn." His incessant claims that he was avoiding strong drink show that he had great difficulty staying on the wagon and suggest that he occasionally fell off it. Three years before his death, he wrote to his wife that he was "as sober as I ever was, & as sad."[50]

Virginia, only forty-three years old when they went to live on the farm in 1868, missed the social activities to which she had been addicted in the prewar years. Activities such as supervising the farm chores, making jelly, mending clothes, and raising flowers and vegetables kept her busy but not happy. Virginia complained to Clement that she was bored, restless, and discontented and blamed him for their financial problems which forced her "to do without what I wd. dearly love to have." Clement, aware of her need to get away from the farm and its isolation, furnished a small apartment for her in his Huntsville office building where she often stayed for several days at a time. She also managed most years a two-week trip to Memphis, Louisville, or St. Louis to visit friends and relatives.[51]

Men continued to seek out Virginia Clay. Jefferson Davis, her husband's old colleague and fellow prisoner, wrote her forty-three letters between 1870 and 1878. Davis, like Clement, was disenchanted with the postwar world, and he found in Virginia a sympathetic woman. "When woman's rights become the law of the land," Davis wrote her, "you will become an available southern candidate for the Presidency." Davis could imagine no higher compliment, but another famous Southerner, L.Q.C. Lamar, who like Davis had been a friend for years, did as much, if not more, for her morale. The Mississippi congressman sent Virginia a poem as overflowing with sentiment as those composed for her during her days as a young belle. Lamar offered to return from the dead if Virginia called. She did not ask him to resurrect himself but requested instead that he endorse a note extending a loan.[52]

Nevertheless, Virginia had changed. No longer the flighty belle, she became the stronger partner during the final years of her marriage. (An essay included in this volume on Ella Gertrude Thomas by Virginia Burr reveals another woman who responded with strength to postwar adversity.) Even in political matters, Virginia was preeminent. Jefferson Davis, as noted, recognized her political abilities, and friends and relatives wrote asking her to endorse their applications for office.[53] As the antebellum correspondence between husband and wife reveals, Virginia always had the potentiality for becoming the dominant personality in their relationship. Clement, in the early years of their marriage, expressed in his letters to his wife a dependence upon her, especially when ill health and self-doubts overcame him. He became more confident following his election to the Senate and his political successes in Washington, and his dependency upon her might have remained only a minor and privately acknowledged component of their relationship had not the Civil War destroyed his health, his political career, and his hopes of prosperity. After the war, he wrote to Virginia that "nothing is worth living for me, but you, and it is only my love for you that saves me from despair and total darkness—I confess this to you, and only with some shame." Her postwar letters are full of compassion for him, but she refused to allow his pessimism to undermine her self-confidence. "You wrong me," she wrote him, "when you think I am not troubled at yr. debts, but it is not my style to die in advance of death's summons."[54]

Although Virginia was able to keep some emotional distance between herself and her self-tormented husband, their letters suggest that their physical desire and affection for one another remained strong despite other changes in their marital relationship. When separated from each other, Clement and Virginia typically wrote how much each missed the other. Off on an insurance trip, Clement wrote that he wished his wife were there to fill his bed. Virginia declared that she missed him especially at night. Trapped by a snowstorm in an overheated Huntsville room, Virginia once wrote, "If I am obliged to be cooked let it be with my old rooster."[55] Given the Victorian unwillingness to discuss sex, these and other statements are indications that intimacy remained an important part of their relationship, even as the marriage drew to a close.

On January 3, 1882, nine years after he had given up the insurance business and had settled back on the farm, Clement Clay died at the age of sixty-five. His health had been poor for many years, and the end could not have come as a surprise to Virginia. She was, at first, melancholic, but she soon recovered enough to make a trip to Europe. Nonetheless, she found life as a widow unsatisfactory. In 1887, Virginia married David Clopton, an old friend and political colleague of her husband in both the United States and Confederate congresses. The bride was sixty-two years old; the groom, five years older, was twice widowed and had six grown children. At the time of their marriage, Clopton was serving as a justice of the Alabama Supreme Court; they lived in Montgomery for five years until Clopton died suddenly in 1892. Virginia inherited one-seventh of his property, much less than she had expected.[56]

Following the death of Judge Clopton, Virginia adopted the name Virginia Clay-Clopton, returned to Wildwood, and supported herself for the remaining twenty-three years of her life apparently with the proceeds of the farm. Virginia, convinced by her own personal observations that woman's talent for politics was equal to that of man's, joined in the crusade to win the vote for women and served from 1896 to 1900 as president of the Alabama Equal Suffrage Association. She remarked that the opponents of equal suffrage thought that women had their own sphere and should not go beyond it, but Virginia noted that "if woman does not now suffer from the absence of political power, it is the only instance in History where a class so deprived has not been the worse because of the disability." Since women are, she declared, "almost as often found in positions of responsibility as men, the same is required of them, and they should be given the same means of attainment and defense," in this case the franchise, to determine their destiny. In her speeches advocating suffrage, Virginia defended women's right to be "strong-minded," and emphasized what she believed was women's increasing responsibility to provide financially for themselves and for their families. Virginia may have been more of an adornment to the suffrage movement than an active leader, but her name carried weight. Interestingly enough, her activities in the suffrage movement do not appear to have damaged her social standing.[57] She also joined and held office in several organizations devoted to keeping alive the memory of the Confederacy, and she particularly enjoyed attending their reunions. At a Confederate gathering in New York City in 1902, she was, she bragged, "the belle of the ball."[58] Her need to feel that she was the center of attention had not at all diminished.

Virginia began working in 1900 on her memoirs, which were published in 1905 under the title *A Belle of the Fifties*. Of the book's thirty chapters, only one discussed her life before her marriage to Clement, nine described Washington society in the 1850s, and an equal number recited her movements and impressions during the Civil War. The final eleven chapters detailed Clement's imprisonment and especially Virginia's role in freeing him. The first ten years of her marriage were omitted entirely, and the period after 1866 received one sentence. She simply blotted out those years which she did not care to recall.

Virginia lived for ten years following the publication of her reminiscences. On January 16, 1915, she celebrated her ninetieth birthday at a party in Huntsville. Hundreds of friends and relatives attended, and almost as many others sent telegrams. Six months later, she died on June 23.[59]

At the time of Clement and Virginia's marriage, their expectations for continued political, economic, and social success rested in part on the assumption that Clement, the able and eldest son of a prominent father, would achieve much in the antebellum world of which they were a part. Their anticipations ignored the fact that Clay, like many other sons in patriarchal families, had remained in a state of prolonged dependency. Although he became a United States senator and an advisor in the Confederacy to Jefferson Davis, Clement's economic and psychological dependence upon his authoritarian father kept him from gaining the self-confidence and maturity necessary to make the most of these opportunities and prevented him from sustaining himself after prominence and prosperity disappeared. Clay, forty-nine years old when he was released from prison in 1866, retreated to the farm, to the bottle, to ill health, and to gloomy thoughts.

After 1865, Virginia emerged as the stronger spouse, demonstrating confidence, buoyancy, and optimism in good times and in bad. Eight years younger than her husband and light years away from him in temperament, Virginia more easily readjusted her sights at war's end, surrendering the lavish, the fashionable, and the expensive to make the best of a simpler style of living. Clement had written Virginia in 1868 that "if it were possible for you to love me & to enjoy my company as I love you and enjoy yrs., we might be happy in our seclusion."[60] He recognized, however, that her preference for city life left her discontented on the farm, and so they worked out an arrangement that enabled her to stay in town often and to take trips out of state to visit friends and relatives. Clay's willingness to reach such an accommodation was a rare occurrence among nineteenth-century Southern husbands.

The study of one marriage does not, of course, prove or disprove a general proposition, but this case study of the marriage of Virginia and Clement Clay seems to support the general hypothesis of the authors that the South's defeat in 1865 and the resulting political, economic, and social changes produced profound alterations in the internal dynamics of many Southern marriages.[61] In the Clays' case, moreover, we know that Virginia, who had seemingly been destined to be a Southern belle in perpetuity, stepped forward after the war to become the stronger spouse. Their reversal of roles did not, however, result in their alienation from one another.

Virginia and Clement's ability to accommodate themselves to each others' needs and their romantic love for one another, which was a constant force in their relationship from their engagement in 1842 until Clement's death almost forty years later, made it possible for their affection to survive in the midst of vast historical change.

10

House and Home in the Victorian South: The Cookbook as Guide

ALAN GRUBB

EVERYONE FAMILIAR WITH Mrs. Trollope and her famous travel book, *Domestic Manners of the Americans*, knows that one of the few things to escape her critical eye was American food. Entering the United States via New Orleans and making her way up the Mississippi past Memphis to Cincinnati and then eventually to the East, while unimpressed by almost everything she saw, she was struck by the abundance and cheapness of our foodstuffs. "Perhaps the most advantageous feature in Cincinnati," she wrote, "is its market, which, for excellence, abundance, and cheapness, can hardly, I should think, be surpassed in any part of the world, if I except the luxury of fruits, which are very inferior to any I have seen in Europe."[1] Of the cooking of the South, which, like its hospitality, was already lore, Mrs. Trollope made no mention, though she had a few kind words for Southerners, noting in a visit to Washington that it was the Southern congressmen who sat politely in their seats, without their hats on, and, above all, without spitting. Like Mrs. Trollope, I approach this subject from a British and Continental perspective, not as a Southern historian but as one who has been working with British Victorian cookbooks. I approach this subject without Mrs. Trollope's ready prejudices but with first-hand experience of the Southern situation, and with a firm conviction that Southern cookbooks have as great a value as historical documents and sources as British cookbooks of the same period do. In his recent book, *Southern*

Food, John Egerton stresses the importance, even the mystique, that food has always had for Southerners. According to Egerton, "Within the South itself, no other form of cultural expression, not even music, is as distinctively characteristic of the region as the spreading of a feast of native food and drink before a gathering of kin and friends. For as long as there has been a South, and people who think of themselves as Southerners, food has been central to the region's image, its personality, and its character."[2] Southern cookbooks make this amply clear. It is, in fact, the point of one of the most interesting of Southern cookbooks—Martha McCulloch-Williams's *Dishes & Beverages of the Old South*, published in 1913. She began by declaring that "Proper dinners mean so much—good blood, good health, good judgment, good conduct. The fact makes tragic a truth too little regarded; namely, that while bad cooking can ruin the very best of raw foodstuffs, all the art of all the cooks in the world can do no more than palliate things stale, flat and unprofitable. . . . Food must satisfy the palate else it will never truly satisfy the stomach. . . . It is said," she wrote, "underdone mutton cost Napoleon the battle of Leipsic [*sic*], and eventually his crown. I wonder, now and then, if the prevalence of divorce has any connection with the decline of home cooking?"[3] McCulloch-Williams added, "it was through being the best fed people in the world, we of the South Country were able to put up the best fight in history, and after the ravages and ruin of civil war, come again to our own. We might have been utterly crushed but for our proud and pampered stomachs, which in turn gave the bone, brain and brawn for the conquests of peace."[4]

Whatever its value as history, Martha McCulloch-Williams's book is testimony to the importance food has had in Southern culture and folklore and to the fact that by knowing what has gone on in the kitchens and dining rooms of the South, we can discover much about its physical health, its economic condition, its race relations, class structure, the status of women, and the state of the family, either ideally or in reality. Egerton commented in *Southern Food* that "On such occasions, a place at the table is like a ring side seat at the historical and ongoing drama of life in the region."[5] This has been the view of cookbook writers themselves. Mrs. Rosser, in her 1895 volume, *Housekeeper's and Mother's Manual*, declared not at all tongue-in-cheek, that "The burning question of the day in America has never been of wars or rumors of wars; the political situation—tariff reform, the unifying of gold and silver, the deportation of John Chinaman, nor woman suffrage—but woman as cooks."[6]

Cookbooks, beyond the recipes they provide, contain a wealth of information concerning the society they were designed to serve. They reflect; they comment on that society; and as such, they are invaluable social documents. They have, however, almost universally been ignored by historians, even by social historians, who have usually drawn upon manuscript sources such as diaries, letters, matrimonial records, various kinds of advice books, and self-help manuals while overlooking the fact that cook-books, too, are similar kinds of documents and full of diverse information reflecting contemporary attitudes and values concerning the home and home life. Indeed, although they vary greatly, very few of them, despite their titles, are simply recipe or receipt books, for besides recipes, they contain sundry advice on etiquette, child rearing, medicine, general house-hold tasks, and marriage. This is especially true in the nineteenth century when Victorian Americans, like their British counterparts, for all their reticence to discuss certain subjects, became quite expansive when it came to expressing their views or opinions on household matters—on woman's lot or "duties," her husband's capacities (and sometimes, incapacities), proper management of the home, kitchen and servants—that is, what for many in the South were indeed "the burning questions of the day." All of which make these seemingly mundane books extremely valuable as social documents. They are perhaps "merely" cookbooks but are often as insight-ful as the other kinds of sources historians have used, at least when read or examined in their historical context.

The South has produced its share of cookbooks, and some early ones have been celebrated—namely the 1770 receipt book and housekeeping notes of Harriott Pinckney Horry (published, however, only in 1984); *The Virginia House-wife* by Mary Randolph, published in 1824; *The Kentucky Housewife* by Mrs. Lettice Bryan, published in 1839; and *The Carolina Housewife* by Sarah Rutledge, published in 1847. But far less attention has been paid to the many Southern cookbooks published after Mrs. Rut-ledge's book (those of the period of the Victorian South), certainly not much by Southern historians, despite the widespread use recently of cook-books by many historians of women. The latter, however, almost totally ignore Southern cookbooks and Southern cookbook writers. Susan Wil-liams in *Savory Suppers and Fashionable Feasts, Dining in Victorian Amer-ica* and Susan Strasser in *Never Done: A History of American Housework*, both of whom draw upon nineteenth-century cookery books as sources (the former exclusively), make no mention of any Southern cookbooks; nor does David M. Katzman in *Seven Days a Week: Women and Domestic Service in Industrializing America*, though he cites other kinds of testimony from Southern housewives. Similarly, Anne Firor Scott in *The Southern Lady: From Pedestal to Politics, 1830–1930* extensively cites memoirs, dia-ries, and letters written by Southern women but not cookbooks, even though these were almost all written by and for women. This is not to say that Southern cookbooks, any more than cookbooks in general, have been completely neglected by scholars. They have not, but they are better known to collectors than to historians, and consequently, little use has been made of them for historical purposes. As John Egerton notes, "by and large, Southern history has seldom held the attention of cookbook writers, and Southern food has been ignored by most historians."[7]

Two of the great problems in using Southern cookbooks (they are problems in using cookbooks generally) are purely bibliographical—identifying
them and then actually locating them. The latter is particularly difficult
since many of these cookbooks were published locally and in limited editions. This is the case of some of the most interesting cookbooks—the
various charity or church-sponsored cookbooks that grew out of the Civil
War and flourished thereafter in both North and South. One of these, *The
Confederate Receipt Book*, a small volume printed on wallpaper in 1863 by
a Richmond, Virginia, publisher, is one of the first wartime cookbooks. It
indicates, as others in the First and Second World Wars were to do, the
impact that war has on households.[8] These charitable cookbooks are, to my
knowledge, a uniquely American phenomenon, and while there were many
more of them published in the North and Midwest than in the South, the
South produced a large number of them, some of which like *The Laurel
(Miss.) Cook Book* and *Housekeeping in Old Virginia* went through several
editions and acquired more than local or regional fame.[9]

Despite their numbers and importance for their communities, such
books are often difficult to locate, and some are now known only by their
titles. Certain Southern states predominate in the publication of the cookbooks examined here—Kentucky, Virginia, South Carolina, and Georgia;
hence this study is admittedly selective, but will illustrate how Southern
cookbooks can be used to document changes in Southern households in the
last half of the nineteenth century. The range or variety of these books is,
however, considerable, from the already mentioned *Carolina Housewife*,
with its recipes reflecting the rice culture of the antebellum South Carolina
plantation economy, to *The Southern Gardener and Receipt-Book* by Mary
L. Edgeworth, a Georgia lady whose 1859 volume provides a final glimpse
of the plantation-era dinner table. Others include *Mrs. Hill's Southern
Cook-Book*, *Mrs. Porter's New Southern Cookery Book or, Housekeeping
Made Easy*, and *Housekeeping in Old Virginia* (three volumes published
during Reconstruction) to *The Dixie Cook-Book and Practical Housekeeper* (first published in 1879, republished in 1883 and 1889, and in many
ways the most Victorian of these books). Finally, there are the often-cited
nostalgic "Mammy" cookbooks published just before and after the First
World War, such as Martha McCulloch-Williams's *Dishes & Beverages of
the Old South* (1913), Laura Thornton Knowles's *Southern Recipes* (1913),
Emma and William McKinney's *Aunt Carolina's Dixieland Recipes* (1922),
and Katherine Bell's *Mammy's Cook Book* (1927).

The books examined here are in many ways so diverse that they reasonably raise a question as to whether there is such a thing as a distinctly
"Southern" cookbook. For instance, some of these books were published
in the North, while others, like Estelle Woods Wilcox's *The Dixie Cook-
Book* and *The New Dixie Cook-Book*, were not compiled by Southerners
at all. One of the most popular cookbook writers in the South as well as

elsewhere, in fact, was the Philadelphia-born Mrs. Rorer, who published *The Queen of the Kitchen, A Collection of Southern Cooking Receipts* in 1886, without the benefit of having been to the South. Later, in 1913, Rorer came to the South, visiting Columbia, South Carolina, where she began her lecture by announcing, "I am opposed to dishwashing. I think dishwashing often makes dishes very dirty."[10] Exactly why Mrs. Rorer was so popular is hard to say, but her popularity in the South may be explained by the fact that her views of woman's place were conservative and that she was a passionate advocate of the chafing dish, a method of serving food well suited to the heat of the South.

But more to the point, although there is a real sense of place and period in these books (some, like Martha McCulloch-Williams's book, positively trade on it), there is also a surprising air of cosmopolitanism in many or most of them, a cosmopolitanism that offsets their presumed provincialism. These are all "women's books" by their own admission, a fact emphasized by many of them, but even the earliest of them are quite cosmopolitan in outlook—from the *Carolina Housewife* with its great number of foreign (particularly French) recipes, to *A (Key) to Good Cooking* (1890), with its inclusion of Continental recipes as diverse as Lyonnaise Potatoes, Polish Tartlets, Biscuit glace à la Charles Dickens, or Prince Albert Pudding, and its advice on carving from *The London Caterer*. Many of these cookbooks, moreover, though supposedly drawn almost exclusively from "personal experience," show great familiarity with popular Northern cookbook writers like Mrs. Rorer, Juliet Courson, Maria Parloa, and Mrs. Lincoln and with British writers like William Kitchiner, Alexis Soyer, and Mrs. Beeton. These are Southern cookbooks but not always provincial in any sense.

Even more interesting, many cookbooks that appeared after the Civil War took the opposite tack than one might expect and are what might be called "reconciliation" cookbooks. There was a lot less looking back in them than one might expect; indeed, as Louis Szathmary points out in the edition he published a decade ago of *Mrs. Porter's New Southern Cookery Book* (the first of these Reconstruction cookbooks), "If one looks for what is generally called Southern cooking or for Southern dishes, he will do so in vain. There are few recipes for hominy grits, hush puppies, gumbo, and red-eye gravies in this 'New Southern' cookbook. It was published only a few years after the Civil War, during a period of history when at least some Southerners wanted to change their image."[11] That famed character of John William De Forest's novel, Miss Ravenel, had, it would seem, her counterpart among many of these writers. *Mrs. Porter's New Southern Cookery Book*, in fact, contains recipes for both a Yankee and a Confederate fruitcake, and it is the Yankee fruitcake she pronounces "unrivaled."[12] Perhaps the operative words here are the rest of the title of her book, "Or, Houskeeping Made Easy: A Practical System for Private Families in Town and Country Especially Adapted to the Southern States." This was a point of view continued and strengthened later in the century by cookbook writers like Mary Stuart Smith (*Virginia Cookery-Book*, 1885), Annie Elizabeth Dennis (*The New Annie Dennis Cook Book*, 1921), and Henrietta Dull (*Southern Cooking*, 1928), each locally celebrated home economists who, as was said of Annie Dennis, having arrived at maturity in "that epochal time in the history of the South when it required every energy of her people to maintain the traditional South with the attenuated revenues of the new South," endeavored to bring Southern women back into the national mainstream, expanding, but not forgetting, Southern traditions.[13] Indeed, by the time Estelle Woods Wilcox's *The Dixie Cook Book* appeared in 1882, even the term "South" had been put in italics; this was perhaps only a printer's decision but nonetheless suggestive.[14]

For many people, cookbooks seem rather formulaic, mere books of recipes, quite utilitarian in purpose, and disposable once their original information or purpose is superceded, and for historians, they do pose definite problems. Even by their collectors like Elizabeth Robins Pennell, nineteenth-century cookbooks, British or American, have not been held in high esteem. Indeed, it was Mrs. Pennell's view that "in the nineteenth century there were, on the one hand, the cookery books, prosaic as primers, that, with their business-like, practical, direct methods, were more useful in the kitchen than entertaining in the library; on the other hand, the books about cookery, so literary in flavor that they were not adapted to the kitchen at all."[15] For historians, particularly social historians, these nineteenth-century cookery and household books may actually be most valuable, for they represent a kind of "populist" literature and enable us to observe the household from within, as those who had the responsibility for domestic tasks experienced things, showing how industrialization altered women's work, how technology and science changed domestic economy, and how political events or wars affected new ideas about women's roles. They are also valuable because other kinds of statistical sources are so often inadequate and direct testimony from housewives' diaries and letters are only beginning to be gathered from family collections, even the richest of them often shedding less light on women's lives than do cookbooks and women's magazines. This is often suggested in cookbook titles themselves, like that of *How We Cook in Tennessee*, and by the fact that these books claim to draw their recipes and advice from "the most experienced housekeepers" of their state, region, town or community.[16]

The shortcomings of these books as "documents" are, of course, that they tell us largely what the writers themselves prescribed, not what most women may actually have done (although the marginalia of some old copies of cookbooks, along with their physical condition, are often quite suggestive). Then, too, some were obviously more important than others. Those books that offered the most information generally sold the best and probably had the most influence—Catharine Beecher wrote the most comprehensive manuals of the period, and the fact that *A Treatise on Domestic Economy*, first published in 1841, was revised and reissued numerous times over the next four decades makes it an especially valuable document of changes in household organization and activities, much as is Mrs. Beeton's equally famous *Book of Household Management*, which first appeared in England in 1859. For the South, there is no comparable volume to either Beecher's or Beeton's, though Estelle Woods Wilcox's 1,288-page *The Dixie Cook Book*, which appeared in at least two editions, comes close in its size, its wealth of information, and, perhaps, its influence.

How important or utilized were such books? Obviously, it is hard to tell. Certainly, we cannot always take them literally as to what Southerners ate, how they prepared food, kept their homes, or comported themselves. Further, in contrast to either Catharine Beecher or Isabella Beeton, about whom we know a great deal, we know relatively little, sometimes nothing, about the women who wrote these books, other than what they themselves reveal, usually in their prefaces. However, what we do learn there, fragmentary though it often is, can be revealing, suggesting the life stories of these women and those for whom they wrote. For example, Abby Fisher, in the "Preface and Apology" of *What Mrs. Fisher Knows about Old Southern Cooking* (1881), as if to excuse in advance the modest nature of her book, explains that since neither she nor her husband could read or write, not having had "the advantage of an education," she had to dictate her book.[17] We learn also, revealed this time in her recipe for "Pap for Infants," that she herself had "given birth to eleven children and raised them all," a fact she considered important at a time of such high infant mortality, and that though she had since taken up residence in San Francisco, she still considered herself "late of Mobile."[18] Similarly, from the preface to *The Warm Springs Receipt Book* (1885), one of the few cookbooks authored by a man (and probably a black man), we learn that the author had been a caterer at Warm Springs, Virginia, for several years and subsequently confined to a "wheeled chair." In Theresa Brown's *Modern Domestic Cookery* (1871) we read that she was a maiden lady and had experienced the particular hardships Reconstruction posed for Southern women.[19]

These biographical revelations are suggestive but brief. At greater length, in Jessie C. Benedict's *The Blue Ribbon Cook Book* (1904), one of the many Kentucky cookbooks written in the latter half of the century, we learn, somewhat surprisingly (in that her book is otherwise simply a recipe book), how her own experience as a homemaker laid the basis of her subsequent "career." In "My Work and How It Grew," a small section at the beginning of her book, she explained how she came to be a caterer, local newspaper columnist, and successful businesswoman through "a desire to prove what a woman can do in the business world without capital, and being confronted with the necessity of falling into rank in the marts of trade."[20] Hers is a story, a mini-autobiography, of personal achievement through traditional womanly skills, hard work, and pluck:

> For those who would like to follow the same business, and there are many, for rarely a day passes that some one does not come in seeking suggestions and advice as to how to take up the work as I did—for the benefit of these, I will say it is not by any means smooth sailing; that there are many *snags* which might be emphasized. First of all, we *must* make sacrifices at every point, and social duties must be wholly abandoned. No business requires more tact, patience, or originality, and surely none requires closer attention or more constant study. One has to fully realize that she must think, plan, and entertain. She must be ready to suggest new menus, originate artistic table decorations, and *carry out* unique ideas in forms of entertainment, being ready with attractive souvenirs, keeping abreast and often *ahead* of the times.[21]

Another interesting book is *Tested Recipe Cook Book*, compiled by Mrs. Henry Lumpkin Wilson and published in Atlanta in 1895. As mentioned earlier, for the most part we know little about these authors, except what they reveal in their prefaces, though by reading their volumes carefully one comes to suspect that their life histories were not unlike Sarah Rorer's, albeit on a local or regional level. Like Mrs. Rorer, they sometimes came to the writing of these books with little training (not even by their mothers if their own statements can be believed) but from a desire to produce something that would be, as another cookbook writer—Jessie Henderson Colville—put it in *A Kentucky Woman's Handy Cook Book*, "very helpful in the every day routine."[22] Mrs. Wilson's small book, however, gives us a better idea than most of the kinds of women who wrote these books, if only because it contains photographs of the women who were on the Committee on Agriculture and Horticulture of the Cotton States and International Exposition held in Atlanta in 1895. This committee produced her book. From these photographs, we gain considerable insight into the women who participated in such groups. They appeared well-dressed and from the middle class—women who took such committees seriously and believed their work important to other women and their communities.[23] These are examples of how these Southern cookbooks can be revealing in sometimes unexpected ways.

The names of recipes themselves are often as suggestive as the titles of the books. Their titles reflect the commonplaces of the age. Witness such titles as *The Way to the Heart: Hints to the Inexperienced*; *Mrs. Hill's Southern Cook-Book, Or, Housekeeping Made Easy: A Practical System for Private Families*; *Mrs. Porter's New Southern Cookery Book, and Companion for Frugal and Economical Housekeepers*; *Dixie Cookery: Or, How I Managed My Table for Twelve Years: A Practical Cook-Book for Southern Housekeepers*; or *Housekeeping in the Blue Grass: A New and Practical Cook Book* with their repetitions of words like "practical" and "economical" and allusions to "domesticity" and "good management," the "key-words" of the age, in the South as elsewhere. Recipes like Robert E. Lee Cake, Jackson Jumbles, Jeff Davis Pudding, Confederate Sponge Cake, Secession Pudding, or Blockade Coffee attest to the Southerner's attachment to the Cause; equally interesting is the recipe for Republican Pudding, named such, one presumes, during Reconstruction for the fact that it skimps on eggs. On the other hand, Southern cookbooks do not exhibit one of the most noticeable characteristics of their British counterparts of the period: the tendency to name recipes after famous people, particularly social superiors. Neither do they contain recipes named after inferiors, for it is only at the end of the period, shortly before and after the First World War, when the New South was displacing the Old, that we find recipe names and cookbook titles more and more assuming an outspoken worship of the old ways and the days of black family retainers, with recipes named after "aunt" or "uncle" somebody. These books presented a nostalgic, idealized view of the Southern household and of black kitchen help in particular and were followed shortly afterward by the so-called "Mammy" cookbooks. Books like *Favorite Southern Recipes* (1912), with recipes contributed by the readers of the *Southern Ruralist*; Laura Thornton Knowles's *Southern Recipes* (1913); Emma and William McKinney's *Aunt Caroline's Dixieland Recipes* (1922); and Katherine Bell's *Mammy's Cook Book* (1929), all with covers depicting "the Old Southern Mammy," projected the stereotypical view of the South, the same view found elsewhere at the time in history books, movies, and popular novels. In cookbooks, however, it is a rather new view, particularly regarding the role of black men and women in Southern households; prior to this period, blacks had rarely, or at least only obliquely, been mentioned.

A food or culinary historian can learn much from the recipes in these books, noting such things as the prevalence of okra dishes; the large number of sweets (reflecting presumably the Southerner's fondness for them); and the comments (often critical) on the Southerner's diet, such as those in *The Dixie Cook Book*, which virtually declare war on grease. There are a large number of recipes for possum. Though one book suggests this was a favorite dish of "colored folk," most of these recipes were aimed at white Southerners, so possum must have been popular with them as well. These books assumed good Southern cooking involved close attention and time ("Gumbo must not be cooked fast," one declares, "it requires from four to six hours to cook properly").[24] Besides what they suggest about daily routines and diet, these recipes (as Louis Szathmary has observed of some of those in *Mrs. Porter's New Southern Cookery*) sometimes reveal simply by their placement the social attitudes and rituals of the age. In the case of Mrs. Porter, her cake recipes could be chapter headings in any of the romantic novels of the day, the story beginning with Bachelor's Cake, followed by Ancient Maiden's Cake, Introduction Cake, Acquaintanceship

Cakes, Sweet Drops, Flirtation Cakes, Love Cakes, Kisses, Rival Cake, Jealousy Puffs, Love Cakes No. 2, Engagement Cake, Wedding Cake, and ending with The Little Folks' Joys.[25] And for much of the period, certainly until around 1900, there is an absence of mention of prepared ingredients, labor-saving devices or what was soon in all cookbooks to be termed "a modern kitchen." This is particularly noticeable in *Mrs. Hill's Southern Cook Book,* published just after the Civil War, in which E. W. Warren of Macon, Georgia, in his introduction reminded husbands that if it were a woman's "duty" to manage the kitchen and home, it was the man's to provide her with "the essentials." He wrote, "Now the consequences of this horrid and unsightly arrangement . . . is that the labor necessary to gather materials for a meal is more fatiguing than its preparation. . . . If you cannot do otherwise, burn that kitchen and smoke-house where they stand. Your dwelling will be in no danger from conflagration. Unite your kitchen with your dwelling, and furnish with a stove, etc."[26]

Along with the details these books can give us of women's daily lives, they also occasionally serve as a kind of memoir—sometimes brief (as in the case of Mrs. Fisher) but often at greater length (as in a book like Martha McCulloch-Williams's *Dishes & Beverages of the Old South*). McCulloch-Williams wrote of her Mammy whose "capacious" skirts she recalled clinging to as a child, of whom she wrote at great length while barely mentioning her parents, the master and mistress of the plantation:

> She was autocratic; a benevolent despot; withal severe. If I displeased her by meddling, putting small grimy fingers into pies they should not touch, she set me to shelling black-eyed peas—a task my soul loathed, likewise the meddlesome fingers—still I knew better than to sulk or whine over it. For that I would have been sent to the back of the house. . . . The house offered only grown-up talk, which rarely interested me. In the kitchen I caught scraps of Brer Rabbit's history, pithily applied, other scraps of song—Mammy always "gave out" the words to herself before singing them—proverbs and sayings such as "cow want her tail agin in fly-time" applied to an ingrate, or: "Dat's er high kick fer er low horse," by way of setting properly in place a pretender.[27]

But the memoir quality of her book is seen not just in her recollection of her near-mythical Mammy but equally in other sections of her remarkable book, a book that is part cookbook (that somewhat randomly), part rumination on food, and part reverie on the antebellum South of her childhood. Three sections stand out in this regard. The first is her description of the Southern custom of the "infare" or dinner to celebrate the bride's coming home to her new house or new family; the second, her lengthy, richly detailed explanation of the centrality of pork in Southern cooking and history; and the third, her remembrance of special festive occasions. Of the first, she recalled: "This etymologically—the root is the Saxon *faran*, to go, whence come wayfaring, faring forth and so forth. . . . Commonly the groom or his family give the *infare*, but often enough some generous and well-to-do friend, or kinsman, preempted the privilege. Wherever held, it was an occasion of keen and jealous rivalry—those in charge being doubly bent on making the faring in more splendid than the wedding. Naturally that put the wedding folk on their mettle."[28] This activity involved not just baking cakes and preparing a memorable repast but also setting the table so that it would outshine other wedding tables. "To this end," McCulloch-Williams recalled, "all the resources of the family, and its friends for a radius of ten miles, were available—glass, silver, china, linen, even cook pots and ovens at need. Also and further it was a slight of the keenest, if you were known as a fine cake maker, not to be asked to help. A past mistress of paper cutting was likewise in request."[29] The cake was in a heart shape—"Heart-cakes were imperative at any wedding of degree," she noted. Further, the baking of it was a ritual since "so many things had to go in it—the darning needle, thimble, picayune, ring, and button. The makers would have scorned utterly the modern subterfuge of baking plain, and thrusting in the portents of fate before the frosting. They mixed the batter a trifle stiff, washed and scoured everything, shut eyes, dropped them, and stirred them well about." The bride, she continued, recalling the occasion, cut the first piece, "hoping it might hold the picayune, and thus symbolize good fortune. The ring presaged the next bride or groom, the darning needle single blessedness to the end, the thimble, many to sew for, or feed, the button, fickleness or disappointment. After the bridal party had done cutting [the cake], other young folk tempted fate."[30]

Of the second, concerning the care and importance attached to slaughtering the hogs, McCulloch-Williams recalled that "Plenty in the smokehouse was the cornerstone of the old time Southern cookery. Hence hog killing was a festival as joyous as Christmas—and little less sacred. . . . There was keen rivalry amongst plantations as to which should show the finest pen of fattening hogs. Though the plantation force was commonly amply sufficient for the work of slaughter, owners indulged their slaves by asking help of each other—of course returning the favor at need."[31] Equally vivid was her memory of such special occasions as Jackson's Day (January 8), dances like the Basket Cotillion, (a combination dance and picnic), and the bran dances, so named, she tells us, because the earth was leveled and pounded hard and smooth and then covered an inch deep with clean wheat bran. "One basket from a plantation," she recalled, "sufficed for bran dances ending at sundown—those running on past midnight demanded two [and] it would never do to offer snippets and fragments for supper. . . . Mammy, and other Mammies, moved proudly about, each a sort of oracle to the friends of her household. They kept sharp eyes on things returnable— plates, platters, knives, spoons, and table-cloths—in any doubtful case, arriving from the fact of similarity in pattern, they were the court of last resort."[32] Such details, which abound not only in the section "Upon Occasions" but also throughout her book, make *Dishes & Beverages of the Old South* a marvelous piece of social or cultural history.

But while Martha McCulloch-Williams's book is perhaps the most evocative of these Southern cookbooks, it is not the only Southern cookbook that functions as much as a memoir as a recipe book. Less well known but equally evocative in its own way is *Famous Old Receipts* (1908). This book contains recipes "used a hundred years and more in the kitchens of the North and South" and much lore concerning Southern cooking and society. A collaborative effort, the book's most important contributors were Mrs. James T. Halsey of Philadelphia and her sister and sister-in-law (Mrs. Charles B. Maury of Washington, D.C., and Mrs. Robert H. Maury of Richmond), all three of the Virginia Maury family. These women contributed not only family recipes but the lore that went with them, lore which, like that in Martha McCulloch-Williams's book, has the quality of a memoir. The short essay contributed by Mrs. James T. Halsey (Sue Mason Maury Halsey), "An Old-Fashioned Christmas Dinner," records a Christmas "befo' the war" in "a rambling, old-fashioned Virginia house, thirty miles from Fredericksburg," with the Southern woman, the "Lady Bountiful" of her domain, surrounded by servants ready to do her bidding:

> . . . She was up with the lark, saw her household in order; she ministered to the sick and comforted the afflicted; bond and free alike had her care. There was as much excitement and anticipation among the negroes at Christmas as among the whites, from the smallest darkey to Uncle Peter, the oldest negro on the plantation. Two weeks before Christmas began the busy time, seeding raisins, cutting citron, washing and drying currants, for these were the days before all this could be bought. Every housekeeper had her own especial receipts handed down from mother to daughter. In the big kitchen at night, before a blazing log fire, would sit the cook, surrounded by several house servants preparing the fruit for cakes, mincemeat and plum pudding. Apple toddy was made by an old family receipt usually a month beforehand, as it improved, like many other things, with age. The menu for a Christmas dinner at this old house was soup, either calf's head or turtle; then a turkey at one end and a young pig or a haunch of venison at the other, with a great variety of vegetables. Wines of different kinds were served throughout the dinner. . . .
> Then came the dessert, to childhood's eyes most important; a bowl of calvesfoot jelly, sparkling in the cut glass bowl, and the oft repeated comparison of Santa Claus in the old nursery jingle, "that he had a round face and a little round belly, which shook when he laughed like a bowl full of jelly," was a good one to juvenile minds. The plum pudding was always brought in, in a blaze of glory, with a sprig of holly in the top, while the blue flame danced around it. . . . Every servant had his share of the good things, and that the sound of the fiddle and the shuffle of many feet gave evidence of a dance in the kitchen for the negroes.[33]

The place of women, as we might expect, is a much discussed topic in these books and, not surprisingly, by inference if nothing else, held to be in the home, the "separate spheres" being fully supported. The patriarchal family structure that came from ownership of slaves and the perpetuation of the idea of the traditional landowning aristocracy was strong in the South, even in other classes, and was reinforced, according to Anne Firor Scott, by Southern plantation novelists and writers of books of advice, most of whom were men.[34] The cookbooks of the period—almost all of them written by women—contain the same view, however. "Home," Theresa Brown of Anderson, South Carolina, declares in *Modern Domestic Cookery* (1871), "is woman's sphere: it is her peculiar mission to make it agreeable and cheerful. To do this successfully she must acquaint herself with the ordinary duties of life, and become a practical operator in the household circle. . . . No external requirements will compensate for a deficiency in a knowledge of the useful and substantial. A woman may play like a professor, sing like a siren, possess the beauty of Arimida, yet a melancholy fate awaits her—her life will be one of gilded misery, if there does not exist the elements of a well-kept home."[35] An unmarried woman herself, writing in the "crisis" period following the Civil War when Southern households faced "a spirit of retrenchment" and "narrow incomes," she was especially critical of the women of her own day. She wrote, "young people, whose domestic employment is chiefly, if not altogether, of a superficial character on the one hand, or left unoccupied on the other, cannot bring their minds to the comprehension of the inferior and less striking virtues. I will here again say, education should be a preparation for *actual, real life*." That "real life" in her view was the home, and she was extremely critical of the attention given "external accomplishments" and "the apathy and indifference with which parents discharge the most sacred observations to their offsprings" and of girls "who talk of little but parties and beaus, and have a thorough knowledge of dress in all its details." Her own book, she said, was to be a correction of these defects in their education and premised on the assumption—she, like so many cookbook writers, particularly in this period, saw herself as a reformer—that domestic science deserved equality with "the other sciences."[36]

Similarly, in *Mrs. Hill's New Family Receipt Book for the Kitchen* (the earlier version of the same book later published as *Mrs. Hill's Southern Cook Book*), the view of woman's place is very traditional, and her happiness is seen in preparing food and enjoying domesticity. This viewpoint is sometimes found in the strangest places, as in her instructions on broiling where she quotes from an unnamed source, "Depend upon it there is a great deal of happiness in a well-dressed mutton chop, or a tidy breakfast table. Men grow sated of music, are often too wearied for conversation, however intellectual; but they can appreciate a well-swept hearth and smiling comfort. Better submit to household duties, even should there be no predilection for them, than doom herself to a loveless home. Women of a higher order of mind will not run this risk; they know that their *feminine*, their *domestic duties*, are their first duties."[37] Also, and again approvingly, Mrs. Hill put at the head of her chapter on pastry this unidentified quote:

> Whether rich or poor, young or old, married or single, a woman is always liable to be called to the performance of every kind of domestic duty, as well as to be placed at the head of a family; and nothing short of a *practical* knowledge of the details of housekeeping can ever make these duties easy or render her competent to direct others in the performance of them. . . . [38]

The Dixie Cook Book, which combines two prevailing Victorian senti-ments, that regarding woman's domestic "nature" and the value of effi-ciency and "system" in household management, carries the same message. "Housekeeping, whatever may be the opinion of the butterflies of the period," according to its author, "is an accomplishment in comparison to which . . . all others are trivial. It comprehends all that goes to make up a well-ordered home, where the sweetest relations of life rest on firm founda-tions, and the purest sentiments thrive. . . . Your husband may admire your grace and ease in society, your wit, your schoolday accomplishments of music and painting, but all in perfection will not atone for an ill-ordered kitchen, sour bread, muddy coffee, tough meats, unpalatable vegetables, indigestible pastry, and the whole train of horrors that result from bad housekeeping."[39]

These books have been cited at length because they are fairly typical of the sentiments expressed in the cookbooks of the period. But even when such sentiments are not expressed at length or overtly, they are indicated by the frequency with which cookbook authors invoked Scriptures, particu-larly Proverbs 31:27, "She looketh well to the ways of her household, and eateth not the bread of idleness," an apt sentiment given the routines indicated in these books. Only at the end of the Victorian age does one find, and nearly always in those cookbooks written by home economists, household hints or recipes for the "busy housewife," though "busy" at what is not always explained. Even then, the view of Southern women and their domestic responsibilities had not changed that much since Mollie Huggins, a prolific late nineteenth-century writer of cookbooks, prefaced her book, *Good Things to Eat,* with the quote, "Home is home when there is a good cook at the helm" and reminded her readers that "A true wife and mother desires above all things to have a happy home; and one of the surest ways to accomplish this is to live within her husband's means, economize as best she can, and have well-prepared, simple, wholesome meals."[40] Similarly, Mrs. Lumpkin included as a frontispiece to *Tested Recipe Cook Book* two recipes—"Recipe for Making a Home Happy" and "Recipe for Cheer-fulness"—that were not really recipes at all but large dollops of Victorian sentiment. The first, for making a home happy, reads, "One ounce each system, frugality and industry, one ounce each gentleness, patience and forbearance, six ounces Paul's Christian charity, that covers a multitude of

failures. These ingredients thoroughly kneaded with the salt of good common sense, flavored with the 'graces of nature and art,' music and flowers,
will make a paradise of a desert, a palace of a hovel"; and the second, for
cheerfulness, "Take two parts of unselfishness, add as much fresh air as can
easily be obtained, stir in two hours of 'beauty sleep,' a silver tongue (from
the tip of which all spite has been removed), and an eye that looks out on
the brighter side of life. Into this mixture throw a pinch of humor and a
sprinkle of the essence of romance. The result is cheerfulness warranted to
stand the test of time."[41] Even Kate Brew Vaughn, and somewhat peculiarly since the stated purpose of her book, *Culinary Echoes from Dixie*,
was to make a case for both women and the home as "producers" in the
economy, concludes that "it is true that man, on a large scale, is a producer,
and woman defines how wealth shall be expended," thus reaffirming the
traditional view.[42]

Interestingly enough, the most emphatic and lengthy elaboration of this
view is found in Mrs. M. F. Armstrong's *On Habits and Manners*, published
by the Hampton Institute in 1888. Mrs. Armstrong was the second wife of
its white founder, Samuel Chapman Armstrong, and for many years before that a teacher at the school. Her book is a remarkable document in
almost every respect and a most unusual cookbook. It qualifies as such
largely because it contains, at the very end, a few recipes; basically,
however, it is a self-help book aimed at middle-class blacks, a combination etiquette and moral-conduct book written by a white woman. The
preface indicates that her book had at least two editions and was used at
the school. Many of Hampton's students were of the first generation of
freed slaves and were destined to become part of the black middle class;
many, too, besides entering the professions, went into domestic service in
the North and South, some in prominent hotels or First Family of Virginia
households.

Like most cookbooks of the period, Mrs. Armstrong's contains sections
on household duties and management, household hints, care for the sick,
and cooking, but she reverses the emphasis; hers is not a cookbook or
recipe book to which other things are added but a discourse on the home
and the woman's—and also the man's—responsibilities to which recipes are
appended. The book spells out the ethos of the period for Christian ladies
and gentlemen "of whatever color" (the author's words), extolling the
value of work, thrift, economy, irreproachable manners (which even for
this period are exceptionally strict) and, above all, the home. The book's
philosophy is contained in her admonition: "And certainly there is no more
honorable ambition for most women than the ambition to be a good housekeeper, taking that word always in its broadest and most beautiful sense,
the Bible sense, whose interpretation we find in that wonderful description
in the last chapter of Proverbs."[43] Her values are those of the white
community—property, the family, work, and the shared, but quite distinct,

roles of men and women in domestic matters. Thus, according to the author:

> The cornerstone of all civilization is the family, the existence of families in-
> cludes the existence of homes, and a home pre-supposes a house, so that we
> are swiftly and easily led to the human race, or at least to all civilized members
> of it, of the houses which shelter them, and which, furthermore, supply so
> large a share of the comforts, the charms, the sweet and powerful influences of
> Home.[44]

This is more than simply the sentiment of domesticity, of the joys of home and home life, so characteristic of cookbooks of the period. For Mrs. Armstrong equates civilization itself with property, and even more specifi-cally with the ownership of homes. "The effect of well built, convenient, attractive houses," she writes, "is hardly to be overrated, they are so su-premely civilizing that men and women can hardly fail to be made, in one way or another, the better for living in them."[45] Further, the advantage of owning a home is not just economic but also a matter of character and self-reliance, of hard work and perseverance, and brings its own rewards since it is "the moral stimulus which he, the husband, and his family receive from living in a house which is their own property, wherein no one has a right but themselves, which they can improve and beautify until it becomes to them, as their home, the pleasantest and most attractive spot on earth. . . . When a man and woman actually own the house which is their home, they find themselves, as a rule, quickly filled with an honorable ambition to make house and garden as neat, comfortable and pretty as possible. They take pride and pleasure in working for the improvement of that which is their own, and receive constant gratification from results achieved by their own labor and thrift."[46]

Yet in striving toward this goal, Mrs. Armstrong asserts that the man's and woman's contributions or duties are different, and it is the husband and father of the family who is responsible for the "thought" and "labor" which lay, sometimes literally, at the foundation of the home. But from the moment the family enters the house, from the moment the house becomes a home, the responsibility shifts and "it is the wife and mother who must bear the chief burden of the housekeeping and become the ruling spirit of the home."[47] She rigorously supports the "separate-spheres" philosophy— "The man, as the bread-winner, finds that his work keeps him during the greater part of the day away from his home and family, and consequently, the duty of regulating and controlling the household falls mainly into the woman's hands, and any conscientious woman will gladly do all in her power to fit herself for the due performance of the work which is so plainly set before her."[48] Cooking, therefore, is a woman's "duty," but in Mrs. Armstrong's view, this is not a simple matter, not merely a matter of sustenance, for it, too, like home ownership, has a "civilizing" function.

For, like many of her day, she believed that there was a correlation between good food and moral conduct and that what is eaten and how it is
fixed were part of, and contributions to, the civilizing force. "It is possible," she writes, "that this principle of the physiological necessity of good
cookery would be sufficient for my present purpose, but there is still another fact which I want you to notice, and that is, that the highest civilization always includes great care in the choice and preparation of food." This
white author, writing for blacks, stated, "uncivilized races live like animals,
eating anything they can get, at any time and in any way; but the gradual
ascent of humanity in the scale of civilization is marked always by an
increase of care in respect to food, both as regards material and cookery."
And thus for women, she concludes, "When you have learned to cook well
and intelligently, you have made yourselves valuable members of any
household, rich or poor, and this is surely no little thing to say, and no
mean ambition for any woman to set before herself, and I would, therefore, urge every woman who reads this to do her best to create healthy and
civilized tastes in regard to food, in all those within your reach."[49] Samuel
Smiles, Harriet Martineau, Isabella Beeton, (three quintessential British
Victorian "philosophers"), or Brillat-Savarin (the source of the oft-quoted
dictum, "You are what you eat") would certainly have concurred.

Given such sentiments, the frequency with which many of these books
allude to a "crisis" in the Southern household following the Civil War is
particularly striking. This had to do only partly with the ravages of war or
"retrenchment" mentioned by Theresa Brown or the difficulties for some
families of adjusting from slave to servant households. It had more to do—
if some of these books can be believed—with the decline of household
skills or the fact, as E. W. Warren declared in *Mrs. Hill's Southern Cook
Book*, that "The race of good cooks among us is almost extinct."[50] This
idea of degeneration or decline is a typical one of the period, however
paradoxical it may seem in an age of such material progress. For British
cookbook writers, this "crisis" sometimes caused regret over the loss of
eighteenth-century manners and elegance; for Southern cookbook writers,
the "crisis" had a similar resonance, fostering a sense that traditional Southern hospitality was in peril; but was also seen as a challenge. "We are not
just now in a condition to sacrifice much to fancy or ornament," Warren
noted, "we must address ourselves to the useful and substantial. Every
mother, wife and daughter must now become a practical operator in the
domestic circle. Each should be emulous to excel in neatness, industry,
usefulness and economy. The days of romance have passed, if they ever
existed; the night for the dreamy visions of elegance and luxury in connection with a life of indolence has suddenly given place to the day of enterprise and industry. . . . A crisis is upon us which demands the development
of the *will* and *energy* of Southern character. Its prestige in the past gives
earnest of a successful future. As woman has been queen in the parlor, so,

if need be, she will be queen in the kitchen; as she has performed so gracefully the duties of the mistress of the establishment in the past, so she will, with a lovelier grace, perform whatever labor duty demands."[51] Southern women, he concluded, should adopt the "system" contained in Mrs. Hill's book—"Make idleness and indolence disreputable, and labor and usefulness honorable. Pluck from the hand of the destroyer the premium awarded to idleness and give it to industry."[52] It was an appeal that made domestic efficiency itself somewhat of a political act.

Part of the "crisis" Warren and others alluded to was "the servant problem" following the Civil War. Thus, according to *The Dixie Cook Book*, "since the surrender the great problem with the Southern matron has been the servant question. Prior to that date, though the mistress had many trials with inefficient, heedless and frequently dishonest servants, yet, as their permanent training was in her hands, she, if competent herself, was likely to have a few, at least, very capable assistants."[53] Still, Southern cookbooks, in my opinion, usually discussed the servant question in ways that have surprisingly little to do with slavery or specifically Southern conditions at all, in ways in which Dinah or Bridget are virtually interchangeable. The assumption in both Mrs. Hill's and Mrs. Wilcox's books, and in the others that appeared in this "crisis" period, is that Southern women, even those who still had servants, or perhaps especially if they had servants, would themselves have to do many more things than simply "managing" the household. While such an assumption is not an unusual one in American cookbooks, it does contrast strikingly with British cookbooks of the period. This was partly by choice, partly of necessity—indeed, according to Marion Cabell Tyree, writing in 1879, a Southern woman should "acquire the practice as well as the theory of bread-making. In this way, she will be able to give more exact directions to her cook. . . . Besides, if circumstances should throw her out of a cook for a short time, she is then prepared for an emergency."[54] And this, she noted, was a distinct possibility since "in this country fortunes are so rapidly made and lost, the vicissitudes of life are so sudden that we know not what a day may bring forth. It is not uncommon to see elegant and refined women brought suddenly face to face with emergencies which their practical knowledge of household economy and their brave hearts enable them to firmly meet and overcome."[55] Even without such a necessity, there were many times, as numerous Southern cookbook writers observed, when a woman would want to cook, or if a popular contemporary lithograph of a drawing by Solomon Eytinge, Jr., entitled "Love in a Cottage" can be believed (which appeared as the frontispiece in *The Dixie Cook Book*), her cook might leave, and she might have to do the cooking and perhaps even be assisted by her husband.

Estelle Woods Wilcox makes much the same point. Taking issue with Northerners who, she said, had "very mistaken ideas about Southern women and their domestic capacities," stemming she thought from their assumption that Southern women had slaves or servants and therefore no household experience, she insisted that they actually had far more experience than their Northern counterparts because:

> A Southern woman must know how to prepare any dish, for she finds no cooks made to order; they must be of her own training, in the minutest particulars of every department. Northern housekeepers, in all the larger towns and cities, do not have to depend on their own skill for the delicacies of every description that make up the dainties of the table, but the Southern housewives, even in our larger towns and cities, all do; and Northern visitors often comment on the filling of our store-houses, and it is difficult to convince them that we must trust these preparations to no one else.[56]

Further, she noted that Southern housewives faced the same "servant problem" as their counterparts in the North and that while many of the black cooks and laundresses of the South had once been noted for their skill—again the notion of some previous golden age—"Now, at the South (as in the North) the 'girls' are birds of passage, though less reliable in their migrations, often coming and going with the weeks instead of seasons."[57]

Surprisingly, while there is a good deal of discussion of the servant problem in these books, there are not many references to blacks, either as cooks or servants. When they are mentioned, it is often in a disparaging or condescending fashion, as in Mary Stuart Smith's *The Virginia Cookery Book*, for instance, which warns housekeepers to watch their black cooks closely because of their tendency to put bacon grease in things; also, in making ice cream, "wherever colored labor is employed, experience has proved that simple contrivances are safest to employ; for, where there is the least complication of machinery with our colored friends, there is ever a screw loose or a button lost, since they have an invincible repugnance to modern improvements."[58] Nor could they be trusted with especially important tasks or meals. Mrs. Hill, at the beginning of her section on cakes, tells her readers that "the process of the compounding and baking of cakes being a delicate operation, it should not be left to careless hands, but should be carried on under supervision."[59] This is a point driven home by the cover of another cookbook, *Favorite Southern Recipes* (1912), which is otherwise undistinguished, showing a black cook throwing up her hands in relief as her white mistress instructs her, which, if John Egerton is right, represents a curious reversal of historical fact.[60]

But for the most part, Southern cookbooks of the period do not mention black cooks or kitchen help at all and only confirm Egerton's observation that "for many years after slavery began in this country the contribution of black cooks—indeed, their very presence in the kitchens of the wealthy— was virtually ignored in cookbooks and other places of public record."[61] Although Egerton has the antebellum home in mind, his observation seems equally applicable to the postbellum household—notwithstanding the prevalence of blacks as servants in Southern households (there being almost no white servants). Indeed, it is only at the end of the post-Reconstruction era that "the creative genius of black cooks" was recognized in books like Martha McCulloch-Williams's *Food & Beverages in the Old South*, Emma and William McKinney's *Aunt Caroline's Dixieland Recipes*, or Katherine Bell's *Mammy's Cook Book*. The popular "Mammy" cookbooks compiled shortly before and after the First World War, though obviously heartfelt and appreciative, were patronizing and created other myths, such as the myth of the "temperamental artist mammies" who could work culinary miracles day in and day out but for the life of them could not explain the recipes of their most important dishes which remained a "mystery," even "accidental." Such inferences can be found in numerous cookbooks after Reconstruction. In *The Virginia Cookery Book*, Mary Stuart Smith noted in 1885 that:

> The most beautiful bread I ever saw was made by a poor creature only one degree removed from idiocy; she had sense enough, however, to *feel* how her bread should be treated, and was, moreover, scrupulously neat. An old "aunty" in a Virginia homestead of the olden time made such exquisitely fair rolls, that a visitor asked leave to be permitted to have her recipe. "Aunt Phyllis," the lady said, "I have come to get your recipe for making the lovely rolls you gave us for breakfast." With a droll and puzzled air the cook answered, "La! missus, I just know I dar'n't make 'em no different." The old woman could give no other recipe; she knew what to do, and did it.[62]

In view of the nature of race relations and the importance of race at the time, this omission of blacks is a curious but not unexpected or unexplainable attitude, just as the endeavor later to give "the turbaned mistress" her just due in the Southern kitchen also is.

On the other hand, though it may be difficult to deduce much from these cookbooks about the actual servant situation—except by indirection or innuendo, these books do detail many other aspects of the Southern household extremely well. Some, like *The Dixie Cook Book*, give especially detailed accounts of the Southern housewife's many labors, not only in the kitchen but also in housekeeping generally—of the routine of cleaning, ridding beds of bedbugs, contending with moths and mildew, caring for children and the sick. And in good melodramatic fashion, they warn of dire consequences if these things are not carefully attended to. "A dirty kitchen and bad cooking," Mrs. Wilcox noted, "have driven many a husband and son, and a daughter, too, from a home that should have been a refuge from temptation."[63] We learn, too, from these books, in particular from the sections on "household hints," something of Southern interiors and how rare store-bought commodities still were in many or most Southern homes—soaps, cleansers, baking powders, medicines, and the like. Such "hints" confirm what Susan Strasser observes in her study that the advice in these books is nearly always for lightening or making the woman's basic tasks more efficient but not for doing away with them.[64] Furthermore, only in the 1890s, and then most often in local cookbooks or cookbooks sponsored by Southern manufacturers, do we find references to store-bought items like Cottolene, Snowdrift shortening, or Sauer's spices and vanilla extract.

Temperance, surprisingly, is not particularly notable in these Southern cookbooks, for even many church-related cookbooks contained numerous recipes for alcoholic beverages and homemade cordials and wines; indeed, one could readily conclude from them that Southerners rather liked their alcohol. Martha Stuart Smith noted in her book the disappearance of many old practices. "Nowadays beaten biscuits are a rarity," she observed in 1885, "found here and there, but soda and modern institutions caused them to be sadly out of vogue"; the reasons she gave for their disappearance were that (1) to make them you had to have a biscuit-block, usually made of the trunk of a solid oak or chestnut tree, felled and sawed off to the right height and planed—"An ordinary table would soon be knocked to pieces, if used for this service"; (2) the axe required, with a short, stout handle "is a condition hard to comply with in a kitchen where servants are careless, as a rule"; and (3) most servants "object nowadays to the trouble of preparing this bread."[65] Mrs. Smith rather deplored the passing of such things, but being a realist, she stood with the professional home economists of her day who were increasingly championing "the modern kitchen."

In the South as elsewhere, cookbooks in the decades after the Civil War had usually only suggested simplifying or "systematizing" the labor or time involved in housekeeping, this in the absence of domestic machinery. This was the fetish for "economy" or efficiency, which though somewhat less noticeable in Southern cookbooks is found there, too. But by the turn of the century, even those cookbooks that desired to perpetuate the South's reputation for hospitality had begun to express different sentiments, much as Mrs. Wilcox did in *The Dixie Cook Book* when she predicted that "All systematic housekeepers will hail the day when some enterprising 'Dixie' girl shall invent a stove or range with a thermometer attached to the oven, so that the heat may be regulated accurately and intelligently."[66] Indeed, even such tradition-minded cookbook writers as Kate Vaughn Brew, herself a cooking instructor, argued in *Culinary Echoes from Dixie*, using and extending an analogy that had long been popular with cookbook writers of the similarity between business and the household, the factory and the kitchen, that this analogy ought also to begin to involve technology and not just organization. "The dissatisfied housekeeper," Kate Vaughn Brew noted, "is usually the one who needs to spend her time in accomplishing her kitchen duties, leaving no time for equally important and more interesting tasks."[67]

Thus, though by the end of the Victorian era the object of many Southern cookbook writers regarding Southern women and their household duties was still (as *The Dixie Cook Book* had earlier put it) "to lessen their perplexities and aid them in their successful and happy reign in Woman's Kingdom—the Home," that kingdom in the South, as elsewhere, had clearly begun to change, and cookbooks not only reflected but helped bring about those changes.

11

A Family Tradition of Letters:
The Female Percys and
the Brontëan Mode

BERTRAM WYATT-BROWN

THE WELL-KNOWN SOUTHERN NOVELIST Walker Percy over-
shadows the accomplishments of those Percy family members who also
adopted literary careers. Like others in the lineage, including his cousin
and guardian William Alexander Percy (an Edwardian poet and author of
the classic memoir *Lanterns on the Levee*), he has had to wrestle with
melancholy. The condition has led at least one Percy to commit suicide or
to be hospitalized for mental illness in each generation since the end of
the eighteenth century. The origins of the disorder may well be genetic;
recent medical findings confirm that hypothesis, although few would
doubt that life events, including the manifestations of depression in parents, would have an emotional effect upon those around them, especially
on the very young.[1]

A claim that Percy family life can be fully explained simply by reference
to depression would be utterly foolish. The members had many more arrows in their collective quiver than that. Nonetheless, in regard to Walker
Percy, concerns over the ailment had a relationship to his deep probing of
French existentialism and the other psychological and philosophical themes
with which his novels are largely involved; these works are: *The Moviegoer*, *The Last Gentleman*, *Love in the Ruins*, *Lancelot*, *The Second Coming*, and *The Thanatos Syndrome*.[2] Although not suicidal, Senator LeRoy
Percy, William Alexander Percy's father, was also subject to the malady.

The Mississippi senator's son shared the condition, owing in part to a failure to work out an independent relationship with his dynamic and rather anti-intellectual father.[3]

Depression is an illness long associated with creativity. As Virginia Woolf observed, "as an experience, madness is terrific I can assure you, and not to be sniffed at; and in its lava I still find most of the things I write about."[4] During its most severe phases, however, the artist—poet, musician, painter, or novelist—has ordinarily been incapable of effective work. As Michael Ignatieff points out, "Of all the painful features of a depression, the worst may be its truth." So long as a part of "our minds believes that our reactions and emotions are exaggerated, we can shield ourselves from the full force of melancholia, . . . but if we convince ourselves that depression lays bare the reality of our existence, we experience our own despair as the scourge of truth, and the scourge of truth always bites deeper than the scourge of error." Over two thousand literary figures have been identified as suffering from one form of serious depression or another.[5]

In the aftermath of such attacks, the imagination soars. Sigmund Freud, who endured the affliction, wrote, "I have long known that I can't be industrious when I am in good health; on the contrary, I need a degree of discomfort which I want to get rid of."[6] Walker Percy himself affirms that his best writing comes after a period of depressive lethargy and ennui.[7] Both Percys—Walker in his novels and Will in his classically styled poetry and his notable memoir—sought through such means not only to cope with the problem itself but also to reach toward more universal meaning in human existence.[8] Such an aim has induced so many thinkers from Socrates to William Styron to challenge through art their worst fears of themselves.[9]

In this respect, the Percy writers were also participating in that peculiarly Southern exercise—the attempt through literature to understand and explain the nature of regional identity. Narrative, as Southern thinkers have long recognized, has the capacity to make communal identifications possible. But beyond that, the act of literary creation in Southern hands has also been part of what psychoanalyst George Pollock calls a healthy mourning process.[10] It permits the articulation of personal feelings of rage, loneliness, or loss through imaginary representations. Particularly after the slave South's surrender in 1865, a need for formal expression arose in order for the section's thinkers to come to terms first with emancipation and military defeat and later with both regional penuriousness and a bewildering array of changes toward economic and social modernity. Through the narrative form, the writer is enabled to remove himself or herself from the risks of self-exposure: the inner thoughts remain sacred territory. Such reticence is almost essential in a culture like that of the American South, which once made so little distinction between private and public spheres. As Walker Percy himself noted, until recently in the Deep South, there had been an "absence of a truly public zone" separate from the interior life of a family.

A consequence was that the latter "came to coincide with the actual public space which it inhabited."[11]

What is so surprising about the twentieth-century Percys' creative experience is not just that they dealt with themes which had, at some level, poignant meaning for them as individuals, artists, and Southerners, but also that their interests had nineteenth-century affinities with other literary configurations within their own family. The Percy writers of the prior century were all women—Catherine Ann Ware Warfield (1816–1877), her sister Eleanor Percy Ware Lee (1819–1849), and their niece Sarah Ann Ellis Dorsey (1829–1879). These fascinating and gifted authors produced fifteen novels and several collections of verse among them. They had a considerably different perspective on life from that of their ingenious male collateral descendants but, given the cultural alterations of a hundred years, much less so than one might expect. Most of our attention will be devoted to the three women (particularly Warfield) rather than to their better-studied twentieth-century relations. Indeed, we know so little of the contributions of early and mid-nineteenth-century Southern women that even a brief review of the Percy novelists' lives and works helps to expand the canon beyond Mary Chesnut, Augusta Evans, and Caroline Hentz. These writers are all relatively familiar figures compared with the dozens, like the Percy women, remaining to be reclaimed.

Although beneficiaries of their fathers' enormous land and slaveholding wealth, the three female writers recognized at some level the constrictions of their roles as thinking women. Moreover, to an astonishing degree, they shared a common, tragic past with the modern Percy writers, despite the intervening years. Furthermore, all of them belonged to the same landed social elite that until recent times dominated the region, and their strong sense of family identity and special destiny came as close to aristocracy—of talent in addition to wealth—as the American nation ever had. Eleanor and Catherine Ann were Walker Percy's great-great aunts; Sarah Ellis Dorsey was his cousin several times removed. All three found similar means of artistic expression and release of deep feelings in their mid-Victorian writing.

We must approach the topic on two intertwined levels: first, the commonality of themes, both secular and religious, linking the two groups of authors, and second, the divergence of motives arising from the women's use of a language of feeling and connection, as it were, and the male Percy writers' discourse based on reason and power. The first set of authors offered an implied critique of male domination; the second, an acceptance of it. But prior to that exploration, something must be said about who these obscure women were and how their understanding of their family's past led them to choose their literary subjects and genres.

Like their twentieth-century successors, the Percy authors responded to the record of despondency and self-dissolution which had already blighted the family's history. Having established himself in British and later Spanish

West Florida, Charles Percy, the founder of the family in America, like Faulkner's Thomas Sutpen, knew the ways to make money from land and slaves. Before his arrival in 1776, however, Charles Percy had deserted a family in England. His thirteen-year-old daughter Sarah and his wife Margaret died destitute and were buried in St. Giles graveyard near High Holborn, the very heart of Hogarth's London slums.[12] Margaret died before her son Robert discovered his father's whereabouts in 1791. Robert, later himself a settler in West Florida (Louisiana), had been sent in 1770 to sea as a Royal Navy cabin boy.[13]

Meantime, with vague hints of an aristocratic relationship to the earls of Northumberland, the former self-styled British army officer established himself as a community leader, receiving a magistracy (*alcalde*), which entitled him to be called "Don Carlos." He designated his place below Natchez as "Northumberland House," the name of the Percys' eighteenth-century London palace at Charing Cross. A gentleman of black moods and dark motives—he was actually twice a bigamist—and of mysterious origins, the Percy progenitor succumbed to acute psychotic depression. In 1794, Charles Percy drowned himself in a rain-swollen creek near his house, leaving a fateful mental legacy, most particularly for the early females in the line. Thirteen at the time of his death, his eldest daughter Sarah Percy, a girl of great beauty by all accounts, married three years later, in 1797, the prosperous and elderly Judge John Ellis of Natchez. By him, she had a son, Thomas George Percy, and a daughter, Mary Jane. Judge Ellis died in 1808. Sarah married again in 1814 the even wealthier and darkly handsome Major Nathaniel A. Ware. Intellectual in his tastes, like Sarah's father, Ware was also too haughty to be popular, although he briefly served as acting governor of the Mississippi territory. In 1819, upon the birth of her second daughter in this second marriage, at age thirty-nine, Sarah fell into deep and permanent melancholia.[14]

The two daughters by Sarah and Nathaniel Ware—Catherine Ann and Eleanor—were raised in Philadelphia. There, the major had consigned his wife Sarah to the Pennsylvania Hospital, the late Benjamin Rush's establishment for the care of the insane.[15] Although the family members treated her with consummate kindness, Sarah never was able to recognize her daughters. Catherine Ann told a journalist, "She would weep sometimes for her baby 'Ellen,' but would repulse caresses of her weeping daughter, who would often try to make her mother understand who she was."[16]

In coping with the unhappy situation, Major Ware gave the girls the best cultural and material surroundings that his great riches from land speculations could provide. Yet, eccentric and reclusive, he rather neglected them. Ware traveled often abroad or on surveying expeditions into the southern and western wilderness. In 1831, the major moved his demented wife to Natchez. Living on the upper story of the large plantation house of Thomas George Percy Ellis, her son by her first marriage, Sarah occupied her days tunelessly strumming on a guitar or painting pictures. Occasionally, she wandered from her nurse "in a mazed state" and had to be retrieved. Sometimes she had seizures that necessitated a straitjacket.[17] Like the Renaissance poet Christopher Hatton's dying swan who "living had no note," Sarah Percy Ware had not recovered her sanity when in 1835 "death approach'd, unlock'd her silent throat" as well as her long imprisoned mind.[18] In like manner, Sarah Ware's daughter Mary Jane, who had married René LaRoche, a prominent Philadelphia physician and yellow-fever specialist, died young after years of insanity. This, too, had an emotional impact because Mary Jane Ellis LaRoche had served as mother to her half sisters Catherine Ann and Eleanor during their early Philadelphia years.[19]

For the two Ware daughters, the double loss under such grievous circumstances encouraged their interest in subjects dramatic, tragic, and romantic. Catherine Ann later remarked how much she enjoyed browsing alone in her father's extensive library, reading through a "ragged regiment of authors"— Walter Scott, a lavishly illustrated Bible, Amelia Opie's *Ruffian Boy* and "the matchless *Madeline*," Maria Edgeworth's *Castle Rackrent*, and other soulful narratives. But she confessed her favorite was *Vathek: An Arabian Tale*, one of the leading gothic stories in the Horace Walpole and Ann Radcliffe tradition. Writing through the medium of a fictional character, Catherine Ann recalled most fondly the eccentric William Beckford's story *Vathek* about a little princess and her feminized brother who vie for the affection of a mad possessor of hidden knowledge. One of the most grotesque and violent romances in the eighteenth-century genre, Beckford describes scenes in which a de-Sade-like character hurls children over a precipice, largely for his own fiendish pleasure.[20] The book, Catherine Ann wrote, "saddened her for days, she scarce knew why, and left its imprint of mournful warning on her heart for life."[21] Indeed, the young woman may well have fancied that she was Princess Nouronihar. Her sister Eleanor appeared as Beckford's creation, the boy-girl Gulchenrouz. Naturally, in this female version of the family romance, Vathek was her fearsome but fascinating father in a fiction of blood and incest. Major Ware himself sanctioned his daughters' intellectual pursuits, even though literature of this kind was thought to be gravely harmful for young impressionable minds.

Both Catherine Ann and Eleanor were extremely gifted, but Catherine Ann was the more sensitive and vulnerable of the pair. As a child, she had reacted so strenuously to her father's long absences that she refused to join her sister at school and had to be tutored at home.[22] Later, isolation and abandonment, emotional as well as physical, were constant themes in their work, especially in Catherine Ann's, much as it was in the fiction of Charlotte Brontë, to whom they and other romantic female writers of their day owed so much, either directly or through popular imitators.

Quite early, the young women found the means to express themselves in literary form. Eleanor at age sixteen wrote an unpublished novel, "Agatha," which proposed the superiority and lofty spirit of her sixteen-year-old heroine, Agatha Murray. The heroine is an orphan who, after some dullish comings and goings, overcomes her grief over her mother's death and hopes to find a dashing eighteen-year-old hero to wed. She does. In the course of the story, however, the pleasure of love, young Eleanor Percy Ware admonished, should be treated with the utmost "suspicion." Romantic love was a dangerous "*sea*, upon whose swelling crest / Floats many a wreck of fond affections lost," editorialized the teenage author.[23]

Whether guided by romance or social convention—one suspects a bit of each—both women married early. In Cincinnati, in 1833, when she was seventeen, Catherine Ann wedded Elisha Warfield, a well-born but unambitious horse breeder of Lexington, Kentucky, with a superb Maryland pedigree.[24] Almost frantic not to be outdone, Eleanor Percy Ware at age twenty followed her sister to the altar in 1840, marrying William Henry Lee, a Virginian from Norfolk. Neither husband was at all intellectual. Yet these undemanding gentlemen of leisure seldom interfered with their wives' remarkable intimacy. Catherine Ann and Eleanor wrote each other almost daily and visited often. In settling slaveholding properties worth over $120,000 on each of his daughters, Major Ware by no means relinquished his paternal supervision. He had established trusts over which he retained control for years ahead with the husbands' presumably genial acquiescence.[25] The funds enabled the women to enjoy plantation life to the fullest and to travel and communicate with ease.

No doubt, in her first immature experimentation in writing, Eleanor Percy Lee, as well as Catherine Ann Warfield, was influenced by the rather busy intellectual life of the Natchez community where they often spent their summers with so many kinsfolk. Such productions as "Agatha" represented an activity that one literary historian has called "almost a social requirement" among the leisure class in the town.[26] Major Ware himself tried his hand at the craft, publishing at his own expense a novel called *Henry Belden*. The adventure story was based on his travels in North Africa. Its melodramatic plot about an enslaved white who escapes from the Moors, however, owed more to works like Beckford's *Vathek* than to Ware's personal experience.[27] The Natchez literary circle, about which there is little record extant, was probably led by Joseph Holt Ingraham, a teacher at the Jefferson Academy and eventually an author of eighty novels.[28]

In the early 1840s, the two Percy women were inspired by and perhaps taught by Eliza Ann DuPuy of Natchez. As one of the very earliest Southern professional writers, DuPuy, author of twenty-five novels, later held a contract with Robert Bonner's New York *Ledger*, a highly popular family magazine. She produced annually one thousand pages of fiction, chiefly of the gothic and adventure type. A Virginian by birth, DuPuy was governess to young Sarah Ann Ellis, daughter of the late Thomas George Percy Ellis and the niece of Catherine Ann Ware Warfield and Eleanor Percy Ware Lee. One would never suspect that Natchez, scarcely known for its intellectual life, would have produced so many among the first professional popular writers in America or that the Percy clan would be so well represented in that group.

A number of the themes of these nineteenth-century Percy authors resemble those in the works of the later Percys. The congruence was partly the function of a common romantic culture in which poets like Shakespeare, Scott, Keats, Southey, Tennyson, and the Brownings set the styles, the subjects of discourse, and the tastes. As conservative as these poets, Will Percy remained a staunch Victorian in his poetic interests well into the 1930s. But in addition, the poetic impulse in him as well as in his great aunts was a response to family concerns regarding honorable conduct and depression, subjects inseparably joined.

Above all, Catherine Ann and Eleanor and their latter day nephew believed in the code of honor. Warfield and Lee accepted it as the current guide to how men and women should behave. Many of their verses sing the praises of noble Indian savages who set examples of meekness and stolid bravery.[29] Will Percy understood honor as a code that *should* but probably would never prevail. In his melancholic *Lanterns on the Levee*, he mourned the loss of his father, the fast disappearance of gentry rule, and the erosion of stoic honor, a loss entailing, he feared, the end of civilization itself.[30] Walker Percy recalled that dwelling with "Uncle Will," his adoptive father, in his book-filled mansion in Greenville, Mississippi, "was to encounter a complete, articulated view of the world as tragic as it was noble."[31] As critics have long pointed out, Walker Percy received from his guardian Cousin Will a thorough inculcation into what it meant to be honorable and stoic in the face of modern-day vulgarity and frailty. Yet the code Walker Percy wrote of in his novels was too narrow spirited and too hierarchical to capture the modern mind. He loved his adoptive father, but he recognized the intellectual weaknesses in the chivalric concepts that Will Percy had espoused.[32] In many ways, Will Percy would have been more comfortable living in the age of his literary Percy forebears than in the twentieth century. That kind of nostalgia for the past, which they also demonstrated in poem after poem, was part of the dejection that they all shared in common. As Carolyn Heilbrun observes, nostalgia can be a mask for unrecognized anger, a canopy of sentiment to cover resentments one would rather not face head on.[33] In one of their longer examinations of broken love, the poets lamented:

> But to the soul
> Where lies a hidden sting of pain, and wrong
> Of vain regret, or darker word—remorse,
> Thou bring'st, O shadowy twilight, brooding gloom,
> And dearth, and restlessness, and agony.[34]

Certainly, Will Percy's poetic themes echoed this sentiment. Dealing with the convention of unrequited love, which was a familiar topic for these nineteenth-century women, the Greenville, Mississippi, poet portrayed himself as Sappho confessing her passion for Phaon, a shepherd boy, to her father Zeus. The handling of the material was much more psychologically sophisticated and more sexually charged than the work of the "Sisters of the West," as Major Ware's daughters, Catherine Ann and Eleanor, styled themselves.[35] Whereas perfidy usually explained the sad breakup of lovers in the Wares' verse, Will Percy probed a little more deeply. Sappho, for instance, worries that "Could Phaon's magic pass, / Yet other snares, perhaps as sweet . . . would trap and madden me."[36]

The Ware sisters never dared to hint at wantonness but selected chaster topics. In a joint publication of their poems, Catherine Ann and Eleanor offered "The Forsaken," verses dedicated to a maiden "who had nursed, / Above all earthly things," a love "destined, in one bitter line," to be "crushed upon its shrine." As one might expect, the subject of the heroic couplets had died of heartbreak after betrayal.[37] In another, a "young maid," whose ghost "wildly roameth" a "Deserted House," has been murdered by her wrongly jealous husband. He had falsely accused her of a "love elicit [*sic*]." The reader was expected to sympathize with the victim, but the husband's fate, the narrators fail to reveal.[38] The female Percys' verse was not unlike that which Mark Twain satirized in *Huckleberry Finn*: Emmeline Grangerford's "Ode to Stephen Dowling Bots, Dec'd."[39] Certainly, Will Percy had improved upon the topic over his ancestors. In his other works, he showed a greater seriousness of philosophical theme, irony, wit, and originality of conceit than they could have mastered. Even so, the social conservatism, stilted Victorianism, and sorrowful tonality of the twentieth-century poet should be evident.

Despite the immaturity of the early poetry, Catherine Ann Warfield learned in time to deal directly and more convincingly with matters of personal grief. (Personal grief was her chief theme until her strong Confederate feelings led her to write militant war poetry.) In a later work, "I Walk in Dreams of Poetry," she rejoices in the gift of language which permits communion of the soul with dead loved ones. The poet had long watched "them in their sorrowing hours, / When, with their spirits tost, / I heard them wail, with bitter cries, / Their earthly prospects crossed." Only "in dreams of poetry" can their memory live. Poetic fancies, she concludes, alone can "make a romance of our life; / They glorify the grave!"[40] Whereas Will Percy constantly returned to the theme of a heroic father in whose shadow the son worshipped, the female Percy writers, though far from feminist, sometimes used the traditional subtext of indirect criticism of men to make their point.

A strong sense of life's problematic character marks the best of Catherine Ann Warfield's verse. The tension of reconciling the joys of creation with pure womanhood may have been an inspiration. In addition, however, she could not forget the family fate, her own shyness, and her desire for solitude. Catherine Ann spoke to the issue of personal identification in an anti-feminist, patriarchal culture. In the first verse of a sonnet, she celebrated her blooming self-confidence: "Oh what joy to Stand / Enfranchised, firm, a Sovereign in the land." But by the end of 'the poem, she reverts to doubt, wondering "Can the freed lark sing [illegible] to the stars—Whose wing was broken on its prison bars?" In another, doubt turns to dejection; the poet says that melancholy is so familiar a companion that it must be welcomed as a friend:

> In my despair I place my chief protection!
> Oh lead me to my prison home again.
> It suits me best to dwell amid the gloom
> of that still solitude, that living tomb
> where sometimes in the darkness I discern
> the phantom forms I idolized so long
> and in my fetters feel my soul grow strong.

Only in melancholy could her desire be satisfied for a reuniting with her mother, so long lost to her.[41] In "Madeline," she mourns, "My smiles are sadder than my tears: / My sky is overcast; / I live with dreams of other years, / And memories of the past." She yearns in the final verse for the presence of "Madeline," who, one suspects, is identified in her mind with her mother.[42]

In 1849, when Eleanor Lee was thirty years old, she died of yellow fever. Yet her influence or at least her memory inspired the first novel that Catherine Ann Warfield published, in 1860.[43] She titled it *The Household of Bouverie; Or the Elixir of Gold*, a two-volume, 783-page gothic romance. The inspiration came in part from Beckford's extravagant fantasy, *Vathek*. Warfield domesticated the plot, however, and in so doing probably took a Brontëan rather than a purely gothic approach. The difference has been explained by Sandra Gilbert and Susan Gubar. They discern in the mid-Victorian novel an implicit but ambivalent protest against the stifling of female identity even as it upheld the current Victorian emphasis on female duty.[44]

The story in *The Household of Bouverie* reveals much about Warfield's conflicting feelings toward her father. Adrienne Rich, the twentieth-century feminist poet, has observed, "It is a painful fact that a nurturing father, who replaces rather than complements a mother, *must be loved at the mother's expense*, whatever the reasons for the mother's absence."[45] Hardly surprisingly, with only one reliable parent upon whom to depend, the young intellectuals sought to please their father. They did so by demonstrating their gifts at such a womanly enterprise as versifying. Lacking a son upon whom to bestow his patrimony and attention, Major Ware tutored the girls himself, read and corrected their creative efforts, and at his own initiative and expense, published their first book of poetry.

Unlike Adrienne Rich, the Ware daughters had no institutional or cultural means to come to terms with their father. Overwhelmed by gratitude for all the wealth and education that he had given them, how could they have challenged the patriarchal order? How could they have found a fully authentic voice of their own? So few in any age find that mastery; among women writers, only geniuses like George Eliot and the Brontës succeeded. Though superbly educated at home and abroad (both of the Ware sisters spoke fluent French), they let themselves be entirely shaped by the cultural order around them. Nor had they any consciousness of a need to find their own singularity, to question, to rebel. Following the deaths of her sister in 1849 and her father in 1853, Catherine Ann gave up writing out of despondency. In the late 1850s, however, with her six children raised, she, like Walker Percy, turned to fiction in middle age to resolve her relationship to her father and to the family's history.

Indeed, in her major novels, *The Household of Bouverie, Ferne Fleming, The Cardinal's Daughter, Miriam Montfort,* and *The Romance of Beauseincourt,* the main action concerns the troubled bond of a young heroine to her father or father-figure—formidable, patriarchal, and often sinister. Although conventional within the romantic genre, this paradigm so often repeated suggests that it served what literary critic Norman Holland has called an "identity theme," affording unity to her novels. Perhaps Warfield herself recognized the relation of life and art when she wrote feelingly of an admiration for Mrs. Gaskell's biography of Charlotte Brontë: "that tragic and strange biography . . . once in a season of deep despondency did more to reconcile me to my own condition, through my pity and admiration for another, than all the condolences that came so freely from lip and pen." For Holland, the literary process often involves what Alan Roland calls "a defensive transformation of unconscious impulses and fantasies" from the various levels of one's experiences, going back to the earliest of them all.[46]

The story of *The Household of Bouverie* (published in 1860) concerns the plight of Lilian de Courcy, orphaned at the age of thirteen. Henry James once claimed to weary of those "precocious little girls" who populated so many sentimental novels of that era.[47] But, whether Warfield intended it or not, Lilian was almost a perfect stereotype to explore father-daughter relations with little attempt at creating a developed figure. Lilian comes to live with her grandmother, Camilla Bouverie, and her collection of eccentric retainers in a decaying plantation mansion vaguely located in an isolated section of a border slave state. Although she has little of the rebelliousness of Brontë's Jane Eyre, Lilian shows enough vigor and curiosity to discover that Erastus Bouverie, Lilian's grandfather, long supposed dead, is secretly living on the second floor (site of her mother Sarah's habitat). No visible access existed but only a secret entry. The original stairs were removed after Bouverie's alleged demise. In his well-appointed hideout, the mad plantation squire conducts alchemical experiments with an elixir that requires measures of human blood and gold. The potion, the Byronic figure claims, is the source of eternal youth. Too proud to submit himself to God, Bouverie anticipates earthly glory and fame for his discoveries.

Instead of a "madwoman in the attic," as in Brontë's *Jane Eyre*, Catherine Ann Warfield has placed a mad grandfather there. Moreover, just as Rochester's hidden wife Bertha Antoinette in crazed fury bites her brother Richard Mason on the chest to suck the blood and "drain" his very heart,[48] so, too, Erastus Bouverie tries to show his power in the drinking of his granddaughter's blood. In portraying the violence of these figures, the authors sought to put into melodramatic form the problem of insanity and its hideous effect upon the sane—something of which Warfield knew firsthand. Neither Brontë's Rochester nor Warfield's Camilla Bouverie had any means of escape from the burden of their marriages. In his own life, as his daughter knew, Major Ware had found that very situation so embittering, so enslaving. In their reading of *Jane Eyre*, Gilbert and Gubar have underestimated the peril that Victorians dreaded: marriage to a partner who might be the very opposite of outward appearance—mad, despicable, weak, or roguish. Brontë dealt with the issue from the perspective of the male victim; Warfield approached it from that of an abused but also resentful wife, no less honorable, no less bound to duty than was Brontë's Rochester. These parallels by no means suggest that Warfield's art was as fully realized as the English novelist's. After all, Brontë's experiences—tragic as they were—were so much more maturing and richer than Warfield's. Charlotte Brontë was the motherless daughter of a poor clergyman who lived, said one of her closest friends, "in a walking nightmare of poverty and self-suppression."[49] In contrast, Catherine Ann Warfield was rich and well-favored throughout her life. Yet both were dealing with issues of which they had personal, immediate knowledge, not just fancies drawn solely from the ample storehouse of romantic tales.

As in all gothic stories, the plot of *The Household of Bouverie* is chaotic to the point of suspenseful incoherence, but two major themes emerge. First, the author casts the worst possible light on the unequal distribution of power in contemporary marriage. Bouverie, the persistent reader learns, has murdered Camilla's first suitor, poisoned her canary and pet dog, spirited away their baby daughter (Lilian's mother) to England and staged a false funeral to deceive his wife, rendered Camilla's later adopted two-year-old boy Jason mute with jolts of electricity from a galvanic battery, tried to blind Camilla herself by the same means, and finally murdered Camilla's second husband whom she had married only because she was under the impression that Bouverie had died on a lengthy diplomatic mission to Russia. Throughout these tribulations, like Susan Warner's Ellen

Montgomery and hundreds of other Victorian heroines, Camilla remains the dutiful wife and successfully fulfills the admonition that "though we *must* sorrow, we must not rebel."[50] She even conspires for ten years to keep her husband Bouverie safe from the law prior to Lilian de Courcy's arrival.

The power of Catherine Ann Warfield's novel is chiefly derived from the author's total engagement in the story. Probably Warfield herself was not fully conscious of what her romance meant. But the anger in it is unmistakable. The forlorn triangle of mad (grand)father, unhappy, essentially neurotic (grand)mother, and teenage (grand)daughter replicated the essential mood of her own family life. How hard it must have been to realize that one's own mother had been too mentally incapacitated to recognize her husband or her children but lived instead in an unhappy world apart. With regard to modern women poets, Diane Hume George points out that the female writer, as she ages, must come to terms with the mother, a task of retrospection more complex than that of dealing with feelings toward the father.[51] So it was in Catherine Ann Warfield's case. Aging herself, and in delicate health, she did not launch her career as a novelist until the last twenty years of her life. In her imagination, she has Lilian de Courcy try desperately to create a believable and affectionate mother out of the hysterical, austere, and sometimes cold-hearted Camilla. To that end, Lilian seeks to bring her adoptive parents together, to create the happy space in which she could mature to adulthood. The couple's estrangement was far too deep—in fiction as in life—for Lilian or the Ware sisters ever to have succeeded. As a result, only in very old age do Erastus Bouverie and his wife reach some rapport. By then, it is too late to have been much help to their young charge. One suspects that Catherine Ann never did quite overcome her sense of loss and angry grief over her mother's illness, so that in her subsequent novels, she repeated themes rather than found new territories of the mind to conquer.

The second theme concerns the issue of depression. The strength of the novel also owes much to the author's almost detached, even clinical approach to madness and to its milder forms of unarticulated black mood. Catherine Ann knew whereof she wrote. She recognized its terrors in herself and in her demented mother, in the restless, morose, and cold-mannered father, Major Ware, in the family stories about Charles Percy's paranoic seizures, and in the "eclipse of reason" that had afflicted her half sister, Mary Jane Ellis LaRoche.[52] She wrote two quatrains after Mary Jane's death following a decade of lunacy. In the last lines, Warfield concluded, how cruel it would be to return her to life; instead the poet would "for thy precious sake—and with tears most bitter—forbid thee to wake."[53]

Her psychological rendering of the main character in *The Household of Bouverie* is logically consistent with what we know of bipolar or manic-depression. Bouverie experiences swift mood shifts in which the "highs," so to speak, feed his sense of omnipotence, and he becomes ruthless, later falling back into remorse and lethargy. The novelist has Erastus Bouverie assume three intermingled roles: a stern patriarch in his self-confined household kingdom; a shrewd masculine manipulator who seduces his disillusioned but still half-mesmerized wife Camilla as well as the beautiful Lilian (from the latter he wins a cup of youthful blood to drink with his gold-laced potion, a Victorian, gothic allusion, of course, to sexual intercourse—incestuous in this case); and an irresponsible child of both wife and granddaughter, playing with his grownup toys—the battery and the elixir—until he accidentally blows up the house and must escape from the attic to a nearby cave (yet another womb). In fact, Camilla's unloving loyalty to Bouverie imprisons him in his guilt just as surely as does his constant fear of exposure and public humiliation for his crimes.

Warfield does not simply report these exotic goings-on; she provides the psychological context as well in a way that may reflect the influence on her writing of Edgar Allan Poe, another Southern victim of depression and student of the interior life. (In reading *The Household of Bouverie*, one is reminded of the hints of incest and the claustrophobic mood of Poe in "The Fall of the House of Usher.") Bouverie, it turns out, was a child abused by Ursus (The Bear) Bouverie, his guardian uncle and rapacious African slave trader, who was based, in part, one suspects, upon the roguish, brutal Charles Percy. Ursus so severely damaged Bouverie's self-confidence that he was unable to learn how to love and was subjected to the numbing feelings of melancholy. Possession, not love, dominates Erastus Bouverie's life; the transference of desire to alchemy and electrical experimentation as a way to gain control of the sore-tried women reveals his inner emptiness. Bouverie hides behind a façade of male power even as he cowers in his hidden sanctuary, completely dependent upon the reluctant loyalty of a wife whose love for him had disappeared years before.

At this point, questions of authorial intent arise because the extravagances of the gothic mode lend themselves to an overly psychoanalytic interpretation. To be sure, Catherine Ann Warfield displayed no signs of emotional and sexual immaturity. If she seethed with an implacable rage against men, her novels do not prove the matter one way or the other. The gothic genre was itself a representation of such feelings but not in any genuinely polemical or outrageous way. That was their appeal. Gothic fiction articulated the unvoiced desires and fears of their writers and readers. Needless to say, the artists were themselves not necessarily neurotic but only aware of such tendencies in themselves and those they knew. Authors like Warfield and Charlotte Brontë found writing to be not exclusively a venting of unmanageable passions but also a means to greater self-understanding and self-identity—as authors enjoying the power derived from building a popular readership. Nonetheless, unquestionably Erastus Bouverie is a refraction of Warfield's grandfather Charles, who had drowned himself long before, and even more clearly of her father, whose irreligion, frosty intellectuality, and interest in science, was shared by the antihero Bouverie. Warfield's bitterness over the abandonment and desolation she felt in her youth found expression in the creation of this memorable figure.[54]

The Household of Bouverie, however, is interesting not only from a psychological perspective but also because of its curious parallel with Walker Percy's *Lancelot*, the story of Lance Lamar, another dark, honor-conscious, scientifically minded, Southern antihero, part child, lover, and patriarch. Lamar, like Bouverie, is locked away in his mad narcissism and melancholia for having killed out of the same kind of sexual jealousy, insecurity, cruelty, and indifference to others, even to his own offspring, that prompted Bouverie's odd but psychologically consistent compulsions. Like Bouverie, Lamar, stricken with depression, does not know who he is and cannot feel, so numbing is his depression and lovelessness of himself and others.[55]

Walker Percy gives us solely the male perspective of the problem of depression, profound and strangely moving though it is. Margot, Lance Lamar's adulterous wife, seems a necessary but not wholly realized figure. Likewise, Warfield's Camilla is rather one-dimensional. Yet Bouverie's long-suffering wife represents attitudes that interestingly contrast with the masculine sensibility which is Warfield's chief moral target. Camilla's devotion to marital duty is so extreme that Warfield risks verisimilitude by stressing the point. In a rare moment of exasperation, Camilla tells her granddaughter, "There are times when a rebellion takes place in our own nature against . . . shallow despotism . . . every drop of my blood . . . cries out within me for peace . . . for a new order of things, a fresher life, a nobler influence!"[56]

Quickly, Catherine Ann Warfield separates herself from her character's momentary lapse of faith and editorializes that the web of Victorian marriage and family cannot be broken without disaster. Wives should "yield" to the "inevitable" and "go down with the boat . . . to the bottom of the deep, rather than stand alone on the gray rock of selfish isolation. . . . The community of suffering is a terrible but established law," the author warns.[57] As a female writer, Warfield sought to affirm the primacy of female connection over male standards of law and power. Freud once pointed out that women "show less sense of justice than men, that they are less ready to submit to the great exigencies of life, that they are more often influenced in their judgement by feelings of affection or hostility."[58] The great psychoanalyst saw it as a problem, but really it was not.

The point is not to defend such opinions. Rather, one should urge that for conservative women of the nineteenth century, a particular female identity was required because of the prevailing cultural sanctions. That model established virtues thought peculiar to femininity: an expansive motherliness, devotion to domestic duty, and a sense of eternal bonding that should outweigh considerations of abstract justice.[59] Thus, women—at least those contemporaneous with Warfield—sought to "define themselves in a context of human relationship" and "judge themselves in terms of their ability to care," as Carol Gilligan puts it.[60] We find these motives disheartening, sentimental, and antifeminist. Indeed, Northern female reformers like Elizabeth Cady Stanton proclaimed that "self-development" was a greater goal than "self-sacrifice"—Camilla's ideal. So it may well be, but women like Catherine Ann Warfield scarcely resembled Margaret Mitchell's Melanie Wilkes. Like Walker Percy, Warfield had little use for the reforms of her time. Nonetheless, her response was intelligent, although even in her own lifetime such views were somewhat dated, at least by contemporary Northern standards.

Like so many gothic romances, even *Jane Eyre*, Warfield's story proposes the virtue of fidelity and nurture for a sick antihero whom modern readers would find undeserving.[61] It celebrates the feminine code of attachment, family bond, and marital obedience. Warfield argues that the virtuous woman can only find herself by being true to her psychological nature, a different and higher standard than that proposed for the male domain of ambition, law, and retribution. Indeed, why should there be "justice" in an allegory about the spiritual sickness and hopeless narcissism of a man's interior life and the sacrifice of a woman who lives up to the moral demands of her nature and sex? Fractured relationships rather than breaches of law, Warfield implies, are the greater tragedies of life; isolation is more to be feared than even the dangers of living with a madman.[62]

Warfield's eight other novels, written after the Civil War, show, however, a timidly growing appreciation of a different style for women to follow. In them, feminine integrity is less tied to social and moral constraints, and some modest degree of autonomy finds expression. Published in 1867, *The Romance of Beauseincourt* reveals that the heroine Miriam Montfort, a Jewish woman of considerable independence of mind, becomes a governess on Colonel Prosper La Vigne's plantation near Savannah.[63] Apparently, Warfield fashioned the story from a tantalizingly undisclosed incident that occurred during a childhood visit to her father's Florida estates near Appalachicola.[64] There, Miriam discovers the inadequacies of the patriarchal order. The reactionary colonel's wife is portrayed as "the constant, self-sacrificing wife," who explains that following "a lifetime of submission, first to my father, next to my husband, I could not commence" a domestic "revolution." After witnessing the colonel's drunken incompetence, the self-employed Miriam recognizes that the result will be a future filled with "sorrow and poverty." In fact, drawing on the old memory from the Florida tragedy, she has the colonel die in a swamp, his eyes plucked out by vultures.[65]

Nor was Warfield uncritical of plantation life. She has her heroine declare, "To vegetate on a Southern plantation, and year by year feel the shackles of prejudice and circumstance more closely confirmed by necessity, did not seem to me the most desirable of conditions, 'noblesse oblige' notwithstanding." Such a life, Miriam continues, was surrounded by "the shadow of mediocrity, self-conceit and dissipation. For me there was no prestige in the mere name of planter."[66] Although an ardent Confederate and an unusually firm supporter of slavery and conservative tradition, Catherine Ann Warfield was no Louisa McCord, the South Carolina intellectual who found very little amiss south of the Potomac. In fact, Warfield had some harsh things to say about plantation management. When Colonel La Vigne gives out the Christmas rations of tobacco, whiskey, fireworks, and other favors, he receives the usual "Thankee, Master, thankee" from the hands. But when a chained bear gets loose and mauls the old reprobate, the field hands stand by and passively watch, before the white observers rescue him.[67] To be sure, these are exceptional passages in the midst of the customary glorification of Southern mores. However, she sets the good qualities against what she calls the "petty vanities and social narrowness" of Southern rural life.[68]

In her most popular postwar novels, *Ferne Fleming* and its sequel *The Cardinal's Daughter*, Warfield created one rather memorable character. Warfield seemed to have turned her attention to the marginality of the kinless, plain-looking but sturdy woman about whom Charlotte Brontë wrote so effectively. Marian Dormer, the heroine's sometime confidante, eventually marries Ferne Fleming's wealthy uncle, much to the family's distress. She is an aggressive woman who speaks her mind. She confesses to Ferne at one point that in her teens, she had married her first husband simply to survive. He was twenty years her senior, an invalid but wealthy— " 'Mediocre women can never choose their fortunes: they must meekly accept them.' "[69] Yet unlike Brontë who sympathizes with her struggling, solitary women, Warfield did not altogether countenance Mrs. Dormer's plainspoken determination. After her last, much deplored match to the well-to-do widower, the character disappears from the narrative.

In one of her last composed works, *Hester Howard's Temptation* (1875), Warfield proved more adventurous still—up to a point.[70] For the first time, she created a spirited heroine who, unlike Camilla Bouverie, deserts her self-serving husband and goes on the stage. But it was all too daring. Warfield has Hester Howard give up the professional career of an actress to return to a Southern plantation inheritance, periodically bedeviled, like Camilla Bouverie, by her unreliable mate. After her husband's fortuitous death from drink and her escape from a feverish, over-repressed lawyer named Mulgrave, Hester unites with a former physician, Confederate blockade-runner, and all-around hero, who turns out to have inherited an English barony. Despite such predictable plots and characters throughout these later works, Warfield denounces men who, eager to put matters straight, "think housework a cure-all" for "weary, broken-spirited" women under the yoke of misfortune and bad husbands.[71]

Such matters as these, needless to say, have not concerned the two male Percy writers of the twentieth century. Neither Will Percy in his poetry and memoir nor Walker Percy in his brilliant novels have been much concerned with the role of women *per se*. To be sure, Walker Percy has had very wise but rather critical things to say about "the lovely, little bitty steel-hearted women" who carried the burden of war at home and "sat in their rocking chairs, and made everybody do right; they were enough to scare you to death."[72] Nonetheless, with such notable exceptions as Rita and Valerie Vaught, his women are not as complex characters as are Binx Bolling, Tom More, Will Barrett, and Lance Lamar. Whether an artistic weakness or not, Percy concentrates on his male creations and their struggles in a modern world of commercial artificiality and spiritual emptiness.

The point at which the nineteenth- and twentieth-century authors come together is in their relation to the family's psychological history. In this respect, all of them made use of family materials, not only for the sake of art but also for some hidden satisfaction of their own. But curiously enough, the third female Percy artist, Sarah Ann Ellis Dorsey, delved most deeply and candidly into the family's "lumber-room" of whispered troubles. Although gifted as a painter in oils, Sarah Dorsey, too, undertook a literary vocation, undoubtedly inspired by her aunts but also by Eliza Ann DuPuy, her governess whom we have suggested may have also stirred the literary ambitions of Sarah's aunts Catherine Ann and Eleanor. Like them, she developed a gothic strain, albeit much less bloodthirsty than Eleanor Lee's narrative poems and Catherine Ann Warfield's romances.

Sarah Dorsey faced losses, too. Her father, Thomas George Ellis, had married Mary Routh, a woman of great plantation wealth in Natchez, but he also devoted himself to the care of his mother who, after release from the Pennsylvania Hospital, lived at his plantation "Woodlawn," near ancestor Charles Percy's "Northumberland House." Sarah remembered her grandmother, for whom she was named, and her sad peculiarities. Within a year or so of her grandmother's death, Sarah's father also died at the age of thirty-four. Her mother then married Charles Dahlgren, a wealthy factor, warehouse owner, and engineer, who built "Dunleith" in Natchez as his mansion, a showcase of Southern splendor on the annual spring tour.

Raised on literature, music, and art in as sophisticated a manner as that afforded her aunts, Sarah Ann Ellis Dorsey wrote her first novel during the early part of the Civil War. *Agnes Graham* is much more explicit about the family predisposition toward depression than the work of Catherine Ann Warfield. The story concerns a young couple who are cousins. The pair is much in love until an aunt informs Agnes that she and Robert Selman had a common grandmother whose insanity was intimately related to the suicide of the grandmother's father. He had been an English army officer of noble lineage who had drowned himself after beginning a family with his wealthy Louisiana wife. The sudden news brings on the obligatory attack of brain fever to which Victorian heroines were peculiarly subject. Agnes recovers, but only because, by her lights, she has promised God never to marry her cousin Robert and thus perpetuate the family curse.

The incest of such a fictional union between Agnes Graham and Robert Selman by no means bothered the novelist. Close cousinly marriages were scarcely condemned in the Old South, where family connections were as thick and tangled as the forest underbrush along the banks of the Homochitto. Disappointed in love, Robert disappears into a life of dissipation, but Agnes fends off a fortune-hunting villain during a European tour—until she marries an elderly family friend to whom she is kind but not emotionally attached. (Like her aunts, Sarah Ann Ellis Dorsey had married a pleasant but much senior planter of impeccable Chesapeake credentials.) Upon his death, Agnes converts to High Anglicanism, only a short step away from Rome. With her sizable fortune, her heroine, Agnes, who, like Sarah Dorsey herself dreamed of such a plan, endows a hospital for the poor of New Orleans, becomes an archdeaconess, and heads an order of nuns of the Episcopal Church who run it. Robert reappears quite suddenly, just as Agnes is recovering from a heart attack. His abrupt appearance throws her into a fatal relapse. She dies happy but chaste and true to her pledge of duty over love. In real life, Sarah Dorsey is best known for having befriended Jefferson Davis in the years following the Civil War.

Despite the convenient endings of *Agnes Graham* and her other novels, Sarah Dorsey wrote in a firm, plain style which had its own realistic merits for pointed social comment, a skill that Eleanor and Catherine Ann never developed. In *Panola*, for instance, Dorsey rather anticipates Kate Chopin with some spirited portraits of Southern vulgarity in her dissection of Louisiana upper-class society. Equally realistic was her fictional rendering of Charles Percy's suicide (in the guise of one Philip St. George Davenant) in *Agnes Graham*. In handling the problem of genetic insanity, her character, Robert Selman, who had studied medicine, takes a modern point of view. Hoping in vain to marry Agnes Graham, he challenges his cousin's fears of divine retribution and Calvinistic notions of "fatality" by saying, "the sins of the fathers are visited upon the children of the fourth generation. I know it is so physically; my medical experience tells me that; and why not morally?"[73] The novelist well demonstrated the concern that the Percy women had in that generation about the fate of the family.

Nor were they exaggerating the problem. In 1879, three years after Sarah Dorsey died of cancer at the age of fifty, her second cousin, Dr. LeRoy Pope Percy of Greenville, Mississippi, so paralyzed by depression that he never ventured to practice his calling, killed himself with an overdose of laudanum the day before a favorite niece died from medical complications for which he, most irrationally, felt responsible.[74] In 1888, Confederate veteran William Alexander Percy, the suicide's brother, died at age fifty-three from chronic overwork, often considered today a sign of what is called "masked depression." That same Colonel Percy's son Walker, a brilliant Birmingham, Alabama, lawyer shot himself in 1917 at the age of forty-seven with an English Greener. As noted earlier, LeRoy Pratt Percy (the son of Walker Percy, Sr.), also a distinguished lawyer of Birmingham, used the same kind of weapon on himself twelve years later in 1929. He was the novelist Walker Percy's father.[75] One should remember that the decision to kill oneself comes neither from frailty nor impulse. Arguing from personal experience, the Southern novelist William Styron reminds us that sufferers of acute depression "are in the grip of an illness that causes almost unimaginable pain." Neither cowardice nor immeasurable losses are involved but rather "blind necessity," the salvation, as it were, of total naughtness.[76] Styron's characterization fits well the situation in the Percy line; all the suicides were men of remarkable dynamism and bravery, perhaps to the point of recklessness.

In coping with the problem of genetic depression, the three Victorian Percy women writers all turned to the most structured and authoritarian forms of Christianity available as the source of redemption. Eleanor Percy Lee became a Catholic under the auspices of Bishop John Chanche of Natchez. Catherine Ann Warfield presented her sister's confidante as Bishop Clare, advisor to Camilla Bouverie. Throughout *The Household of Bouverie* and her other novels, Warfield made her own attraction to Catholicism obvious, though she never formally converted to that faith. Likewise, Sarah Ann Ellis Dorsey devoted herself to the practices of High Church Episcopalianism, the American version of the Anglican Oxford movement.[77] We should remember that Will Percy had been raised in the Catholic faith, and though he rejected it in favor of Aurelian stoicism as his ethical guide, he may have planted the seed that his adopted son Walker Percy was to cultivate in himself. Following his marriage at the end of the Second World War, Walker Percy and his wife joined the church, and he remains one of the leading Catholic authors in the nation.[78]

Religious experience can take so many forms, creeds, and sects that clearly more than coincidence was involved in drawing the Percys toward the magnet of Rome. Nor was it an accident that of all the Christian denominations, the Catholic faith is the most hostile to the taking of one's own life. To gain some insight, one may best turn to Charlotte Brontë, whose gifts far outshone those of the Percy women. In Brontë's brilliant novel *Villette* (1853), Lucy Snow suffers from unremitting depression. Her mother had died; her father had abandoned her without offering much explanation for his departure. These were familiar events in the life of all three of the Percy women. Similar tragic losses had struck Charlotte Brontë herself. The early death of her mother was later compounded by the desolation and grief that came with the deaths of her sisters and brother. At one point, Brontë has Lucy Snow attend confession in hope of some emotional relief. A surprised but understanding Catholic priest declares: "You were made for our faith: depend upon it our faith alone could heal and help you—Protestantism is altogether too dry, cold, prosaic for you."[79] Even though Charlotte Brontë makes clear in the novel her own deep suspicions of the Catholic Church, her words provide us with an understanding of its appeal to the suffering depressive. Dryness, coldness of death, one recalls, were the conditions associated with black bile or melancholy, one of the four antique Galenic humors.

For all three Percy women, and perhaps for Walker Percy, the Catholic Church, though patriarchal, personified the feminine in the worship of Mary. In Brontë's *Villette*, Lucy Snow finds the rule of masculine Reason "vindictive as the devil. . . . Often has Reason turned me out by night . . . and harshly denied my right to ask better things." But a different voice beckons her away from the despair that austere rationality exacted. She calls that countering force "this daughter of Heaven" with powers "divine, compassionate, succourable. . . ." The nurturing spirit, Lucy Snow says, "saw me weep and she came with comfort: 'Sleep sweetly—I gild thy dreams!' "[80] In Catholic terms, that spirit materialized in the form of the mother of mankind—the mother that Catherine Ann and Eleanor had known and loved and yet not known at all.

Yet, attracted though Catherine Ann Warfield was to the faith that had captured her beloved sister Eleanor, she, like Charlotte Brontë, held deep prejudices against it. In her books *Ferne Fleming* and *The Cardinal's Daughter*, she has a Southern planter abruptly leaving his wife to join the Roman priesthood and finally receiving the cardinal's hat from Pio Nono himself. Once again, Warfield seems in search of a father. Taciturn, book-minded, Ferne's father, who calls himself Salvano, never explains his decision to take up holy orders, never acknowledges the pain and bitterness he caused his wife or the vacancy he left in his daughter's upbringing. In some ways, Salvano is another Bouverie, although only fanatical, not mad. Yet the portrait is not altogether dark. The novelist, through her heroine, Ferne, admires the intellectuality and even the formality of the Catholic father; at the end, Salvano gives his hearty blessing to her marriage, the customary close to romance.

Despite her religious misgivings, Catherine Ann Warfield, like the other Percys, recognized that order, structure, hierarchy, and a moral imperative that could challenge depression and offer hope in this life and the next were to be found within the Catholic realm. Such was the faith of the Percy lineage. And such was their grand creative record. Wealth, fame, and power were theirs but so was a somber dark heritage, which both the daughters and the sons tried to conquer through the alchemy of art, an elixir of gold, indeed, with its own form of immortality.

12

The Political Economy
of Sharecropping Families:
Blacks and Poor Whites in
The Rural South, 1865–1915

JACQUELINE JONES

ANTEBELLUM SLAVEHOLDERS liked to boast that cotton was the perfect crop because it could not be eaten by the people who grew it. But the "New South" of the 1870s offered up a different lesson to William Holtzclaw, the son of black sharecroppers in Alabama. Later in life, Holtzclaw recalled his bewilderment each December upon hearing his family's employer tell them that they had already "eaten" their share of the cotton they had produced that year. The white landowner meant that the "furnishings" he advanced to the household—food, clothes, and supplies purchased on credit—had consumed any cash they might otherwise have received from the sale of the crop. Yet these advances routinely ceased between July and September, the late summer slack season. As a result, in Holtzclaw's words, "All the rest of the time we had to find something to do away from the plantation in order to keep supplied with bread and clothes, which were scanty enough."[1] In the late nineteenth-century rural South, a perverse relationship seemed to exist between the richness of the soil and the well-being of its tillers; a bountiful cotton crop, nevertheless, left Black-Belt families hungry and impoverished.

For the Holtzclaw household, survival depended on the efforts of every member, young and old, male and female, to grow cotton, earn wages, and forage for food. Holtzclaw's mother "cooked for the 'white folks,' " a job that at times kept her away from her own home overnight. Together, the children spent hours in the nearby swamps and marshes, "wading in the slush" above their knees in search of the tasty hog potato, which, together with the persimmons, nuts, berries, and muscadines they managed to scrounge up, kept "body and soul together during those dark days." Holtzclaw's father, "to keep the wolf from the door," along with poor white men from the area, hauled logs at a nearby sawmill for sixty cents a day until the mill moved out of the neighborhood in search of fresh timber. Then, he left the family behind for a year and found a job working on a railroad fifty miles from his family, returning home every three months (a journey that consumed two weeks) to deliver the proceeds of his labor, forty to fifty dollars to their landlord; all of it went to pay for the "furnishings" used by the household in his absence. As a ten year old, William split two thousand rails one fall to pay for his own clothes. That same year, he hired out to work for a white man and became "morose [and] disheartened" by the abrupt termination of his schooling.[2]

In 1880, Holtzclaw's father realized that the family would never advance by farming on shares and decided to rent a forty-acre farm; "He bought a mule, a horse, and a yoke of oxen, and so we started out for ourselves." The children were ecstatic; "we were so happy at the prospects of owning a wagon and a pair of mules and having only our father for boss that we shouted and leaped for joy." But misfortune wore many faces—that of a mule, suffering from a "peculiar" ailment that kept it from getting on its feet in the morning; an ox, its neck broken from a farm accident; and a horse, "so poor and thin that he could not plow." The father suffered a crippling accident when he stepped on a stub of cane in the field one day, and then their "splendid" crop of corn, gathered by the other family members and carefully piled in heaps, washed away after a storm. It was this last blow "from which we were never wholly able to recover." His father, by this time recovered, took a job off the farm. Still, after four years, the family's struggles had yielded only a monstrous debt which prompted creditors to "clean them out"—"they came and took our corn and, finally, the vegetables from our little garden as well as the chickens and the pig." At the end of the year, the Holtzclaws "applied to a white man for a home on his place—a home under the old system," and the father was never able again to lift himself out of the status of sharecropper.[3]

The story of William Holtzclaw is an extraordinary one, because he went on to graduate from Tuskegee Institute and soon after, in Mississippi, founded a school on the same principles of vocational education—the Utica Normal and Industrial Institute. However, viewed as part of the history of the South's rural poor during the latter part of the nineteenth century, the story of the Holtzclaw family was all too ordinary. In the course of a year, black and white fathers routinely alternated between work in the cotton fields and wage work in the nearby rural nonagricultural sector. Mothers performed child care and other homemaking chores, labored in the cotton crop according to seasonal dictates, and managed the farm in their husbands' absence. Over their life histories, these families could represent a peculiar blend of resourcefulness and fatalism; in any case, their relatively modest ambitions—"the prospects of owning a wagon and a pair of mules and having only our father for boss"—bespoke the circumscribed nature of upward social mobility in the rural South.

While the Holtzclaw family conformed to general patterns of life among the landless of both races, they also faced liabilities that set them apart from their poorest white neighbors. From the end of the Civil War until the collapse of the sharecropping system in the 1930s, blacks predominated in the lowest categories of agricultural labor—wage hands and sharecroppers. (In 1920, 80 percent of all black farmers were landless, about one-half of them sharecroppers, and black croppers outnumbered their white counterparts in absolute numbers by three to two. On the other hand, 40 percent of all white farmers in the South worked someone else's land, but three-quarters of those families occupied the higher status of tenant and had more control over their own productive energies compared to sharecroppers.)[4] For the most part, these households remained confined to a rather narrow geographical area and "shifted" from one plantation to another without appreciable change in their material condition. They lacked opportunities (comparable to those of whites) to travel throughout the South and seek work elsewhere, especially in the new textile mills that dotted the Piedmont landscape. Segregated in inferior schools and on the bottom rungs of the agricultural tenure ladder, black people confronted a racial caste system that thwarted the "big eyes and high hopes"[5] of the most efficient and talented farming families.

White southerners, no matter how poor, continued to hold specific advantages over the mass of blacks in day-to-day dealings with landlords. In areas with workers of both races, planters often hired as many black sharecroppers as they could (under the least favorable terms for those workers as possible) and only then began to make concessions to whites—offering them tenancies or renters' contracts, for example. In the upcountry, some landless whites toiled on the holdings of their kinfolk, preserving family bonds in the midst of transformations in class relations; in contrast, whatever blood ties black employees might have shared with white landowners (through common paternal ancestors) were, of course, never acknowledged in any formal or informal way. And finally, white husbands and sons who sought gainful employment along the byways of the rural South, in turpentine camps or sawmills, could travel in search of work free of the fear that they would be arrested and convicted of vagrancy and then "sold" to the highest convict-lease bidder—in Meriweather, Georgia, for instance, on the block "after the style in vogue before the war."[6] In the late 1870s, the dramatic rise in the number of black prisoners held in southern jails offered eloquent testimony to the demise of Radical Reconstruction and the effects of a regional depression that threw male agricultural workers into the vicious embrace of chain-gang foremen. Thus, until well into the twentieth century, as members of the two races made their separate ways across the southern landscape, they passed black convicts with shovels and pick axes laying railroad tracks and repairing bridges, improving a transportation network that would facilitate the task at hand for "Judge Lynch" and his minions.

The passage of time meant very little to people who owned nothing; despite transformations in the South's staple-crop economy between 1865 and 1915, years punctuated by severe depressions and radical agrarian protest, the material basis of the households of sharecroppers and tenants showed remarkable continuity. In their social organization and economic function, these families remained distinct from the Victorians (the northern upper and middle classes, and southern planters and urban elites) as well as the industrial working class. In the South, the rural poor abided by a family system of labor, in contrast to the individualism implicit in urban economies. They lacked also the cash to participate in the burgeoning consumerism that shaped the household and leisure-time spending patterns of the middle class and city folk all over the country. For people who stayed on the countryside over the life cycle of a family, or the course of generations, increases in well-being came in exceedingly small increments—a mother freed from field work for part of the year, a mule that lifted the household out of the cropper status and into tenancy, a cabin with screens in place of the old one infested with flies. Despite the persistently high demand for agricultural labor during this period, the crop lien system kept the poorest families indebted and on the move.

"Negroes rove from place to place," declared a Texas cotton planter in 1868. "They love change, and a month's work at a place, and are reluctant to make a year engagement."[7] Landowners throughout the former Confederate states seemed to agree that the slave as "fixed capital" had quickly degenerated into the wartime runaway and then to the freedman, with his family's confounding habits of "anxious locomotion."[8] The lament of the Texas planter, in particular, represented an emerging mythology, a portrait of the postbellum South blending fact with fiction and painted in the stark blacks and whites that defined the contemporary social landscape. He continued, "white people love home, take interest in making it pleasant, comfortable—as the spot from which issue all their money and comforts."[9] In his view, then, the slave South had yielded to a New South in which black households would continue to wander, forever "taking a mind to move," oblivious to the benefits of steady toil; while whites, regardless of class, would prosper through capital accumulation, the fruits of devotion to place.

Soon after Appomattox, in pockets of the South, the system of share-cropping emerged in response to a number of factors—the planters' lack of capital and their need for a year-round resident work force as well as the freedpeople's desire to work in family groups rather than neo-slavery gangs. When southern (and northern) white men issued a blanket condemnation of "roving" blacks, they had in mind specific offenders: husbands who deserted the cotton fields early in the afternoon to go fishing; the wife who cut short her work week to visit an ailing niece nearby; sons who earned a few dollars chopping wood off the plantation during the slack season; families that "drifted" down the road or into town after "reckoning time" in December; and whole kin groups that migrated hundreds of miles so that their members could piece together a living, no matter how precarious, from jobs less closely supervised by whites. An elastic unit of production, the sharecropping household responded to seasonal demands in cotton cultivation—the busiest times came in the spring with plowing and in the early fall with harvesting. Families often fragmented during the slack season, when fathers and older children sought out nearby wage work off the plantation. Planters counted on this arrangement to eliminate the *"irregularity and uncertainty of the system of labor"* characterized by freedpeople who "work when they please and do just as much as they please . . . and rely largely upon hunting and fishing for what they lose in the field."[10]

Conspicuous in their absence from the postwar debate over real and potential sources of field hands were the poorest whites of the South, men and women who had a history of "wandering" all their own. Members of the white elite, preachers of the South's old-time civil religion based on the supremacy of racial considerations and the irrelevance of class, only infrequently acknowledged their fears that "the elevation of the blacks will be the degradation of the whites."[11] Yet during the Reconstruction era, increasing numbers of white husbands and fathers found themselves competing with blacks, not for property but for the sharecropping contracts that promised families only a bitter life of transience. By the late nineteenth century, a large, dependent rural white proletariat would also lack the "money and comforts" associated with a settled home life.

Despite their loud lamentations about "irresponsible" black women and men and regardless of the shape of their individual longings for the past, southern ideologues could not reconcile the emergence of a large class of white agricultural laborers with their vision of the future. When postbellum southern writers praised the virtues of farm life, they did so with planters and sturdy, independent, white yeomen in mind; when they extolled the productive abilities of whites of the "lower classes," they did so with mill workers in mind.[12] Nevertheless, the process of postwar economic reconstruction drew increasing numbers of small white landowners into the commercial staple-crop economy; in need of loans to rebuild their homesteads after the devastation of war, these white families (especially in the Piedmont) found themselves beholden to bankers and lending agencies. A poor crop or drop in the price of cotton could strip them of their land and reduce them to tenantry.[13]

Changes wrought in household routine and organization by the growth of landlessness among whites varied according to specific groups. Men and women who before the war roamed the backwoods, herding cattle and squatting on someone else's land, found intensive crop cultivation a severe break with the past indeed.[14] It is difficult to know what percentage of this group became sharecroppers during Reconstruction, but certainly their traditional "habits" of restlessness might help to account for high rates of labor turnover among whites on postbellum plantations. Now reduced to the status of dependent workers, men who were formerly proud republican-minded farmers and respectable tenants also experienced a radically new kind of life; as tenants and sharecroppers, they labored for landlords who monitored their every move in the fields and deprived them of the power to make modest decisions affecting the work and welfare of their families. These men were obliged to put their wives and children in the fields chopping cotton and worming tobacco plants and to forego any kind of household industry that would have rendered their families independent of local store-keepers. The reduction in household agricultural production—the ears of corn replaced by cotton bolls, the vegetable patches prohibited by annual contracts, the hogs and cattle denied an open range for grazing—amounted to the most compelling symbol and potent cause of rural southerners' abject poverty in the late nineteenth century.[15]

By 1900, state and federal agricultural officials saw little reason to distinguish between the poor of the two races in condemning "shiftlessness." Based on his work at the state experiment station, a Georgia professor indicted both blacks and whites: "Few rise to the top to take advantage of opportunities and secure homes, but the large majority . . . are in the same condition that they have been for years past—that is, they live 'from hand to mouth' and are content at the end of the year to have a few dollars to spend for Christmas, and are willing to start out on a new year, and do so cheerfully, without having laid up a single dollar's worth of anything."[16] This statement ignored two crucial facts related to the family life of the rural poor. First, planters within a subregion colluded (albeit informally) to maintain a system of "localized labor" that prevented workers from accumulating much of anything, let alone a home. Second, these households demonstrated tremendous energy and initiative in exploiting wage-work opportunities, as well as their natural environment, to provide for themselves.

Referring to the tendency of blacks to take jobs off the plantation during the contract year, a planter observed in 1900, "Under our farming system the negroes catch at every little thing. . . . Under the tenant system he takes a good deal of time and has liberty to come and go as he pleases."

The white man added that the "disposition to get away from the farm to other employment" was shared by "both the white and colored" tenants.[17] Together, the rural poor caught at "every little thing" that a local economy might have to offer in terms of ready cash-making. Wages offered in the rural nonagricultural sector were on a par with farm wages; hence, fathers and sons traveled regularly between the two kinds of work, which often complemented each other on a seasonal basis.

The Mississippi Yazoo Delta, though characterized by a general lack of industry, offered jobs to blacks in cotton gins as crewmen and engineers (for from $1 to $1.50 per day) and on levees (at the same wage rates). A public-works project in the area might draw workers from a four-mile radius seeking the daily paydays that lasted until a levee was repaired or a road built. The availability of work in various extractive industries might inflate agricultural wages within a limited area; for example, lumbering and oil businesses helped to insure relatively higher compensation for workers in the rice belt of Louisiana compared to cotton croppers elsewhere in the South. A particularly poor crop in northern Alabama drove dependent farm laborers and their sons to the iron mines or the railroads, again during the slack season in both the summer and winter months. In the North Carolina Piedmont, white tobacco farmers routinely earned cash off their farms, by cutting lumber, repairing farm equipment for their neighbors, and working for the railroad.[18]

Such work was considered temporary; the young men who left the farms for the Birmingham mineral district "always come back. They go there and work a few months and generally drift back to the plantations."[19] In Virginia, small landowners cultivated their patches and supplemented their meager diets in the summer with tonging for oysters during cold weather (along the tidewater) or working in the small, diverse industries among the rolling hills of the predominantly agricultural counties inland for money to buy food. Until a disastrous hurricane demolished the phosphate mines along the South Carolina coast in 1893, Sea Island blacks depended on wage work in the mines for cash to buy clothes and pay taxes; thereafter, Georgia and Florida sawmills and turpentine camps and dock work in Savannah offered hope to breadwinners who "had to keep the family up during the cold months."[20] Though some young people used wage work off the plantation as a stepping-stone north, fathers often felt a strong obligation to return to the family fold and the duty of farming for planting and picking time.[21]

The heavy work associated with the construction, extractive, and processing industries favored the employment of able-bodied men. Nevertheless, other family members found ways to add to the household income in the course of the year. Wives earned "patch" money by marketing small surpluses of vegetables and dairy products. Black women took in laundry, served as midwives, and labored as domestic servants at times for their poor white neighbors as well as their landlords. Children of all ages helped their fathers cut firewood and fat pine to sell and hired themselves out as cotton pickers on nearby farms once they had fulfilled harvest-time duties at home. Local truck farms employed women and children to pick berries and vegetables during the slack season. And finally, country folk all over the South congregated on cotton plantations in the fall to earn some cash (usually between 75 cents and $1.50 per day). In Florence, South Carolina, a community with both tobacco and cotton farming, tobacco tenants could gather their own crop and then move down the road and find a job "while there is any cotton left to pick, sometimes even until Christmas."[22] Planters in Leflore County, Mississippi, annually paid white labor agents to bring "hill negroes" down to the Delta, where "Labor for picking is very hard to get indeed."[23] Some employers safeguarded themselves against the possibility that their own flowering cotton fields would turn to dust for want of pickers—people who failed to return home in the fall—by offering wage work at local, plantation-based enterprises during the off-season. Gristmills and sawmills, for example, paid cash wages over and above any share of the crop and served to hold labor to a particular plantation and insure sufficient hands for harvest.[24]

Foraging, including fishing and hunting, represented for many blacks and whites a subeconomy that might yield small amounts of cash and rescue families from complete dependence on merchants' stores and planters' advances. Most elite whites (and some blacks, like Booker T. Washington) condemned fishing and hunting as leisurely pursuits, more akin to recreation than productive labor; but for the black women of the Sand Hills district in Sumter County, South Carolina, "muddying" for eels or mullet and fishing in nearby creeks and rivers afforded a major source of sustenance. In contrast, their menfolk "went to nearby mills or into the forest to cut crossties for the railroad."[25] These households depended on the ability of "women and children [to] pick up a precarious living out of the assets of the community—fruit, fowls, game and fish."[26] Such pursuits often required considerable skill and physical exertion. The Sand Hills women who "muddied" the Wateree River "would hike their dresses up and wade in, taking up the fish in baskets or nets," certainly not a simple task for the uninitiated.[27] Seasoned fishermen of the Delta concocted elaborate recipes for bait and engaged in time-consuming preparations that paid off in large catches.[28] The young boys who, bleary-eyed, stumbled their way through thickets on moonlit possum hunts with their fathers would have disputed their employers' contention that hunting appealed to the "lazy" instincts of men of both races.[29]

The tendency of sharecroppers to move down the road to another plantation at the end of each year provoked a chorus of complaints from planters, government officials, and visitors to the South, all of whom lamented the failure of poor people to remain rooted in one place for very long. In 1874,

journalist Edwin DeLeon described the freedman as "restless and roving, . . . getting poorer and shabbier and sulkier at each remove instead of
bettering his condition. . . ." The latter-day children of the Old Testa-
ment's Reuben, blacks were "'made like unto a wheel,' ever rolling, never
resting, and never accumulating either money or realty."[30] A quarter of a
century later, a federal commission heard testimony from several southern
whites who described the "restless disposition" of blacks, leading one panel
member to cite the "natural shiftlessness of the negro . . . his carelessness,
and his transient condition, travelling from one spot to another, losing time
and opportunities."[31] Nevertheless, around this time such assessments had
become more generalized to take into account the growing numbers of
whites reduced to perpetual tenantry, "losing time and opportunities" after
their own fashion. By 1910, scholar-jeremiads could see the phenomenon
of annual plantation turnover as the root of "all social and religious problems" that plagued the rural South.[32]

Shifting occurred within such a small geographical area that many families managed to retain ties not only to kin and friends but also to local
churches, schools, and cultural institutions. Nevertheless, the seemingly
straightforward act of picking up one's family and furniture exacerbated
the hardships endured by poor households. A study of Mississippi workers
who moved from plantation to plantation concluded that "as the share
tenant was supplied not only with a house but with most of his furniture,
farm implements and stock, moving was a relatively simple operation, in
many cases consisting of loading all his household goods and family into a
one-horse wagon and moving to another farm without losing any time from
work."[33] And yet such moves often extracted considerable costs from families. For example, illness and childbirth at times coincided with the end-of-
year departure:

> Emergencies similar to the following were not unknown: A mother confined in
> January said that during the latter part of her pregnancy her husband was
> taken ill, and the family was obliged to move to make room for other tenants.
> The mother had to assume the whole burden of moving and settling in the new
> home. She cut enough wood to last throughout the period of her confinement,
> and when labor pains began she was building a hogpen.[34]

The passability of local roads and the endurance of a mule or ox, usually
borrowed, all shaped journeys that could range from family routines to
family ordeals.

The phenomenon of shifting, so baffling to historians and econometricians alike, merits detailed attention, for it reveals some of the sources of
fundamental estrangement between rural blacks and whites, despite apparent similarities in their material condition. These households exhibited a
high degree of geographical mobility[35] that gained them little in the way of
better housing and better contractual arrangements. In fact, the matrix of

motives that produced shifting—those of landlord and black and white employees, motives borne of desire and violence—had a complexity that went beyond mere financial considerations and ultimately reflected political issues that lay at the heart of the postbellum South's system of power and domination.

Both blacks and whites resisted the close supervision that was the sharecropper's lot in life. The former slaves sought to embrace a freedom that would set them apart from their forebears in bondage. Together in family groups, they institutionalized the annual practice of running away, though they could only deprive one particular white man (a current employer) of their labor and not planters in general. On the one hand, whites feared that they might become the South's first slaves with the same skin color as antebellum masters. On the other hand, the initiative for shifting often lay with an employer and not with the people he excoriated. A state agricultural commissioner put the balance of interests in perspective: "Sometimes you have a tenant on a place, and he finds he can do a little better somewhere else, and he moves off and goes to the next place. Sometimes the landlord finds that he can get a better tenant than the one he has. He lets this fellow go and gets the other fellow."[36] Thus, at times workers were forced off a plantation by an employer anxious to import hands more to his liking; but in other cases, the separate histories of blacks and whites converged in the form of annual shifting, a turnover that did in some respect conform to critics' charges that it represented movement "for its own sake," without apparent rational rhyme or economic reason.

In 1898, Alfred H. Stone, self-proclaimed agricultural reformer and race-relations expert, initiated a five-year experiment to achieve an "assured tenantry" on his expansive Delta plantation. With annual turnover rates ranging from 22 percent to 45 percent during the course of the experiment, Stone eventually pronounced the effort a failure, acknowledging that he was unable to "create a satisfied and satisfactory force of reasonably permanent tenants." In fact, he faced a planter's dilemma that the practical application of economic principles just could not solve: the best tenants were bound to leave, while the worst stayed behind. Employers might expel the lazy ones in hopes of attracting the "better kind" of tenants, but this annual turnover necessarily undermined continuity of plantation operations.[37]

An examination of the South's agricultural tenure ladder reveals that although annual turnover was higher for whites than blacks, black people actually shifted to a greater extent than whites. White families demonstrated higher rates of social mobility, both up and down the ladder; by 1920, about 40 percent of all southern white farm families tilled someone else's land, compared to an antebellum tenancy rate of about 20 percent region wide.[38] The Piedmont, in particular, showed a steady erosion of its small-farmer class. On the one hand, some plantation turnover resulted from the introduction of new families into a state of landless dependency. On the other hand, to a greater extent than blacks, white sharecroppers and tenants worked the land of kin and moved up the tenure ladder by means of bequests and gifts of cash; thus, young white families might move off a plantation and buy their own land at the end of the year. And finally, wage work in textile mills and certain kinds of jobs in cities beckoned to whites and took them out of the plantation economy altogether; black families lacked comparable opportunities off the countryside and (until 1916) up North.

Ultimately, the options of rural folk depended more upon the preferences and priorities of the local landholding elite than upon their own initiative in wringing a living from the soil. Planters throughout the South expressed strong convictions about the appropriate tenure arrangements for their particular holdings. They based their labor-force assessments on seasonal crop demands and on the age, race, and marital status of their workers. Conventional wisdom about such matters varied according to region and changed in response to patterns of local labor supply and demand.[39] Within neighborhoods, planters need not have banded together in formal associations to keep all blacks in their area from owning or renting land. In this sense, the agricultural tenure ladder conformed to the overt political convictions and economic interests of large landowners, to the extent that these white men enjoyed an abundance of willing workers. On the eve of the First World War, more than half of all tenants and croppers lived on plantations employing ten or more families; many employers, then, had some flexibility in determining the proportion of wage hands, sharecroppers, tenants, and renters they wanted to hire.[40]

In general, planters preferred young, unmarried (black) men as wage hands, large black families as sharecroppers, and large white families as tenants and renters. Since whites often refused to work in the same field with blacks, the tendency to group croppers near the owner's and overseer's quarters and to rent out more remote parcels to whites, provided for the close supervision of blacks while keeping the races segregated. Yet, time and necessity wrought transformations in the most dearly held principles of plantation organization. Most whites probably agreed that "the negro renter's foot is poison to the land,"[41] but the disastrous drop in cotton prices during the 1890s convinced more and more planters that their own economic salvation depended upon the shifting of a larger proportion of risk onto their workers, and the prevalence of cash renting increased.[42]

Few landlords showed the same equanimity toward white and black workers as the cotton planter in Polk County, Georgia, who approved of the performance of previously self-sufficient yeomen now reduced to tenancy: "as producers of cotton, whites can be just as efficient [as blacks] in this part of the country" if subjected to close supervision, he believed.[43] Echoing their Reconstruction-era forefathers, most employers cited (once again) the "lesser needs" of blacks ("hog and hominy, blackberries and plums"), their ability to withstand, "it seems, a great deal of discomfort," and their reluctance (or inability) to voice demands for better working and living conditions.[44] Black families had accommodated themselves "to the primeval curse"[45] in a way their white counterparts had not, or so the argument went. Moreover, black fathers showed a greater "willingness" to send their wives and children to the fields, probably a reflection of their desperate need to farm every acre intensively; in general, black croppers and tenants were allocated smaller parcels of land than whites.

In the end, planters would not have expressed a preference for black workers had members of that race been less vulnerable or less easily manipulated than whites. The favorable caste status of whites, no matter how poor, helps to account to some degree for their relatively greater rates of plantation turnover; as desired workers, blacks were held to certain plantations by a variety of means, voluntary and forced, while planters (and southern law-enforcement agents) allowed whites to move more freely simply because they were more expendable and because they were white.

The South abounded in examples of peonage, pure and simple, enforced by legal contract as well as by the pistol. Around the turn of the century, James M. Smith's huge work force on Smithsonia in Oglethorpe County, Georgia, consisted not only of convicts leased from the state but also of "hundreds of laborers on wages, many of them bound by voluntary indenture for terms as long as five years."[46] An employer need not wield a whip "to impose . . . a practically coerced service. The mere moral prestige of the white and the fear of physical violence, rarely employed, but always a potentiality, are often sufficient."[47] For Ned Cobb, "a practically coerced service" stemmed from signing a "note" with an employer; for others, from an unpaid lien that advanced to the next year; and for still others, a merchant's refusal to accept a debt payment at all, with the disclaimer that "he did not care whether his good customers paid [up] or not, just so they kept on paying."[48]

The notorious "close outs" and "clean ups" that deprived families of all their worldly goods served not only as a mandate for acquiescence among all tenants but also as a way of appropriating every bit of proceeds from a family's year-long labor before sending them on their way. Ollie Smith, a black woman, remembered that indebted croppers on the North Carolina plantation where she worked were "free" to leave at the end of the year, but "if you left, they took everything."[49] Close outs reveal then that indebtedness was not necessarily incompatible with high rates of shifting; a family's future depended largely on the self-interest of a planter who wanted them either to go or to stay. Indeed, croppers and tenants often left debts behind—first, because such "debts" were more contrived than real and, hence, an integral part of the labor system; and second, because they were so generally accepted by both parties, prospective employers rarely considered them a barrier to hiring new workers.

Assumed by some scholars to be "vigorous and competitive,"[50] the labor markets of southern subeconomies operated on a planter's principle best summarized as the endless quest for the perfect (that is, perfectly subordinate) laborer. Within regions, contracts rarely differed much from one to another;[51] employers offered workers essentially the same terms, with only modest variations. Consequently, the system relied on an elaborate set of tradeoffs—a smaller share of the crop for a better cabin (one with a porch) one year, an extra five dollars Christmas bonus in return for poorer quality soil the next. In fact, more favorable contractual arrangements inevitably carried a price tag, hidden or otherwise—the end-of-year bonus charged to next year's account or the garden plot in return for reduced furnishings at higher interest rates. When a planter agreed to assume the debt of a family from a neighboring planter, he often simply added the amount to their current statement of charges; at best, he allowed them to begin the new year with a clean slate, that is, "free" from debt, with nothing at all.

Given the myriad potential sources of conflict between employer and employee, it is not difficult to understand the reasons for December expulsions. "Reliable tenants" were those who were "public-spirited and loyal to the planter and who exercise a good influence over those inclined to become dissatisfied." The counterpoint to croppers' "irresponsibility" in moving so frequently was their employer's conviction that the "undesirable ones" should be evicted "as soon as possible," to be replaced by workers leaving neighboring plantations for whatever reasons.[52]

In evaluating the causes and consequences of evictions, it is often difficult to assess which departures came as a result of overt pressure and which ones followed more subtle means of discouragement. For example, tenants might voluntarily pick up and leave in disgust when faced with rent increases, a continuation of an unfavorable tenure status, trouble from poor white neighbors, or an employer bent on cheating them out of their year's compensation. In 1901, a congressional representative from North Carolina acknowledged the unspoken rules of plantation labor management: "There is a great deal of fraud perpetrated on the ignorant; [employers] keep no books, and in the fall the account is what the landlord and the store man choose to make it. [The workers] can not dispute it; they have kept no accounts."[53] Subjected to the injustices of such a system in Arkansas, an elderly black woman named Cora Gillam recalled, "We was just about where we was in slave days."[54] In essence, many planters, by "the cajolery of promises never intended to be kept"[55] (promises rarely committed to paper in any case), secured a short-term work force which they prepared to relinquish at the end of each year.

The ideal sharecropping family was not only large but also male-headed. Consequently, household members had their fate sealed by the absence or contrariness of fathers and husbands. On the one hand, when a father left during the slack season to work at a sawmill but failed to return at harvest time or when a husband died during the year, a family found itself unable to negotiate for the coming year and was forced to move.[56] On the other hand, the Department of Justice's Peonage Files reveal cases of wives and children held, virtually as hostages, until the return of a father who remained away from the plantation, even if he had been "run off" by his employer. This situation was unique to black families.[57] In addition, whole groups of families could fall out of favor, depending on the age of the head of the household. Planters rarely hesitated to bid farewell to older tenants, failing in "energy and strength," to make way for newly formed households.[58] In a strict sense, then, croppers, tenants, and renters were judged not on the basis of their worthiness as field hands but in relation to the household of which they were a part; they labored, and stayed or left, as members of corporate bodies rather than as individuals.

Indeed, exclusive attention to the fate of nuclear families or individual households obscures the prominent role played by kin in determining patterns of shifting throughout the South. Planters rarely understood the intricate webs of mutual assistance and dependence that kept relatives together; but these white men did recognize the phenomenon of kin clusters to the extent that they watched extended families leave on their own in a group at the end of a year, and they saw the close kin of an evicted family pick up and move as well. Around the First World War, on Runnymeade Plantation in Leflore County, Mississippi, "a policy is followed of encouraging a tenant to get his relatives to move on to the plantation and to live near him, as this seems to develop a more stable tenantry."[59]

Landless families often relied on each other for sustenance, but at least some whites had the added advantage of working for kin. Black croppers drew upon a slave tradition of "mutuality" in establishing networks of self-help. A group "down there together, all connected, kind of kinfolks"[60] might induce a young family to join them. These "corporate or quasi-corporate descent groups"[61] often paid homage to an aged leader, either male or female, and swapped workers at planting and harvesting time, as well as food, money, and child-care services. For whites, who depended to some extent on family connections to landlords in order to advance, a lack of kin in an area could signify a household's particularly desperate situation. A study of fifty-one white tenant families in North Carolina contrasted the one-half who were "living on and cultivating family lands" with those who lacked such ties, the latter "pilgrims, strangers, and sojourners in the land, with little or no workstock and farm implements of their own, and a minimum worldly wealth in household goods and utensils. . . ."[62]

Community-based obligations served the same function as blood ties in sustaining households and easing the burdens produced by illness, seasonal crop demands, and old age. Ollie Smith remembered that on the North

Carolina plantation where she lived for many years, sharecropping families rarely thought of themselves as isolated entities; when "neighbors [would] get sick, we'd all throw our work down and go there and help them. Work and iron, clean up the house, work the farm—whatever they needed. They do the same to us."[63] Within the small parameters of shifting households, then, each racial group developed its own set of expectations among neighbors, expectations that at once form the basis of communal life and transcended annual disruptions caused by residential turnover.

Emblematic of the South's stunted social structure was the plight not of the lowliest wage hand but of the small owner-operator, a family man who relied on a mule, fifty acres, and the labor power of his own household. Beset by creditors and reliant on wage work to hold onto their property (real and personal), these owners achieved an often illusory, often temporary, form of independence from planters and overseers. Their precarious status revealed the erosion of the South's yeomanry class after the Civil War. For example, the 175,000 black farm owners in 1910 were for the most part concentrated on small patches of thin soil in Virginia and on the South Carolina Sea Islands; to hold onto their land, they often had to sacrifice the education of children kept hard at work in the fields.

Most farmers, regardless of tenure status, had to live on credit during the year, unless they could earn enough in wages or from the sale of chickens and eggs to support their families. In Alabama, Sara Brooks's landowning father cut and rolled logs "at a place called Pineland" during the winter, returning home only on weekends. He also made some extra money by digging and cleaning wells and by working on the railroad—"now he did that most often than anything else." The children hoed and picked cotton for a neighboring white man for fifty cents a day. An older son left school and "went to workin out" in Springfield, where he would saw logs during the week and bring some of his earnings to his father on the weekends. In the end, property taxes and mortgages enforced a type of subordination that was as financially costly as it was personally demeaning; even the most industrious farmer could count on a creditor to "ride out and see if it's promisin enough to let you keep on takin up."[64] A drop in cotton prices, a fire in the barn, or a drought or sudden cold snap could send a family back into tenancy or off the land altogether.

Between 1865 and 1915, southern cities drew off the countryside individual households possessed of the aspirations that country life could not fulfill. Loyalty to kin—the satisfaction of being "at home anywhere I went amongst my mother's and daddy's folks,"[65] a love of the land, and pride in one's farming abilities, no matter how sparsely rewarded, kept some men of exceptional abilities on the treadmill of an agricultural tenure ladder. Nevertheless, in the words of W. E. B. Du Bois, "there is little to inspire the laborer to become a better farmer. If he is ambitious, he moves to town or tries other kinds of labor."[66] According to Du Bois, then, the structure of the land tenure ladder reflected (black) ability only insofar as a few families managed to buy small plots of land; the rest relinquished this "hopeless" struggle altogether. The sociologist Charles S. Johnson agreed that "the more alert and ambitious of the men" left their rural homes for southern and, after 1916, northern cities.[67]

Still, a town dweller might mourn the loss of a modest, rural-based independence or even the dream of it. The death of a male household head often brought to a bitter end a family's search for a settled home in the country. Interviewed in the late 1930s by a Federal Writers' Project worker, one black woman expressed deep regrets that the strenuous efforts of her farming father and husband had amounted to so little. Mary Anne Gibson had grown up in east Texas, where, soon after the Civil War, her father sold charcoal, farmed on halves, and presided over frequent moves to new plantations. Her mother cooked for whites; her sister served as a nurse for their children; and Mary Anne worked in the fields. She described her father as a "noble man" who died at age thirty-eight, while he was in the process of "trying to build a house" for his family. Mary Anne's three marriages kept her on the farm (or rather, a farm), but at the age of seventy-six, she found herself living in Austin: "I was bawn in de country, and lived in de country. I lak de country, and always did. I wouldn't be in town now, if I had a way to live on the farm."[68] Just a couple of generations removed from slavery, the Gibson households worked to redeem themselves from their past history; unlike their forebears in bondage, they lived a semi-nomadic existence but never lost sight of the ideal of owning a home.

White families pushed out of the mountains and off the Piedmont and into a city or mill village could also leave behind them a trail of regrets. Ernest Hickum's father wrested a living from his farm in the mountains of North Carolina; the family raised tobacco, corn, and wheat and never lacked for food from their garden. However, in the 1920s, trucks owned by local lumber companies eliminated a significant portion of the family's income when Hickum could no longer make money hauling logs with his wagon. His son remembered the time: "Now it wasn't but a year or two that they got to bringing them other kinds of trucks in there and just cut the poor farmer plumb out of the sawmill hauling lumber." The family sold their farm and moved to a Piedmont textile mill village to find work; but the father "just studied and grieved about selling everything he had and coming down here. He got around that machinery and he never seen nothing like it. You know what a racket machinery makes. I think the machinery scared him too much to try to run a job. . . . My daddy didn't like that. He couldn't work in no cotton mill, so he went back to the mountains." [69]

Working in the mills was an option for white husbands and fathers who wanted to keep their families together at all costs. Black sharecroppers, tenants, and small owners lacked this option; for them, life in the towns and cities meant not a harmony between work and family life but disrupted households—wives and daughters in the white folks' kitchens; sons and husbands dependent on low-wage, temporary, unskilled work that kept them constantly on the move, away from home. In the end, it is difficult to compare the subjective experiences of, on the one hand, poor white families slipping from the yeomanry into tenancy or into the textile mills with, on the other hand, the descendants of slaves being stripped of small parcels of land that possessed for them as much symbolic as real value. All of these families, regardless of race, aimed to make a home for themselves on the land. But if the eventual fate of their children is any indication, they failed. For aspiring tenants and sharecroppers, the rural South operated according to a strange system of incentives and rewards, with hard work enforced and ambition scorned.

It is possible to argue that the many children born to the poorest black and white families in the rural South were themselves the instruments of class subordination. Large families, though economically necessary under the sharecropping system, were in the long run economically dysfunctional; the land could not withstand a high rate of population growth combined with falling crop prices within a stagnant staple-crop economy.[70] This argument would suggest that farming was a doomed enterprise, bound to leave the majority of rural dwellers impoverished regardless of the political system under which they lived. Nevertheless, this system did produce prosperity for a very few, the largest planters, and it opened avenues of escape to those men, women, and children with white skins. For black households in particular, a patch of land in the country represented their last best hope for freedom from white employers, though that freedom came at the expense of creature comforts and the vital social life afforded by the city. By the mid-twentieth century, almost all blacks would find themselves not in the vortex of industrial capitalism but on its fringes—marginalized in northern cities the way freedpeople were enclosed in the late nineteenth-century rural South.

The theme of labor mobility among sharecropping households sheds light on a number of issues currently under debate by historians and econometricians. As a chapter in postbellum Afro-American history, the peripatetic moves of black households contrast with the enforced immobility of slaves. Plantation turnover among black croppers resembled less the "ambivalence" of first-generation factory workers, North and South, and more the determination of another group of black workers—domestic servants—to deny their white employers regular and unlimited power over their productive energies. At the same time, the routine fragmentation of families, especially those that sent out fathers and sons to seek wage work for part of the year, calls into question those sanguine assessments of the stability of rural life in the late nineteenth century, a lull between slavery in the South and ghettoization in the North. It is possible that federal census takers, who usually made their rounds on April 15 at the start of each decade, seriously overestimated the integrity of nuclear households, since this was planting time, when men were most likely to be at home.

Scholars have speculated on the betrayed promises represented by biracial political activism during the last two decades of the nineteenth century. But within regions of the South and on individual plantations, blacks and whites often occupied different tenure statuses and perceived different possibilities for their children; hence, it is not clear that they constituted a single class with identical interests. In fact, the upward struggle of some black families into landownership,[71] juxtaposed to the declining status of hundreds of thousands of whites, helped set the stage for the racial violence that erupted on the southern countryside in the 1880s, 1890s, and beyond. If Jim Crow laws established a new code of racial-caste order in the cities, then lynchings amounted to retaliation against a new generation of blacks in the rural areas: women and men who exasperated their employers even as they infuriated their poor white neighbors, men and women filled with caste pretensions and class anxieties.

Finally, the polarized interpretations of the southern labor economy—as either a system of neo-slavery or as a highly competitive market—have failed to take into consideration the phenomenon of sharecroppers shifting from place to place. Coercive labor-management policies coexisted with high rates of plantation turnover, and families were as likely to be evicted as they were to move on "voluntarily." Localized labor markets—revealed by the narrow geographical range of shifting, by the identical wages afforded by plantation work, and by work in rural nonagricultural enterprises—provided planters with a supply of subordinate labor, if not always all the appropriately subordinate households they desired. In 1866, a Freedmen's Bureau agent in Alabama observed that employers who routinely cheated their workers "think that there will be plenty of freedmen in the same condition as they have left their own and that in the general confusion that will then exist they can find some more willing to try the experiment again, and again defraud their Freedmen of their just wages."[72] Three generations later, a United States Department of Agriculture official described the same situation in slightly different terms: before the 1920s, "local restlessness [among workers] had never been a cause of anxiety or alarm to plantation operators . . . because the shifting labor was replaced by other shifting labor and no particular inconvenience was experienced."[73]

Around the time of the First World War, a black housewife in rural Georgia named Martha Brown told her young son, "If the white people would forget my color and I would forget slavery, we could all be Christians together."[74] During the half century after the Civil War, groups of blacks and whites would continue to work in the cotton fields near to each other and, in some cases, side-by-side, and at times, their families even exchanged cabins at the end of the year. Together, in certain areas, black and white poor families would descend into a state of permanent transiency as a new class of migratory workers emerged on the East Coast in the 1880s. Yet, Martha Brown's vision of a world of color-blind souls, united in religious faith and bereft of historical memory, would find no place, no home, in rural southern society.

13

A Woman Made to Suffer and Be Strong: Ella Gertrude Clanton Thomas, 1834–1907

VIRGINIA I. BURR

O N N E W Y E A R ' S N I G H T in 1859, Ella Gertrude Clanton Thomas, writing in her journal, addressed her three-month-old daughter who was sleeping in her crib nearby, ". . . and oh, may you realize what a glorious thing it is to be a *woman* in the *proper sense*. A woman made 'to suffer and be strong.' " She went on to say that as a child she had been struck with an expression she read—"I was a woman my Lord, and *of course* unhappy. . . . I had an idea then that the one was not a necessary consequence of the other, nor do I think so now. Yet I do think that a woman is so constituted as to be very easily affected."[1]

At that time she was seven years into a marriage that lasted fifty-four years. She was financially and emotionally stressed. She had already tasted grief and suffering, but even her spirited imagination could not have envisioned what the future held for her. A few years later, she must have had some idea when she said, "It is indeed a kind Providence which hides from us the future and I would not have the veil drawn aside and know what the coming years will bring to pass if I could."[2]

In an uncommon parallel, Gertrude Thomas's life span is almost identical to the period of Queen Victoria's reign in England, 1837–1901. Gertrude was born in Georgia in 1834 and died there in 1907. For forty-one years, beginning in 1848 when she was fourteen years old and ending in 1889 when she was fifty-five years old, she wrote an articulate account of her life and times in the South from the antebellum era through the first post-Reconstruction decade. For forty years, from about 1860 to 1900, she also kept scrapbooks which enhanced and extended her story.[3] Her writing, private and public, is that of an intelligent, perceptive woman speaking to the social and political issues of half a century. Her life is strikingly analogous to that composite lady described by Anne Firor Scott in *The Southern Lady: From Pedestal to Politics*.[4] The difference is in the extremes of her experiences—from wealth and privilege to overwhelming trials and impoverishment to survival and a phoenix-like redemption. Her journal is valuable especially because it is the sustained record of one woman's life before, during, and after the Civil War. The emphasis in this paper will be on her suffering, both physical and psychological, her almost buried hopes, and her strong-willed personal growth.

Ella Gertrude Clanton was born in Columbia County, Georgia, about fifteen miles north of Augusta. She was the second child of Mary Luke and Turner Clanton and one of seven Clanton children who lived to adulthood. Both Mary Luke and Turner Clanton came from families who emigrated from Virginia at the end of the eighteenth century and became well-to-do slaveholding planters in Columbia County. Turner was thirty-one years old, already a successful planter, when he married eighteen-year-old Mary Luke. He was a handsome man of impressive appearance and character, owner of considerable land and a large number of slaves, and his business acumen was well respected. Those qualities were not lost on his daughter, who revered him throughout her life. By the mid-1850s, he was reputed to be one of the richest men in the entire Southeast.[5] When he died in 1864, he was worth over $2,500,000 in Confederate assets.

In addition to owning five plantations, Turner Clanton built a twenty-four-room mansion on affluent Greene Street in Augusta. The three story, white-columned, brick structure of Greek Revival architecture, boasted solid-silver door knobs, door plates, and other hardware. It was said to be the first house in Augusta with indoor plumbing and caused people to comment that Colonel Clanton was spoiling his womenfolk. It was in this milieu, country home in summer and city mansion for the winter social season, that the adolescent Ella, also called Gertrude, and her siblings enjoyed growing up. Turner Clanton lavished gifts and jewelry from Tiffany's on his wife and daughters and provided travel opportunities for his family and higher education for his children. Mary Luke Clanton was the consummate wife and mother and, as later proven, a capable business woman herself.[6]

After attending private schools in Columbia County and Augusta, Gertrude entered Wesleyan Female College in Macon, Georgia, as a sophomore in January 1849 at age fourteen. Her schooling does not fit neatly into the genre of female education described by Stephen Stowe in his essay, "The Not-So-Cloistered Academy: Elite Women's Education and Family Feeling in the Old South," though there were similarities—as in the experience of the "immediate intimacy of shared womanhood" and in the emphasis on religion.[7] All of the professors at Wesleyan were men, most of them ministers—no mothering or coddling there. Wesleyan was the first four-year female college in America chartered to grant degrees to women, and the courses corresponded to those of all-male Emory College at Oxford, Georgia. The Reverend George F. Pierce, Wesleyan's first president, was a zealous champion of higher and equal education for women. He spoke derisively of the popular mode of female education prevalent at the time— female academies. He felt that the college diploma should be a voucher of superior education. Gertrude invoked that term "superior education" many times. The Reverend Mr. Pierce also advocated making the mind "self-dependent" and to have "as the object of ambition, the usefulness of a lifetime."[8] From her earliest years, Gertrude Clanton had an independent mind, but the concept of a useful life lay mostly dormant in her mind until fertilized with adversity.

At Wesleyan, the environment was intensely evangelical with nightly prayer meetings and exhortations. Under this influence, Gertrude was converted to Methodism, and though her strong faith faltered in later years, indeed collapsed at times, she remained faithful to the Methodist Church. Yet, her intellectual curiosity led her to examine other religions and even to delve into spiritualism and the philosophy of Emanuel Swedenborg.

Gertrude graduated from Wesleyan in July 1851 at the age of seventeen. The same summer, her "beau ideal," twenty-year-old J. Jefferson Thomas, graduated from Princeton. Jeff Thomas (1831–1916) was the oldest child of Joseph Darius Thomas and Louisa Kettles Thomas of Waynesboro in Burke County, Georgia. Joseph Thomas was a prosperous planter-slaveholder, not nearly so wealthy as Turner Clanton but with the same aspirations for his children.

In the fall of 1851, Jeff began reading medicine in Augusta with plans to become a doctor. During the winter, he courted Gertrude Clanton, who made her formal debut to society in January at an extravagant party for more than three hundred guests. Early in 1852, the young couple became engaged, and Gertrude wrote, "Jeff thinks of leaving off the practice or rather the study of medicine for another year." Gertrude's account reveals that her father was not enthusiastic about the match, and though no reason for his reluctance is given, it seems probable that Turner Clanton, with his wise instincts, may have foreseen problems. He finally yielded to his daughter's wishes, however, and Gertrude and Jefferson were married on December 16, 1852.[9]

The adjustment to marriage apparently interfered with keeping a journal, for when Gertrude resumed writing two-and-a-half years later, in April

1855, she was the mother of a sixteen-month-old son, Turner Clanton Thomas. The Thomases lived on a small, ninety-acre estate (named Belmont by Gertrude) six miles south of Augusta. This land and the house along with its slaves came from Gertrude's generous dowry. Not by chance, her parents now lived just one mile away in the summer season. Mr. Thomas, as she would call her husband for the remainder of her life, was planting in Burke County, twenty-five miles south, on land provided by his father.

The Thomases' marriage, at least for Gertrude, was one of romantic love. Jeff was not her first or only suitor, but she thought him handsome and charming, worthy of her love and respect—respect being of equal importance to love in her mind. She commented on his moral qualities and affectionate heart with just the "master will" to suit her nature. "[F]or true to my sex, I delight in *looking up* and love to feel my woman's weakness protected by man's superior strength. . . . I have selected my destiny and am content with it." With these parrot-like sentiments of her day, she showed herself to be a true daughter of patriarchy and a disciple of "woman's sphere."[10]

Gertrude described a tranquil life as a young plantation mistress, but frustrations surfaced soon enough. She admitted having an aversion for sewing, a serious flaw for a young wife, and one she never overcame. Making "drawers and undershirts" for her husband and clothes for her young son held no charm for her. She found cutting out clothes for a large number of slaves irksome, and supervising the killing of hogs was not congenial with her nature. Gardening and raising poultry were somewhat more compatible. Her discontentment with housekeeping could be heard when she moaned, "Oh at times what a perfect longing I have for increased knowledge. How much valuable time I fritter away upon things which are useless."[11] Even after the Civil War when her lifestyle had changed dramatically, she found household duties bothersome and "utterly uncongenial."

There is no evidence that Jefferson Thomas was any fonder of planting than Gertrude was of housekeeping. His decision to give up the study of medicine, a decision which later proved unwise, was most likely influenced by Gertrude who wanted a husband in the very same image of her father— a successful planter. Doctors, although highly respected, did not enjoy the status or wealth of elite antebellum planters. With his wife's potential wealth for security, as well as some of his own, and with Turner Clanton and his father as mentors, Jeff probably saw little risk in becoming a planter rather than pursuing a career as a doctor.[12]

Gertrude and Jeff had been somewhat spoiled and accustomed to a gay social life, and the confinement of marriage was probably disillusioning, but as propriety demanded, they settled into the conventional roles of husband and wife in the Victorian South. Along with five pregnancies in the first six years of marriage came personal grief for the Thomases. Within a two year period, 1856 and 1857, they buried a three-week-old baby boy on New Year's Eve; Gertrude suffered a serious miscarriage, or as she termed it, "an abortion"; and a six-month-old daughter died four days before Christmas. Gertrude praised her husband's solicitous concern and acknowledged a new emotion, "Now I do indeed begin to know what are the trials of life."[13]

The miscarriage merits special mention. During a visit to their Burke County plantation in the summer of 1856, Gertrude engaged in a heated argument with Mr. Thomas and some of his family regarding the treatment of pregnant slave women working in the fields. "I know that had I the sole management of a plantation," she wrote later, "pregnant women would be highly favored. A woman myself I can sympathize with my sex, whether white or black." At her father-in-law's home that night, Gertrude, still perturbed, did not join the family gathering after evening tea but retired to her room. The next morning, she was aware of her physical distress. She and Mr. Thomas returned home and called for the doctor. "Nothing that he did," she said, "(in fact he did nothing) proved efficacious and on Monday I had an abortion." She reported that her parents were very kind during her convalescence and Pa expressed his sympathy by saying to Mr. Thomas, "[A]s Gertrude wishes to have a piazza in front of the house, if you will see Goodrich [an Augusta builder] I will pay for it." Turner Clanton's generosity, which included substantial help in running the plantation, continued until his death. "Surely I have one of the very kindest dearest fathers in the one world," Gertrude later noted.[14]

Although the economy was good in the 1850s, Mr. Thomas's planting efforts did not go well. Gertrude alluded in her journal to lack of money and said she was trying to be economical. She thought her husband more liberal than he could afford to be and expressed the opinion that if she was to have a husband who gambled and drank to excess, she would spend more money and have her own expenses more in proportion to his. Then, as if denying the thought, she added, "As it is I endeavor to economize in some degree and assist Mr. Thomas in disengaging himself from his embarrassments." If she harbored any suspicion of her own husband's dissipations, she put such thoughts aside. She rationalized that "After the first romance of life begins to wear away, it is well for it to be supplied by the rational, calm, trusting happiness which we can only feel when we know and understand each other's faults. The only remedy for faults discovered must be to *love them down*."[15] Eighteen months earlier, she had written of an experience which was too intimate to confide to her journal, but she inferred that in the flash of an eye she was changed from a gay, thoughtless girl into a woman with all a woman's feelings. "Years hence," she wrote, ". . . this page will awaken emotions and cause a heart perhaps grown cold . . . to wonder at the wild tumultuous throbbings of early womanhood."[16]

Gertrude's journal was her companion in times of trouble and loneliness and her "confidante" to which she expressed thoughts she could not voice—for instance, her strong opinions "on the subject of woman and her wrongs." She deplored the double standard applied to the conduct of men and women and in her journal asked why a husband was considered justified in refusing to forgive an erring wife, while a deserted wife was expected to show woman's love, "or rather woman's weakness," and receive the wanderer back again. She thought more blame should be directed where it was due—at men. Although she sympathized with ill-treated wives, nevertheless, "I look upon the separation of a married couple," she asserted, "very nearly equivalent to a disgrace." She was aware in the early years of her marriage of the women's movement in the North but insisted, "I am no 'Woman's Rights Woman' in the northern sense of the word." Still she read the literature with more than passing interest, and her attitude on this subject later changed.[17]

Gertrude also contemplated the evils of slavery, especially those that affected the "standard of morality in southern homes." Like some of her contemporaries, she concluded that all Southern women were abolitionists at heart, "but then," she added, "I expect I have made a very broad assertion but I will stand to the opinion that the institution of slavery degrades the white man more than the Negro." She was disturbed over the number of white children of slave women belonging to her father's estate, "as well as others," and she noticed the favored treatment of mulatto women, but she knew that was "a subject thought best for women to ignore." Her concern turned into genuine worry in the mid-1860s when she considered the consequences of emancipation. Gertrude never confronted directly the issue of miscegenation, and therefore adultery, within her own family—few plantation wives did. She did write about it explicitly in her journal, however, betraying her own tortured thoughts and apprehensions.[18]

By August 1861, Gertrude was wrapped in fierce patriotism for the Confederate cause. A son, named Jefferson for his father, was born that year and the Thomases later added "Davis" to his name to show their esteem for the president of the Confederacy. Mr. Thomas was at the front, an officer in the Richmond Hussars, a cavalry unit in General Thomas R. R. Cobb's legion. His absence from home rekindled romantic love and taught Gertrude, "to appreciate more fully," she said, "his many noble traits of character" and "those quiet domestic virtues which render home so happy." One year later, he resigned from the army with her approval (having hired a substitute because he felt his honor had been tarnished when he was passed over for promotion). He immediately joined a home defense cavalry, the Wheeler Dragoons. Gertrude's happiness at having her husband home again was soon tinged with some embarrassment caused, in part, by the fact that her young brother and two of Mr. Thomas's brothers fought on and were seriously wounded. Later, she confessed to being proud of the time he spent in active service.[19]

In the early years of the war, Gertrude did not suffer the terrible misfortunes that many Southern women endured. There were periods of stress and anxiety, to be sure, inconveniences and inflation to deal with, but her father, Colonel Clanton, was there to provide necessities and give moral support. On New Year's Eve 1863, she reflected on the gloomy prospects for peace, the gay parties which belied the reality of war, and, again, on Mr. Thomas's extravagances (as his paying $100 for a saddle for his five-year-old daughter). She prayed for a renewal of Christian strength and character to help her in aiding her husband. She concluded by saying, "I have great faith in that innate courage which all women are said to possess when great trials come upon them." "Providential trials," she added.[20]

In 1864, the war came near. The Thomases' plantations in Burke County were looted and burned. People lived in fear of raids and prepared to flee their homes. With Mr. Thomas at the plantations or off skirmishing with the Wheeler Dragoons, Gertrude was often alone at home with four small children (two of whom were born during the war), except for the servants in the yard quarters. Generally, she was calm and unafraid, but after one unusually harrowing week, when Sherman's troops threatened Augusta and thousands of bales of cotton were piled in the streets ready to be torched if the enemy approached, she confessed in her journal, "I have experienced a new sensation. I have *been frightened.*" She wondered, "Oh God, will this war never cease?"[21]

In 1864, with the unraveling of the Confederate cause, she suffered a traumatic personal tragedy—the death of her father. Still worse, the contents of his will and accounts sent her faith reeling and threatened her health. The records disclosed that her husband, without her knowledge, had borrowed large sums of money from Colonel Clanton. The Thomases had expected a sizable legacy, but they were, instead, in debt to the Clanton estate. The news of her husband's deception shattered Gertrude emotionally. She wrote that she had no faith in God or man. God had deserted her; her father was dead; and her husband had deceived her. Her mind was tormented under "the weight of a nightmare." She feared that her prayers went no higher than her head. Racked with grief and doubts, she wanted "to read some healthy, strong, woman's writing. . . . Nothing sentimental, no romance of fiction. . . . No it is the writing of some sensible, practical woman, one who has suffered and grown strong."[22] Gertrude, pampered in her youth, knew with certainty that in the future she would have to rely on her own strength to deal with the uncertainties of life.

As the war dragged on, she struggled to resolve her feelings on the issue of slavery, seeking answers from her Bible as well as from proslavery and abolitionist literature.[23] "Yet the idea has gradually become more and more fixed in my mind," she wrote, "that the institution of slavery is not right . . . and taking my stand upon the moral view of the subject, I can but think that to hold men and women in perpetual bondage is wrong." Facing the real possibility of Southern defeat and the loss of so much personal property, she considered that she might someday have to earn her own living. Teaching school seemed the logical solution, and in her mind she planned for that eventuality. "Poverty is not the worst evil which can befall us," she wrote. "The enemy can take all else—Thank God they cannot deprive me of [my] education."[24]

The Confederate surrender brought a sense of despair to the countryside, "[A]nd yet," wrote Gertrude, "strange to say I feel bright and somewhat hopeful. The war is over and I am glad of it. What terms of agreement may be decided upon—I cannot say, but if *anything* is left us—if we can count with certainty upon enough to raise and educate our children, I shall be grateful."[25] A week later, in May 1865, she summed up her feelings, "Our Negroes will be freed—our lands confiscated and imagination cannot tell what is in store for us, but thank God I have an increased degree of faith. . . . [I] am not the person to permit pecuniary loss to afflict me as long as I have health and energy. As to the emancipation of the Negroes, while there is of course a natural dislike to the loss of so much property, in my inmost soul I cannot regret it."[26]

Nevertheless, the reality of emancipation and the dilemma it produced unnerved her, causing uncharacteristic bitterness and even physical illness. In July 1865, a baby boy was born prematurely and lived only a few hours. She felt sure that the constant strain on her nervous system was the cause, and she came dangerously near to fulfilling her fear of dying in childbirth. She also had another crisis of faith when she realized the enormity of her financial loss in slaves. Because she, like so many others, interpreted the Bible as sanctioning slavery, her faith in "God's Holy Book" was shaken. She lost interest in the church and for a time doubted God.[27]

The Thomases' immediate postwar problems were lack of money and hired labor. Confederate money was worthless. Mr. Thomas had invested $15,000 in Confederate bonds, now worthless as well. The sudden transition from slave labor to free labor produced uncertainty and confusion among whites and blacks alike. Former slaves were free to remain or leave, and slowly, one by one, they left. The Thomases, like everyone else, were forced to hire domestic labor and field hands, a situation complicated by financial instability. In contrast to Gertrude's optimistic attitude, her husband was gloomy, "cast down, utterly spirit broken." This difference in temperament became more and more pronounced and supports the view of some historians that women emerged from the war stronger, more resourceful, and more self-reliant, while many men found it difficult, even impossible, to adjust. Gertrude and Jefferson Thomas became conspicuous prototypes of that theory. Imbued with a new spirit of independence, Gertrude declared, "I think and think boldly, I act—and act boldly."[28]

Shortly after the war, Mr. Thomas invested in a porcelain and crockery store in Augusta—no doubt looking for a more reliable income. While Gertrude was delighted (for it meant spending the winters in town and a pleasant social life), she was still haunted by the idea of having to support herself and her children and disquieted at her husband's continuing squandering habits. At the end of 1866, the Thomases still owned their home—Belmont—an adjoining farm, the Burke plantations, and a house and business in Augusta. There was also the prospect of inheriting more from Turner Clanton's estate as it was arbitrated periodically when his minor children came of age.

Two years later, when Gertrude's account resumed in October 1868, the Thomases' situation had worsened drastically. The painful truth of that dark period gradually emerged from her journal as she mingled the recent past with the anguished present.[29] She was heartsick that her sixteen-year-old son, Turner, had been taken from school to plough and do farm work alongside black labor. She was tired from unaccustomed housework. There was no money. She wrote that her head and her heart ached. Her only comfort was her baby son, Julian, born in January 1868, "who has come," she said, "since our change of fortune. The little baby who in my anxiety to avoid adding to Mr. Turner's expense, I scarcely provided clothing enough for a change."[30]

The presidential election of 1868, the first for the freed blacks, caused heated politics and potential trouble, which Gertrude minimized by referring to as the "unsettled state of affairs among Negroes and white people." She reported in her journal that while white men armed themselves and spied on the Negroes, she walked to the servants' quarters alone at night to talk with them and calm their excitement. When neighbor women moved into town in fear of violence, she refused to leave, saying, "[A]s a woman I dislike to show that I am afraid to remain at home. Indeed, I think the women of the country are *very wrong* in showing this exhibition of fear. . . . True, the colored people are not now as they were during the war, but we trusted ourselves to them then. Why not now?" Gertrude approved of the blacks voting the radical (Republican) ticket. She did not underestimate the power of the vote. Taking it a step further, she said, "If the women of the North once secured to me the right to vote, whilst it might be an honor thrust upon me, I think I should think twice before I voted to have it taken from me."[31]

Once the excitement of the election had passed, Gertrude dropped her armor of pride and wrote candidly, "Old friend! dark days are gathering around me, heavy clouds obscure my future. . . . Mr. Thomas's affairs are so complicated, & he is so depressed." Six months later, she unburdened her agitated mind further: "The crisis has come at last," she confessed, "For two years I have watched a death struggle, have heard every sigh, every groan, have seen the anguished brow, the convulsed lip—have seen

the *mask off* and have known that my husband's affairs were terribly involved, have known too that we were living beyond our means and have
been utterly powerless to avert the blow which I knew was coming. I am
glad it has come." She believed that if the crisis had happened earlier, the
debt would not have reached such magnitude. Now, she was tormented by
the knowledge that members of her own and Mr. Thomas's families would
suffer from loans and mortgages made to her husband. Her younger
brother had cosigned an unsecured note for a large amount with Mr.
Thomas and was in danger of losing all he owned. "Oh my God," she cried,
"I have been so proud a woman. . . . My life, my glory, my honor has been
so intimately blended with that of my husband and now to see him broken
in fortune, health and spirits."[32]

In 1869, Gertrude received a plantation and four valuable city lots from
her father's estate, but they merely furnished more collateral for Mr.
Thomas to juggle his debts. Under the terms of Turner Clanton's will, all of
Gertrude's property was held "in trust" for her lifetime use only, after
which it passed to her children. It was "not liable for the debts of her
husband."[33] Therefore, she had to legally transfer her interest to Mr.
Thomas in order for him to use it as security. Her mother warned her to be
careful how she signed papers for Mr. Thomas, but having signed once,
there was no end to it. Each time she surrendered her interest in a piece of
property, she worried that she might be jeopardizing her children's inheritance. When she tried to talk with her husband, he became blasphemous.
"I might render my journal more spicy," she said, "were I to relate conversations verbatim, but I omit the garniture with which Mr. Thomas clothes
most of his remarks to render them emphatic, alas, a habit into which he
has fallen since the war." She noted that God was "too near" and "the
heavens too far away." She protested in vain and declared, "[M]y nature,
never gentle, becomes indignant and I am no meek and lowly disciple, but
like Peter, am hot-headed and say words for which I am sorry."[34]

Although Gertrude never admitted that her husband had a drinking
problem, one that became much worse in the aftermath of defeat and loss
of fortune, innuendos were frequent and unmistakable. She referred to a
"family skeleton," and she wrote despondently of a cross to bear, her
"thorn in the flesh." Family pride would have prevented her from acknowledging it in her journal—she often noted that others might someday read
her words—but there is little doubt that alcohol contributed to Mr.
Thomas's problems, his moodiness and ill temper, and that it added significantly to the suffering of his wife.[35]

Such conditions strained their marriage bonds and Gertrude's indignation spilled over into her journal. "Most men," she wrote, "dislike to admit
that their [wives] own anything. It is all the masculine 'my' and 'my own'
which they use and in polite circles it would be considered in bad taste for a
woman to say 'my plantation, my horse, my cows' although they are really

as much her own as the dress she wears." Gertrude attempted to advise her husband, but he resented her advice and asked her not to interfere. "But, I appear to see so clearly when things are wrong," she wrote, "that it is impossible to resist telling [him], not in a fault finding manner. . . . I have read a great deal of woman's endurance under pecuniary trials, a great deal of romantic, beautifully written sentiment about cheering a despondent husband. . . . I wonder if it ever occurred to anyone to imagine how a proud woman feels under such circumstance? A woman who is identified so completely with the interest of her husband that his success or failure is hers."[36]

"Oh Pa, Pa," she implored, "if you were living this would not be so. You would help us with your good judgement or cheer me with some kind word." She wondered if she were a better woman for the chastening of her pride but decided that she was not. "At heart, I am rebellious still. Yet in my own conscience I think a great deal of what we call bad luck is bad management. . . . there is no use talking about bad luck when one places themselves in the very way to produce that ill luck." Yet, she was often sympathetic. "My poor dear husband . . . ," she lamented, "has tried so hard," and she wrote that she never loved him more than when the day was darkest. As she had done since the early years of marriage, she vacillated between rationalizing her husband's faults and acknowledging his weaknesses.[37]

The Thomases' downward spiral for the next twenty years begs description. Strapped with enormous debts, unable to pay interest (sometimes as high as 20 percent) much less principal, they lived on a treadmill of foreclosures and legal threats. By the end of 1870, Thomas's porcelain business was bankrupt and their Augusta house had been sold for debt. A few months later, their Burke plantations—including land, livestock, and crops—were sold at public auction to satisfy mortgages held by his brother and sister. He was sued by the court receiver for the Clanton estate, by his factor, and by the bank for unpaid notes. The final blow was a levy against Belmont. "I don't think that I would wish the worst enemy I have any greater trial than to be encumbered with debt," Gertrude wrote.[38]

The humiliation of being sued by her family and the knowledge that she might lose her home, Belmont, were almost more than Gertrude could bear. She poured out her resentment and mortification in her journal and looked to the one source that had never failed her. "I wanted Pa worse than God," she wrote. Even more painful was the realization that her relatives were rebuilding their lives while she was hopelessly burdened with debts, which she called her "Sisyphus stone." She grieved that her children were so deprived of the advantages she had known as a young girl. "My pride suffers," she said, "when I think of my children as the poor relations of the family." Her mother, Mary Luke Clanton, relieved her of much of the responsibility for the older children—sending them to school and to dancing classes and providing them with clothes. Gertrude was genuinely grateful for kindnesses extended by her family, but she found the taste of "[h]umble pie" bitter indeed.[39]

Each time a public notice appeared in the newspapers, Gertrude was embarrassed. She compared herself to Hester Prynne in Nathaniel Hawthorne's *The Scarlet Letter*. "[B]ut I do not refer to her concealment," she wrote. "But it was the publicity, the being set apart, the being conspicuous, the branding which was torture to a proud spirit. Who can imagine what I have felt? How humiliated." Nevertheless, she displayed a brave front and high spirits, which deceived even her mother who thought Gertrude did not know how deeply Mr. Thomas was involved. Torn between accommodation to her husband and protecting the interests of her children, she was bewildered. "Ah my journal," she confessed, "in my effort not to reduce my children to beggary . . . and my wish to oblige Mr. Thomas, I have a hard time. . . . A few more turns of fortune's wheel and I will be at the bottom, but *there I will not remain.*"[40]

The Thomases' financial problems created a fair amount of irritability and discord. They argued over his stubborn manner of handling their affairs and particularly over where to take a homestead. In any case, Gertrude found the homestead exemption humiliating.[41] Within the home, she was plagued with domestic problems and was convinced that her husband did not appreciate her efforts to economize. Unable to pay for good help, she was forced to tolerate inexperienced servants whom she thought "indolent and impertinent." "I do not often complain . . . of my domestic annoyances," she wrote. "Sometimes I think it would be better if I did and kept a record of the trials to which Southern housekeepers are exposed. . . . when I complain to Mr. Thomas he tells me 'so much for the blessings of freedom,' not realizing that in this reply he gives me comfort instead of dissatisfaction." Emancipation was a point upon which she and Mr. Thomas did not agree.[42]

In those troubled times, Gertrude's joy and comfort were in her children. "Have I not my children?" she asked, "But this is an unshared joy with Mr. Thomas who while he loves and will take care to the best of his ability of these I have, has so morbid a dread of our having more mouths to feed and little feet to cover that he chills my womanly heart and makes me untrue to my better nature." Despite Gertrude's melancholy sentiment, Jefferson Thomas was generally portrayed as being a good and caring father. Her last entry for the year 1871, on May 28, was poignant:

When I place you aside dear friend, I leave a record of one portion of my life I would not live over again. I say this while I have a dim consciousness that those very events and the thoughts which they have given rise to, have enlarged and strengthened my character. I am not able to decide whether I have been benefited spiritually. . . . My children are a great comfort to me . . . I love my husband . . . I know that I love God and I will trust him.[43]

The journal after May 28, 1871, through December 30, 1878, is not among the extant volumes. Considering the staggering adversity of that period, it seems likely that the book, which did exist, was deliberately destroyed by someone, perhaps by Gertrude herself, at a later time. On the opening page of the new volume begun on New Year's Eve 1878, she wrote, "I have been reading over my last journal. . . . I was [almost] eight years writing that book."[44] During those years, a five-year hiatus from pregnancies ended, and the Thomases had another son and daughter, bringing to ten the number of children born of their marriage.[45] They also endured another critical loss. In April 1875 (possibly 1876), Gertrude's beloved home, Belmont, burned to the ground—nothing could be saved. The undated newspaper account of the fire is pasted in a scrapbook. How her journals and scrapbooks survived is a mystery, but she did write later that some of her possessions were in Augusta at her mother's home at the time.

After the fire, the Thomases moved into a farmhouse on the property which adjoined Belmont. It was a smaller, much less imposing home than they were accustomed to, and Gertrude named it Dixie Farm. Mr. Thomas farmed that land as well as his wife's few remaining properties. After years of thinking about the possibility, Gertrude was teaching a county school in one room of the house. The tone of her writing was perceptibly changed—it was resignation. "I know that I will not be mistress of my own time," she wrote, "but with that thought comes the reflection that I will be profitably employed. . . . This New Year [1879] finds me more contented than the two last years. Taxes are still to be paid, debts are pressing, but I am more sanguine."[46]

Gertrude was more content, but she had a new set of problems. She was constantly on guard against those who wanted her teaching job, and the challenge of keeping twenty children regularly enrolled, as required by law, was extremely difficult in a farm community. For the years that she kept the school, it was a love-hate relationship. She took genuine pleasure in teaching the young children—sometimes; at other times, she was weary, frustrated, and wished desperately not to teach. This latter happened, she wrote, "when worries outside of my schoolroom unfitted me to cope with the trials within." In December 1880, after wrestling with indecision for days, she went into town and resigned. She felt ecstatic relief only to be told by Mr. Thomas when she returned home that he did not see how they could get along without the school. "We are dependent upon the salary you earn," he told her. "I knew what that meant," she added. She promptly withdrew her resignation and continued her school.[47]

Her real pleasure came from spending the salary she earned, thirty-five dollars a month plus an allowance for firewood. She also sold old dresses and hats to the servants for extra money, and she kept a detailed account of every penny she received, spent, owed, and repaid. She bought clothes for her children, furniture, and household items; to feed her own soul, she subscribed to *Harper's* and *Scribner's*. "Everything is so low," she noted, "that a great deal can be bought with a small amount of money, but oh the scarcity of money." There were times, too, when Gertrude paid the taxes and the farmhands with her teaching salary and felt hurt that Mr. Thomas had not one kind word of appreciation for her help. Gertrude signed notes for the farming supplies, liens on crops and livestock, and in some instances, she arranged for credit when his efforts failed.[48] She could no longer depend on her husband for emotional or financial support.

As Gertrude became more independent, she made practical suggestions for meeting their financial obligations, but they were ignored. Mr. Thomas's habits had not improved, and he was no more successful with crops. "There are some thoughts we utter not," she wrote, "some experience of which we make no record in our journals. . . . I suppose everyone has a cross—well mine, like a diseased limb, I have become somewhat accustomed to."[49] Gertrude thought of trying to write for publication, perhaps publishing something from her journal, "alas, not for fame, for money." It was not the first or the last time that she expressed a desire to write and publish. The journal does, in fact, contain many fascinating accounts of special interest, several of which were published later on, and there are hundreds of cheerful, absorbing vignettes describing a happy life with children, family, and friends. Downward mobility and suffering are but two of the themes that intermingle throughout Gertrude Thomas's long record.[50]

In August 1879, however, Gertrude suffered another paralyzing providential trial. Her youngest son, Clanton, died of a fever two days before his seventh birthday. Her lengthy account is heartrending. For a brief time, Mr. Thomas gave her sympathy and support, and they shared the common emotion of grief. Vulnerable in her sorrow, the last months of 1879 found Gertrude utterly forlorn. Her health was poor, and she reckoned with morbid humor that she was at a critical period in a woman's life when the purchase of her lifetime interest "might prove a bad speculation." After she had pledged her last remaining asset—the lifetime interest in her father's estate—Gertrude succumbed to self-pity. "I could not realize my situation or the importance of the new trouble with which I shall have to grapple," she wrote, "I only felt that Mr. Thomas could not help me, the children could not. I had not one friend upon whom I could rely. . . . Hope, there was none for me . . . I sank on my knees by the sofa and said not one word. My heart and my brain were alike, dumb—utterance, I had none. . . . What the future has in store for me God only knows."[51]

Gertrude's ability, however, to rally was remarkable. A few months after recording her dire despair, she was writing articles for the Augusta *Chroni-*

cle and the Augusta *Constitutionalist* and proudly proclaimed, "[I] signed my name Gertrude Thomas. . . . I am a public woman now." Heretofore, she had signed her name Mrs. J. Jefferson Thomas. "Am I trying my wings for bolder flights," she wondered?[52] Her greatest anguish concerned her six remaining children. She worried over her boys—that she could not send them to college—and over her two older daughters. For them, the absence of social advantages translated into fewer and, perhaps, less desirable marriage opportunities. "Keep me from the sin of envy," she prayed. "I can stand poverty for myself, but oh my children!" She compared her everyday trials to "wearing a shirt of hair—a daily torment," and concluded, "I think that it is infinitely more easy to be amiable when one is rich."[53]

After 1881, Gertrude wrote infrequently in her journal. If it were not for the scrapbooks, the reason might be lost, for she never mentioned that she was becoming involved outside the home in the newly flourishing women's organizations—particularly the Ladies Missionary Society of the Methodist Church and the Women's Christian Temperance Union. Duty became the watchword of her life, and she observed, ". . . duty is not always pleasant. Sometimes it is very hard."[54] Her duty, as she saw it, was to her children and her husband, in that order. As she devoted herself to the teaching that helped support her family and also worked energetically with other women, Mr. Thomas's name all but disappeared from her writing.

When her mother died in 1884, Gertrude's usual common sense deserted her. She resigned her school and, in a sentimental act of folly, arranged to move her family into her mother's Augusta mansion until it was sold, agreeing to pay the other heirs $500 a year rent to be deducted from her share of Mrs. Clanton's estate when it was settled. The impractical scheme lasted three years, with Gertrude forced to rent out rooms in the house to obtain money for bare necessities. Crop failures continued for Mr. Thomas, and whatever income he derived was used to satisfy creditors and to support the farm operations. Once more, the Thomases were disappointed in their expectations of a legacy from her mother to aid their financial imbroglio, for Mrs. Clanton's personal wealth had dwindled away. A year after the great earthquake of August 31, 1886, about which Gertrude wrote graphic descriptions, but during which she was terrified and ill, the Thomases moved back to Dixie Farm.[55]

Gertrude made only five entries in her journal from 1887 until she abandoned it in 1889. Except for one occasion of immense pride when her son Julian graduated from medical college, they were years of miserable deprivation. In January 1887, she wrote, "Business cares have pressed upon me and I have written [almost] nothing for two years in my journal and very little for publication. . . . Julian will be nineteen . . . this month and in March he hopes to receive his diploma as a doctor." Then in April 1888, she wrote, "I expect I shrink from what is before me. Tomorrow I will be fifty-four years old and I could not obtain credit for fifty dollars. . . . I own land, much of it, and it does not support my family. . . . There is nothing to be obtained from my mother's estate. . . . I think my long [malarial] illness last summer was owing to the strain on my nervous system."[56] On August 30, 1889, she described a pleasant day at Dixie Farm and then wrote, "In the August number [of the *Old Homestead* magazine] was a paper I wrote on *Henry IV*. In September will be a paper on Ophelia. I read both of them before the [Paul Hamilton] Hayne circle. I have received many complimentary notices, but little substantial encouragement to write."[57] With those words, she closed her journal and ended her account of forty-one years.

Gertrude's married life was not the one she had envisioned: poverty in place of wealth, privation rather than privilege, illness rather than health, emotional stress rather than harmony, and failure in place of success. Her enduring joy was in her children, and in some singular way, she loved her husband, or at the very least felt a deep loyalty to him. Mary Elizabeth Massey, in her essay on Gertrude Thomas, "The Making of a Feminist," noted that with only Gertrude's records available, it is impossible to present both sides of this couple's story but added that "Mrs. Thomas was unusually level-headed [and] fair-minded." Gertrude Thomas, apparently, managed in a remarkable way to keep the spark of integrity and hope alive in her life. Jefferson Thomas, like many other Southern men of his class, was unable to cope with defeat and loss of fortune. The Thomases' marriage, though lasting, never settled into the kind of companionate liaison described by Carol Bleser in her essay, "The Perrys of Greenville: A Nineteenth-Century Marriage."[58]

If the story of Gertrude's life had ended with the journal, it would have been a familiar one of post-Reconstruction poverty and failure. Her scrapbooks, however, record her active public life that began in earnest during the 1880s, when she was approaching the age of fifty. These books are crammed full of hundreds of newspaper clippings, many of which were written by Mrs. Thomas. The articles reflect her passionate interest in education, women, temperance, and the "Lost Cause" and reveal a woman who traveled extensively while representing the Women's Christian Temperance Union (WCTU) and the United Daughters of the Confederacy. Gertrude's lifelong interest in education was emphasized in 1887 when she wrote articles in favor of the Blair bill, then before Congress, for national aid in support of common schools for whites and blacks alike. She pointed out the importance of an educated electorate, saying, "Education should be compulsory, nor would I permit a man to vote who could not read and write." She added that she "would rather be taxed to educate the colored families whose fathers labored faithfully for us, than to pay a pension to support the Union soldiers who fought against us." She also published her opinions on political matters, and she commended a WCTU convention in 1889 where black and white women worked together. Except for a few bitter years following Emancipation, her views on race were always more liberal than those of her contemporaries.[59]

Gertrude and Jefferson Thomas moved to Atlanta in 1893 to live with their son Dr. Julian Thomas, who had established a successful clinic there. Whatever her feelings may have been about leaving Augusta, Gertrude responded with extraordinary energy and enthusiasm to the opportunities in her new environment. Through the WCTU, she met Frances Willard and, later, Rebecca Latimer Felton and Mary Latimer McLendon. In Gertrude, the reformers found an enthusiastic worker and an eloquent spokeswoman. She wrote fervent appeals for temperance and prison reform. She railed against wife abuse and against discrimination in women's education and employment. She worked to establish an industrial school for girls, saying, "There are ambitious girls in the state. . . . Make those girls educated women and the influence will be felt in the history of Georgia."[60] She attended the annual meeting of the National Woman Suffrage Association held in Atlanta in 1895—as a fraternal delegate from the WCTU—where she met Susan B. Anthony. Inevitably, her path led to the suffrage movement.

In 1899, at age sixty-five, Gertrude was elected president of the Georgia Woman Suffrage Association. The sum of her life experience was expressed when she addressed the convention that year and declared, "woman was not taken from the head of man—she is not his superior; she was not taken from his foot—she is not his inferior; but she was taken from his side, and there she should stand, his equal in the work of the world."[61]

Until a short time before her death in 1907 at the age of seventy-three, Gertrude led an active life that brought her fulfillment and wide recognition throughout the Southeast. While she was thus engaged, Jefferson Thomas, ironically, busied himself in the role of Confederate veteran, riding his sorrel pony, Dixie-Will-Go, in Atlanta parades. He attended meetings of the Princeton alumni and, in time, became something of a celebrity as the oldest living graduate of Princeton University in the state of Georgia. He outlived his wife by nine years.

In 1880, a tenacious Gertrude had written, "If a higher field of usefulness is intended, a way will be made for me. Of this I am sure so I go on my way content."[62] Ella Gertrude Clanton Thomas was "a woman made to suffer and be strong."

The baby in the crib, addressed by Gertrude Thomas in the first paragraph of this essay, was my grandmother, Mary Belle Thomas Ingraham. Contrary to her mother's fears, Mary Belle married well.[63] She was older, at age twenty-five, than her mother and grandmother had been when they married at age eighteen, but that was not unusual in the postbellum years. When I was growing up in Atlanta, the Thomas and Ingraham ancestors were living history, larger than life and ever present. They were spoken of as if they were alive and well and might appear at any moment to elucidate the conversation. "Grandmama" Thomas was a dynamic presence. Her legacy continued well into my generation and shows signs of yet another reincarnation.

Appropriately, it has been Gertrude Thomas's female descendants who have preserved and perpetuated her existence. In all my childhood memories, in all my research and interviews with close and distant relatives, and most of all through constant study of her journal, Gertrude Thomas emerges as an intelligent, loving, honest, strong woman—not without faults but, ultimately, indomitable.

14

A Victorian Father:
Josiah Gorgas and His Family

SARAH WOOLFOLK WIGGINS

ONE EVENING, when his son William Crawford was twelve, Josiah Gorgas mused in his diary:

> As he lies asleep before me now, how earnestly I pray for his future welfare. How my heart yearns toward him; & how glad I would be to shield him from the troubles of life. It makes me understand, & in some measure respect the desire people have to *accumulate*, in order that they may leave their children in affluence. It is the natural desire of the parent to protect & watch over the offspring—to *work hard*, & bear the brunt of the struggle of life, that the child may be saved the same struggle in some degree.[1]

Famous as Confederate chief of ordnance, Josiah Gorgas (1818–1883) became a father in the midst of the Victorian era in America, a transition age in childrearing patterns. Mid-nineteenth-century fathers had moved away from the severity of Puritan evangelical attitudes that the child's will must be broken and had come to believe that children were pliable and could be bent and shaped as young plants by careful pruning. Such parents exercised authoritative influence, not authoritarian power, over their offspring. Relying on moderate discipline and voluntary obedience, Victorian parents nurtured their children and welcomed them into the world, anticipating their children's growth to maturity as responsible community members. But there were limits. They did not believe in sinful or dangerous indulgence so that children became undisciplined, too free in behavior, spoiled, vain, or arrogant. The essential issue was that children voluntarily obeyed their parents.[2]

Josiah Gorgas's parenting exemplifies the family patriarch as "source, provider, protector, example, and judge." His journal "dedicated to my children" and the voluminous family correspondence offer an unusual opportunity for insight into the relationship between a nineteenth-century American father and his children over a period of twenty-five years.[3]

A career United States Army officer from Pennsylvania, Josiah met and married Amelia Gayle while he was stationed at the Mount Vernon Arsenal near her home in Mobile, Alabama, in 1853. He was thirty-five. Few couples could have had more dissimilar family backgrounds. The youngest of ten children, Josiah was born into a family where the father moved from one job to another as clock maker, mechanic, farmer, innkeeper, and the older boys contributed to the family's support. Much of Josiah's childhood was spent on a Pennsylvania farm where few educational opportunities existed. At seventeen, he moved in with a sister's family in Lyons, New York, and became an apprentice to a printer. Soon he was reading law in the office of a local congressman who secured Josiah an appointment to West Point. Josiah passed the years between his graduation and the Civil War with service in the Mexican War and at various army posts. His was a self-made success, the product of keen intelligence and persistent hard work.[4]

Amelia Gayle (1826–1913) came from an entirely different world, the "Old Guard" South. Her paternal and maternal ancestors included distinguished veterans of the Revolutionary War in the South who migrated to Alabama when it was part of the Mississippi Territory. Her father, John Gayle, graduated from Mt. Bethel Academy in the Newberry District of South Carolina, probably when Elisha Hammond, James Henry Hammond's father, was principal. From South Carolina College he went on to a distinguished career in Alabama—a member of the territorial legislature, judge on the Supreme Court, speaker of the House of Representatives, governor for two terms, congressman, and district judge in Mobile at the time of his death. Amelia accompanied her congressman father to Washington. There, her companion on sunrise walks through the grounds of the nation's capitol was Senator John C. Calhoun of South Carolina, who discussed with Amelia such topics as the French Revolution of 1848 and its probable effects in Europe. Calhoun was almost seventy, and Amelia was twenty-two. The Gayles and the Calhouns became such good friends that they set up housekeeping together in Washington, and the senator arranged for Amelia to sit on the platform for the ceremonies for the laying of the cornerstone of the Washington Monument.[5]

Amelia's mother, Sarah Haynsworth Gayle, an only child, descended from an equally distinguished South Carolina family and is the subject of an essay in this volume by Elizabeth Fox-Genovese. Sarah's maternal great-grandfather signed the South Carolina "Declaration of Rights," and Furman University was named for one of her maternal grandmother's brothers. Her parents migrated to Alabama while the area was a territory, settling in the plantation country north of Mobile. A great beauty, Sarah Gayle was also a gifted writer whose talents are evident through her surviving journal.[6]

The third of six children, Amelia attended Columbia Female Institute in Tennessee as a teenager and then returned to Mobile. The oldest daughter at home, she assumed responsibilities of assisting with the family's young children, a practice that continued over the next ten years and led to her romance with Josiah. He always insisted that as he overheard Amelia reading daily to children on the veranda next door to the Mount Vernon Arsenal, he fell in love with her voice before they met. Amelia was then twenty-eight.[7]

Amelia and Josiah had six children between 1854 and 1864; the eldest and youngest were boys. The parents' favored their eldest, Willie, of whom they expected the most and upon whom they lavished their love and affection—a situation that could not have been painless for the other children. Because William Crawford is the child most often discussed in family correspondence and Josiah's journal, Josiah's relationship with Willie is the paternal relationship in this family that is most apparent. Amelia especially doted on her eldest son; although she was grateful for her four girls, she said, "my pride & chief jewel . . . will ever be Willie my first born," "my dearest child and the very pride of his Father's heart." When her son was twenty-one, she wrote him that she thanked "God every day for the blessing he gave me in my first-born darling."[8] Yet, nowhere in correspondence that numbers thousands of letters is there an expression of sibling jealousy about the parental preference that Willie enjoyed.

The family's rootless military life before the Civil War carried them to assignments at Kennebec Arsenal in Maine, Charleston Arsenal in South Carolina, and Frankford Arsenal near Philadelphia before Josiah resigned his commission in 1861 to become chief of ordnance for the Confederacy. During most of the years of the Civil War, the family lived in Richmond in the Virginia State Armory. Wherever they landed, Amelia knew someone—childhood friends, schoolmates, Washington acquaintances, or family friends. No sooner did Amelia arrive than a veritable parade of callers appeared.[9]

Josiah's decision in 1861 to side with his wife's South evolved from his experiences over the previous eight years since his marriage. Josiah had married into Amelia's aristocratic Mobile family, not she into his of Pennsylvania farmers. Amelia's family steadily absorbed Josiah, while he had infrequent contact with his own, even while he was stationed in Maine and Pennsylvania. One of the few visits of members of Josiah's family occurred while the Gorgases were in Maine. He rarely mentioned his relatives in his journal, while accounts of Amelia's appeared on virtually every page. His closest friend was Thomas L. Bayne, husband of Amelia's youngest sister,

Maria. In his journal, Josiah described Bayne as the "most amiable and best man to get along with" that he had ever known. The friendship lasted the rest of Josiah's life. "No brother could be kinder than Mr. Bayne & he was the man my husband loved best in the world," Amelia wrote one of her sisters. When Josiah was dying in 1883 and Amelia asked if he wanted to see Bayne, he whispered, " 'Yes, oh yes, Bayne & I are very intimate. We are brothers.' " Josiah also deeply admired Amelia's father. "It is strange," he wrote Amelia, "what an attraction he exercises toward even me, a stranger to his blood. But I owe him 'Heavens last best gift' my darling wife, and he is associated with all the happiest periods of my life. . . . Talk of battles, politics, travel! A man has no experience worth mentioning until he loves the woman he weds & has children born to him by her."[10]

Josiah not only became deeply attached to members of his wife's family, but he and Amelia also often kept house with one of Amelia's sisters and her family, and individual relatives lived with them for extended periods. This pattern characterized their household life-style throughout their marriage. For example, in Charleston the Gorgas household included Mary Gayle, her husband Hugh Aiken, and their children. When the family settled in Richmond, they combined households for two years with Maria Gayle, her husband, T. L. Bayne, and their children. In 1865, when Josiah and Bayne fled Richmond, the two sisters remained, and Amelia moved in with Maria. Soon their brother Richard arrived from a federal prison and joined them.[11]

Amelia's family not only absorbed Josiah, influencing his decision in 1861, but also made his household their headquarters, their home, throughout and beyond his and Amelia's lifetimes. Once when Josiah was on the brink of financial disaster, he calmly noted in his journal that the family then included "8 grown white people, and 10 children with 4 colored Servants." Two more children were expected with Amelia's stepmother the following week. "Besides," he added, "we expect some visitors soon! Mamma seems to think the more the merrier." Obviously, Josiah did not consider Amelia's family "visitors." On another occasion, Josiah noted that in addition to his own family of a wife, six children, and a nurse, his household then included Amelia's stepmother, a daughter with her baby and nurse, Maria, Bayne, and four of their children. After the Civil War, wherever the Gorgases lived, there was rarely a time when at least one of Amelia's siblings and family was not living with them. The older generation came home to die, and the younger generation came home to give birth. Years after Amelia's death, when a niece came home to have her baby, Willie wrote his sister Jessie, "One more born in the old house but Mother not there. I know that she is interested and sympathizes."[12]

The voluminous sources that chronicle the peregrinations of this large family reflect much about Josiah as a father in the Victorian era. He emerges as a man who found his children fascinating, who viewed male and female children differently, who asserted his paternal authority up to a point, who was not hesitant to judge his eldest son's growth harshly, who lacked the financial resources to be an indulgent or even benevolent father in a material sense, who saw fatherhood in terms of love and duty, not love and fear.

Josiah's journal demonstrates that he was a deeply caring father who lavished time and affection upon his children, nurturing them and providing opportunities for their observation and imitation. He delighted in their activities, and they sensed his genuine interest in their amusements, their health, their world. Family outings included everyone, even the children's nurse. They often went driving—in winter they took sleigh rides; in summer, carriage rides. When the weather was too bitter for such pleasures in Maine, Josiah lamented that he and Amelia sighed "for the sunny days at Mt. Vernon," when they would take daily rides with the children in that mild climate.[13]

He often observed his children at play and involved himself in their activities. Once while Josiah watched Willie coasting on his sled in the snow, the boy dove off the top of a hill at full speed. Fearing the child would go over a nearby wall and into the river, Josiah threw off his cloak "to head him off." Fortunately, the sled stopped itself, but Josiah got himself a case of "rheumatics" for his "parental anxiety." Josiah shared their delight as Willie and his younger sister Jessie romped on the beach picking up shells or amused themselves at a circus. On another occasion, he lamented when rain ruined his plans to take Willie to the races. One mild day, he described himself as "loitering about the grounds all morning," carrying his new infant Mamie, and watching "Willie and a playmate carrying and placing sods with considerable skill," as they had seen workmen do the day before.[14]

When Josiah was ordered to Charleston in 1858, he was again separated from his wife and three children. Willie was ill with typhoid fever. No sooner did he recover than Amelia fell sick, and Josiah went to his assignment alone "with heavy heart." He did not view separation with relief as an escape from parental responsibility. Instead, his letters to Amelia are those of a man passionately in love with his wife and wild about his children. They sensed his devotion. Amelia wrote that the children talked of Josiah all day, and Willie had a "good cry for his dear Papa." A few days later, she wrote that Willie had dreamed of his father and waked saying "how lonesome" he was for his papa. The father was as lonesome as the son. Josiah promised that he would be away no longer than necessary, as he yearned to see his wife and babies. They were constantly in his thoughts. As he celebrated the birthday of his wife's brother-in-law with ice cream and peaches, Josiah thought of Willie and Jessie, who "would have split their little stomachs—at least Willie would—over them."[15]

When Josiah did not receive letters from Amelia on schedule, he worried. "No letter from you to-day nor yesterday," he wrote. "Perhaps you are too ill to write—perhaps Willie is sick—or Jessie—or baby has had convulsions." He pleaded with his wife to write him at least every other day. "I have hardly known myself how my heart is wrapped up in you until I am so far away from you." He asked Amelia to send pictures of herself and the children to keep him company in his loneliness. When the pictures arrived, he stood them "all in a row on the mantel-piece" to form a "perfect family library." He could not help observing to Amelia that Willie was a "fine looking little fellow" and on another occasion "a noble little fellow." When he held another boy the age of Willie, he found that the child would hardly compare with their "noble boy." Very proud of his wife and children, he saw "none like them" in Charleston.[16]

Every letter to Amelia not only discussed the children but also closed with "kisses to our babies" or "kiss the dear ones" or "kiss the little orphans" or "kiss them 'five times' for me." He feared that he could not bear another separation from his family: "I am constantly thinking of you, longing for you and my little pets."[17]

As he anticipated a reunion with his family, he worried that the children might not recognize him. "My little darlings—how I shall rejoice over them. Mamie will look at me wonderingly & even Jessie will have half-forgotten me." He counted the weeks until he rejoined his family. "The 7 or 8 weeks yet to be passed alone afford but a dreary perspective," he noted in his journal. Then, "five weeks from to-day I . . . hope to be sitting with my arm around my wife . . . '& my babies on my knee,' " he wrote Amelia. And, "four weeks now," he rejoiced, and "I shall hold the little darlings in my arms, & their mama—can't leave you out of the kissing & caressing." A few days later, "I would give anything to have my arm around your waist & my babies about me. . . . God willing we shall be reunited in less than four weeks." Time passed too slowly for Josiah during this separation. "I wish with all my heart," he wrote his beloved Amelia, that "it would take the bit into its teeth and run away with me."[18]

His musings in his journal repeat the devotion to his family expressed in his letters. "Suppose that they were all lost to me, as has happened to men before now—what would become of the remainder of my life! It is a thought which, like that of annihilation, the mind refuses to contemplate." When Willie was four, his father pondered the ageless question of how one transmitted the wisdom of experience to the next generation. "Would that there were some way of impressing others with a truth we have ourselves acquired by hard experience. But outside of mathematics, & some of the physical sciences, there is no such thing as impressing *conviction* on the mind of another."[19]

During the Civil War, separation from his family still pained Josiah, although the children were older. In 1862, when the war threatened Richmond where Josiah was stationed, Amelia and the children refugeed to the home of her sister Mary Gayle Aiken near Winnsboro, South Carolina. The children now numbered five. A daughter had been born in Charleston, and another daughter arrived after their move to Richmond. Amelia's cheerful letters made him quite happy, as happy, he said, as he could be "away from wife and babies without whom the world is indeed very dull." He again closed his letters with directions for his wife to "kiss the babies all round for their papa who would be glad to have them all together on his knee." When Amelia prepared to return to Richmond, he urged her not to "leave any of the children." He wanted "very much to have them all together." He said, "I never saw too many of them," fearing that "the little rogue" Willie might forget him.[20]

Josiah's journal and correspondence reveal also the difference in his attitudes toward male and female children. He openly deferred to Amelia's judgment in matters relating to their four daughters; the unstated assumption was that Josiah decided about their two sons. To Josiah, the education of boys had a different goal from that of girls, as he plainly wrote his daughter Jessie away in boarding school. "Your mother will decide for you whether you are to stay or come away before the exam, should you desire to do so," wrote Josiah. "I am not in favor of publicity in the examination of girls. For boys who must be *hardened* for their work in life it does very well." Amelia grieved whenever Willie was separated from Josiah's influence, for, she said, "I have not sufficient decision of character to train children particularly boys. . . . Willie loves me dearly & I control him entirely through his affection but I am too weak to insist upon duties repugnant to him."[21]

Gifts for the children were typical ones. Jessie received dolls for her birthday and Christmas, while Willie received gardening tools and "a *real gun*." Willie, Josiah noticed early, was a child whose temper improved when he played outdoors; "confinement to the house worries him." Josiah's journal and correspondence are full of anecdotes about Willie's childhood—sports, school, and hunting. However, the other children received little comment; the longest of these described a very domestic scene: Amelia discovering Jessie busily ironing Willie's handkerchief.[22]

Josiah was a father who did not consider it demeaning to his masculinity to tend sick children at night or to be involved in dosing them with medicine by day. He was sensitive to the fact that Amelia was "very much worn out" after several sleepless nights with Jessie's teething and worried that he was "such a poor nurse" that he could do little to relieve his tired wife. His masculine presence early on made a powerful impression on his eldest son. Once when Willie was ill, Josiah described the child as taking a dose of calomel and rhubarb "like a little hero." The next day when Willie clinched his teeth and defied all efforts to give him his medicine, Josiah had only to appear, and Willie swallowed the dose of oil "like a man."[23]

The fatherly attention to the children continued despite the demands of the Confederate Ordnance Department. Wartime Richmond was a heady place for the Gorgas children, living as they did in the Virginia State Armory at the center of military activity, while their father went back and forth on the business of the Confederacy. Here, the soldier-father made time in a busy schedule to enjoy his children, to fence part of the Armory grounds as a playground, to take them to church, to walk seven miles with Willie in pleasant spring weather, and to bathe with his son one summer evening in a river near Richmond.[24]

The children saw southern heroes close at hand. In the spring of 1863, Josiah took eight-and-one-half-year-old Willie and seven-year-old Jessie to the Virginia capitol to view the body of General Stonewall Jackson. Children could hardly forget such an experience. One Sunday in the fall of 1863, when Willie met General Robert E. Lee for the first time, he sat on the general's lap. Afterward, the nine year old "seemed disappointed" because the general did not look sufficiently "heroic."[25] Despite Willie's disappointment in the appearance of General Lee, the role model of respected soldier-father "took" on the impressionable little boy. When Willie ran a fever so high as to cause hallucinations, Amelia reported to her husband that the boy's brain was "filled with Ord. matters" and that he had "passed hours trying to invent a *point for a bayonet.*" To her niece, she described her ten year old as "a *big boy* longing for the time he will enter the army."[26]

As Richmond fell in April 1865, Josiah and T. L. Bayne left the city with the Confederate secretary of war. The two sisters and their children stayed behind. At this time, Amelia had six children, ranging from eleven-year-old Willie to five-month-old Richard. Maria had three and was expecting another. After news at Danville of Robert E. Lee's surrender at Appomattox, the men moved south to Charlotte, North Carolina, to join Jefferson Davis. Then came word of General Joseph E. Johnston's surrender, and the Confederate government dissolved, each member to go his own way. The two brothers-in-law were not far from the Winnsboro, South Carolina, home of Mary Aiken, their wives' sister, so they rode in that direction. Bayne obviously intended to go home to New Orleans, but for Josiah, it was a different matter. In the past, he and his brothers had been very close, according to his sister, "until North and South became the all important words." Now somewhere in flight, Josiah decided to shelter with Amelia's relatives in Alabama, probably assuming that he would not exactly be welcomed if he sought refuge with his own family. After all, he had cast his lot with the South in 1861, and now he must live with the consequences of that decision. During the next several weeks, Josiah and Bayne crossed the South to join Amelia's widowed stepmother in Greensboro, Alabama, where the two men parted. As Josiah settled in, he waited daily to see if he would be arrested and imprisoned. In late 1865, as he saw his fears were needless, Josiah searched for a way to earn a livelihood for his family, who were by then in Cambridge, Maryland, where they had taken refuge with the father of one of the Yale classmates of Bayne. There, Amelia remained until April 1866, when Josiah had a home ready at Brierfield, near Montevallo, Alabama, where he had opened an iron furnace.[27]

The year-long separation deeply distressed Josiah. "It seems a loss to me that I am separated from my children . . . when I have so much leisure to be with them & I feel now like amusing them," he wrote Amelia. Visits to them only deepened his anguish. "I leave my wife and babies behind with great reluctance," he moaned in his journal. "I had hoped we would never again separate."[28]

In this interim, Willie, bereft of the parent with whom he had been so close, replaced the absent father as the "man" of the family. About the wedding of old friends in Baltimore, Amelia wrote, "I think I shall don my one silk dress & attend with Willie as escort. His grey suit shall be freshly trimmed with red & he shall appear as much as possible in the uniform of his lost but beloved Confederacy." On another occasion, she reported to Josiah that she and Willie had attended several activities intended "for the benefit of the suffering poor at the South." Also, she and Willie had dined recently with some of Josiah's old military friends.[29] Amelia contemplated sending Willie to join his father in Alabama, admitting, however, that this move would be a "privation" to her. "He is so manly & obedient that I find myself growing quite dependent upon him. He is my escort to any part of the city at night & my messenger by day." Despite her dread of separation from her eldest son, Amelia reported that Willie was "wild with delight" and "crazy" to join his father. The boy had sometimes been unable to sleep, "wishing now you were only here."[30]

Soon after the family was reunited at Brierfield in 1866, new strains appeared, as financial calamity reduced Josiah to despondency that was near suicidal. Too, the boy Willie that Josiah had left behind in Richmond had grown into an adolescent. The child whom Josiah had petted and played with and loved was now a maturing son to be trained for manhood's responsibilities. During the long separation, the roles of husband and son had become confused. The son had attempted to replace the absent husband and had become a rival for the mother's affection. The father now reasserted his position in the family as husband and father. The warm, affectionate parent became the stiff critic of Willie's shortcomings, using the powerful weapon of the need for paternal approval. Nowhere in the family correspondence or Josiah's journal is there any suggestion of the use of corporal punishment to discipline the children, nor is there any intimation of parental wrath that might crush a child's spirit. Josiah never presided over a fearful, subservient household. Rather, affection and approval that had been freely given to Willie now had to be repeatedly earned by the young man, and earning it was tough. Discipline was thereby achieved by the threat of the withholding of paternal approval, a terrifying prospect for a boy deeply attached to his father. Above all else, the eleven-and-one-half-year-old Willie wished to please his father, to make him proud. After a childhood of lavish paternal affection and then a year's separation when the son tried desperately to be the man of the family, the reunion at Brierfield opened a new phase in the father-son relationship. Now Josiah stiffly disciplined and silently loved his eldest son, as he prepared the boy for the harsh world beyond his home.[31] It was as if Josiah unconsciously focused his parental attention on Willie, the eldest son, who then would assume a parental role for the younger children. At this point, Josiah's parenting centered upon his father-son relationship with Willie.

Josiah did not try to educate and shape his son in his own image to equal or to surpass his own accomplishments. Quite the opposite, for Josiah strongly objected to his son's pursuit of a military career. Josiah commanded no economic authority, no "hold" over his son to influence his educational and career choices. Unlike a planter, he possessed no property on which to establish his son. What seemed at the time to be a financial deprivation may have been a blessing in disguise. The nine-teenth-century patriarchal family has been termed a "school for subordina-tion," although fathers desired to train sons to take their place and to dominate. Sons expecting to inherit fortunes often remained subservient to parental wishes.[32] Josiah and Willie had no such problems, as Josiah possessed nothing for Willie to inherit. The growing poverty of the Gorgas family restricted educational opportunities and would dictate fu-ture contributions from Willie for the family's financial well-being. In the 1870s, Josiah's health began a gradual decline, and it grew increasingly clear that Willie's education must eventually produce a career through which he could support himself and probably his parents and siblings. Josiah saw education as more than classroom performance. He instructed his son to keep an accurate record of his "little expenses" to know "ex-actly how to account" for money. "You can not too soon learn the value of money, for the prospect is very strong, my boy, that you will have to do as I did before you, make your own way in the world. This will be no disadvantage to you in the end."[33] Josiah quietly fostered a sense of pride in achievement and encouraged independence in his son.

It was Willie's great misfortune to have a gifted, intelligent sister eigh-teen months his junior. Beginning during Josiah's separation from his family in 1865–1866, Willie suffered from his parents' comparison of his talents with those of his younger sister. "Jessie has the best mind," wrote Amelia wistfully when Jessie was nine years old. "After a gigantic effort poor Willie produces a letter in pencil, pen & ink are beyond him yet a while." However, she noted, "He wrote it of his own free will feeling a great longing to communicate privately with you." She asked her husband to reply to the boy, urging him to "persevere & expressing gratification at this rude attempt."[34]

Josiah's withering responses continued the invidious comparison. The quality of Jessie's letter genuinely surprised him, but he supposed "Willie could not compete with her in this respect." He wrote, "Tell Willie his sister is getting ahead of him, and will leave him quite out of sight unless he practices daily. . . . Jessie's letter is really very creditable"; Willie, he hoped, "will persevere and improve his writing. Jessie does remarkably well." Eventually, Willie did improve, and Josiah observed with satifaction in his diary in March 1866 that he had received a letter that was "very well written. I am glad to see he improves."[35] It was very hard for Josiah to allow his son the luxury of failure.

Conscious of Josiah's increasing impatience with their eldest son, Amelia tried to intercede for Willie. On one occasion, she enclosed with her own a letter Willie had proudly written to his father:

> I have not looked over his note but you must not be too hard on him for he is more than willing to practice if I had time & patience to attend to him. Jessie is uncommonly bright & writes with as much ease as I do. It is a pretty sight to watch her leaning over Willie assisting him to copy some thing he has written on his slate. She is so motherly & gentle to him, correcting all his funny, boyish mistakes as gravely as if she were his grand mother.[36]

After the family had been reunited at Brierfield, the educational deprivations of living at an iron furnace in rural Alabama distressed both Josiah and Amelia. In February 1867, Willie was sent off to school in Greensboro, Alabama, Josiah noting in his diary that the "little fellow went off courageously." However, the next term Willie remained at home, where Josiah attempted to find the time to teach Willie and Jessie a "little Latin."[37]

In November 1867, Willie went to New Orleans to go to school and to live with Amelia's sister Maria and her husband, T. L. Bayne. Accounts of Willie's success there made Amelia ecstatic: "your proud Father & fond Mother offer their congratulations upon your success this month. To stand first in your class is no mean triumph & certainly more than I hoped for or expected." She admonished him to determine "to stand *first* in whatever pursuit or profession you decide to adopt." Josiah, however, was more restrained in acknowledging his satisfaction in his son's accomplishments: "Your mother & I are extremely gratified to hear your industry & obedience so highly commended." Even in his journal Josiah was restrained about this improvement in Willie's scholarship: "His mother is of course very proud to hear every one speak in praise of him." Unfortunately for all concerned, Willie's scholastic accomplishments were short-lived, and Josiah resumed his criticism of his son. Willie's spelling was particularly poor, and the best the father could say was that his son had "perseverance."[38] And Willie did try, especially because he wanted to earn his father's approval.

Facing financial disaster at the Brierfield ironworks, Josiah took the position of headmaster of the Junior Department at the University of the South at Sewanee, Tennessee, in 1868. It was decided to send Willie to Tennessee with him, while Amelia and the other children remained at Brierfield. The arrangement would permit Josiah time to make living arrangements for the family at Sewanee and allow Amelia to salvage what could be salvaged at Brierfield. Amelia was also pregnant and would suffer a miscarriage in September. This move of the father and son signaled another shift in their relationship. For the first time, the son was alone under the unremitting gaze of his father. Willie was then almost fifteen, and he unconsciously began to assert himself in his relationship with his father. The balance was slow to change, but gradually the son became the prime mover in the relationship as Josiah's parenting grew increasingly confined to reactions to his adolescent son's actions.

Leaving Brierfield was painful for Willie. His father described him at Sewanee as homesick, lonesome, downcast, and shy but believed it was well for him to go "where he stands on his own bottom, & has to make his way among the boys without assistance." Later, Josiah observed that his son did not "look quite happy," did not "laugh often," was "deficient," and could do "little for himself." He also fretted over his son's companions. "I am sorry to see he does not consort with the best & most *uppish* boys. I don't think he feels himself quite at home yet. He is a little less important than he was at home, & this I think he don't [*sic*] quite understand. Perhaps it is best so."[39]

At Sewanee comparisons were now with the other boys. In his father's eyes, Willie fared no better than he had at home in comparisons with his sister. "Perhaps you had better write a letter to Willie," suggested Josiah to Amelia, "urging him for your sake to apply himself. He is now 15 & should begin to feel his responsibilities. I don't like to say too much to him. He is not doing as well as I had hoped in any of his studies. I feel disappointed in him, very much disappointed. Perhaps he had better go to some other school. . . ." Occasionally, Josiah enclosed "poor Willie's scrawl" in a letter to Amelia, adding, "I fear he is hopeless," and, "letter writing is evidently not his *forte*."[40] The relentless catalog of the boy's failings continued. Willie was "terribly, shamefully backward; and I am really at a loss what to do with him. I try not to tell him so, but he is not over sensitive, & can bear pretty hard reproofs. I think he writes a good deal worse now than he did six months ago." Josiah often attached critical postscripts to Willie's letters to his mother. "Poor Willie has apparently done his best above, but you see how terribly deficient he is in spelling." Willie tried to satisfy his father. "He has just handed me a letter . . . to put a stamp on for him. The superscription is all right at least. I think he feels solicitous about his spelling now, as he asked me several times how many errors I found in his letter to you, and says he did not mean to write 'grownd' but 'u.' "[41]

Josiah continued to correct his son even after Willie turned twenty-one.

"Apply yourself to improving your hand. Write a little more *roundly* & very slowly & carefully. Form your letters if you can a little more like this: a c m n o p q r and so on; and don't spell *remarcable* with a c!" And "Be careful about your letters, I note 3 errors '*Greenville*' has an *e*, '*predecesor*' another s, '*compeditors*' this is of course a slip. In writing the congressman's name write McFarland. You wrote McFarland—perhaps it is MacFarland. Be careful as to proper names—people are touchy."[42]

Willie ultimately proved to be a late bloomer scholastically. At Sewanee he "turned student" in 1870 and won the Alabama medal for scholarship, "a very beautiful gold medal. His mother & sisters are very proud of it & him to say nothing of my feelings on the subject."[43] Josiah's cold restraint had for a moment melted in pride in his son. It is a tribute to the character of William Crawford that Josiah's criticisms did not become self-fulfilling prophecies in his son.

Not unexpectedly, the boy whose temper improved outdoors, who was a less than satisfactory student, whose father was a general, and whose mother dressed him to appear as much as possible in the uniform of his lost but beloved Confederacy developed an early fascination for guns and hunting. The fascination continued throughout his lifetime. When there was a possibility that Willie might join his father in Alabama in the summer of 1865, Josiah told Amelia to allow the boy "to bring his gun, some powder & shot." Confederate General Joseph E. Johnston sent Willie a Christmas present in 1866 of a powder flask and shot pouch. The boy shot his first bird one day while the general was visiting Josiah, and Willie burst in upon the two generals, glowing with joy. Johnston was "delighted." On another occasion, Josiah observed in his journal that Willie and one of his friends had returned from a day's shooting, "proud of a crow, a lark & a dove!"[44]

When Willie went off to school at Sewanee, he pined for hunting at home at Brierfield. "He is impatient to get home," Josiah wrote Amelia, "but gloats chiefly over the prospect of hunting." Only a broken arm could prevent a shooting excursion during winter vacation. From Sewanee, Willie wrote his sister that he and one of his classmates planned "to try a hunt tomorrow but do not expect to kill much as it is most too early to find many birds." Later that fall, Willie spent his school vacation hunting with a friend in Texas.[45] For a boy who loved guns, hunting, and the out-of-doors, a military career would naturally be attractive.

Willie chose a military career over the vehement objections of his father. When the boy was only six years old, Josiah noted in his journal in the midst of his reassignment from Charleston to Philadelphia that "I do not want Willie to take or retain a commission in the army. My great regret is the wandering life we are obliged to lead."[46] The father never changed his mind about the army as a career for his son. Unfortunately for Josiah, the dream of a military career snared Willie as a boy, and he could never completely shake it off. Maybe it was that lyrical image of the Confederate soldier that Faulkner said lurks in the heart of every southern boy. After all, this boy had sat on the lap of Robert E. Lee and had seen Stonewall Jackson in his casket. Years later, when Willie was in his sixties, he wrote a condolence letter to a childhood friend after the death of the friend's father. He remembered the man going out to a sawmill near Brierfield every morning. "He was just from the Army and had one of the finest horses that could be found in the country. He still wore his slouch hat, and I recollect him as one of the finest and most soldierly figures when mounted on his horse that I have ever seen. I was a boy of twelve at that time and he was my ideal and I fairly worshipped him."[47]

Military figures were Willie's heroes. In the harsh eyes of the world, Josiah was a success as a soldier and a failure as a civilian. A lengthy separation from his family divided the periods of success and failure in his life, and during that separation, the son became the man of the family. While Josiah resisted a military career for his son, the family unwittingly reinforced Willie's determination to choose the same occupation as his father by proudly reminiscing about Josiah's successful years as a soldier. The status, respect, and gracious life-style accorded Josiah before 1865 contrasted sharply with the genteel poverty of his postwar career as a civilian in a failing iron business or as a harassed teacher in a school teetering on the edge of bankruptcy. Like so many other fallen southern families, all that the Gorgases had left after 1865 was a sense of pride in the family's past. As Josiah agonized over the possibility that he might fail in his responsibility to see his son well settled in the world, he plunged into deep depression, and the family attempted to boost his morale by emphasizing his earlier successes.[48] Certainly, by this point in Willie's life, the boy was aware of the near miracle his father had performed in keeping the Confederate armies supplied during the Civil War. He was immensely proud of his father, and his "pride grew as he grew older."[49]

After Willie completed his work at Sewanee in December 1874 and at his parents' urging, he went to New Orleans to work in the law office of his Uncle T. L. Bayne. Exactly when Willie decided upon a military career for himself is uncertain, but while he was in New Orleans, if not before, the decision became definite, and he began preparing for his West Point examinations. Ten years later, Willie described this period in New Orleans as one in which certain "things" seemed "unendurable at the time, but I have found out from experience could have been cured in a short time." Josiah grieved to see his son "so infatuated about West Point, & so opposed to the law, in which he would have so capital an opportunity with his uncle Bayne."[50]

Willie's desire to escape a legal career with his uncle in New Orleans may have been motivated by more than an infatuation with West Point. The oldest of the Bayne children was Mamie. The two cousins had practically grown up together as the two families had made their homes together for extended periods of time. Willie had lived with the Baynes in 1867 and 1868 while he attended school in New Orleans. Willie's letters to "Coz" were among his first efforts at letter writing. Whenever the Gorgases received a letter from Mamie or news about her in a letter from the Baynes, it was always Willie who was presumed to be interested in hearing about her. For example, Amelia wrote Josiah that she had received notes one morning from Bayne and Mamie, and now she enclosed "Mamie's as it will interest Willie."[51] On another occasion, Josiah commented to Amelia about Willie answering that "really charming letter of Mamie Bayne." Two days later, he wrote that Willie was "concocting something" to Mamie. Later, Josiah wrote Amelia that Willie had "filled one page & 2 lines on the next to his Coz (which he spells *Couz*)." In one letter from Bayne to Josiah, Mamie enclosed a letter to Willie teasing him about his bashfulness. Still later, Josiah reported to Amelia that their son had heard Mamie's letter read with "lively pleasure," and "Willie promises to write to his Coz to-day, from whom he has rec'd another letter."[52] Mamie was the only person whom the family mentioned as a regular correspondent with Willie other than his parents.[53]

Willie tried the legal profession while he lived with the Baynes for much of 1875. Willie was then almost twenty-one, a handsome young man from the country (Brierfield and Sewanee). Mamie was then twenty, a stunningly beautiful and stylish young lady from the most cosmopolitan city of the New South. Six years earlier, Amelia had commented prior to a visit of the Baynes to Sewanee that Mamie would "turn the heads of half the boys. She is so bright & attractive." From New Orleans, Willie wrote his mother about his pretty cousin, and Amelia answered, "Yes, I know how sweet Coz is in party dress. I dont blame the gentlemen for admiring her; do you? Her lovely disposition is more to me, than the white neck & arms & is worth a fortune to any man." She concluded her letter saying "I did not give you my darling boy the orthodox motherly council when you left us because I knew that no temptations would ever entice you to bring grief to the hearts of the loved ones at home."[54] Perhaps Amelia understood the ageless dictum that one can gauge a man's interest in a woman by how often her name pops up in his conversation or letters.

A few months later, Josiah visited the Baynes and saw Willie off to Tennessee to pursue his dream of admission to West Point. "He writes cheerfully, both to me & to Mamie," Josiah recounted to Amelia. "I wish he could give up this entanglement but I suppose that is hardly to be hoped for until Mamie gets married."[55] Willie's decision to forego what his father termed "so capital an opportunity" to pursue a legal career with his uncle was influenced by the problem of an attraction to his first cousin.

To satisfy his determination for a military career, Willie had to win an appointment to West Point. Unfortunately, he had forfeited his Tennessee residency by his year in his uncle's law office. At the end of 1875, he sought to establish residency in any congressional district in Alabama or Tennessee where there appeared to be a chance for an appointment.[56] Josiah resigned himself to doing all he could to help Willie achieve the desired goal. As Willie acknowledged a decade later, Josiah "acquiesced without a word in what must have been a great disappointment to him." He swallowed his pride and solicited recommendations from President Ulysses S. Grant, and he did not chide his son about the spectacle of an ex-Confederate general trying to get his son into West Point. Josiah admitted to Amelia that he expected nothing from his efforts, but he acted "to satisfy Willie that everything has been done that I could do."[57] Meanwhile, Josiah suggested to his son that he cultivate "social relations" with the family of one congressman from whom Willie sought an appointment, adding, "Women move the world you know."[58]

Amelia, too, wrote letters and advised Willie about his quest. "Call on the Episcopal minister & introduce yourself. He may be of some service to you." She also admonished him "to be extra careful in your dress, knowing how much it influences strangers & how vastly my handsome boy is improved by it."[59]

Willie had already begun taking the examinations for West Point. When he failed the first one, his father did not assume his customary posture of criticizing his son and badgering him to improve. Instead, Josiah tried to bolster his son's morale: "you must make up your mind . . . to suffer disappointment after all your labors," and *don't make yourself unhappy over the past*. Work for the future. You still have June & Sept next, & I hope something may turn up. . . . keep your book open for any future examination that you may get access to."[60] Privately, he expressed his fear to Amelia that there was a "predetermination in these cases. Of course the Examiner can mark as they please, with a perfect appearance of fairness." Josiah hoped that Willie had "made up his mind to failure at last. I think the President might reach his name in a year or two, if Willie could wait. I have little hope of it this year."[61] Josiah was very supportive of an effort of which he disapproved highly and wherein he expected Willie to fail. Earlier, he had withheld approval and criticized his son to spur him to greater effort and achievement.

As Josiah had predicted, the efforts proved futile. In the fall of 1876, Josiah observed in his journal that Willie had "exhausted himself, trying to get to West Point, & attended several competitive examinations, until on the 3rd of this month he passed beyond the prescribed age (22)."[62]

Josiah and Amelia presumed that the issue of a military career for Willie was closed, but they underestimated their son's determination. Having failed to achieve a military career along the customary route via West Point, Willie entered Bellevue Hospital Medical College in New York City in September 1876. Josiah accepted this course at face value and expressed pride in his son's choice of a medical career. "We are all very much gratified at your success. It is your first step . . . in your professional life—a success-ful life I hope it will be." Amelia saw medicine as a career that would make Willie a "good useful & great man."[63]

Then news came that placed Willie's interest in medicine in a new light. A letter to Josiah from T. L. Bayne in 1878 recounted the latter's recent visit with Willie in New York and warned Josiah that Willie would "get into the Army yet, if he can." Josiah did not wish to believe that Willie intended to become an army doctor, and after Willie had visited him, he wrote Amelia about discussions with their son. "What dreams flow thro' the boy's mind. . . . I fear he is very impractical. But he has worked well & thus far been successful. We must keep him at his profession, hold him to a high standard—theoretically. Practically I should be glad if he had $600 a year at the [Alabama Insane] Assylum [*sic*] & could stay with us."[64]

To his son, Josiah wrote about financial opportunities. One was "worth looking into, provided you still harp upon the Army. I confess I had rather see you assume the position (at Utica) with a salary of $1200 a year. I am afraid the Army *might* switch you off the track of your grand profession."[65] Clearly, no confrontation occurred between father and son over the son's career choice. Willie just quietly persisted in his medical studies and al-lowed events to take their course. Josiah had schooled Willie well in self-reliance and independence.

Until Willie went to New York, his education had cost Josiah little more than what the father called a "very irksome" mode of life—"the charge of boys" at Sewanee. Now Josiah sent his son money to cover some expenses, and he feared that occasionally Willie's finances must be "pretty low." However, he assured Willie that no matter how bleak matters appeared to be, there would be money to pay for his medical studies. Bayne had prom-ised Josiah that he would gladly advance funds to complete the boy's educa-tion if necessary, "so," Josiah wrote, "that if anything should happen to me I feel safe, & you may feel safe that you need not abandon your studies."[66] As a successful New Orleans attorney, Bayne obviously could provide mate-rial benefits for Willie that Josiah could not. Yet, there is no evidence in either the family correspondence or Josiah's journal that the father felt threatened by the relationship between Willie and Bayne.

Willie's move to New York and medical school coincided with Josiah's rapidly failing health and his difficulties with the Sewanee trustees who were forcing him out of his position as headmaster of the Junior Depart-ment. Josiah's financial future was grim as he approached the age of sixty. In his journal, he expressed the hope that when Willie was sixty, his son would be an "honored member of his high profession, & *will have attained a competency*, without which old age is not honored & may become a burden." An old southern friend came to Josiah's rescue in 1878. N.H.R. Dawson, a distinguished attorney in Selma, Alabama, telegraphed Josiah of his election as president of the University of Alabama. Josiah immediately resigned his position at Sewanee after ten years' service and boarded a train for Tuscaloosa.[67]

A few months later, the entire family joined him. However, just as they were "very comfortably established" with Josiah's pleasant new job—not to mention a fine salary and the use of the splendid president's mansion— Josiah suffered a severe stroke in February 1879. He was four months from his sixty-first birthday. Never fully recovering, he resigned as university president in September. The trustees appointed him university librarian, a post Amelia and their daughters could cover for him when necessary, and gave him a residence on campus. In the months immediately after Josiah's stroke, the family was frantic about Josiah's health and their financial situation. Willie was warned that he might have to find a job to pay his expenses, and Amelia urged him, "Do what is best for your future, for your old Mother & Father may be your dependents & you must do whatever will promote your interests and success."[68]

Amelia did not need to remind Willie of his duty on his parents' behalf, for deference and duty had long been integral to Willie's psychological makeup. Father and son felt a deep sense of obligation to each other. Paternal duty, as Josiah saw it, dictated that he provide for his children in a material sense and that he teach them to be honest and self-reliant and to make something of their lives. Obligations were reciprocal. Josiah and Willie saw parents' and sons' duties as lifelong, to provide mutual comfort and respect. When Willie was in medical school in New York, Josiah expressed the hope that his son's life would be one of "usefulness, and of distinction."[69] He admonished him not to sleep late in the morning. "Sluggishness in the morning is not conducive to a good day's work. I want you to accomplish more in life than I did. I feel the effect of time wasted." Despite his relentless criticism of his son, Josiah had never tried to appear as a moral or physical superman to Willie. In admitting his own failures, he set the stage for his son not only to mature and achieve at the father's level but also to excel in his chosen career.[70]

After Josiah's stroke, all of the older children except Willie quit school and made plans to contribute to the family income. Amelia wrote her eldest child that "we must help ourselves as long as we can & you can save your earning for the time of need" and enclosed the usual check. She proposed to delay a decision about the family's future for a few weeks to see if Josiah could resume his work as university president. If not, "then we will consult & decide upon our future." After Josiah's stroke, he relinquished the role of provider and guardian of the family to Willie, who was then twenty-four. The façade of stern patriarch also faded, and the depth and the intensity of Josiah's love for his son was visible. Amelia urged Willie to write often because "Your Father is constantly thinking of you I know for he frequently calls your name aloud."[71] On Willie's twenty-fifth birthday, she recounted that the "first words your Father said when he

awoke was 'This is Willie's *birth*day, dear boy how I long to see him.' "
Josiah prayed that the dear Lord "permit me to clasp my boy to my heart
once more, else I could hardly bear the increasing burdens of our lives."
Later, she wrote that Josiah looked forward "with eagerness" to his son's
visit.[72]

Eventually, the checks to Willie had to stop, and Amelia "grieved" to
think "how sorely you must need funds and how helpless we are to send
you money just now. . . . Don't grieve over W Point or anything else that
cannot be remedied. All was done for the best. You are putting yourself in
a position to assist your family far more materially than you could possibly
have done in the army." Amelia understood reciprocal obligations, too. "I
am strong," she wrote, "& able to exert myself for years to come & by that
time your loving arms will sustain & rest me. Your Father's devotion to you
knows no bounds," she concluded. Recently, Josiah had told Amelia that if
he could see his son for a few days, Willie could "do something for me." He
would place himself in his son's hands "with the utmost confidence."[73]

Two years after the checks from Amelia to Willie stopped, the son began
to send his mother money with increasing frequency and in increasing
amounts. This practice continued for thirty-nine years. The father's admonition to record expenses had profoundly impressed the son, and Willie
maintained detailed account books. Copies for the years 1877 through 1919
still survive. These reflect even the most minute expenditures—oranges
and oysters, cigars and haircuts, buttons and underwear—and depict
Willie's frugal life-style as a young man and as an adult. They also reflect
how seriously he took his financial duty to his family, as he sent his mother
approximately one-third of his army salary, while he supported a wife and a
daughter. As his salary rose, so did the amount that he sent to Amelia.
After his mother died in 1913, he sent checks to his sisters, mailing the last
one from London four days before he suffered a fatal stroke in 1920.[74]

After his father's stroke in 1879 Willie assumed personal responsibility
for his brother Richard, then fifteen. As the youngest of six children,
Richard had not received the intense supervision that Josiah had given to
Willie, the eldest. In a parental role, the brother was far more relaxed than
the father had been. Willie wrote Richard, "Next spring . . . I shall probably be able to pay your school expenses. By the time you are 18 we can all
have laid by enough for your Univ. course, either at the Univ. of Va. or any
other school you prefer." A few months later, Willie wrote again about
Richard's future education and career. "You will have to look around you
in the next four or five years & decide what course you will pursue in life."
He hoped to be able to allow his brother to finish his education as he
pleased and then choose a profession. "I must confess," he wrote wistfully,
"I should like to see you at West Point. But I believe that every man should
follow his own tastes when he has any decided likes or dislikes."[75]

Richard eventually graduated from the University of Alabama and tried his hand in T. L. Bayne's law office in New Orleans. "Richie is not in love with the law but he has plenty to do," Amelia wrote Willie, who doubtless found such comments sounding very familiar.[76]

Josiah's paternal duty to transform his eldest son into a responsible, self-supporting adult had now been met, actually well met, as the illustrious medical career of William Crawford Gorgas and his role as a conscientious family man himself attest. In June 1880, one year after graduation from medical school, Willie entered the United States Army as an assistant surgeon. He gained fame first as chief sanitary officer with the United States Army in Havana (1898–1902), where he applied Walter Reed's theories on the transmission of yellow fever. Even more significant was his role in sanitation efforts that made possible the building of the Panama Canal, during which he was chief sanitary officer and later a member of the Isthmian Canal Commission. Without his work, thousands of lives would have been lost, and the United States could have met failure as had the French earlier. After his success in Panama, William Crawford Gorgas served as surgeon general of the United States Army from 1914 to 1918. The son had become even more famous than the father.[77]

Paternal approval had disciplined the adolescent and shaped his education. Only in asserting the primacy of his own career aspirations did the son balk in his customary deference to parental authority. With Josiah's stroke in February 1879, the tug-of-war between the father and the twenty-four-year-old son ended, and the two reversed their roles.

Clearly, Josiah Gorgas as a father was a product of his age. Parenting in a transition era, he embodied the Victorian father intent on nurturing his children while at the same time exercising discipline. Sternness and sympathy alternated in his relationship with his son, with sympathy tempering sternness; and sternness, sympathy. Although the defeat of the South in the Civil War destroyed Josiah's military career, Reconstruction was far more devastating to his relationships with his family. It crushed his hopes for prosperity, thus threatening his role as provider. It also separated Josiah from his family, creating a vacuum in which his son attempted to fill his place, and, thereafter, father and son subconsciously competed for the mother's affections.

Over a lifetime, Josiah always closed the many letters that he wrote to Willie with "Affy." or "Affy your father," usually the latter. In what appears to have been his last letter to his son, Josiah unconsciously acknowledged that the process of molding Willie the adolescent into William Crawford Gorgas the man was complete, that he was relinquishing his paternal role. Only in his letter of May 10, 1880, did he close with "Good-by. Affy yr son."[78]

Epilogue

DREW GILPIN FAUST

"AT THE CENTER OF Victorian life was the family," Walter Houghton wrote in his classic study *The Victorian Frame of Mind*.[1] As the foundation generally of Victorian society throughout the Anglo-American world, the family assumed perhaps even greater significance in the nineteenth-century American South, where it served as the bulwark of the Southern social order and as the region's central social institution. Because slavery required concentration of power in the slaveholders' hands and because it inhibited the development of urban life, the South of the early nineteenth-century was an "underinstitutionalized" world. It lacked the developed infrastructure of much of the rest of the nation, where social functions ranging from work to education to responsibility for social control and social welfare had moved outside the home and had become public concerns. In the South, these activities lingered within the private realm, closely connected to family life. As Elizabeth Fox-Genovese has argued, "in contrast to the North," white Southern households held within themselves the "decisive relations of production and reproduction" and "retained a vigor that permitted Southerners to ascribe many matters to the private sphere, whereas Northerners would increasingly ascribe them to the public spheres of market and state."[2] The private sphere, the family, thus in a paradoxical sense took on such importance in the white Southern social order as to become political in significance, the essential foundation of Southern public life and values.

Yet, family is always necessarily more than a static bulwark or foundation. As the central institution in the transmission of culture from generation to generation, the family serves as both agent and mediator of social and ideological change. Change must be at the heart of any understanding of the South during this period, an era that encompasses the experience

253

and devastation of Civil War and the transition from bondage to freedom of four million slaves. The task Carol Bleser set for the Fort Hill Conference was to investigate these broad-scale political, social, and cultural developments by examining them through the prism of family life, while simultaneously exploring the family through its refraction of such social and political transformations.

An important source or dynamic of change that *In Joy and in Sorrow: Women, Family, and Marriage in the Victorian South, 1830–1900* forcefully illustrates derives from the persisting tensions within the ideology of nineteenth-century family, as well as between these ideas and the social practice of family life. Examples of white Southerners' prescriptions for family relations and their self-conscious reflections about family ideals abound in this collection of essays. Familial values, Eugene Genovese reminds us, "lay at the core of the slaveholders' world view." Even their cookbooks, as Alan Grubb shows us, were as concerned with recipes for domestic life as for food or drink. Yet, these nineteenth-century Southerners clearly recognized that many of the issues that confronted them were not easily resolved, that conflicting imperatives were at work within their systems of belief about family life.

Peter Bardaglio's essay, dealing with the comparatively neat abstractions of appellate justice, may demonstrate this ideological uncertainty most explicitly and compellingly. There was a "tension," he argues, "between marriage as a voluntary contractual act and as an organic institution that provided the foundations of the social order." The South, in other words, particularly in the years before the Civil War but continuing into the postwar period, embraced parts of two conflicting notions of family. The first was the traditional and hierarchical conception in which persons were defined—and defined themselves—by their relations with others; the second was the "bourgeois" belief in self-identity and, thus, marriage based upon romantic love.

These essays show in rich detail how these ideologies operated in the lives of particular Southerners. Wylma Wates describes women of the Izard family struggling to define the criteria by which to choose husbands. Anne Izard rejects wealth as a consideration out of hand; such dynastic considerations appear to her clearly outdated. But she is somewhat hesitant to embrace fully the ideal of companionate marriage. "I asked myself if I thought I could be happy with him and as it really appeared that I could, I thought I acted right in accepting him." Virginia Burr finds Gertrude Thomas a few decades later making, in face of her father's reservations, what proves to be in many ways an unfortunate marital choice by basing her decision squarely on the dictates of romantic love. And Carol Bleser and Frederick Heath identify the same motive operating in Virginia Tunstall's 1843 marriage to Clement Claiborne Clay: "she was eager to marry Clement for she loved him."

Yet despite the growing significance of the ideals of companionate marriage, reverence for hierarchy persists: Elizabeth Fox-Genovese notes that Sarah Gayle seeks a "protector" in a husband; Gertrude Thomas finds in her spouse "just the 'master will' to suit her nature. '[F]or true to my sex, I delight in *looking up* and love to feel my woman's weakness protected by man's superior strength.' " In these antebellum years, Gertrude Thomas, Burr reminds us, "showed herself to be a true daughter of patriarchy." Any embryonic egalitarianism in views about the place of men and women in the family certainly is not evident in the attitudes these elite white Southerners display toward children of different sexes. Both the Gayles and the Gorgases baldly acknowledge male children to be of paramount emotional and social importance.

For families of the white elite, growing attention to the affective dimensions of domestic experience was made possible in many cases by the underpinnings of economic independence and personal autonomy. Treatments of free black, slave, and sharecropping families in this collection remind us of other family functions and of structural factors retarding the movement toward the growing emphasis on individual feeling and emotional fulfillment as the purposes of family life. James Roark and Michael Johnson have stressed the importance of "strategies of survival" in the shaping of family practice, a kind of "safety-first" imperative. Before free blacks could think about racial solidarity with slaves or the possible benefits of female self-realization through autonomy, they had to consider survival. We must, Johnson and Roark remind us, think about families historically, "in the context of their world, not ours." In late twentieth-century America, where so many of the social and political functions of the family have been assumed by other institutions, we automatically stress the affective, psychological functions of family. Such an emphasis in our examination of historical families may produce serious misunderstanding. Free black families had first and foremost to devise strategies to prosper economically and thus to remain free. The postwar sharecroppers in Jacqueline Jones's essay confronted a not dissimilar imperative—though in their case the threat was not slavery but peonage or, if they were not too unlucky, perhaps a lower rung on the tenancy ladder.

Such an emphasis on the defensive functions of family reminds us of some of the distinctive features—even threats—inherent in the world of the nineteenth-century South, a world in which unfettered independence, Johnson and Roark warn us, might have been "dangerous," where the personalistic foundations of justice, wealth, and power gave individual autonomy a far less clearly positive value than it holds in our own time. This was a society in which the protection of belonging, of associating oneself with a white male, was often a political necessity, however ultimately undesirable it might have seemed. As Eugene Genovese quotes George W. Armstrong in 1858, "of all the unreal visions which 'the foolish heart, darkened' has conjured up, none is more unreal than the vision of man standing by and for himself." Freedom and autonomy have not always been the highest desiderata in human life. We must historicize them and understand the nineteenth-century South as a society in which their import and appeal changed over time. Freedom without power could be meaningless. Affective considerations were in many cases luxuries that could be addressed only after survival was assured.

Nevertheless, there seems to be during this period—especially among the elite white families—a kind of ideological continuum, progressing from traditional to increasingly bourgeois notions of family, from fatherhood based on traditional "authoritarian power" to child rearing (as Sarah Wiggins describes the family of Josiah Gorgas) by "authoritative influence." Like many of the white Southerners portrayed in these essays, Gorgas found himself "in a transition era" of family life, combining in his paternal role nurturance and discipline, "sternness and sympathy." Elizabeth Fox-Genovese and Eugene Genovese would associate this movement with the increasing ideological incursions of the capitalist world into the slave society of the Old South and ultimately with the disappearance during the Civil War of the social formation of slavery itself.

Several of these essays do illustrate with compelling specificity how the Civil War undermined the hierarchy of white male power within the Southern family. Women like Gertrude Thomas, *"looking up"* to be "protected by man's superior strength," found themselves greatly disappointed by both their individual men and the Confederacy more generally. Jefferson Thomas followed his desultory military service with financial miscalculations and deceits that ruined his family, thrusting Gertrude largely on her own resources as manager and classroom teacher. Clement Claiborne Clay proved equally incompetent in the face of postwar economic upheavals and became, Bleser and Heath tell us, "more and more depressed and dependent" upon his wife. He felt, he said, he had lost " 'all self confidence and courage.' " Both Clement Clay and Jefferson Thomas turned to drink, while their wives embraced the movement for women's suffrage. It was a considerable journey from Gertrude Thomas's prewar celebrations of patriarchy and Virginia Clay's belledom.

The theme of male failure is central to *In Joy and in Sorrow*, and the disastrous choice white Southern men made in favor of civil war represents only a small part of the record against them. The white men in this collection of essays are not a very admirable lot. With the exception of Josiah Gorgas, whom we may excuse as a Northerner by birth in any case, we might most charitably characterize them as feckless. Sarah Gayle harangues against their disappearance into grog shops and shuffleboard games. Jefferson Thomas and Clement Clay disappear into the bottle. The Percy men Bertram Wyatt-Brown describes offer us a multi-generational "record of despondency and self-dissolution." But these fissures in the patriarchy seem minor in the larger context of this collection. At least the Percys only kill themselves. Nineteenth-century white Southern men sexually abuse women and children, committing incest and rape with only mild legal reproof, Peter Bardaglio tells us. And Catherine Clinton and Brenda Stevenson remind us of the realities of "Southern dishonor," of the very great distance between the ideology of Christian slaveholding and the day-to-day practices of familial and sexual exploitation of slaves. Black families, cast in the historiography of the last decade as models of strength and humanity, are in this collection deromanticized; they are, Stevenson tells us, deeply affected—driven themselves to violence and disintegration—by the contagion of white male aggression. The "brutality that whites imposed on their slaves," she remarks, "undoubtedly influenced the ways in which bondsmen treated their own children and other dependents."

The most fundamental threat to the patriarchy of the South, the most compelling force pushing for change, thus ironically becomes the patriarch himself. His abuses of his own power are undercutting its very foundations; his lack of competence in face of wartime reversals reinforces his military and political failures. "Men without pity or honor," as Faulkner's Rosa Coldfield describes them in *Absalom, Absalom!*, could not maintain the foundations on which the Southern social order was based. The master class had apparently forgotten both its *noblesse* and its *oblige*. "Is it any wonder," as Rosa pointedly asks after Confederate defeat, that "Heaven saw fit to let us lose?"[3]

So if it is the white men who are the unwitting revolutionaries undermining the legitimacy of their own rule, what political role does this leave for women and blacks? Those we have seen in these essays are not overtly rebellious, hardly even resistors of the domination of white males. The current historiographical return to an interest in the damage done by slavery is evident here. These essays place far more emphasis upon the constraints the system imposed than the possibilities it offered. And white women, too, are limited in their expressions of opposition. Catherine Clinton, despite her disclaimers, casts them largely as victims. Elizabeth Fox-Genovese would vigorously dissent from such a portrayal, but certainly not because she regards them as active or effective opponents of the social order. Both Fox-Genovese and Genovese find elite antebellum women to be eager supporters of their world, as well as of the slave system upon which it rests. The "discernible influence of the ladies," Eugene Genovese notes, "came down hard on the side of proslavery and political extremism." Bertram Wyatt-Brown discovers Catherine Ann Warfield's 1860 novel, *The Household of Bouverie*, to be suffused with anger, yet judges her protest against male domination only muted. After the Civil War, her attitude changes somewhat, but in Warfield's eight post-bellum novels, only a "modest degree of autonomy finds expression." Gertrude Thomas, with her important contributions to woman suffrage, moves closest to a self-consciously oppositional feminist position. Yet within the context of her life, we can perhaps most accurately characterize her reformist efforts as a dimension of the strategic coping that serves as a theme in almost all these essays. Nineteenth-century Southerners, black and white, and their families confronted enormous difficulties—as oppressed slaves or free blacks, as defeated and impoverished Confederates, even as depression-haunted artists in the Percy mode. Above all, these essays chronicle how their subjects deal with adversity, not so much in celebration of their triumphs, for they were few, but in more quiet admiration of the less-dramatic heroism of their survival.

Were the stresses these families confronted markedly different from those faced by other families in other times and places? Do their experiences of slavery and civil war make nineteenth-century Southern families entirely exceptional? Do these families represent an embodiment of Tolstoy's oft-quoted maxim that "every unhappy family is unhappy in its own way"? *In Joy and in Sorrow* tantalizes us with suggestions of both the uniqueness and the typicality of nineteenth-century Southern families. The label "Victorian" urges further comparison with transatlantic counterparts. Exploration of familial attitudes and experiences of the English upper class would undoubtedly reveal much about the nature of Southern planters' lives, just as comparisons between European workers and the sharecropping families Jacqueline Jones describes would help illuminate the degree of peculiarity of the South's post-Civil War labor arrangements. The potential richness of comparisons with primal West African family forms is also striking. The centrality of the notion of belonging and of relational foundations for identity in Africa suggest that the "household" form Elizabeth Fox-Genovese attributes to the American South may be as much West African as European in origin.

The essays in this volume suggest another important dimension of comparison as well. The Fort Hill Conference sought simultaneously to address the experiences of black and white families. Such ventures are quite new; with only a few recent exceptions, scholars have tended to explore such issues within separate black and white histories. This collection thus prompts us to think about models and methods for this newly integrated effort. Several of the essays in fact offer implicit assumptions or theories about how the experiences of black and white families are related. Roark and Johnson see free-black family behavior shaped largely as a defense against potential white oppression; Brenda Stevenson portrays slave families deeply affected by white cruelty; Catherine Clinton shows black and white women abused by white males. In an essay that endeavors systematically to ask the same questions about black and white families, Jacqueline Jones finds that even in apparently similar economic situations, the factor of race renders the experiences of the two groups quite different. And, of course, in the analytically powerful notion of the household, Elizabeth

Fox-Genovese and Eugene Genovese offer a theoretical as well as a descriptive model of how Southern families, black and white, were connected socially, economically, and ideologically. All these essays make important statements about the ways in which black and white families in the South were interrelated, by structure and function, as well as by blood, about their influences upon one another, and about the potential sources for familial change. As Bertram Wyatt-Brown so eloquently phrases it, Southern "family connections were as thick and tangled as the forest underbrush along the banks of the Homochitto."

It is true that the essayists of *In Joy and in Sorrow* have not been easy on Southern families—black or white, slave or free. But serious discussion of family—be it historical or personal—seems to me almost always to be critical. Our expectations for this institution are so protean and so high that the experience of family life almost always falls short of our prescriptions. That is why families are so interesting. And that is why novelists from Faulkner, Percy, Warren, and Welty to Walker, Crews, Morrison, and Tyler have made Southern families the stuff of great fiction. But the essays in this volume, *In Joy and in Sorrow*, show that we hardly need to turn to fiction for compelling characters and arresting stories that cannot but bring us to reflect upon our own lives.

Appendix for
"An Outrage upon Nature"

Southern Appellate Cases Cited

I. INCEST CASES

Alabama

Morgan v. State, 11 Ala. 289 (1847)
Baker v. State, 30 Ala. 521 (1857)
Smith v. State, 108 Ala. 1 (1895)
Elder v. State, 123 Ala. 35 (1898)

Arkansas

State v. Fritts and Phillips, 48 Ark. 66 (1886)
Martin v. State, 58 Ark. 3 (1893)
State v. Ratcliffe, 61 Ark. 62 (1895)
Nations v. State, 64 Ark. 467 (1897)

Florida

Brown v. State, 27 So. 869 (1900)

Georgia

Cook v. State, 11 Ga. 53 (1852)
Powers v. State, 44 Ga. 209 (1871)
Raiford v. State, 68 Ga. 672 (1882)
Taylor v. State, 110 Ga. 150 (1900)

Louisiana

State v. Guiton, 51 La. An. 155 (1898)

261

Mississippi

Chancellor v. State, 47 Miss. 278 (1872)
Newman v. State, 69 Miss. 393 (1891)

North Carolina

State v. Kessler, 78 N.C. 469 (1878)
State v. Laurence, 95 N.C. 659 (1886)

South Carolina

State v. Reynolds, 48 S.C. 384 (1896)

Tennessee

Ewell v. State, 14 Tenn. 364 (1834)
Owen v. State, 89 Tenn. 698 (1891)
Shelly v. State, 95 Tenn. 152 (1895)
Wilson v. State, 100 Tenn. 596 (1898)

Texas

Tuberville v. State, 4 Tex. 128 (1849)
Freeman v. State, 11 Tex. App. 92 (1881)
Compton v. State, 13 Tex. App. 271 (1882)
McGrew v. State, 13 Tex. App. 340 (1883)
Mercer v. State, 17 Tex. App. 452 (1885)
Johnson v. State, 20 Tex. App. 609 (1886)
Jones v. State, 23 Tex. App. 501 (1887)
Sauls v. State, 30 Tex. App. 496 (1891)
Schoenfeldt v. State, 30 Tex. App. 695 (1892)
Simon v. State, 31 Tex. Cr. R. 186 (1892)
Burnett v. State, 32 Tex. Cr. R. 86 (1893)
Clements v. State, 34 Tex. Cr. R. 616 (1895)
Stewart v. State, 35 Tex. Cr. R. 174 (1895)
Waggoner v. State, 35 Tex. Cr. R. 199 (1895)
Cummings v. State, 36 Tex. Cr. R. 256 (1896)
Coburn v. State, 36 Tex. Cr. R. 257 (1896)
Jackson v. State, 40 S.W. 998 (1897)
Bales v. State, 44 S.W. 517 (1898)
Kilpatrick v. State, 39 Tex. Cr. R. 10 (1898)
Clark v. State, 39 Tex. Cr. R. 179 (1898)
Poyner v. State, 48 S.W. 516 (1898)
Adcock v. State, 41 Tex. Cr. R. 288 (1899)

Virginia

Attorney General v. Broaddus, 20 Va. 116 (1818)
Hutchins v. Commonwealth, 2 Va. Cas. 331 (1823)
Commonwealth v. Leftwhich, 5 Rand. 83 (1827)
Commonwealth v. Perryman, 29 Va. 717 (1830)

II. OTHER CASES

Alabama

Beggs v. State, 55 Ala. 108 (1876)

Arkansas

Kelly v. Neely, 12 Ark. 657 (1852)

Louisiana

State v. Smith, 30 La. An. 846 (1878)
State v. DeHart, 109 La. 570 (1903)
State v. Couvillion, 117 La. 935 (1906)

Mississippi

Ward v. Dulaney, 23 Miss. 410 (1852)

North Carolina

State v. Shaw, 25 N.C. 532 (1843)

South Carolina

State v. Barefoot, 32 Rich. 209 (1845)
Bowers v. Bowers, 10 Rich. Eq. 551 (1858)
Ex parte Hewitt, 11 Rich. 326 (S.C. 1858)

Texas

Alonzo v. State, 15 Tex. App. 378 (1884)

Virginia

Dr. Stahan's Opinion, 2 Va. Col. Dec. Barradall's Rep. B20 (1724)
Kelly v. Scott, 46 Va. 479 (1849)

Notes

Preface

1. For the details of the personal lives of the Clemsons and the Calhouns, see Ernest M. Lander, Jr., *The Calhoun Family and Thomas Green Clemson: The Decline of a Southern Patriarchy* (Columbia: University of South Carolina Press, 1983), and John Niven, *John C. Calhoun and the Price of Union: A Biography* (Baton Rouge: Louisiana State University Press, 1988).

Foreword

1. Julia Cherry Spruill, *Women's Life and Work in the Southern Colonies* (Chapel Hill: Univ. of North Carolina Press, 1938).

2. Arthur S. Link and Rembert W. Patrick, eds., *Writing Southern History: Essays in Historiography in Honor of Fletcher M. Green* (Baton Rouge: Louisiana State Univ. Press, 1965).

3. The article was by Anne Firor Scott, "The 'New Woman' in the New South," *South Atlantic Quarterly* 61 (Autumn 1962): 417–83; this article became a chapter in *The Southern Lady: From Pedestal to Politics, 1830–1930* (Chicago: Univ. of Chicago Press, 1970).

4. Jacquelyn Dowd Hall and Anne Firor Scott, "Women in the South," in John B. Boles and Evelyn Thomas Nolen, eds., *Interpreting Southern History: Historiographical Essays in Honor of Sanford W. Higginbotham* (Baton Rouge: Louisiana State Univ. Press, 1987), 454–509.

5. Black women's history is, as one might expect at the outset, being written by a group of unusually talented young black women scholars. Excellent dissertations, many articles, a few guides to sources, and a few books are already available, and more are on the way. Brenda Stevenson is one of this exemplary group.

6. Jane Turner Censer, *North Carolina Planters and Their Children, 1800–1860* (Baton Rouge: Louisiana State Univ. Press, 1984), offers indirect evidence of this point.

7. Evelyn Brooks, "The Woman's Movement in the Black Baptist Church 1880–1920" (Ph.D. diss. Univ. of Rochester, 1984). Brooks found women quite

successfully battling the patriarchy which characterized the leadership of the church.

8. As that great liberal James L. Petigru put it, speaking of his niece, "Well done for little Carey! Has she not done her duty . . . two sons and four daughters and only nine years a wife? Why the Queen of England hardly beats her." James Petigru Carson, *Life, Letters and Speeches of James Louis Petigru: The Union Man of South Carolina* (Washington, D.C.: W. H. Lowdermilk and Co., 1920), 441.

9. Dubose Heyward, *Jasbo Brown and Selected Poems* (New York: Farrar and Rinehart, 1931), 30.

1. Precursor to the Victorian Age: The Concept of Marriage and Family as Revealed in the Correspondence of the Izard Family of South Carolina

1. Margaret Izard Manigault to Georgina Izard Smith, Aug. 8, 1811, Manigault Family Papers, South Caroliniana Library, Univ. of South Carolina, hereafter cited as MFP, SCL.

2. There are significant collections of their letters in the South Caroliniana Library, Univ. of South Carolina; the South Carolina Historical Society; the Southern Historical Collection, Univ. of North Carolina; the William Perkins Library, Duke Univ.; and the Library of Congress.

3. "Memoirs of General George Izard," unpublished manuscript at the South Carolina Historical Society, Charleston, S.C.

4. Ralph Izard to Peter Manigault, July 1, 1764, Ralph Izard Papers, South Caroliniana Library, Univ. of South Carolina, hereafter cited as RIP, SCL.

5. Alice DeLancey Izard to Margaret Izard Manigault, Sept. 14, 1801, MFP, SCL.

6. Lyman Butterfield, ed., *Diary and Autobiography of John Adams*, vol. 4(New York: Atheneum Publishers, 1964), 70–71.

7. They were: Margaret, born in Charleston in 1768; Elizabeth, born and died in New York in 1769; Charlotte, born in New York in 1770; Henry, born at sea in 1771 on a journey from Charleston to New York and left with his grandmother DeLancey in New York when the family went to England; Ralph, who was born and died in London in 1771; Charles, born in London in 1773 and died aged eleven soon after their return to Charleston; George, born in Richmond, Surrey, where the family was forced to retrench in 1776; another Elizabeth, born in Paris in 1777 and died in Charleston in 1784; Anne (or Nancy as she was always called in the family), born in Paris in 1779; another Ralph, born in Charleston in 1785; Caroline, born in Charleston in 1786 and died two years later; Henrietta, born and died at The Elms in 1788; William, born and died in New York in 1789; and Georgina, born in Philadelphia in 1792.

8. The other two daughters, Charlotte, who married William Loughton Smith in 1786 and died six years later, and Georgina, who married Joseph Allen Smith in 1809, left no surviving letters, or at least not any that have been located yet, that give us insight into their views on marriage. George, who married the twice widowed Elizabeth Farley Banister Shippen in 1803, after an earlier entanglement with a French refugee from Santo Domingo, and Ralph, who married Elizabeth Middleton, niece of his brother-in-law Gabriel Manigault in 1808, both had happy and

successful marriages which bear out the conclusions to be drawn from their sisters' and brother's experiences. Ralph's second marriage to Eliza Lucas Pinckney in 1824 was so brief (he died later that year) that there is little to say about it.

9. Ralph Izard to Alice DeLancey Izard, 1795, Papers of Ralph Izard and Family (microfilm), Library of Congress, hereafter cited as PRIF, LC.

10. Scattered letters between Ralph and Alice DeLancey Izard can be found in PRIF, LC and in RIP, SCL.

11. Mary Wollstonecraft, *Vindication of the Rights of Woman: With Strictures on Political and Moral Subjects* (London: J. Johnson, 1792).

12. Alice DeLancey Izard to Margaret Izard Manigault, May 29, 1801, MFP, SCL.

13. Ralph Izard to Alice DeLancey Izard, Dec. 28, 1781, RIP, SCL.

14. Charles Izard Manigault Memoir, unpublished manuscript, Southern Historical Collection, Univ. of North Carolina.

15. Margaret Izard to Mary Stead, Feb. 24, 1785, RIP, SCL.

16. Gabriel Manigault to Margaret Izard Manigault, Nov. 7, 1787, Manigault Family Papers, South Carolina Historical Society, Charleston, S.C. , hereafter cited as MFP, SCHS.

17. Margaret Izard Manigault to Gabriel Manigault, Nov. 8, 1787, MFP, SCHS.

18. Charles Izard Manigault Memoir, *loc. cit.*

19. Anne Izard to Elizabeth Farley Banister Shippen, Apr. 6, 1798, Shippen Family Papers, Library of Congress, hereafter cited as SFP, LC.

20. Ibid., Aug. 15, 1798, SFP, LC.

21. Ibid., Sept. 16, 1798, SFP, LC.

22. Ibid., Oct. 25, 1798, SFP, LC.

23. Margaret Izard Manigault to Alice DeLancey Izard, Feb. 2, 1804, PRIF, LC.

24. "Excerpts from a Memoir of Joshua Francis Fisher (1807–1873)," p. 143, published as an appendix in *The Diary of Harriet Manigault 1813–1816*, vol. II (Philadelphia: The Colonial Dames of America, 1976). William Allen Deas and Alexander Inglis fought a duel on Mar. 30, 1791, in which Inglis, a kinsman but not an uncle of Deas, received a gunshot wound from which he died a few days later. See *South Carolina Historical Magazine*, 21 (Apr. 1920): 77–78.

25. George Izard to Henry Izard, Nov. 26, 1806, RIP, SCL.

26. Alice DeLancey Izard to Margaret Izard Manigault, Mar. 14, 1816, MFP, SCL.

27. Ralph Izard to Edward Rutledge, Sept. 27, 1791, RIP, SCL.

28. Ibid., Sept. 28, 1792, PRIF, LC.

29. Alice DeLancey Izard to Ralph Izard, Dec. 11, 1794, PRIF, LC.

30. Henry Izard to Margaret Izard Manigault, June 21, 1809, RIP, SCL.

31. Henry Izard to Margaret Izard Manigault, Apr. 26, 1813, MFP, SCL.

32. Anne Izard Deas to Margaret Izard Manigault, Feb. 5, 1813, MFP, SCL.

33. Alice DeLancey Izard to Margaret Izard Manigault, Apr. 22, 1814, PRIF, LC.

34. George C. Rogers, Jr., *William Loughton Smith: Evolution of a Federalist* (Columbia: Univ. of South Carolina Press, 1961), 402.

35. U.S. Census, Population Schedules, 1850, Charleston District, South Carolina (NARS Microcopy 432, Roll 850).

36. Quoted in correspondence of Alice DeLancey Izard to Margaret Izard Manigault, May 16, 1814, PRIF, LC.

37. Margaret Izard Manigault to Alice DeLancey Izard, May 15, 1814, PRIF, LC.

38. Alice DeLancey Izard to Margaret Izard Manigault, May 16, 1814, PRIF, LC.

39. Elizabeth Farley Banister Izard to William Shippen, Apr. 11, 1816, SFP, LC. In her next letter she made it clear that she had not meant "so refined a word as 'Love' . . . tho' some unrefined souls might consider it entitled to so pure an appellation." Ibid., May 14, 1816, SFP, LC.

40. Anne Izard Deas to Margaret Izard Manigault, Mar. 5, 1813, MFP, SCL.

2. Family and Female Identity in the Antebellum South: Sarah Gayle and Her Family

1. Sarah Furman Haynsworth to Sarah Ann Haynsworth Gayle, 28 Mar. 1820, Gayle Papers, Library of the City of Mobile; also in Alabama Department of Archives and History.

2. Ibid.

3. Ibid.

4. Laurel Thatcher Ulrich, *Good Wives: Image and Reality in the Lives of Women in Northern New England, 1650–1750* (New York: Oxford Univ. Press, 1982); Linda K. Kerber, *Women of the Republic: Intellect and Ideology in Revolutionary America* (Chapel Hill: Univ. of North Carolina Press, 1980).

5. "Sarah Haynsworth Gayle and Her Journal," Alabama Department of Archives and History, Montgomery, Alabama. This account was written by one of Sarah Gayle's descendants for the family. See also "John Gayle," *Dictionary of American Biography*, 20 vols., Allen Johnson and Dumas Malone, eds. (New York: Charles Scribner's Sons, 1928–36), vol. 7, 197–98; and Mary Tabb Johnston with Elizabeth Johnston Lipscomb, *Amelia Gayle Gorgas: A Biography* (University: Univ. of Alabama Press, 1978). Sarah Gayle's recollections of the journey from South Carolina to Alabama can be found in Sarah Haynsworth Gayle, Diary, William Stanley Hoole Special Collections, Amelia Gayle Gorgas Library, Univ. of Alabama (henceforth *Diary*). For other discussions of the early migration to Alabama, see Weymouth T. Jordan, *Hugh Davis and His Alabama Plantation* (University: Univ. of Alabama Press, 1948); Ray Mathis, *John Horry Dent: South Carolina Aristocrat on the Alabama Frontier* (University: Univ. of Alabama Press, 1979); J. Mills Thornton, III, *Politics and Power in a Slave Society: Alabama, 1800–1860* (Baton Rouge: Louisiana State Univ. Press, 1978).

6. On Greensboro, see William E.W. Yerby and Mabel Yerby Lawson, *History of Greensboro, Alabama, from Its Earliest Settlement*, 2nd ed. (Northport, Ala.: Colonial Press, 1963). See also "John Gayle," *American Dictionary of Biography*; *Diary*; and Sarah Ann (Haynsworth) Gayle, Journal, Bayne and Gayle Family Papers, Southern Historical Collection, University of North Carolina at Chapel Hill (henceforth *Journal*).

7. Johnston and Lipscomb, pp. 1–9 passim.; Elizabeth Fox-Genovese, *Within the Plantation Household: Black and White Women of the Old South* (Chapel Hill: Univ. of North Carolina Press, 1988), 1–28 passim.

8. For a fuller elaboration of this argument, see Fox-Genovese, *Within the Plantation Household*. For a contrasting interpretation that stresses the extent to

which southern slaveholders accepted the emerging values of bourgeois individualism beginning in the mid-eighteenth century, see Daniel Blake Smith, *Inside the Great House: Planter Family Life in Eighteenth-Century Chesapeake Society* (Ithaca: Cornell Univ. Press, 1980), and his "Autonomy and Affection: Parents and Children in Eighteenth-Century Chesapeake Families," in N. Ray Hiner and Joseph M. Hawes, eds., *Growing Up in America: Children in Historical Perspective* (Urbana: Univ. of Illinois, 1985), 45–58; and for the nineteenth century, see, Jane Turner Censer, *North Carolina Planters and Their Children, 1800–1860* (Baton Rouge: Louisiana State Univ. Press, 1984).

9. For an elaboration of the argument, see Fox-Genovese, *Within the Plantation Household*. See also Linda K. Kerber, "Separate Spheres, Female Worlds, Woman's Place: The Rhetoric of Women's History," *Journal of American History* 75 (June 1988): 9–39; Jeanne Boydston, Mary Kelley, and Anne Margolis, *The Limits of Sisterhood: The Beecher Sisters on Women's Rights and Woman's Sphere* (Chapel Hill: Univ. of North Carolina Press, 1988); and Mary Kelley, *Private Woman, Public Stage: Literary Domesticity in Nineteenth-Century America* (New York: Oxford Univ. Press, 1984).

10. The best evidence for the familial identification of non-slaveholding women lies in religious history: sermons and, especially, church records.

11. See, especially, Thomas Roderick Dew, "Influence of Slavery on the Condition of the Female Sex," in *Review of the Debate in the Virginia Legislature of 1831 and 1832* (1832; repr. Westport, Conn.: Greenwood Press, 1970), 35–38, and his "Dissertation on the Characteristic Differences between the Sexes, and on the Position and Influence of Woman in Society," *Southern Literary Messenger* 1 (July, Aug. 1835): 621–32, 672–91; H[ershel]. V. Johnson, *Address by the Hon. H.V. Johnson, at the Commencement Exercises of the Wesleyan Female College, Macon, Georgia, on the 14th of July, 1853* (Macon: Georgia Telegraph Print, 1853); Charles Colcock Jones, *The Glory of Woman Is the Fear of the Lord* (Philadelphia: William S. Martien, 1847); William Harper, *Memoir on Slavery, Read before the Society for the Advancement of Learning at Its Annual Meeting in Columbia, 1837* (Charleston, S.C., 1838); John Fletcher, *Studies on Slavery, in Easy Lessons* (1852; repr., Miami: Mnemosyne, 1965); Frederick A. Ross, *Slavery Ordained of God* (1857; repr. Miami: Mnemosyne, 1969). And for a general development of the argument, see Eugene D. Genovese in this volume.

12. Elizabeth Fox-Genovese and Eugene D. Genovese, *Fruits of Merchant Capital: Slavery and Bourgeois Property in the Rise and Expansion of Capitalism* (New York: Oxford Univ. Press, 1983), ch. 11. See also Elizabeth Fox-Genovese, "Women in the Age of Enlightenment," in Renate Bridenthal, Claudia Koonz, and Susan Mosher Stuard, eds., *Becoming Visible: Women in European History*, 2nd ed. (Boston: Houghton Mifflin, 1987); Elizabeth Fox-Genovese, "Introduction," in Samia Spencer, ed., *French Women in the Age of Enlightenment* (Bloomington: Indiana Univ. Press, 1985); Smith, *Inside the Great House*; Anne L. Kuhn, *The Mother's Role in Childhood Education: New England Concepts, 1830-1860* (New Haven: Yale Univ. Press, 1947); Mary Sumner Benson, *Women in Eighteenth-Century America: A Study in Opinion and Social Usage* (New York: Columbia Univ. Press, 1935); Sylvia D. Hoffert, *Private Matters: American Attitudes toward Childbearing and Infant Nurture in the Urban North, 1800–1860* (Urbana: Univ. of Illinois Press, 1989).

13. For Sarah Gayle's papers, see Bayne and Gayle Family Papers, esp. the journal (1829–1835) and correspondence (1820) of Sarah A. (Haynsworth) Gayle, Southern Historical Collection, Univ. of North Carolina at Chapel Hill (henceforth SHC); the Gayle and Crawford Family Papers, SHC; and Sarah Haynsworth Gayle Diary (1827–1831), Hoole Special Collections, Univ. of Alabama (henceforth HSC). Citations will be to *Journal* and *Diary* respectively.

14. *Diary*, 10 Sept. 1828, HSC.

15. Ibid.

16. *Diary*, Thursday morning, n.d., 1828, HSC.

17. *Diary*, Monday, 22 [Sept.] 1828, HSC.

18. *Diary*, Saturday, 20 [Sept.] 1828, HSC.

19. Ibid.

20. Ibid.

21. Sarah Gayle to John Gayle, 19 May 1831, SHC.

22. *Diary*, 19 Feb. 1828, HSC.

23. Ibid.

24. *Diary*, 23 Feb. 1828, HSC.

25. Ibid.

26. *Diary*, 7 Mar. 1828, HSC.

27. Ibid. Her mother, Ann Haynsworth, died in 1822 at the age of 42.

28. *Diary*, 7 Mar. 1828, HSC.

29. Ibid.

30. *Diary*, 17 Apr. 1828, HSC.

31. *Diary*, 21 Apr. 1828, HSC.

32. Ibid.

33. Ibid.

34. See, for example, Nancy Choderow, *The Reproduction of Mothering* (Berkeley: Univ. of California Press, 1978).

35. On the relations between mothers and daughters, see Fox-Genovese, *Within the Plantation Household*. On the age of wealthy Alabama women at marriage (significantly lower than wealthy Bostonian women), see Ann Williams Boucher, "Wealthy Planter Families in Nineteenth-Century Alabama" (Ph.D. dissertation, Univ. of Connecticut, 1978), esp. ch. 2; and on the general propensity of slaveholding women to marry younger than their northern counterparts, Catherine Clinton, *The Plantation Mistress: Woman's World in the Old South* (New York: Pantheon Books, 1982). We do not, in fact, have enough systematic studies of either age at marriage or fertility of slaveholding women throughout the antebellum South to evoke scientific precision, but the private papers of slaveholding women strongly suggest that young women were commonly marrying around, or slightly before, the age of twenty through 1860, when the age of marriage for northeastern women had risen to twenty-four or twenty-five. Similarly, the fertility of slaveholding women seems not to have dropped as rapidly as that of northeastern women, although among white southern women there may have been significant variation according to class and region. On the general problem of the "demographic transition," see Robert V. Wells, "Family History and Demographic Transition," in Hiner and Hawes, eds., *Growing Up in America*, pp. 61–77.

36. *Diary*, 1827, date unclear, HSC.

37. *Diary*, 16 Dec. 1827, HSC.

38. *Diary*, 23 Dec. 1827, HSC.
39. *Diary*, 2 Dec. 1827, HSC.
40. Ibid.
41. Ibid.
42. Ibid.
43. *Diary*, 12 Jan. 1828, HSC.
44. Ibid.
45. *Diary*, 8 Mar. 1828, HSC.
46. *Diary*, 15 Jan. 1828, HSC.
47. Ibid.
48. *Diary*, 18 Jan. 1828, HSC.
49. Ibid.
50. *Journal*, 17 Nov. 1832, HSC.
51. Ibid.
52. Ibid.
53. *Diary*, 30 Dec. 1830, HSC.
54. See, e.g., Kuhn, *The Mother's Role in Childhood Education*; Benson, *Women in Eighteenth-Century America*; Hoffert, *Private Matters*.
55. Although education for slaveholding women improved considerably toward the end of the antebellum period, attendance at school typically remained brief, normally no more than a year or two. Especially during the later part of the period, young girls might episodically attend such schools as were available near their homes, but they continued to receive much of their education from their mothers and, when available, a governess or a tutor. See Catherine Clinton, "Equally Their Due: The Education of the Planter Daughter in the Early Republic," *Journal of the Early Republic* 2 (Spring 1982): 39–60; Steven M. Stowe, "City, County, and the Feminine Voice," in Michael O'Brien and David Moltke-Hansen, eds., *Intellectual Life in Antebellum Charleston* (Knoxville: Univ. of Tennessee Press, 1986), 295–325, and his "The Not-So-Cloistered Academy: Elite Women's Education and Family Feeling in the Old South," in Walter J. Fraser, Jr., R. Frank Saunders, Jr., and Jon Wakelyn, *The Web of Southern Social Relations: Women, Family, and Education* (Athens: Univ. of Georgia Press, 1985), 90–106.
56. See, e.g., *Journal*, 31 June 1832, 2 July 1832, SHC. She dwells with increasing frequency on religion as she and her children get older, in part, no doubt, because of her own fears of death; in part because of her concern that her children have an adequate religious grounding with which to face the temptations of adolescence.
57. *Diary*, 7 Mar. 1828, HSC.
58. Ibid.
59. For a fuller discussion of Sarah Gayle's relations with her slaves, see *Within the Plantation Household*, pp. 20–27, and *Journal* and letters to John Gayle, 1833–35, SHC.
60. *Diary*, 15 Aug. 1830, HSC.
61. *Diary*, 5 July 1831, HSC.
62. *Diary*, 20 Nov. 1830, HSC.
63. *Diary*, 30 Oct. 1831, HSC.
64. *Diary*, Saturday night, n.d., Sept. 1830, HSC.
65. *Diary*, 30 Oct. 1831, HSC.

66. *Journal*, 13 July 1833, HSC.

67. *Diary*, 30 Oct. 1831, HSC.

68. *Diary*, Sunday n.d., Apr. 1831, HSC.

69. Augusta J. Wilson, *Beulah. A Novel* (Atlanta: Evans, Martin and Hoyt Co., 1887; first ed., 1859).

3. "An Outrage upon Nature:" Incest and the Law in the Nineteenth-Century South

I would like to thank the many people who commented on and raised questions about an earlier draft of this paper delivered at the Fort Hill Conference on Southern Culture. I am grateful particularly to Carol Bleser, Drew Gilpin Faust, and Steven Stowe for their insightful suggestions and criticisms. The American Historical Association Littleton-Griswold Research Grant and a Goucher College grant from the Elizabeth Nitchie Fellowship Fund helped support the research and writing of this study.

1. The South is defined in this study as the eleven Confederate states. Although arbitrary in some ways, such a definition of the region concentrates on those states where slavery was strongest and where a sense of Southernness was so deeply rooted that the states left the Union.

2. William Faulkner, *Absalom, Absalom!* (New York: Vintage Books, 1972), 347. The involvement of James Henry Hammond with his wife's four teenaged nieces, although it allegedly fell short of sexual intercourse, also underscored the relationship between patriarchy and incest in the Old South. For further details regarding the Hammond incident, see Carol Bleser, ed., *Secret and Sacred: The Diaries of James Henry Hammond, a Southern Slaveholder* (New York: Oxford Univ. Press, 1988), xi–xii, 164–76; and Drew Gilpin Faust, *James Henry Hammond and the Old South: A Design for Mastery* (Baton Rouge: Louisiana State Press, 1982), 241–54, 287–92, 338–39.

3. Bertram Wyatt-Brown, *Southern Honor: Ethics and Behavior in the Old South* (New York: Oxford Univ. Press, 1982), xv, 14–15, 198–99, 383–85; and Edward L. Ayers, *Vengeance and Justice: Crime and Punishment in the 19th-Century American South* (New York: Oxford Univ. Press, 1984), 13–14, 18–19.

4. Charles S. Sydnor, "The Southerner and the Laws," *Journal of Southern History*, 6 (Feb. 1940): 3–23; Ayers, *Vengeance and Justice*, pp. 15–16, 21–22; Elliot J. Gorn, " 'Gouge and Bite, Pull Hair and Scratch': The Social Significance of Fighting in the Southern Backcountry," *American Historical Review*, 90 (Feb. 1985): 18–43; Dickson D. Bruce, Jr., *Violence and Culture in the Antebellum South* (Austin: Univ. of Texas Press, 1979), introduction and ch. 1; Steven M. Stowe, "The 'Touchiness' of the Gentleman Planter: The Sense of Esteem and Continuity in the Antebellum South," *Psychohistory Review*, 8 (Winter 1979): 6–17; and W.J. Cash, *The Mind of the South* (New York: Alfred A. Knopf, 1941), 32–35.

5. Little exists on the development of incest law in the nineteenth-century United States, but historical investigations dealing with incest in Victorian America and England include Bryan Strong, "Toward a History of the Experiential Family: Sex and Incest in the Nineteenth-Century Family," *Journal of Marriage and the Family*, 35 (Aug. 1973): 457–66; Stephen Kern, "Explosive Intimacy: Psycho-

dynamics of the Victorian Family," in *The New Psychohistory*, Lloyd deMause, ed. (New York: Psychohistory Press, 1975), 29–53; and Anthony S. Wohl, "Sex and the Single Room: Incest Among the Victorian Working Classes," in *The Victorian Family: Structure and Stresses*, Anthony S. Wohl, ed. (New York: St. Martin's Press, 1978), 197–216; and Linda Gordon, *Heroes of Their Own Lives: The Politics and History of Family Violence* (New York: Viking Press, 1988), 204–49. For general discussions of strains in Victorian families and sexuality in nineteenth-century America, see Steven Mintz and Susan Kellogg, *Domestic Relations: A Social History of American Family Life* (New York: Free Press, 1988), 43–65; and John D'Emilio and Estelle B. Freedman, *Intimate Matters: A History of Sexuality in America* (New York: Harper and Row, 1988), part two, esp. 73–84.

6. On the southern commitment to the family as the key to social control, see Thomas Virgil Peterson, *Ham and Japheth: The Mythic World of Whites in the Antebellum South* (Metuchen, N.J.: Scarecrow Press, 1978), 48–56.

7. *Compton v. State*, 13 Tex. App. 271 (1882), p. 275; and *Beggs v. State*, 55 Ala. 108 (1876), p. 112.

8. *Chancellor v. State*, 47 Miss. 278 (1872), p. 280; and *Ward v. Dulaney*, 23 Miss. 410 (1852), p. 426.

9. *Ex parte Hewitt*, 11 Rich. 326 (S.C. 1858), p. 329.

10. For useful theoretical discussions of how law perpetuates patriarchy, see Janet Rifkin, "Toward a Theory of Law and Patriarchy," *Harvard Women's Law Journal*, 3 (Spring 1980): 83–95; Nadine Taub and Elizabeth M. Schneider, "Perspectives on Women's Subordination and the Role of Law," in *The Politics of Law: A Progressive Critique*, David Kairys, ed. (New York: Pantheon Books, 1982), 117–39; and Diane Polan, "Toward A Theory of Law and Patriarchy," in Kairys, *The Politics of Law*, pp. 294–303.

11. Recent studies that emphasize the patriarchal nature of the white southern family include Orville Burton, *In My Father's House Are Many Mansions: Family and Community in Edgefield, South Carolina* (Chapel Hill: Univ. of North Carolina Press, 1985), 99–109; Catherine Clinton, *The Plantation Mistress: Woman's World in the Old South* (New York: Pantheon Books, 1982), esp. ch. 3; Michael P. Johnson, "Planters and Patriarchy: Charleston, 1800–1860," *Journal of Southern History*, 46 (Feb. 1980): 45–72; Anne Firor Scott, *The Southern Lady: From Pedestal to Politics, 1830–1930* (Chicago: Univ. of Chicago Press, 1970), 16–17; and Wyatt-Brown, *Southern Honor*, part two. On the development of patriarchalism in the eighteenth-century Chesapeake, see Allan Kulikoff, *Tobacco and Slaves: The Development of Southern Cultures in the Chesapeake, 1680–1800* (Chapel Hill: Univ. of North Carolina Press, 1986), ch. 5.

For investigations that offer an alternative approach and instead stress the role of affection in family relations among southern whites, see Daniel Blake Smith, *Inside the Great House: Planter Family Life in Eighteenth-Century Chesapeake Society* (Ithaca: Cornell Univ. Press, 1980); Jan Lewis, *The Pursuit of Happiness: Family and Values in Jefferson's Virginia* (New York: Cambridge Univ. Press, 1983); and Jane Turner Censer, *North Carolina Planters and Their Children, 1800–1860* (Baton Rouge: Louisiana State Univ. Press, 1984).

Rhys Isaac, *The Transformation of Virginia, 1740–1790* (Chapel Hill: Univ. of North Carolina Press, 1982); and Elizabeth Fox-Genovese, *Within the Plantation Household: Black and White Women in the Old South* (Chapel Hill: Univ. of North

Carolina Press, 1988) prefer the term "paternalism" to "patriarchy" in characterizing southern relations of dependence and inequality. In particular, Isaac emphasizes the role of republicanism and sentimentalism after the American Revolution in bringing about a more individualistic and contractual conception of social relations. As Isaac observes, however, "Patriarchy, and its adaptation, paternalism, continued to be a powerful principle in a thoroughly agrarian society where households small and great were still the social units of production." See Isaac, *Transformation of Virginia*, pp. 308–10, 320–22; and Fox-Genovese, *Within the Plantation Household*, pp. 63–64.

The important point here is that patriarchy was not a static social system and that simply because it did not assume ancient Roman form in the nineteenth-century South is no reason to deny its existence in a more modern guise. Indeed, I would argue that the legal foundation of patriarchy in the South changed in crucial ways before and after the Civil War and that patriarchy persisted alongside, and in tension with, competing forces of individualism, contractualism, and domesticity. Much of the present study aims at illuminating the ways in which these changes and tensions manifested themselves in the legal sphere.

12. Wyatt-Brown, *Southern Honor*, p. 293. For evaluations of the strengths and weaknesses inherent in the use of appellate decisions as historical sources, consult G. Edward White, "The Appellate Court Opinion as Historical Source Material," *Journal of Interdisciplinary History*, 1 (Spring 1971): 492–93; Mark Tushnet, "The American Law of Slavery, 1810–1860: A Study in the Persistence of Legal Autonomy," *Law and Society Review*, 10 (Fall 1975): 125–31; and Jane Turner Censer, " 'Smiling Through Her Tears': Antebellum Southern Women and Divorce," *American Journal of Legal History*, 25 (Jan. 1981): 25–26.

13. Brenda Z. Seligman, "The Incest Barrier: Its Role in Social Organization," *British Journal of Psychology*, 22 (Jan. 1932): 250–76; Talcott Parsons, "The Incest Taboo in Relation to Social Structure," in *The Family: Its Structures and Functions*, 2d ed., Rose Laub Coser, ed. (New York: St. Martin's Press, 1974), 13–30; and Claude Lévi-Strauss, *The Elementary Structures of Kinship* (Boston: Beacon Press, 1969), esp. chs. 1–4. On Lévi-Strauss and his theory of the incest taboo, see Mark Poster, *Critical Theory of the Family* (New York: Seabury Press, 1978), 97–102.

Other recent studies by social scientists of incest include Robin Fox, *The Red Lamp of Incest* (New York: Dutton, 1980); Joseph Shepher, *Incest: A Biosocial View* (New York: Academic Press, 1983); Judith Lewis Herman, *Father-Daughter Incest* (Cambridge: Harvard Univ. Press, 1981); and Sarah Begus and Pamela Armstrong, "Daddy's Right: Incestuous Assault," in *Families, Politics, and Public Policy: A Feminist Dialogue on Women and the State*, Irene Diamond, ed. (New York: Longman, 1983), 236–49. Joseph Shepher, in the study cited above, criticizes the structural-functionalist approach and advances a biosocial explanation of the incest taboo.

14. Claude Lévi-Strauss, "The Family," in *Man, Culture, and Society*, Harry L. Shapiro, ed. (New York: Oxford Univ. Press, 1956), 276; Jane Lloyd, "The Management of Incest: An Overview of Three Interrelated Systems—The Family, the Legal and the Therapeutic," *Journal of Social Welfare Law*, (Jan. 1982): 17; Anthony H. Manchester, "Incest and the Law," in *Family Violence: An International and Interdisciplinary Study*, John M. Eekelaar and Sanford N. Katz, eds. (Toronto: Butterworths, 1978), 487–88; and Frederic P. Storke, "The Incestuous Marriage—Relic of the Past," *University of Colorado Law Review*, 36 (Summer 1964): 473–74.

15. Michael Grossberg, "Law and the Family in Nineteenth-Century America" (Ph.D. diss., Brandeis Univ., 1979), 121; Randolph Trumbach, *The Rise of the Egalitarian Family: Aristocratic Kinship and Domestic Relations in Eighteenth-Century England* (New York: Academic Press, 1978), 18; Michael P. Einbinder, "The Legal Family—A Definitional Analysis," *Journal of Family Law*, 13 (1973): 782, 782n; James Schouler, *A Treatise on the Law of Domestic Relations*, 2nd ed. (Boston: Little, Brown, 1874), 26–28; and Joel Prentiss Bishop, *Commentaries on the Law of Marriage and Divorce* (Boston: Little, Brown, 1852), 171.

16. Julia Cherry Spruill, *Women's Life and Work in the Southern Colonies* (New York: Norton, 1972), 141–42; Va., *Statutes at Large* (Hening, 1820), vol. 4, pp. 245–46 (Act of 1730); and S.C., *Statutes at Large* (Cooper, 1837), vol. 2, pp. 241, 243, 475–76. For North Carolina legislation, see N.C., *Colonial Records*, (Saunders, 1886), vol. 2, pp. 212–13. Discussions of colonial laws in the South include George E. Howard, *A History of Matrimonial Institutions*, vol. 2 (Chicago: Univ. of Chicago Press, 1904), 234, 251, 260; Arthur W. Calhoun, *A Social History of the American Family*, vol. 1, (Cleveland: Arthur H. Clark Co., 1917), 264, 304, 315; and John E. Semonche, "Common-Law Marriage in North Carolina: A Study in Legal History," *American Journal of Legal History*, 9 (Oct. 1965): 330–31.

For colonial cases dealing with the prohibited degrees of marriage, see Dr. Strahan's Opinion, 2 Va. Col. Dec. Baradall's Rep. B20 (1724); and Mattie Erma Edwards Parker, ed., *North Carolina Higher-Court Records, 1697–1701* (Raleigh: State Department of Archives and History, 1971), 468–69.

17. Ga., *Code* (Clarke, Cobb, and Irwin, 1861), ch. 1655, p. 331; and Ga., *Acts of the General Assembly* (1865–1866), p. 244.

18. Ala., *Digest of the Laws* (Toulmin, 1823), p. 578; Ark., *Revised Statutes* (Ball and Roane, 1838), ch. 94, sec. 3, p. 535; La., *Digest of the Civil Laws* (1808), title 4, ch. 2, arts. 9–10, pp. 24–26; Miss., *Revised Code* (Poindexter, 1824), ch. 102, sec. 8, pp. 447–48; N.C., *Revised Code* (Moore and Biggs, 1855), ch. 68, sec. 9, p. 392; Tenn., *Compilation of the Statutes* (Caruthers and Nicholson, 1836), ch. 23, sec. 18, pp. 318–19; Tex., *Digest of the Laws* (Dallam, 1845), p. 103; and Va., *Revised Code* (1819), vol. 1, ch. 106, sec. 17, p. 399.

19. Ala., *Code* (Ormond, Bagby, and Goldthwaite, 1852), chs. 1942–43, p. 375; Ark., *Revised Statutes* (1838), ch. 94, sec. 3, p. 535; La., *Digest* (1808), title 4, ch. 2, arts. 9–10, pp. 24–26; and Tex., *Digest of the General Statute Laws* (Oldham and White, 1859), p. 503. The Texas restrictions dealt solely with half-blood relatives. In addition, Mississippi and Virginia had antebellum legislation specifically banning marriages between half brothers and half sisters. See Miss., *Revised Code* (1824), ch. 102, sec. 8, pp. 447–48; and Va., *Revised Code* (1819), vol. 1, ch. 106, sec. 17, p. 399.

20. Va., *Revised Code* (1819), vol. 1, ch. 106, sec. 17, p. 399.

21. Louisiana abolished all such barriers in 1827. La., *Civil Code* (Upton and Jennings, 1838), title 4, ch. 1, art. 98. For the lack of affinal prohibitions in the other three states, consult Ark., *Digest of the Statutes* (Gould, 1858), ch. 51, pt. 8, art. 1, sec. 6, p. 368; Fla., *Digest of the Statute Law* (Thompson, 1847), p. 499; and N.C., *Revised Code* (1855), ch. 68, sec. 9, p. 392.

22. Bernard Farber, *Kinship and Class: A Midwestern Study* (New York: Basic Books, 1971), 14–16; Grossberg, "Law and the Family," p. 125; and Trumbach, *Rise of the Egalitarian Family*, pp. 18–19.

Despite the traditional stricture against marriages between a widower and his deceased wife's sister or between a widow and her late husband's brother, it appears that such unions were actually not uncommon in the antebellum South. See Clinton, *Plantation Mistress*, pp. 78–79; Wyatt-Brown, *Southern Honor*, p. 219; and Censer, *North Carolina Planters*, p. 88.

23. Virginia finally lifted its legal sanction against contracting matrimony with a deceased wife's sister in 1849. In its 1859–60 session, the Virginia legislature also abolished the prohibition against marriage with a brother's widow. Georgia, another southern state that had followed English tradition closely on these matters, dropped the two marital bans in 1861. Compare Va., *Digest of the Laws*, (2nd ed., Tate, 1841), pp. 500–501 with *Code* (Patton and Robinson, 1849), ch. 108, sec. 10, pp. 470–71, where the prohibition against marrying a deceased wife's sister does not appear. For the dropping of the ban on marrying a brother's widow, see Va., *Code* (1860), ch. 108, sec. 9, p. 524. For Georgia, see Ga., *Code* (1861), ch. 1655, p. 331.

24. Michael Grossberg, "Guarding the Altar: Physiological Restrictions and the Rise of State Intervention in Matrimony," *American Journal of Legal History*, 26 (July 1982): 213; Howard, *Matrimonial Institutions*, vol. 2, pp. 397–98, 473–75; and Helen I. Clarke, *Social Legislation: American Laws Dealing with Family, Child, and Dependent* (New York: D. Appleton-Century, 1940), 97.

25. *Kelly v. Neely,* 12 Ark. 657 (1852), p. 660. See also *State v. Shaw,* 25 N.C. 532 (1843).

26. On the growing role of voluntary consent and mutual affection in influencing marital decisions, see Carl N. Degler, *At Odds: Women and the Family in America from the Revolution to the Present* (New York: Oxford Univ. Press, 1980), 9–14; Mary Beth Norton, *Liberty's Daughters: The Revolutionary Experience of American Women, 1750–1800* (Boston: Little, Brown, 1980), 229–30; Jay Fliegelman, *Prodigals and Pilgrims: The American Revolution Against Patriarchal Authority, 1750–1800* (New York: Cambridge Univ. Press, 1982), 132–37; and Mintz and Kellogg, *Domestic Revolutions*, pp. 46–48.

Analyses of southern marriage that emphasize free choice and affection include Smith, *Inside the Great House*, pp. 140–50; Lewis, *Pursuit of Happiness*, pp. 188–91; Censer, *North Carolina Planters*, pp. 65–70, 72, 79–81; Russell L. Blake, "Ties of Intimacy: Social Values and Personal Relationships of Antebellum Slaveholders" (Ph.D. diss., Univ. of Michigan, 1978), 64–70, 81–82; and Steven M. Stowe, *Intimacy and Power in the Old South: Ritual in the Lives of the Planters* (Baltimore: Johns Hopkins Univ. Press, 1987), 124–28. Stowe's study is distinctive in its approach because it examines the role of anxiety and fear, as well as affection, in southern courtship, but the emphasis is clearly on the emotional dimension. Carol Bleser, "The Perrys of Greenville: A Nineteenth-Century Marriage," in *The Web of Southern Social Relations: Women, Family, and Education*, Walter J. Fraser, Jr., R. Frank Saunders, Jr., and Jon L. Wakelyn, eds. (Athens: Univ. of Georgia Press, 1985), 72–89 presents an interesting case study of a southern marriage based on voluntary consent and romantic love.

For a contrasting point of view that stresses continued parental control and financial considerations, consult Wyatt-Brown, *Southern Honor*, pp. 207–13; Clinton, *Plantation Mistress*, pp. 59–60, 64–65; Johnson, "Planters and Patriarchy," pp. 65–66; and Suzanne Lebsock, *The Free Women of Petersburg: Status and Culture in a Southern Town, 1784–1860* (New York: W.W. Norton, 1984), 16–22.

27. See Ala., *Code* (1852), ch. 1942, p. 375; Ga., *Code* (1861), ch. 1655, p. 331; Miss., *Revised Code* (Sharkey, Harris, and Ellett, 1857), ch. 40, art. 8, p. 333; Tenn., *Code* (Meigs and Cooper, 1858), chs. 4836–37, p. 867; Tex., *Digest* (1859), p. 503; and Va., *Code* (1860), ch. 108, sec. 9, p. 524.

28. Farber, *Kinship and Class*, pp. 40–41. See the discussion of Farber's analysis in Michael Grossberg, *Governing the Hearth: Law and the Family in Nineteenth-Century America* (Chapel Hill: Univ. of North Carolina Press, 1985), 112.

29. Wyatt-Brown, *Southern Honor*, pp. 217–21; Clinton, *Plantation Mistress*, pp. 57–58, 61; and Turner, *North Carolina Planters*, pp. 84–87. But see Burton, *In My Father's House*, pp. 119–23, for evidence that cousin marriage occurred more frequently among wealthier white families than among those not so well off. On the taboo against cousin unions in the slave community, see Herbert G. Gutman, *The Black Family in Slavery and Freedom, 1750–1925* (New York: Pantheon Books, 1976), 880–90.

30. Jeffrey Weeks, *Sex, Politics and Society: The Regulation of Sexuality Since 1800* (London: Longman, 1981), 31; Graham Hughes, "The Crime of Incest," *Journal of Criminal Law, Criminology and Police Science*, 55 (Sept. 1964): 322–23; and David Royce and Anthony A. Waits, "The Crime of Incest," *Northern Kentucky Law Review*, 5 (1978): 191–92.

31. Georgia and Louisiana in 1817, Tennessee in 1829, Florida in 1832, Arkansas in 1837, Mississippi in 1839, Alabama in 1841, and Texas in 1848 all authorized serious criminal penalties for both incestuous marriages and sexual relations. Ga., *Digest* (1822), p. 365; La., *Consolidation and Revision of the Statutes* (Peirce, Taylor, and King, 1852), p. 188; Tenn., *Compilation* (1836), ch. 23, sec. 18, pp. 318–19; Fla., *Compilation* (1839), p. 120; Ark., *Revised Statutes* (1838), ch. 44, art. 7, sec. 5, p. 254; Miss., *Code* (Hutchinson, 1848), ch. 64, title 7, sec. 5, p. 978; Ala., *Supplement to Aikin's Digest* (Meek, 1841), ch. 6, sec. 6, p. 239; and Tex., *Digest of the Laws* (Hartley, 1850), ch. 557, p. 212.

In 1878 the Louisiana State Supreme Court overturned a conviction for incest under the 1817 law on the grounds that the statute did not provide a definition of what constituted the crime of incest. In response, the legislators passed a bill in 1884 which pronounced cohabitation and marriage within the forbidden degrees as incest. See *State v. Smith,* 30 La. An. 846 (1878); and *Revised Laws* (Wolff, 1897), p. 189. The Louisiana Supreme Court, in *State v. Guiton,* 51 La. An. 155 (1898) and *State v. DeHart,* 109 La. 570 (1903), held that the 1884 definition of incest was legally sufficient, and it affirmed incest convictions under the new legislation.

In Mississippi, only persons within the prohibited degrees of consanguinity who had sex could be convicted of incest. No penalties existed in the state's incest regulations for close affines who engaged in intercourse, even though some of these affines were not allowed to contract matrimony. In other words, a stepfather who had sexual intercourse with his stepdaughter could not be punished for incest in Mississippi, despite the fact that marriage between them was considered incestuous. Compare ch. 64, title 7, sec. 5, p. 978 with ch. 34, art. 1, sec. 8, p. 494 in Miss., *Code* (1848). See also *Chancellor v. State,* 47 Miss. 278 (1872), in which the Mississippi Supreme Court decried its inability under the state's incest laws to punish a man who had sex with his stepdaughter.

Although antebellum Virginia, North Carolina, and South Carolina enacted legislation prohibiting marriages between near kin, these three states waited until the late nineteenth century to classify incestuous sexual relations as a crime. Va., *Code* (1887), ch. 3786, p. 899; N.C., *Code* (Dortch, Manning, and Henderson, 1883), vol. 1, chs. 1060–61, p. 429; and S.C., *Revised Statutes* (Breazeale, 1894), vol. 2, ch. 258, pp. 349–50. Virginia's Act of 1730 gave colonial courts the power to fine at their discretion any person who copulated within the prohibited degrees, but this law was repealed and replaced by the Act of 1788, which did not provide any punishment for incestuous intercourse. See *Statutes at Large* (Hening, 1820), vol. 4, p. 246; and *Statutes at Large* (Hening, 1823), vol. 12, pp. 688–89.

32. Fla., *Digest* (1847), p. 499; and La., *Statutes* (1852), p. 188. For legislation in other southern states, see Ala., *Code* (1852), ch. 1945, p. 376; and ch. 3234, p. 583; Ark., *Digest* (1858), ch. 51, pt. 8, art. 1, sec. 7, p. 368; and ch. 109, sec. 3, p. 760; Ga., *Code* (1861), ch. 1657, p. 331; and ch. 4418, p. 860; Miss., *Revised Code* (1857), ch, 64, art. 9, p. 574; and ch. 64, art. 184, p. 603; N.C., *Revised Code* (1855), ch. 68, sec. 9, p. 392; Tenn., *Code* (1858), chs. 4836–37, p. 867; Tex., *Digest* (1850), ch. 557, p. 212; and *Digest* (1859), p. 503; and Va., *Code* (1860), ch. 109, sec. 1, p. 529; and ch. 196, sec. 3, p. 803.

33. For discussions of the distinction between void and voidable, see Paul J. Goda, "The Historical Evolution of the Concepts of Void and Voidable Marriages," *Journal of Family Law*, 7 (Summer 1967): 297–308; Schouler, *Domestic Relations*, pp. 24–25; and Bishop, *Marriage and Divorce*, pp. 37–46.

34. Aside from these forty-nine criminal cases that reached southern appellate courts between 1800 and 1900, another thirteen state supreme-court cases from the South touching on the issue of incest have been consulted for this paper. The forty-nine cases regarding incest prosecutions are all that were heard at the appellate level, as far as the author was able to determine from an examination of the published opinions. See the Appendix for a listing of the individual cases.

Unfortunately, appellate-court opinions in the overwhelming majority of these criminal cases provide little if any information on the social background of the legal parties. In only one instance is race mentioned: the uncle whose incest conviction is upheld in an 1898 Louisiana opinion and his niece are referred to as "a colored man and . . . a colored woman." See *State v. Guiton*, 51 La. An. 155 (1898), p. 159. Furthermore, there is little indication of socioeconomic position in these cases. The only exceptions are five state supreme-court decisions in late nineteenth-century Texas that involved small-farm and farm-laborer households. See *McGrew v. State*, 13 Tex. App. 340 (1883); *Mercer v. State*, 17 Tex. App. 452 (1885); *Johnson v. State*, 20 Tex. App. 609 (1886); *Clements v. State*, 34 Tex. Cr. R. 616 (1895); and *Waggoner v. State*, 35 Tex. Cr. R. 199 (1895).

35. *Smith v. State*, 108 Ala. 1 (1895), p. 3.

36. *Mercer v. State*, 17 Tex. App. 452 (1885), p. 464. See also *Powers v. State*, 44 Ga. 209 (1871); *Raiford v. State*, 68 Ga. 672 (1882); *Alonzo v. State*, 15 Tex. App. 378 (1884); *Schoenfeldt v. State*, 30 Tex. App. 695 (1892); and *Stewart v. State*, 35 Tex. Cr. R. 174 (1895).

37. Of these three females, one was convicted of cohabitation with her uncle, another of marrying her uncle, and the third of marrying her deceased husband's brother. See *Newman v. State*, 69 Miss. 393 (1891); *Hutchins v. Commonwealth*, 2 Va. Cas. 331 (1823); and *Commonwealth v. Perryman*, 29 Va. 717 (1830).

In *State v. Fritts and Phillips*, 48 Ark. 66 (1886), both parties (first cousins) were indicted for incest, but the court quashed the indictment, a decision that was upheld by the Arkansas Supreme Court on appeal from the state. *Burnett v. State,* 32 Tex. Cr. R. 86 (1893) stemmed from an indictment of the father and daughter for incest. But only the father was found guilty at the trial, and so he was the only party in the appellate decision, which affirmed his conviction.

Besides *State v. Fritts and Phillips,* cases that involved appeals by the state included *State v. Ratcliffe,* 61 Ark. 62 (1895); *State v. Keesler,* 78 N.C. 469 (1878); and *Attorney General v. Broaddus,* 20 Va. 116 (1818).

38. *State v. Barefoot,* 2 Rich. 209 (S.C. 1845), pp. 213, 218.

39. Ibid., pp. 221, 227, 223.

40. *Bowers v. Bowers,* 10 Rich. Eq. 551 (S.C. 1858), p. 555.

41. See also *Attorney General v. Broaddus,* 20 Va. 116 (1818); and *Commonwealth v. Leftwich,* 5 Rand. 83 (Va., 1827).

42. For example, in Virginia (where the courts had long possessed such authority) appellate judges in 1823 upheld the criminal conviction of a woman who had married her uncle. But the high court made certain that its decision had sufficient legislative basis: "upon examination of the Act of the Assembly it is seen that the offence is . . . laid in the very words of the Act" and "it seems to all the Judges that there is all the certainty which reason, or the Law of the Case requires." *Hutchins v. Commonwealth,* 2 Va. Cas. 331 (1823), p. 259. See also *Commonwealth v. Perryman,* 29 Va. 717 (1830), in which the court declared a marriage between a man and his brother's widow void; and *Kelly v. Scott,* 46 Va. 479 (1849), in which the court upheld the invalidation of a union between a man and his deceased wife's sister.

43. *Ewell v. State,* 14 Tenn. 364 (1834), p. 376.

44. *Cook v. State,* 11 Ga. 53 (1852), p. 57 (emphasis in original). See also *Morgan v. State,* 11 Ala. 289 (1847); and *Baker v. State,* 30 Ala. 521 (1857). In these two cases the Alabama Supreme Court decided that the state's incest statute applied to illegitimate as well as legitimate relations within the forbidden degrees, even though the statute did not explicitly state so.

45. *Tuberville v. State,* 4 Tex. 128 (1849), p. 130.

46. Compare Miss., *Revised Code* (Campbell, Johnston, and Lovering, 1871), ch. 1762, p. 373, with *Revised Code* (1857), ch. 40, art. 8, p. 333. For Virginia and Georgia, see Va., *Code* (Munford, 1873), title 31, ch. 104, sec. 9, p. 844; and Ga., *Code,* 4th ed. (Lester, Rowell, and Hill, 1882), ch. 1700, p. 392.

47. Ark., *Digest of the Statutes* (Mansfield, 1884), ch. 4592, p. 911; and La., *Acts* (1900), p. 188. While the Arkansas Supreme Court upheld the ban on first-cousin marriages and argued that intercourse between first cousins could also be punished as incest, the Louisiana high court struck down the first-cousin prohibition on a technicality. See *Nations v. State,* 64 Ark. 467 (1897); and *State v. Couvillion,* 117 La. 935 (1906).

48. Compare Ala., *Code* (1852), ch. 1942, p. 375, with *Revised Code* (Walker, 1867), ch. 2331, p. 481; and consult N.C., *Code* (1883), vol. 1, ch. 1811, p. 689. On the uncle-niece ban in Mississippi, contrast *Revised Code* (1871), ch. 1763, p. 373, with *Revised Code* (Campbell, 1880), ch. 1146, p. 335. On the prohibition against marrying one's grandparent, compare *Revised Code* (Campbell, 1880), ch. 1145, p. 335, with *Annotated Code* (Thompson, Dillard, and Campbell, 1892), chs. 2857–58, p. 677.

49. Grossberg, "Guarding the Altar," pp. 214–17. See also Grossberg, *Governing the Hearth,* pp. 144–46.

50. *State v. Fritts and Phillips*, 48 Ark. 66 (1886), pp. 68–69.

51. N.C., *Code* (1883), vol. 1, chs. 1060–61, p. 429; S.C., *Revised Statutes* (1894), vol. 2, ch. 258, pp. 349–50; and Va., *Code* (1887), ch. 3786, p. 899. Apparently, the North Carolina statute was passed at the urging of the state supreme court, which in a case the year before had declared that an indictment for incest could not be maintained because the offense was not indictable at common law and there was no state legislation making incestuous sexual intercourse a criminal offense. Following passage of the act, the state court held that the incest statute affected illegitimate as well as legitimate persons. See *State v. Kessler*, 78 N.C. 469 (1878); and *State v. Laurence*, 95 N.C. 659 (1886).

52. *Johnson v. State*, 20 Tex. App. 609 (1886), p. 615. See also *Compton v. State*, 13 Tex. App. 271 (1882).

53. *Wilson v. State*, 100 Tenn. 596 (1898), p. 597. For another case in which strict constructionism played a major role in the reversal of an incest conviction, see *State v. Smith*, 30 La. Ann. 846 (1878).

54. *Owen v. State*, 89 Tenn. 698 (1891), p. 703.

55. *Newman v. State*, 69 Miss. 393 (1891).

56. *State v. Fritts and Phillips*, 48 Ark. 66 (1886); and *Martin v. State*, 58 Ark. 3 (1893), p. 6. See also *State v. Ratcliffe*, 61 Ark. 62 (1895).

57. Daniel J. Flanigan, "Criminal Procedure in Slave Trials in the Antebellum South," *Journal of Southern History*, 40 (Nov. 1974): 549–50. See also A. E. Keir Nash, "Fairness and Formalism in the Trials of Blacks in the State Supreme Courts of the Old South," *Virginia Law Review*, 56 (Feb. 1970): 79–81; and Nash, "The Texas Supreme Court and Trial Rights of Blacks, 1845–1860," *Journal of American History*, 58 (Dec. 1971): 628–29.

58. See, for example, *Chancellor v. State*, 47 Miss. 278 (1872); and *State v. Keesler*, 78 N.C. 469 (1878).

59. Flanigan, "Criminal Procedure in Slave Trials," p. 549.

60. *Clark v. State*, 39 Tex. Cr. R. 179 (1898), p. 182; and *McGrew v. State*, 13 Tex. App. 340 (1883), p. 343. For other cases dealing with proof of relationship, see *Simon v. State*, 31 Tex. Cr. R. 186 (1892); *Cummings v. State*, 36 Tex. Cr. R. 256 (1896); and *Elder v. State*, 123 Ala. 35 (1898).

61. *Burnett v. State*, 32 Tex. Cr. R. 86 (1893); *State v. Reynolds*, 48 S.C. 384 (1897); and *Taylor v. State*, 110 Ga. 150 (1900).

62. *Compton v. State*, 13 Tex. App. 271 (1882); and *State v. Reynolds*, 48 S.C. 384 (1896), p. 388. See also *Owen v. State*, 89 Tenn. 698 (1891); and *Stewart v. State*, 35 Tex. Cr. R. 174 (1895).

63. See, for example, *Brown v. State*, 27 So. 869 (Fla., 1900); *Powers v. State*, 44 Ga. 209 (1871); *Jones v. State*, 23 Tex. App. 501 (1887); *Shelly v. State*, 95 Tenn. 152 (1895); and *Waggoner v. State*, 35 Tex. Cr. R. 199 (1895).

64. *Taylor v. State*, 110 Ga. 150 (1900), pp. 154, 157. For other discussions of corroborative evidence, see *Powers v. State*, 44 Ga. 209 (1871); *Mercer v. State*, 17 Tex. App. 452 (1885); *Sauls v. State*, 30 Tex. App. 496 (1891); *Schoenfeldt v. State*, 30 Tex. App. 695 (1892); *Clements v. State*, 34 Tex. Cr. R. 616 (1895); *Jackson v. State*, 40 S.W. 998 (1897); *Bales v. State*, 44 S.W. 517 (1898); *Kilpatrick v. State*, 39 Tex. Cr. R. 10 (1898); *Poyner v. State*, 48 S.W. 516 (1898); and *Adcock v. State*, 41 Tex. Cr. R. 288 (1899).

65. *Freeman v. State*, 11 Tex. App. 92 (1881); *Stewart v. State*, 35 Tex. Cr. R. 174

(1895); *Coburn v. State,* 36 Tex. Cr. R. 257 (1896); *Clark v. State,* 39 Tex. Cr. R. 179 (1898); and *Taylor v. State,* 110 Ga. 150 (1900).

66. *Mercer v. State,* 17 Tex. App. 452 (1885), p. 465. See also *Freeman v. State,* 11 Tex. App. 92 (1881).

67. *Mercer v. State,* 17 Tex. App. 452 (1885), pp. 465–66, 455, 457.

68. *Coburn v. State,* 36 Tex. Cr. R. 257 (1896), p. 258. See also *Shelly v. State,* 95 Tenn. 152 (1895); *Stewart v. State,* 35 Tex. Cr. R. 174 (1895); and *Clark v. State,* 39 Tex. Cr. R. 179 (1898).

69. *Taylor v. State,* 110 Ga. 150 (1900), pp. 155–56. The age of the girl was not stated in the facts of the case, but elsewhere in the appellate opinion, the judges referred to her as a "female of tender years," indicating that she was in her early teens, at most.

70. *Powers v. State,* 44 Ga. 209 (1871), p. 214 (emphasis in original). The Georgia Supreme Court appeared to reaffirm the notion of psychological coercion in *Raiford v. State,* 68 Ga. 672 (1882). The court considered the woman in this case an accomplice, however. The corroborating testimony of a servant provided the necessary evidence to convict her uncle of incestuous fornication.

71. Psychological coercion was important in the employment of patriarchal control over subordinate males as well as female members of the household. See Johnson, "Planters and Patriarchy," pp. 56–60.

72. For a recent discussion of how the accomplice testimony rule hinders the successful prosecution of incest, see Donald E. Wood, "Characterization of the Daughter as an Accomplice in Incest Prosecutions: Does Texas Immunize the Father?" *Houston Law Review,* 20 (1983): 1129–56.

73. *Porath v. State,* 63 N.W. 1061 (Wis. 1895), p. 1064; and *People v. Burwell,* 63 N.W. 986 (Mich. 1895), pp. 987–88. See also *State v. Chambers,* 53 N.W. 1090 (Iowa 1893).

74. *State v. Dana,* 10 Atl. 727 (Vt. 1887), p. 729. See also *State v. Kouhns,* 73 N.W. 353 (Iowa 1897); and *People v. Jenness,* 5 Mich. 305 (1858).

75. D'Emilio and Freedman, *Intimate Matters,* pp. 31–32; Karen A. Getman, "Sexual Control in the Slaveholding South: The Implementation and Maintenance of a Racial Caste System," *Harvard Women's Law Journal,* 7 (Spring 1984): 136–39; and Elizabeth Pleck, *Domestic Tyranny: The Making of Social Policy Against Family Violence from Colonial Times to the Present* (New York: Oxford Univ. Press, 1987), 94–96.

4. "Southern Dishonor":
Flesh, Blood, Race, and Bondage

1. W.E.B. Du Bois, *Darkwater: Voices from Within the Veil* (New York: Harcourt Brace, 1921), 172.

2. Toni Morrison, "A Bench by the Road," *The World: Journal of the Unitarian Universalist Association,* vol. 3 (Jan/Feb 1989): 4.

3. Orlando Patterson, *Slavery and Social Death* (Cambridge: Harvard Univ. Press, 1984).

4. Cambridge: Harvard Univ. Press, 1987.

5. Richard Sutch, "Slave Breeding," *Dictionary of Afro-American Slavery,* ed. by Miller and Smith (New York: Greenwood Press, 1988).

6. See Paul Escott, *Slavery Remembered: A Record of Twentieth Century Slave Narratives* (Chapel Hill: Univ. of North Carolina Press, 1979), 44–45; also Catherine Clinton, "Caught in the Web of the Big House: Women and Slavery," *The Web of Southern Social Relations*, ed. by Fraser, Saunders, and Wakelyn (Athens: Univ. of Georgia Press, 1985), 23–24.

7. Betty Wood, "Some Aspects of Female Resistance to Chattel Slavery in Low Country Georgia," *The Historical Journal*, 30, no. 3, (1987).

8. George Washington Carleton, ed., *The Suppressed Book About Slavery* (New York: Arno Press, 1968), 176.

9. Joel Williamson, *New People: Miscegenation and Mulattoes in the United States* (New York: Free Press, 1980), 7. See also Catherine Clinton, *The Plantation Mistress: Woman's World in the Old South* (New York: Pantheon Books, 1982), 202–3.

10. Williamson, *New People,* p. 8.

11. Ibid.

12. Karen A. Getman, "Sexual Control in the Slaveholding South," *Harvard Women's Law Journal*, no. 7 (1984): 120–27.

13. For Louisiana, see Virginia Dominguez, *White by Definition* (New Brunswick: Rutgers Univ. Press, 1986); and for Mississippi, see *Executor v. Bridault and Wife*, 37 Miss. 209 (Apr. 1859) Helen Catterall, *Judicial Cases Concerning American Slavery and the Negro*, vol. 3 (reprinted, New York: Negro Universities Press, 1968), 360.

14. As cited in Ronald Takaki, *Iron Cages: Race and Culture in Nineteenth Century America* (New York: Alfred A. Knopf, 1979), 53.

15. Sidney Kaplan, "The Miscegenation Issue in the Election of 1864," *Journal of Negro History*, 34, (Apr., 1949): 274–343.

16. Du Bois recounts: "As I remember through memories of others, backward among my own family, it is the mother I ever recall. . . . All the way back in these dim distances it is the mothers and mothers of mothers who seem to count, while fathers are shadowy memories. . . ." in *Darkwater*, p. 168.

17. I am willing to concede that women might subscribe to the male system of honor, they even might contribute to its power within the larger society—but they lacked the essential ingredient of "autonomy." Female influence was a sop patriarchs used to keep women enthralled.

18. Clinton, *Plantation Mistress*, p. 94.

19. Ibid., pp. 228–31.

20. From *Totem and Taboo*, quoted in Werner Sollers, "Never Was Born: The Mulatto, An American Tragedy?" unpublished essay, p. 13.

21. Getman, pp. 137–38.

22. Ibid.

23. Ibid., p. 136.

24. See Getman and Williamson. See also James H. Johnston, *Race Relations in Virginia and Miscegenation in the South* (Amherst: Univ. of Massachusetts, 1970).

25. Williamson, pp. 52–53.

26. See Susan Brownmiller, *Against Our Will: Men, Women and Rape* (New York: Simon & Schuster, 1975).

27. Du Bois, *Darkwater*, p. 172.

28. See Terry Alford, *Prince Among Slaves* (New York: Harcourt Brace Jovanovich, 1977).

29. Leland Meyer, *The Life and Times of Colonel Richard M. Johnson of Kentucky* (New York: Columbia Univ. Press, 1932), 317, 322–23, 341–422.

30. Clinton, *Plantation Mistress*, p. 204.

31. Pauli Murray, *Proud Shoes* (New York: Harper and Row, 1978), 33, 47–49.

32. Lucius Versus Bierce, *Travels in the Southland, 1822–23* (Columbus: Ohio State Univ. Press, 1966), 100.

33. Carol Bleser, ed., *Secret and Sacred: The Diaries of James Henry Hammond, Southern Slaveholder* (New York: Oxford Univ. Press, 1988), 18.

34. Ibid., p. 19.

35. See *Ingram v. Fraley*, 29 Ga. 553 (Nov. 1859) in Catterall, *Judicial Cases Concerning American Slavery, and the Negro*, vol. 3, p. 72.

36. See *Shaw v. Brown*, 35 Miss. 246 (Apr. 1858) in Catterall, vol. 3, p. 354; and see also in 1856 *Berry v. Alsop*, 45 Miss. I (Apr. 1871).

37. *Carter's Heirs v. Carter's Administrators*, 39 Ala. 579 (Jan. 1865) in Catterall, vol. 3, p. 261.

38. Williamson, pp. 48–49.

39. *Walker v. Walker*, 25 Ga. 420 (June 1858) in Catterall, vol. 3, p. 62.

40. See *Pool's Heirs v. Pool's Executor*, 33 Ala 145 (June 1858) in Catterall, vol. 3, p. 228; and *Mathews v. Springer*, 16 Fed Cas 1096 [2 Abb. U.S. 283] (Jan. 1871) in Catterall, vol. 3, p. 384.

41. *Mitchell v. Wells*, 37 Miss. 235 (1859) in Catterall, vol. 3, p. 385.

42. *Cobb v. Battle*, 34 Ga. 458 (June 1866) in Catterall, vol. 3, p. 72.

43. *Barksdale v. Elam*, 30 Miss. 694 (Apr. 1856) in Catterall, vol. 3, p. 342.

44. *Dupree v. State*, 133 Ala. 80 (Jan. 1859) in Catterall, vol. 3, p. 229.

45. Carleton, p. 129.

46. George P. Rawick, ed., *The American Slave*, vol. 13 (Westport, Conn.: Greenwood Press, 1972), 4.

47. Jean Yellin, ed. (Cambridge: Harvard Univ. Press, 1986).

48. John Thompson, *The Life of John Thompson, A Fugitive, Containing His History of Twenty-Five Years in Bondage, and His Providential Escape Written by Himself* (Worcester, Mass.: John Thompson, 1856), cited in Marion Wilson Starling, *The Slave Narrative* (Washington, D.C.: Howard Univ. Press, 1988), 181.

49. Du Bois, p. 171.

50. They do make bold and vivid appearances in the diaries of Mary Boykin Chesnut, Lucy Minor Blackford, James Henry Hammond, to name but three of a dozen prominent white Southerners who included extensive commentary on this issue.

51. See in Catterall *Cocke v. Hannum*, 39 Miss. 423 (Oct. 1860) in Catterall, vol. 3, p. 371; *Harrison v. Harrison*, 20 Ala. 629 (June 1852) in vol. 3, p. 181; *Ex Parte Smith*, 23 Ala. 94 (June 1852) in vol. 3, p. 1; *Stripling v. Ware*, 36 Ala. 87 (Jan. 1860) in vol. 3, p. 238; *Jeter v. Jeter*, 36 Ala. 391 (June 1860) in vol. 3, p. 243; *Pulliam v. Pulliam*, Miss. Ch. 348, (1842) in vol. 3, p. 294; *Adams v. Adams*, 36 Ga. 236 (June 1867) in vol. 3, pp. 94–95; *Mosser v. Mosser*, 29 Ala. 313 (June 1856) in vol. 3, p. 212; and *Stallings v. Finch*, 25 Ala. 518 (June 1854) in vol. 3, p. 199.

52. *Mark V. Tushnet, The American Law of Slavery, 1810–1860* (Princeton: Princeton Univ. Press, 1981), 85–86.

53. Margaret Burnham, "An Impossible Marriage: Slave Law and Family Law," *Law and Inequality*, 5 (July 1987): 219.

54. Ibid.

55. *Alfred* (a slave) *v. State,* 37 Miss. 396 (Oct. 1859) in Catterall, vol. 3, p. 362.

56. See accounts of Clinton, "Caught in the Web of the Big House," pp. 19–32.

57. See *Fundi,* film tribute to Ella Baker, documentary produced and directed by Joanne Grant, 1984.

58. Baton Rouge: Louisiana State Univ. Press, 1988.

59. Frederick Law Olmsted, *Journey in the Seaboard States*, p. 240.

60. *Bryan v. Walten* (1864) in Catterall, vol. 3, p. 88.

61. C. Vann Woodward and Elisabeth Muhlenfeld, *The Private Mary Chesnut* (New York: Oxford Univ. Press, 1984), 42.

62. V. S. Naipaul, *A Turn in the South* (New York: Alfred A. Knopf, 1989), 109. Some even insist that the presence of mulattoes in the South can be blamed on the Union Army.

63. The 1974 indictment of Joan Little, a twenty-year-old black woman who killed her jailer after he raped her in Beaufort County, North Carolina, took place in the South, but the sexual abuse of African-American women cannot be confined to regional boundaries.

5. "Our Family, White and Black": Family and Household in the Southern Slaveholders' World View

1. Benjamin Morgan Palmer, *The Family, in Its Civil and Churchly Aspects: An Essay in Two Parts* (Richmond: Presbyterian Committee of Publication, 1876), 9–10. Palmer, the son of a prominent South Carolina minister of the same name, established his reputation at Columbia, where he was closely associated with James Henley Thornwell. In the 1850s, he moved to New Orleans, where he served as Presbyterian pastor and emerged as a pro-secession firebrand. See Thomas Cary Johnson, *The Life and Letters of Benjamin Morgan Palmer* (Richmond: Presbyterian Committee of Publication, 1906); and James Oscar Farmer, *The Metaphysical Confederacy: James Henley Thronwell and the Synthesis of Southern Values* (Macon, Ga.: Mercer Univ. Press, 1986).

2. Palmer, *Family*, pp. 174–75.

3. Ibid., pp. 14–15.

4. On the ministers' contribution to the proslavery argument, see William Sumner Jenkins, *Pro-Slavery Thought in the Old South* (Gloucester, Mass.: Peter Smith, 1960); and Larry E. Tise, *Proslavery: A History of the Defense of Slavery in America, 1701–1840* (Athens: Univ. of Georgia Press, 1988). For a critique of Tise's controversial thesis, see Eugene D. Genovese, "Larry Tise's *Proslavery*: A Critique and an Appreciation," *Georgia Historical Quarterly*, 72 (Winter 1988): 670–683. For a stunning illustration of the tribute paid scriptural arguments by secular theorists and politicians, see J.B. Thrasher, *Slavery, A Divine Institution, A Speech Made before the Breckenridge and Lane Club, Nov. 5, 1860* (Port Gibson, Miss.: Southern Reville Book & Job, 1861). For a particularly pithy statement of the common view of the relation of the subordination of women to that of slaves, see Frederick A. Ross, *Slavery Ordained of God* (Philadelphia: J.B. Lippincott, 1857), 106, 164ff.

5. Joseph R. Wilson, *Mutual Relation of Masters and Slaves as Taught by the Bible. A Discourse Preached at the First Church, Augusta, Georgia . . . Jan 6, 1861* (Augusta, Ga.: Chronicle & Sentinel, 1861), 7, 8, 9, 12–13. Here and elsewhere, all words in italics designate original emphasis.

6. H.N. McTyeire, "Plantation Life—Duties and Responsibilities," *DeBow's Review* 30 (Sept., 1860), excerpted in James O. Breeden, ed., *Advice among Masters: The Ideal of Slave Management in the Old South* (Westport, Conn.: Greenwood Press, 1980), 58, 110.

7. George W. Armstrong, *The Theology of Christian Experience, Designed as an Exposition of the "Common Faith" of the Church of God* (New York: C. Scribner, 1858), 165–69; quotations from pp. 165, 168.

8. George W. Armstrong, *The Christian Doctrine of Slavery* (New York: Negro Universities Press, 1967 [1857]), 158. For a discussion of the slaveholders' interpretation of the history of Western Civilization, see Eugene D. Genovese, *Western Civilization through Slaveholding Eyes: The Social and Historical Thought of Thomas Roderick Dew*, the Andrew W. Mellon Lecture (New Orleans: The Graduate School of Tulane Univ., 1986). Dew's lectures at the College of William and Mary were posthumously published and remain well worth reading for their historical insights. See *A Digest of the Laws, Customs, Manners, and Institutions of the Ancient and Modern Nations* (New York: D. Appleton & Co., 1854).

9. Ross, *Slavery Ordained of God*, p. 118.

10. This discussion and that which immediately follows owe much to Gavin Wright, *The Political Economy of the Cotton South* (New York: W.W. Norton, 1978), esp. chs. II and III; and to Elizabeth Fox-Genovese, *Within the Plantation Household: Black and White Women of the Old South* (Chapel Hill: Univ. of North Carolina Press, 1988), esp. ch. I. For the colonial period see esp. Edmund S. Morgan, *Virginians at Home: Family Life in the Eighteenth Century* (Williamsburg: Colonial Williamsburg, 1952); and Allan Kulikoff, *Tobacco and Slaves: The Development of Southern Cultures in the Chesapeake, 1680–1800* (Chapel Hill: Univ. of North Carolina Press, 1986).

11. Andrew P. Butler to Waddy Thompson, July 16, 1852, in the Waddy Thompson Papers, Univ. of South Carolina.

12. Carol Bleser, ed., *Secret and Sacred: The Diaries of James Henry Hammond, a Southern Slaveholder* (New York: Oxford Univ. Press, 1988), Jan. 29, 1848, p. 188. On Hammond, see Drew Gilpin Faust, *James Henry Hammond and the Old South: A Design for Mastery* (Baton Rouge: Louisiana State Univ. Press, 1982); and Carol Bleser, ed., *The Hammonds of Redcliffe* (New York: Oxford Univ. Press, 1981). For a colonial observation of the compatibility of stern treatment of slaves with a sense of them as part of the family see Hunter Dickinson Farish, ed., *Journal and Letters of Philip Vickers Fithian: A Plantation Tutor of the Old Dominion* (Charlottesville: Univ. Press of Virginia, 1957), esp. 145.

13. William Cabell Bruce, *John Randolph of Roanoke, 1773–1833,* vol. 1 (New York: Octagon Books, 1970), 624.

14. Lawrence M. Keitt, *Slavery and the Resources of the South* (Washington, D.C.: Congressional Globe, 1857), 7. This speech was originally delivered in the U.S. House of Representatives, Jan. 15, 1857.

15. J.P. Holcombe, *Address Delivered before the Seventh Annual Meeting of the Virginia State Agricultural Society, Nov. 4, 1858* (Richmond: MacFarlane & Ferguson, 1858), 5.

16. George W. Freedman, *Rights and Duties of Slaveholders: Two Discourses Delivered on Sunday, Nov. 27, 1835, in Christ Church, Raleigh, North Carolina* (Raleigh: J. Gales & Son, 1836), 5–6.

17. William O. Prentiss, *A Sermon Preached at St. Peter's Church, Charleston, . . . Nov. 4, 1860* (Charleston, S.C.: Evans & Cogswell, 1860), 14. See also Meade Minnigerode, *The Fabulous Forties: A Presentation of Everyday Life* (New York: G.P. Putnam & Sons, 1924), 102–4, for the controversy over birth control in the North, which in itself shocked public opinion in the South.

18. John Fletcher, *Studies on Slavery, in Easy Lessons* (Miami: Mnemosyne Publishing Co., 1969 [1852]), 9, 23.

19. For the debate, see Eugene D. Genovese, *Slavery Ordained of God: The Southern Slaveholders' View of Biblical History and Modern Politics*, the Robert Fortenbaugh Memorial Lecture (Pennsylvania: Gettysburg College, 1985).

20. Ross, *Slavery Ordained of God*, pp. 151–52.

21. Armstrong, *Christian Doctrine of Slavery*, pp. 56–60.

22. Thornton Stringfellow, "The Bible Argument; Or Slavery in Light of Divine Revelation," in E.N. Elliott, ed., *Cotton is King and Pro-Slavery Arguments* (New York: Negro Universities Press, 1969 [1860]), 481–84; also p. 462n. For similar arguments from the Southwest, see Fletcher, *Studies on Slavery*, p. 290 and passim; William T. Hamilton, *The "Friend of Moses;" Or, a Defence of the Pentateuch as the Production of Moses and an Inspired Document against the Objections of Modern Skepticism* (New York: M.W. Dodd, 1853), 125. Fletcher lived in New Orleans; Hamilton, in Mobile.

23. Palmer, *Family*, p. 173.

24. Ibid., pp. 172–73.

25. Ibid., pp. 226–27.

26. Ibid., p. 173. For earlier projections of the slaveholders as guardians and "fathers" of their slaves, see Tise, *Proslavery*, p. 61 and passim.

27. For an elaboration, see Eugene D. Genovese, *Roll, Jordan, Roll: The World the Slaves Made* (New York: Pantheon, 1974), book one, part one; and "Master-Slave Relations," in Randall M. Miller and John David Smith, eds., *Dictionary of Afro-American Slavery* (New York: Greenwood Press, 1988), 449–54.

28. George W. McDuffie, *Governor McDuffie's Message on the Slavery* (New York: A. Lowell & Co., 1893 [1835]), p. 8.

29. Omo, "Negro Houses—Plantation Hospitals," *Southern Cultivator*, XIV (Jan. 1856), excerpted in Breeden, ed., *Advice among Masters*, p. 191.

30. M.W. Phillips, "Preserving Health," *South-Western Farmer*, 2 (Aug. 1843), excerpted in Breeden, ed., *Advice among Masters*, pp. 164–65; Foby, "Management of Servants," *Southern Cultivator*, XI (Aug. 1853), excerpted in Breeden, ed., *Advice among Masters*, p. 306. Breeden also excerpts a number of other articles that stress plantation household and the religious duty attached thereto. See pp. 44–49.

31. Quoted in William Mercer Green, *Memoir of the Rt. Rev. James Hervey Otey* (New York: James Pott & Co., 1885), 94. Otey was echoing a long-standing southern lament. See, e.g., James Smylie, *Review of a Letter from the Presbytery of Chillicothe to the Presbytery of Mississippi on the Subject of Slavery* (Woodville, Miss.: A. Norris, 1836), 60–61. For that matter, not a few Northerners, including Ralph Waldo Emerson, chided the abolitionists on the same point.

32. Maria Genoino Caravaglios, *The American Catholic Church and the Negro Problem in the XVII–XIX Centuries* (Charleston, S.C.: n.p., 1974), quoting Bishop Hughes on p. 165; William Henry Elder, *Civil War Diary (1862–1865)* (Jackson, Miss.: n.p., n.d.).

33. Quoted by Bleser in her introduction to *Secret and Sacred*, p. 19.

34. George Fort Milton, *The Eve of Conflict: Stephen A. Douglas and the Needless War* (Cambridge, Mass.: Houghton Mifflin Co., 1934). There were various other embarrassments. Consider, e.g., the case of Jonathan Worth, a prominent civic leader in North Carolina, who was almost ruined politically by false rumors that he allowed his slaves to eat at the family table. Richard L. Zubin, *Jonathan Worth: A Biography of a Southern Unionist* (Chapel Hill: Univ. of North Carolina Press, 1965), 62–63.

35. Armstrong, *Christian Doctrine of Slavery*, p. 120n., asserted that he never knew of a slave family being broken up. He was not alone in making such an assertion.

36. *State v. Mann* in J.G. de Roulhac Hamilton, ed., *The Papers of Thomas Ruffin*, 4 (Raleigh, N.C.: Edwards & Broughton, 1918), 256.

37. Mark V. Tushnet, *The American Law of Slavery: Considerations of Humanity and Interest* (Princeton: Princeton Univ. Press, 1981), esp. 54–65.

38. Hamilton, ed., *Papers of Thomas Ruffin*, 4: 250 ("Rough Draft") and 4: 251 ("Second Draft").

39. William Brockenbaugh to Thomas Ruffin, Feb. 7, 1831, in Hamilton, ed., *Papers of Thomas Ruffin*, 2: 28.

40. Thomas Ruffin to John Holt, Mar. 4, 1850, in Hamilton, ed., *Papers of Thomas Ruffin*, 2: 420. Holt agreed on condition that he be allowed to immerse the girl in proper Baptist fashion.

41. "Address of Thomas Ruffin Delivered before the State Agricultural Society of North Carolina, October 18, 1855," in Hamilton, ed., *Papers of Thomas Ruffin*, 4: 332–33.

42. "Address of Thomas Ruffin," Hamilton, ed., *Papers of Thomas Ruffin*, 4: 333–34.

43. For the divines' espousal of the doctrines of "slavery in the abstract," see Eugene D. Genovese and Elizabeth Fox-Genovese, "The Social Thought of the Antebellum Southern Divines" (forthcoming).

44. Thomas R.R. Cobb, *An Inquiry into the Law of Negro Slavery in the United States* (New York: Negro Universities Press, 1968 [1858]), esp. the long historical introduction.

45. John C. Calhoun, quoted by Augustus Baldwin Longstreet, "Review of Ex-Gov. Perry's Sketch of John C. Calhoun," *The XIX Century*, 2 (Jan. 1870): 623.

46. Hunt's text appears in W. Way, *New England Society of Charleston* (Charleston, S.C.: published by the Society, 1920), 216–17.

47. Henry Hughes, *Treatise on Sociology, Theoretical and Practical* (New York: Negro Universities Press, 1968 [1854]), 82–83.

48. Smylie, *Review of a Letter from the Presbytery of Chillicothe*, p. 53.

49. Jacksonville, Ala., *Republican*, Jan. 17, 1861; and Atlanta, Ga., *Gate-City Guardian*, Feb. 12, 1861, quoted in Donald E. Reynolds, *Editors Make War: Southern Newspapers in the Secession Crisis* (Nashville: Vanderbilt Univ. Press, 1961), 177.

50. Quoted in David Edwin Harrell, Jr., *Quest for a Christian America: The Disciples of Christ to 1866* (Nashville: Disciples of Christ Historical Society, 1966), 104–5.

51. J.J. O'Connell, *Catholicity in the Carolinas and Georgia: Leaves of Its History* (Westminster, Md.: Ars Sacra, 1964), 72.

52. Wilson, *Mutual Relation of Masters and Slaves*, p. 5; also, W.H. Rivers, *Elements of Moral Philosophy* (Nashville: Methodist Publishing House, 1860), 220–21.

53. Fletcher, *Studies on Slavery*, pp. 19, 81, 182–83, 187–88, 203.

54. For Thornwell's view of property in labor and service, see John B. Adger and John Girardeau, eds., *The Collected Writings of James Henley Thornwell*, vol. 4 (Richmond: Presbyterian Committee of Publication, 1871), 4: 415. Also, Robert L. Dabney, *Defence of Virginia (and through Her of the South) in Recent and Pending Contest against the Sectional Party* (New York: Negro Universities Press, 1960 [1867]), 94.

55. Stringfellow, "Bible Argument," p. 462n.

56. William A. Smith, *Lectures on the Philosophy and Practice of Slavery, as Exhibited in the Institution of Domestic Slavery in the United States, with the Duties of Masters to Slaves* (Nashville: Stevenson & Evans, 1856), 39–40.

57. Dabney, *Defence of Virginia*, pp. 305–6.

6. Strategies of Survival: Free Negro Families
and the Problem of Slavery

1. Frederick Douglass, *Life and Times of Frederick Douglass* (New York: Collier Books, 1962; original edition, 1892), 27. See also Dickson J. Preston, *Young Frederick Douglass: The Maryland Years* (Baltimore: Johns Hopkins Univ. Press, 1980); Waldo E. Martin, Jr., *The Mind of Frederick Douglass* (Chapel Hill: Univ. of North Carolina Press, 1984); and William L. Andrews, *To Tell a Free Story: The First Century of Afro-American Autobiography, 1760–1865* (Urbana: Univ. of Illinois Press, 1986).

2. On the slave family, see especially Herbert G. Gutman, *The Black Family in Slavery and Freedom, 1750–1925* (New York: Vintage Books, 1976); Eugene D. Genovese, *Roll, Jordan, Roll: The World the Slaves Made* (New York: Pantheon Books, 1974); George Rawick, *From Sundown to Sunup: The Making of the Black Community* (Westport, Conn.: Greenwood Press, 1972); John W. Blassingame, *The Slave Community: Plantation Life in the Antebellum South* (New York: Oxford Univ. Press, 1972); Willie Lee Rose, *Slavery and Freedom*, edited by William W. Freehling (New York: Oxford Univ. Press, 1982); Elizabeth Fox-Genovese, *Within the Plantation Household: Black and White Women of the Old South* (Chapel Hill: Univ. of North Carolina Press, 1988); Jacqueline Jones, *Labor of Love, Labor of Sorrow: Black Women, Work, and the Family from Slavery to the Present* (New York: Basic Books, 1985); Deborah Gray White, *Ar'n't I a Woman? Female Slaves in the Plantation South* (New York: W. W. Norton, 1985); Anne Patton Malone, "Searching for the Family and Household Structure of Rural Louisiana Slaves, 1810–1864," *Louisiana History*, 28 (Fall 1987): 357–79.

3. Ira Berlin, *Slaves Without Masters: The Free Negro in the Antebellum South* (New York: Pantheon Books, 1974); Michael P. Johnson and James L. Roark, *Black Masters: A Free Family of Color in the Old South* (New York: W.W. Norton, 1984).

4. Leon F. Litwack, *North of Slavery: The Negro in the Free States, 1790–1860* (Chicago: Univ. of Chicago Press, 1961); Benjamin Quarles, *Black Abolitionists* (New York: Oxford Univ. Press, 1969); R.J.M. Blackett, *Building An Antislavery Wall: Black Americans in the Atlantic Abolitionist Movement, 1830–1860* (Baton

Rouge: Louisiana State Univ. Press, 1983); C. Peter Ripley, ed., *The Black Aboli-tionist Papers*, vol. 1, *The British Isles, 1830–1865* (Chapel Hill: Univ. of North Carolina Press, 1985), and vol. 2, *Canada, 1830–1865* (Chapel Hill: Univ. of North Carolina Press, 1986).

5. Genovese, *Roll, Jordan, Roll*, pp. 408, 412.

6. Among the important state studies are Jeffrey R. Brackett, *The Negro in Maryland: A Study in the Institution of Slavery* (Baltimore: Johns Hopkins Univ. Press, 1899); John H. Russell, *The Free Negro in Virginia, 1619–1865* (Baltimore: Johns Hopkins Univ. Press, 1913); James M. Wright, *The Free Negro in Maryland, 1634–1860* (New York: Columbia Univ. Press, 1921); Charles S. Sydnor, "The Free Negro in Mississippi Before the Civil War," *American Historical Review*, 32 (1927): 769–88; Ralph B. Flanders, "The Free Negro in Antebellum Georgia," *North Carolina Historical Review*, 9 (1932): 250–72; James M. England, "The Free Negro in Ante-Bellum Tennessee," (Ph.D. diss., Vanderbilt Univ., 1941); Luther P. Jackson, *Free Negro Labor and Property Holding in Virginia, 1830–1860* (New York: D. Appleton-Century, 1942); John Hope Franklin, *The Free Negro in North Carolina, 1790–1860* (Chapel Hill: Univ. of North Carolina Press, 1943); Morris R. Boucher, "The Free Negro in Alabama Prior to 1860," (Ph.D. diss., State Univ. of Iowa, 1950); Edward F. Sweat, "The Free Negro in Antebellum Georgia," (Ph.D. diss., Univ. of Indiana, 1957); Herbert E. Sterkx, *The Free Negro in Antebellum Louisiana* (Rutherford, N.J.: Fairleigh Dickinson Univ. Press, 1972); Marina Wikramanayake, *A World in Shadow: The Free Black in Antebellum South Carolina* (Columbia: Univ. of South Carolina Press, 1973); Larry Koger, *Black Slaveowners: Free Black Slave Masters in South Carolina, 1790–1860* (Jefferson, N.C: McFarland, 1985); Barbara Jeanne Fields, *Slavery and Freedom on the Middle Ground: Maryland during the Nineteenth Century* (New Haven: Yale Univ. Press, 1985).

Other important studies include Ulrich Bonnell Phillips, "Slave Labor in the Charleston District," *Political Science Quarterly*, 22 (1907): 416–39; Phillips, *American Negro Slavery* (New York: D. Appleton, 1918); E. Franklin Frazier, *The Free Negro Family: A Study of Family Origins Before the Civil War* (Nashville: Fisk Univ. Press, 1932); E. Horace Fitchett, "The Traditions of the Free Negro in Charleston, South Carolina," *Journal of Negro History*, 25 (1940): 139–51; Fitchett, "The Origins and Growth of the Free Negro Population of Charleston, South Carolina," *Journal of Negro History*, 26 (1941): 421–37; Fitchett, "The Status of the Free Negro in Charleston, South Carolina, and His Descendants in Modern Society," *Journal of Negro History*, 32 (1947): 430–51; Donald E. Everett, "The Free Persons of Color in New Orleans, 1830–1865," (Ph.D. diss., Tulane Univ., 1952); David C. Rankin, "The Forgotten People: Free People of Color in New Orleans, 1850–1870," (Ph.D. diss., Johns Hopkins Univ., 1976); Leonard P. Stavisky, "The Negro Artisan in the South Atlantic States, 1800–1860: A Study of Status and Economic Opportunity with Special Reference to Charleston," (Ph.D. diss., Columbia Univ., 1958); James Hugo Johnston, *Race Relations in Virginia & Miscegenation in the South, 1776–1860* (Amherst: Univ. of Massachusetts Press, 1970); Letitia Woods Brown, *Free Negroes in the District of Columbia, 1790–1846* (New York: Oxford Univ. Press, 1972); Leonard P. Curry, *The Free Black in Urban America, 1800–1850: The Shadow of the Dream* (Chicago: Univ. of Chicago Press, 1981); Michael P. Johnson and James L. Roark, eds., *No Chariot Let Down: Charleston's Free*

People of Color on the Eve of the Civil War (Chapel Hill: Univ. of North Carolina Press, 1984).

Studies that examine the activities of individuals or families include William Ranson Hogan and Edwin Adams Davis, eds., *William Johnson's Natchez: The Antebellum Diary of a Free Negro* (Baton Rouge: Louisiana State Univ. Press, 1951); Edwin Adams Davis and William Ranson Hogan, *The Barber of Natchez* (Baton Rouge: Louisiana State Univ. Press, 1954); Gary B. Mills, *The Forgotten People: Cane River's Creoles of Color* (Baton Rouge: Louisiana State Univ. Press, 1977); T.H. Breen and Stephen Innes, *"Myne Owne Ground": Race and Freedom on Virginia's Eastern Shore, 1640–1676* (New York: Oxford Univ. Press, 1980); David O. Whitten, *Andrew Durnford: A Black Sugar Planter in Antebellum Louisiana* (Natchitoches, La.: Northwestern State Univ. Press, 1981); Willard B. Gatewood, Jr., ed., *Free Man of Color: The Autobiography of Willis Augustus Hodges* (Knoxville: Univ. of Tennessee Press, 1982); Juliet E. K. Walker, *Free Frank: A Black Pioneer on the Antebellum Frontier* (Lexington: Univ. Press of Kentucky, 1983); Loren Schweninger, ed., *From Tennessee Slave to St. Louis Entrepreneur: The Autobiography of James Thomas* (Columbia: Univ. of Missouri Press, 1986).

7. C.L.R. James, *The Black Jacobins: Toussaint L'Ouverture and the San Domingo Revolution* (London: Allison & Busby, 1980; original 1938), 38.

8. For a summary of the proscriptive legislation, see Berlin, *Slaves Without Masters*, pp. 316–40.

9. *Population of the United States in 1860*, pp. 598–605; Berlin, *Slaves Without Masters*, pp. 136–37, 397–99. In the entire South, the proportion of the Afro-American population that was free reached a peak in 1810 at 8.5 percent. It declined slowly to 8.3 percent by 1830, then slumped more quickly to 6.2 percent by 1860. Derived from population data in Berlin, *Slaves Without Masters*, pp. 46–47, 136–37.

10. George Fitzhugh, "What Shall Be Done with the Free Negroes: Essays Written for the Fredricksburg *Recorder,*" *Recorder,* Fredricksburg, Va., 1851, p. 6.

11. In South Carolina in 1832, the informal practice of local whites determining the free status of Afro-Americans was formally accepted as a legal test for the freedom of those who were not subject to the 1800 manumission law, either because they were free earlier or because they were freeborn. In the case of *State v. Harden*, Justice John Belton O'Neall wrote, "Proof that a negro has been suffered to live in a community for years, as a free man, would, *prima facie*, establish the fact of freedom." Helen Tunnicliff Catterall, ed., *Judicial Cases Concerning American Slavery and the Negro*, vol. 2 (Washington, D.C.: Carnegie Institute of Washington, 1929), 350.

12. The antebellum achievement of successful free Negroes was usually made possible by their ability to shelter themselves from the ruthless force of the law and to carve out a niche in what David M. Potter termed the "folk culture" of the South. Potter emphasized that personal, face-to-face relations played a crucial role in southern folk culture, imparting a distinctive style to social life that he termed "personalism." *The South and the Sectional Conflict* (Baton Rouge: Louisiana State Univ. Press, 1968), 15–16. The codes, customs, and values that regulated community life impinged on all southerners, white and black. But the social assignment for free Negroes was even murkier than for whites. Bertram Wyatt-Brown, *Southern*

Honor: Ethics and Behavior in the Old South (New York: Oxford Univ. Press, 1982).

For guardianship, see Berlin, *Slaves Without Masters*, pp. 215, 318, 357. In other states, much the same effect was achieved by laws requiring each free person of color to register with the local courthouse. Ibid., pp. 317, 319, 327–33.

13. Suzanne Lebsock, *The Free Women of Petersburg: Status and Culture in a Southern Town, 1784–1860* (New York: W.W. Norton, 1984), 87–111.

14. Johnson and Roark, *Black Masters*, pp. 209–12; Fox-Genovese, *Within the Plantation Household*, p. 52; Lebsock, *The Free Women of Petersburg*, pp. 87–111.

15. For a discussion of gender roles among northern free Negroes, see James Oliver Horton, "Freedom's Yoke: Gender Conventions Among Antebellum Free Blacks," *Feminist Studies*, 12 (Spring 1986): 51–76. For patriarchy among whites, see Anne Firor Scott, *The Southern Lady: From Pedestal to Politics, 1830–1930* (Chicago: Univ. of Chicago Press, 1970); Catherine Clinton, *The Plantation Mistress: Woman's World in the Old South* (New York: Pantheon Books, 1982); Jean E. Friedman, *The Enclosed Garden: Women and Community in the Evangelical South, 1830–1900* (Chapel Hill: Univ. of North Carolina Press, 1985); Steven M. Stowe, *Intimacy and Power in the Old South: Ritual in the Lives of the Planters* (Baltimore: Johns Hopkins Univ. Press, 1987).

16. Johnson and Roark, *Black Masters*, pp. 81–117.

17. Fox-Genovese, *Within the Plantation Household*, p. 30.

18. Data on families were derived from an analysis of every free Afro-American household in South Carolina outside the city of Charleston that was listed in the manuscript schedules of the 1860 federal census. In all, there were 1,387 free Negro households outside Charleston.

19. Carter G. Woodson, "Free Negro Owners of Slaves in the United States in 1830," *Journal of Negro History*, 9 (Jan. 1924): 41–85. Studies that investigate, rather than merely mention, slaveholding among free Negroes include Calvin Dill Wilson, "Black Masters: A Side-Light on Slavery," *North American Review*, 171 (Nov. 1905): 685–98; John H. Russell, "Colored Freemen as Slave Owners in Virginia," *Journal of Negro History*, 1 (July 1916): 233–42; R. Halliburton, Jr., "Free Black Owners of Slaves: A Reappraisal of the Woodson Thesis," *South Carolina Historical Magazine*, 76 (July 1975): 129–42; Philip J. Schwarz, "Emancipators, Protectors, and Anomalies: Free Black Slaveholders in Virginia," *Virginia Magazine of History and Biography*, 95 (July 1987): 317–38; Koger, *Black Slaveowners*.

20. James Oakes, *The Ruling Race: A History of American Slaveowners* (New York: Alfred A. Knopf, 1982), 47–48.

21. In 1838, for example, James Patterson, a free man of color who lived in Columbia, South Carolina, petitioned the South Carolina legislature for permission to free his wife Sarah and his two children George and Mary whom he had purchased and currently owned as his slaves. Despite the endorsement of prominent white citizens, including Pierce M. Butler's praise of Patterson as "an industrious well behaved boy, respectful & always knowing his place," the legislators denied Patterson's request. Petition of James Patterson (1838), Slavery Petitions, South Carolina Department of Archives and History, Columbia, South Carolina. See also, Schwarz, "Emancipators, Protectors, and Anomalies," pp. 329–32.

22. N. Webster Moore, "John Berry Meachum (1789–1854): St. Louis Pioneer,

Black Abolitionist, Educator, and Preacher," *Bulletin of the Missouri Historical Society*, 29 (Oct. 1972): 96–103; Lebsock, *The Free Women of Petersburg*, p. 98.

23. Hogan and Davis, eds., *William Johnson's Natchez*; Davis and Hogan, *The Barber of Natchez*.

24. Whitten, *Andrew Durnford*, pp. 58–59.

25. Johnson and Roark, *Black Masters*.

26. Schweninger, ed., *From Tennessee Slave to St. Louis Entrepreneur*, p. 120.

27. All the 1830 data are from Carter G. Woodson, compiler and ed., *Free Negro Owners of Slaves in the United States in 1830 Together with Absentee Ownership of Slaves in the United States in 1830* (c. 1924; reprinted, New York, 1968), to p. 42. For summaries of the Woodson data, see Tables 6.1 and 6.2. We have checked the accuracy of the Woodson data for the entire state of South Carolina and found only a few errors. These do not materially affect the general pattern. Free Negro masters with ten or more slaves owned 44 percent of the slaves owned by free Afro-Americans in the lower South; in the upper South, they held just 13 percent. In all, 27 masters in the upper South possessed 10 or more slaves. Fifteen lived in Virginia, 11 in Maryland, and 1 in Tennessee. The lower South contained 184 such slaveholders. South Carolina had 99, Louisiana 65, North Carolina 9, Alabama 6, Florida and Mississippi 2 each, and Georgia 1.

28. For a convenient summary of laws regarding manumission, see Berlin, *Slaves Without Masters*, pp. 138–39, n. 2.

29. Nonetheless, free Afro-Americans in Virginia continued to purchase and free family members well after 1806 and still remain in the state. Between 1784 and 1806, free Afro-Americans were responsible for about one-sixth of the manumissions in Petersburg, Virginia. After 1806, they emancipated about one-third of the slaves freed in Petersburg (133 out of 410). Since free Negroes made up about one-third of the town's free population, they were no more involved in freeing slaves after 1806 than the town's white masters were. See Lebsock, *The Free Women of Petersburg*, pp. 91, 96, 106; Schwarz, "Emancipators, Protectors, and Anomalies," pp. 321–22.

30. John H. Russell points out that while free Negroes often owned family members, they also "purchased and held slaves with the same considerations of profit in view as governed the actions of white owners of slaves." *The Free Negro in Virginia*, p. 93.

31. The data for this analysis were compiled from the manuscript schedules of the federal census of Maryland, North Carolina, and South Carolina in 1790, 1800, and 1810, and Virginia in 1810. Ideally, one could use the manuscript census schedules to compile a list of all free Negro slaveholders in the nation between 1790 and 1810. In fact, the Virginia schedules for 1790 and 1800 have not survived, a major loss since free Afro-American Virginians accounted for 40 percent and 33 percent of the total southern free Negro population in the two census years respectively. Estimates of the total number of free Negro slaveholders in 1790 and 1800 can be obtained, however, from examination of the manuscript census schedules of Maryland, North Carolina, and South Carolina, which together contained 46 percent and 49 percent of the southern free Negro population in the two census years. Virginia census data exist for 1810 and when added to that from the other three states allow the 1810 estimate to be based on evidence from states that contained 73 percent of all southern free Negroes. Estimates of the total numbers of free Negro masters and their slaves were derived by

assuming that free Afro-Americans in the other states owned slaves at the same per-capita rate and that they owned about the same number of slaves. It is unlikely that these assumptions significantly overestimate the extent of slaveholding in the remaining states. For summaries of the data, see Tables 6.3 and 6.4.

32. For a brief summary of data on slaveholding in the United States in 1790 and 1850, see United States Bureau of the Census, *Negro Population, 1790–1915* (Washington, D.C.: 1918), 56.

33. Data on all free Afro-American slaveholders in South Carolina were compiled from the manuscript schedules of the 1820 federal census. See Table 6.5 for a summary. Slaveholding in the city of Charleston might plausibly be thought to be a special case. However, the pattern of slaveholding among free Negroes outside Charleston did not differ dramatically from that in the city. Of the 35 free Afro-American masters who lived outside the city of Charleston in 1820, only 3 (9 percent) appear likely to have owned members of their immediate family; they owned a total of 4 (2 percent) of the 169 slaves owned by these masters. Since the similarity between the city and the rest of the state holds true for all the subsequent analysis of the 1820 South Carolina data, the Charleston data have not been disaggregated from the statewide totals.

34. Suzanne Lebsock has observed that after the Panic of 1819 lowered the price of slaves, a good many free women of color bought slaves for the first time and during the 1820s consolidated their greatest economic gains. Lebsock, "Free Black Women and the Question of Matriarchy: Petersburg, Virginia, 1784–1820," *Feminist Studies*, 8 (Summer 1982): 281–82.

35. Gatewood, ed., *Free Man of Color*, p. 7.

36. The information about the Lee brothers is from E. Horace Fitchett, "The Free Negro in Charleston, South Carolina," (Ph.D. diss., Univ. of Chicago, 1950), 345–49. The graffiti on the walls of the *Mercury* office are reported in "The Fall of Charleston," New York *Tribune*, Mar. 2, 1865.

7. Distress and Discord in
Virginia Slave Families, 1830–1860

1. Several important works are available which are discussions of the general life-styles as well as family and marriage problems of antebellum Southerners. For free blacks in antebellum Virginia, see Luther P. Jackson, *Free Negro Labor and Property Holding in Virginia, 1830–1860* (New York: Athenaeum, 1969 [c 1942]; reprint ed., 1986). See also: "Free Women of Color" in Suzanne Lebsock, *The Free Women of Petersburg: Status and Culture in a Southern Town, 1784–1860* (New York: W.W. Norton, 1984), 87–111. For a general discussion of free blacks in the antebellum lower South, see Ira Berlin, *Slaves Without Masters: The Free Negro in the Antebellum South* (New York: Vintage Books, 1976), 174.

Concerning slavery and the slave family, the most impressive, scholarly treatments are found in John W. Blassingame, *The Slave Community: Plantation Life in the Antebellum South* (New York: Oxford Univ. Press, 1972), Deborah Gray White, *Ar'n't I A Woman? Female Slaves in the Plantation South* (New York: W.W. Norton, 1985); Eugene Genovese, *Roll, Jordan, Roll: The World the Slaves Made* (New York: Pantheon Books, 1974), and particularly Herbert G. Gutman, *The Black Family in Slavery and Freedom, 1750–1925* (New York: Pantheon Books, 1976).

For the most thoughtful descriptions of antebellum white familial relations, see Elizabeth Fox-Genovese *Within the Plantation Household: Black and White Women in the Old South* (Chapel Hill: The Univ. of North Carolina Press, 1988); Catherine Clinton *The Plantation Mistress: Woman's World in the Old South* (New York: Pantheon Books, 1982); Bertram Wyatt-Brown, *Southern Honor: Ethics and Behavior in the Old South* (New York: Oxford Univ. Press, 1982); Anne Firor Scott, *The Southern Lady: From Pedestal to Politics, 1830–1930* (Chicago: Univ. of Chicago Press, 1970); and Lebsock, *Free Women of Petersburg.*

2. Richard Sutch, "The Breeding of Slaves for Sale and the Westward Expansion of Slavery, 1850–1860," in Stanley L. Engerman and Eugene Genovese, eds., *Race and Slavery in the Western Hemisphere: Quantitative Studies* (Princeton: Princeton Univ. Press, 1975), Appendix, Table 4, p. 207.

3. Donald M. Sweig, "Northern Virginia Slavery: A Statistical and Demographic Investigation" (Ph.D. dissertation, College of William and Mary, 1982), 206.

4. Sutch, "The Breeding of Slaves for Sale," Appendix, Tables 4 and 5, pp. 207, 209.

5. JoAnn Manfra and Robert R. Dykstra, "Serial Marriage and the Origins of the Black Stepfamily: The Rowanty Evidence," *Journal of American History* 72 (June 1985): 32. These authors state that 35.3 percent of slave marriages terminated in their sample from Dinwiddie County, Virginia was due to involuntary separation. Comparatively, Blassingame in his compilation of causes of slave marriage termination records that 39 percent in Mississippi, 26.8 percent in Tennessee and 29.2 percent in Louisiana ended as a result of forced separation. Blassingame, *Slave Community*, Table 2, p. 90.

6. Manfra and Dykstra, "Serial Marriage," p. 36.

7. The slave narratives which comprise this sample were the 142 included in Charles L. Perdue, Jr., Thomas E. Barden, and Robert K. Phillips, eds., *Weevils in the Wheat: Interviews with Virginia Ex-Slaves* (Charlottesville: Univ. Press of Virginia, 1976).

8. Ibid., p. 1.

9. Ibid., p. 3.

10. Ibid., pp. 1, 3.

11. Ibid., pp. 3–4.

12. "Slave List," Bruce Family Papers, Virginia Historical Society, Richmond, hereafter referred to as VHS.

13. Robert S. Starobin, ed., *Blacks in Bondage: Letters of American Slaves* (reprinted, New York: Markus Wiener Publishing, 1988), 72.

14. Anthropologist Nancy Tanner offers one of the most viable definitions for matrifocality. She describes the term in part as (1) "kinship systems in which (a) the role of the mother is structurally, culturally, and affectively central and (b) this multidimensional centrality is legitimate; and (2) the societies in which these features coexist, where (a) the relationship between the sexes is relatively egalitarian and (b) both women and men are important actors in the economic and ritual spheres." Matrilocal families are those in which the majority of the functional members reside in the home of the mother. Nancy Tanner, "Matrifocality in Indonesia and Africa and Among Black Americans," in Michele Zimbalist Rosaldo and Louise Lamphere, eds., *Woman, Culture and Society* (Stanford: Stanford Univ. Press, 1974), 131.

15. William Waller Hennings, ed., *The Statutes at Large: Being a Collection of All the Laws of Virginia*, vol. 2 (Richmond: Samuel Pleasants, 1832), 170.

16. Perdue et al., eds., *Weevils in the Wheat*, passim. See, for example, Frank Bell's description of his Uncle Moses Bell's relationship with his family, p. 26.

17. Perdue et al., eds., *Weevils in the Wheat*, passim.

18. Norman Yetman, ed., *Voices from Slavery* (New York: Holt, Rinehart and Winston, 1970), 26.

19. Perdue et al., eds., *Weevils in the Wheat*, p. 161.

20. Sutch, "Breeding of Slaves for Sale," Appendix, Table 5, p. 209.

21. Information for computation of the average age of Virginia slave mothers at first birth, 19.71 years, was compiled from slave lists dated during the period 1800–1865, located in the William H. Gray Farm Book, Gray Family Papers, VHS; Ledger of George Saunders, Saunders Family Papers, Virginia State Library, Richmond, Virginia. Ledger of William Gatewood and Samuel Vance Gatewood, Gatewood Family Papers, VHS; Stringfellow Family Bible, Stringfellow Family Papers, VHS; Allen T. Caperton Family Papers, VHS; Slave Lists, John Young Mason Papers, VHS; Slave Lists, William Bolling Papers, VHS; Slave List, Baskerville Family Papers, VHS.

Trussel and Steckel estimate that the mean age of first birth for slave mothers throughout the antebellum South was 20.6 years. James Trussel and Richard Steckel, "The Age of Slaves at Menarche and Their First Birth" *Journal of Interdisciplinary History*, 8 (Winter 1978): 492.

22. Perdue et al., eds., *Weevils in the Wheat*, p. 199.

23. Ibid., p. 33.

24. Ibid.

25. Eugene Genovese also argues, and rightfully so, that "inherent" in the "paternalism" of slave owners, "were dangerously deceptive ideas of 'gratitude,' 'loyalty,' and 'family.' Inherent also was an intimacy that turned every act of impudence and insubordination—every act of unsanctioned self-assertion—into an act of treason and disloyalty, for by repudiating the principle of submission it struck at the heart of the master's moral self-justification and therefore at his self-esteem." Genovese, *Roll, Jordan, Roll*, p. 91.

For more detailed discussions of these issues, see Thomas L. Webber, *Deep Like the Rivers: Education in the Slave Quarter Community, 1831–1865* (New York: W.W. Norton, 1978), 63–79, passim; and Brenda Stevenson, " 'Seemed Like Your Children Belonged to Everyone But You': The Rearing of Slave Children in Antebellum Virginia," presented at the annual conference of the Organization of American Historians, Apr. 12, 1987, Reno, Nevada.

26. Perdue et al., eds., *Weevils in the Wheat*, p. 68.

27. Ibid., p. 150.

28. Ibid., p. 317.

29. Ibid., p. 245.

30. Ibid., p. 15.

31. Ibid., pp. 16–17.

32. Ibid.

33. Ibid., p. 108.

34. In late May 1861, General Benjamin F. Butler of the United States Army, then commander of Fortress Monroe at Old Point Comfort, Virginia, decided to

accept slaves escaping from Confederate owners as "contraband" of the Civil War, that is, property which belonged to the enemy that could have been used against the Union in the war effort. His decision set an important precedent in the war, and before its end, thousands of slaves escaped and sought protection in Union-held camps and forts as "contraband." See, for example, Robert Francis Engs's discussion in *Freedom's First Generation: Black Hampton, Virginia, 1861–1890* (Philadelphia: Univ. of Pennsylvania Press, 1979), 18–22.

35. Henry Swint, ed., *Dear Ones At Home: Letters from Contraband Camps* (Nashville: Vanderbilt Univ. Press, 1966), 39, 55–56, 73.

36. Perdue et al., eds., *Weevils in the Wheat*, pp. 108–9.

37. Ibid., pp. 255–57.

38. James O. Breeden, ed., *Advice to Masters: The Ideal in Slave Management in the Old South* (Westport, Conn.: Greenwood Press, 1980), 282.

39. Swint, ed., *Dear Ones at Home*, p. 161.

40. Ibid., p. 123.

41. Perdue et al., eds., *Weevils in the Wheat*, p. 317.

42. Ibid.

43. Ibid., p. 161.

44. Quoted in *The Negro in Virginia*. Compiled by the Virginia Federal Writers' Project of the Work Projects Administration in the state of Virginia (New York: Hastings Publishers, 1940), 83–84.

45. Perdue et al., eds., *Weevils in the Wheat*, p. 161.

46. Ibid., p. 209.

47. Ibid., p. 161.

48. For information on sources consulted in the computation of the average age of Virginia slave mothers at first birth, see note 21 above. James Trussell and Richard Steckel estimate that the mean age at first birth for antebellum Southern white women was "about two years" later than the projected 20.6 years they estimated for age at first birth for slave mothers in the antebellum South. Trussell and Steckel, "The Age of Slaves at Menarche and Their First Birth," p. 492.

49. Consider, for example, the child:woman ratios for slaves and whites in Virginia when distributed in the age cohorts 1–14 years (children) and 14/15–49 years (women) represented in Table A.

TABLE A

Census Year	Slave	White
1820	1.916678	2.499881
1830	1.818838	1.358570*
1840	1.960139	2.172618
1850	2.057590	2.162029
1860	2.012159	2.191168

* The unusually low ratio produced from census information available for 1830 is probably indicative of a substantial undercount of white children aged 0–14 years old. This error also is reflected in the white child:woman ratio for 1830 descriptive of the age cohorts 0–9 years (children) and 10–49 years (women), and to a lesser extent for blacks during this census year in both categories of compilation.

Table B includes child:woman ratios for slaves and whites in Virginia distributed in the age cohorts 0–9 years (children) and 10–49 years (women).

TABLE B

Census Year	Slave	White
1820	—	1.237707
1830	1.311458	.950202*
1840	1.346319	1.226515
1850	1.079547	1.3326
1860	1.047343	1.015537

* This ratio probably reflects an undercount of children aged 0–9 years during this census year.

Sources: Census for 1820 (Washington, D.C.: G504, 512, 518, Gales and Seaton, 1821), 23–26; *Fifth Census or Enumeration of the Inhabitants of the United States, 1830* (Washington, D.C.: Duff Green, 1832), 87, 89; *Compendium of the Enumeration of the Inhabitants of the United States* (Washington, D.C.: Department of the Interior, 1841), 32–33, 36–38; J.D.B. DeBow, *Statistical View of the United States . . . Being a Compendium of the Seventh Census . . .* (Washington, D.C.: A.O.P. Nicholson, 1854), 215, 253–55, 257; Joseph G. Kennedy, *Population of the United States in 1860, Compiled from the Original Returns of the Eighth Census* (Washington, D.C.: Government Printing Office, 1864), 507–8, 512.

50. William Bolling Slave Register, 1752–1865, Bolling Family Papers, VHS.

51. Yetman, ed., *Voices from Slavery*, p. 92.

52. William Still, ed., *Underground Railroad* (New York: Arno Press, 1968), 411.

53. "A Slave's Story," *Putnam Monthly Magazine* 9 (June 1957): 617.

54. John W. Blassingame, ed., *Slave Testimony: Two Centuries of Letters, Speeches, Interviews and Autobiographies* (Baton Rouge: Louisiana State Univ. Press, 1977), 118.

55. *Negro in Virginia*, p. 84; "A Slave's Story," p. 617.

56. Perdue et al., eds., *Weevils in the Wheat*, p. 117.

57. Ibid., p. 207.

58. Ibid.

59. Ibid.

60. Manfra and Dykstra, "Serial Marriage," p. 32.

61. "A Slave's Story," p. 617.

62. Ibid.

63. Ibid., pp. 617–18.

64. Swint, ed., *Dear Ones At Home*, pp. 123–24.

8. Toward a Kinder and Gentler America: The Southern Lady in the Greening of the Politics of the Old South

After-dinner talk on Tuesday, April 11, 1989, celebrating the 150th wedding anniversary of Anna Maria Calhoun to Thomas Green Clemson, at the Fort Hill Conference held at Clemson University.

1. See E. Genovese, " 'Our Family, White and Black': Family and Household in the Southern Slaveholders' World View," in this volume.

2. John C. Calhoun to Anna Maria Calhoun, Mar. 10, 1832, in J. A. Jameson, ed., *Calhoun Correspondence*, Annual Report of the American Historical Association for the Year, 1899, vol. 2 (Washington, D.C.: American Historical Association,

1900), 316; also, Charles M. Wiltse, *John C. Calhoun: Nullifier, 1829–1839* (Indianapolis, Ind.: Bobbs-Merrill, 1944), 167.

3. Stanford M. Lyman, Jr., ed., *Selected Writings of Henry Hughes: Antebellum Southerner, Slavocrat, Sociologist* (Jackson: Univ. Press of Mississippi, 1985), 185–86.

4. William Cabell Bruce, *John Randolph of Roanoke, 1773–1833: A Biography Based Largely on New Material*; vol. 2 (New York: Octagon Books, 1970; originally published in 1922), 417.

5. Carol Bleser, ed., *Secret and Sacred: The Diaries of James Henry Hammond, a Southern Slaveholder* (New York: Oxford Univ. Press, 1988), Dec. 15, 1850, p. 213, and pp. 82, 261, 294.

6. David Outlaw to Emily Outlaw, Feb. 14, 1850, Outlaw Papers in the Southern Historical Collection, Univ. of North Carolina.

7. Ibid., Dec. 10, 1849.

8. See John A. Quitman to Eliza Quitman, Jan. 19, Feb. 2, 1828; Jan. 10, 1836; Oct. 1, 1850, Quitman Papers in the Southern Historical Collection, Univ. of North Carolina.

9. For samples, see Ulrich B. Phillips, ed., *The Correspondence of Robert Toombs, Alexander H. Stephens, and Howell Cobb*, Annual Report of the American Historical Association for the year 1911, vol. 2 (Washington, D.C.: American Historical Association, 1913); A.L. Hull, ed., "The Correspondence of Thomas Reade Rootes Cobb, 1860–62," *Publications of the Southern Historical Association*, 11 (1907): 147–56, 163, 164, 170; and the letters in J. Marion Sims, *The Story of my Life* (New York: D. Appleton & Co., 1884).

10. Lollie Belle Wyles, ed., *Memoirs of Judge Richard H. Clark* (Atlanta: Franklin Printing and Publishing Co., 1898), 345. Also, Elizabeth Tyler Coleman, *Priscilla Cooper Tyler and the American Scene, 1816–1889* (University: Univ. of Alabama Press, 1955), 75; "Jabez Lamar Monroe Curry" and "Augusta Jane Evans" in Jon L. Wakelyn, ed., *Biographical Dictionary of the Confederacy* (Westport, Conn.: Greenwood Press, 1977), 156, 180; Ben H. Proctor, *Not Without Honor: The Life of John H. Reagan* (Austin: Univ. of Texas Press, 1962), 145–46.

11. *Magnolia*, 9 (April, 1842): 249.

12. Eliza Maria Pinckney, *The Quintessence of Long Speeches, Arranged as a Political Catechism, by a Lady for Her God-Daughter* (Charleston, S.C.: E.A. Miller, 1830); George C. Rogers, Jr., *Charleston in the Age of the Pinckneys* (Columbia: Univ. of South Carolina Press, 1969), 153.

13. Grady McWhiney, *Braxton Bragg and Confederate Defeat: Field Command* (New York: Columbia Univ. Press, 1969), 217, 324–25.

14. Una Pope-Hennessy, ed., *The Aristocratic Journey: Being the Outspoken Letters of Mrs. Basil Hall . . .* (New York: G.P. Putnam & Sons, 1931), 209; Fredrika Bremer, *Homes of the New World; Impressions of America*, vol. 1 (New York: Harper & Bros., 1853), 276.

15. Beth E. Crabtree and James W. Patton, eds., *Journal of a Secesh Lady: The Diary of Catherine Ann Devereux Edmonston, 1860–1866* (Raleigh, N.C.: Division of Archives and History, 1979), Nov. 20, Dec. 30, 1864, pp. 638, 651).

16. Bertram H. Groene, *Ante-Bellum Tallahassee* (Tallahassee: Florida Heritage Foundation, 1971), 108; James C. Bonner, *Milledgeville: Georgia's Antebellum Capital* (Athens: Univ. of Georgia Press, 1978), 64.

17. [Rev. George Rogers], *Memoranda of the Experience, Labors and Travels of an Universalist Preacher, Written by Himself* (Cincinnati: John A. Gurley, 1845), 266.

18. Jack K. Williams, *Dueling in the Old South: Vignettes of Social History* (College Station: Texas A & M Univ. Press, 1980), 19.

19. H.A. Kinen, *Music in New Orleans: The Formative Years, 1791–1841* (Baton Rouge: Louisiana State Univ. Press, 1966), 32.

20. James Holmes, *"Dr. Bullie's" Notes: Reminiscences of Early Georgia and of Philadelphia and New Haven* (Atlanta: The Cherokee Publishing Co., 1976), 112–13.

21. Mary Blount Pettigrew to James Johnston Pettigrew, Aug. 10, 1843, in Sarah McCulloch Lemmon, ed., *The Pettigrew Papers*, vol. 2 (Raleigh, N.C.: Division of Archives and History, 1988), 584.

22. Georgia King to Tip King, Nov. 13, 1860, Thomas Butler King Papers, Southern Historical Collection, Univ. of North Carolina.

23. Alvy L. King, *Louis T. Wigfall: Southern Fire-eater* (Baton Rouge: Louisiana State Univ. Press, 1970), 122, 125, 141. See also pp. 36–37 for the southern-extremist views of Wigfall's Rhode Island–born wife.

24. David Duncan Wallace, *The History of South Carolina*, vol. 3 (New York: The American Historical Society, 1934), 152.

25. Quoted in Roy F. Nichols, *The Disruption of American Democracy* (New York: Macmillan, 1948), 367.

26. Mary Jones to C.C. Jones, June 20, 1851, in Robert Manson Myers, ed., *A Georgian at Princeton* (New York: Harcourt Brace Jovanovich, 1976), 193.

27. Nicholas, *Disruption of American Democracy*, p. 291.

28. Susan Cornwall Diary, Jan. 31, 1861; Kate S. Carney Diary, Apr. 8, May 3, 1861, both at the Southern Historical Collection, Univ. of North Carolina.

9. The Clays of Alabama: The Impact of the Civil War on a Southern Marriage

This essay is revised for this collection and appeared in an earlier version as "The Impact of the Civil War on a Southern Marriage: Clement and Virginia Tunstall Clay of Alabama," in Civil War History, *30, (Sept. 1984): 197–220. The authors appreciate the cooperation of the editor, John Hubbell, in granting permission for revisions and reprinting of the essay.*

1. Margaret Mitchell, *Gone with the Wind* (1936; reprint, Garden City, N.Y.: Garden City Books, 1954), 67. C. Vann Woodward, ed., *Mary Chesnut's Civil War* (New Haven: Yale Univ. Press, 1981), and Elisabeth Muhlenfeld, *Mary Boykin Chesnut: A Biography* (Baton Rouge: Louisiana State Univ. Press, 1981), describe and analyze the most quoted woman of the nineteenth-century South. See also Woodward and Muhlenfeld, eds., *The Private Mary Chesnut: The Unpublished Civil War Diaries* (New York: Oxford Univ. Press, 1984).

2. For information on Virginia's early years and biographical information on all the Clays, see Ruth Nuermberger, *The Clays of Alabama: A Planter-Lawyer-Politician Family* (Lexington: Univ. of Kentucky Press, 1958), 82, hereafter cited as Nuermberger. Bell Irvin Wiley, *Confederate Women*, Contributions in American History, no. 38 (Westport, Conn.: Greenwood Press, 1975), includes a chapter on

Virginia Clay. Wiley stresses Virginia's eagerness to play the belle, but his conclusions differ substantially from ours. Ada Sterling, *A Belle of the Fifties: Memoirs of Mrs. Clay of Alabama, Covering Social and Political Life in Washington and the South, 1853–66; Put into Narrative Form by Ada Sterling* (New York: Doubleday, Page & Company, 1905), hereafter cited as *Belle*. This source must be used with caution as it contains many exaggerations and numerous errors.

3. For information on Henry Collier and Alfred Battle see Matthew W. Clinton, *Tuscaloosa, Alabama: Its Early Days, 1816–1865* (Tuscaloosa: Zonta Club, 1958), 18, 23, 64, 104–5, 109; William Garrett, *Reminiscences of Public Men in Alabama for Thirty Years* (Atlanta: Plantation Publishing Company's Press, 1872), 718–19; Thomas M. Owen, *History of Alabama and Dictionary of Alabama Biography*, vol. 3 (Chicago: S.J. Clarke Publishing Co., 1921), 112, 115, 380; and U.S. Census Records, Alabama, 1840, Population Schedules, Tuscaloosa County, pp. 194, 201, 252, 254. Virginia had other prominent Alabamans among her relatives, including her uncle Thomas B. Tunstall, who served as secretary of state while Clement Comer Clay was governor of Alabama.

4. An acquaintance of Dr. Tunstall recalled he was "too careless of money matters." Thomas J. Green to Clement Claiborne Clay, Sept. 9, 1854. Unless otherwise indicated, all manuscripts and other unpublished sources cited in this paper are from the Clement Claiborne Clay Papers at Duke Univ.. This collection contains over 8,500 items. On Tunstall, see also his obituary in the *Florida Democrat*, reprinted in *Huntsville Democrat*, Oct. 13, 1847; and Whitemore Morris, *The First Tunstalls of Virginia and Some of Their Descendants* (San Antonio: privately published, 1950), 52. The voluminous Clay Papers at Duke contain no letters from Virginia's father, and there are only a few references to him. As late as 1873, Virginia was able, however, to provide the home address of her father's widow, Virginia to Clement, July 5, 1873.

5. Diploma, Virginia Caroline Tunstall, Nashville Female Academy, Dec. 9, 1840; volume of poems to Virginia Tunstall, Clay Papers, Duke, Box 2; "Little Mag" to Virginia, Jan. 12, 1848; Martha Fort to Virginia, July 13, 1845; and F. Garvin Davenport, *Cultural Life in Nashville on the Eve of the Civil War* (Chapel Hill: Univ. of North Carolina Press, 1941), 42–43.

6. *Belle*, pp. 10–13.

7. Nuermberger, pp. 1–68, 85–87. Frances Cabaniss Roberts, "Background and Formative Period in the Great Bend and Madison County," (Ph.D. diss., Univ. of Alabama, 1956), provides an excellent study of the early history of the Huntsville area. Clement Comer Clay's early land transactions are recorded in Deed Books B, pp. 3, 177–78; F, p. 27; G. pp. 246–47; H. pp. 44–45, 621–22; K, pp. 23–24; L, pp. 54–55; M, pp. 319–20, 472–73; N, p. 387; P, pp. 498, 532, Madison County Courthouse. The number of his slaves can be found in U.S. Census Records, Alabama, 1830, Population Schedules, Madison County, p. 101; and 1840, Madison County, pp. 169–70, and Jackson County, p. 70.

8. Clement Claiborne to Ann E. Withers, Dec. 25, 1834, Levert Family Papers, Univ. of North Carolina at Chapel Hill; Clement Claiborne to Susanna, Dec. 26, 1834. See also other letters in the Clay Papers and Nuermberger, pp. 75, 77, 88, 89–90.

9. Clement to Virginia, Jan. 5, 1843. The poem which followed Clement's confession contained the less than immortal lines:

Oh! Ginnie dear, I do declare
You ought to have a lickin!
Unless in mercy you forbear
Your arrows in me stickin!

10. Virginia Clay-Clopton, "Clement Claiborne Clay," *Transactions of the Alabama Historical Society* 2 (1898): 82. See also Maria to "Dear Cousin" [Virginia], Jan. 1, 1843; *Belle*, pp. 15–16. Ann Williams Boucher, "Wealthy Planter Families in Nineteenth-Century Alabama," (Ph.D. diss., Univ. of Connecticut, 1978), 42, arrives at 18.5 as the average age of first marriage of 39 women born between 1820 and 1839 and married to wealthy Alabama planters in 1860. Two other statistical studies of upper-class Southern women in the early nineteenth century agree that the average age of first marriage was twenty. Jane Turner Censer, *North Carolina Planter Families and their Children, 1800–1860* (Baton Rouge: Louisiana State Univ. Press, 1984), 91–92. Catherine Clinton, *The Plantation Mistress: Woman's World in the Old South* (New York: Pantheon Books, 1982), 60, 233. The difference between Boucher's figure of 18.5 for Alabama and Censer's statistic of 20.5 for North Carolina may reveal significant differences between older and more recently settled Southern areas.

11. Boucher, "Wealthy Planter Families," p. 42, and Censer, *North Carolina Planter Families*, pp. 92–93, agree that the average age of marriage for upper-class men was 26.

12. Clement Claiborne to Clement Comer, Jan. 18, 1843; and Clement Claiborne to Susanna, Dec. 23, 1842. Censer, *North Carolina Planter Families*, pp. 65–95, in the best discussion of the topic, maintains that children often informed their parents of an engagement only after a proposal had been accepted and that parental consent, when sought, was seldom refused. Carl Degler, in his book *At Odds: Women and the Family in America from the Revolution to the Present* (New York: Oxford Univ. Press, 1980), 9–14, is in agreement with Censer's findings. Bertram Wyatt-Brown, *Southern Honor: Ethics and Behavior in the Old South* (New York: Oxford Univ. Press, 1982), 206–12, disagrees and claims that the opposition of fathers, other family members, and community opinion often served to block an unacceptable union. Russell Blake, "Ties of Intimacy: Social Values and Personal Relationships of Antebellum Slaveholders," (Ph.D. diss., Univ. of Michigan, 1978), 63–70, asserts that couples were uncertain over whether or not they were obligated to request parental consent prior to becoming engaged. For a recent work on the history of the Southern planter family in the antebellum years, see Steven M. Stowe, *Intimacy and Power in the Old South* (Baltimore: The Johns Hopkins Univ. Press, 1987).

13. Virginia Clay, "Biographical Sketch of Clement Clay," n.d., p. 2, Clement Claiborne Clay Papers, Univ. of Alabama; Clement Claiborne to Clement Comer, Feb. 3, 1843. The home in which the marriage of Virginia and Clement took place is still standing. Frank L. Owsley, "The Clays in Early Alabama History," *The Alabama Review* 2 (Oct. 1949): 243–68, stresses the political dimensions of this marriage.

14. Clement to Virginia, Feb. 15, 1846.

15. Clement to Susanna, Dec. 23, 1842; and Clement to Virginia, Jan. 20, 1843; Mar. 20, 1846.

16. Susanna Clay lacked Virginia's interest in society. Susanna to Ann E. Withers, Dec. 16, 1830, Dec. 3, 1831, Feb. 10, 21, 1832, Levert Family Papers. See also Nuermberger, pp. 81, 84–85, 87; Susanna to Clement Comer, Jan. 4, 1847; and Virginia to Susanna, Jan. 1, 1850; Virginia to Susanna, Dec. n.d., 1844. See also Wiley, *Confederate Women*, p. 44; Nuermberger, p. 96.

17. Woodward, ed., *Mary Chesnut's Civil War*, p. 32; Mary Boykin Chesnut, *A Diary from Dixie*, ed. by Ben Ames Williams (Cambridge: Harvard Univ. Press, 1980, first published 1949), 382; and Clement Claiborne to Virginia, Feb. 22, 1846. Wyatt-Brown, *Southern Honor*, p. 236, claims that "barrenness in women . . . had always been a point of shame, and sufferers were contemptible or at best pitiable in the eyes of others."

18. Clement Claiborne to Clement Comer, Dec. 18, 1846. See also Lawson Clay to Susanna, Dec. 15, 1845; Clement Claiborne to Virginia, Mar. 8, Apr. 26, 1846; and Nuermberger, pp. 15–17, 85–86, 103–5. For Clay's salary as a legislator, see J. Mills Thornton III, *Politics and Power in a Slave Society: Alabama, 1800–1860* (Baton Rouge: Louisiana State Univ. Press, 1978), 80.

19. Clement to Virginia, Apr. 2, 1846. See also Clement to Virginia, Mar. 8, Apr. 9, 26, 1846; Clement Claiborne to Clement Comer, Dec. 18, 1846; and Lawson to Clement Comer, Dec. 19, 1846. The deeds recorded at the time Clay purchased the house and lot state that he paid only $555. He wrote his father, however, shortly before closing the transaction, that he would offer $2,700 for the property. Clement, whatever the original price had been, more than doubled his money when he sold it. Deed Books W, pp. 313–14, 616; Y, pp. 392–93, Madison County Courthouse.

20. Clement to Virginia, June 27–28, 1852, quoting a letter from Virginia which is no longer extant. See also Virginia to Clement Claiborne, June 10, July 20, 1852; Susanna Battle to Susanna Clay, Oct. 22, 1852; and Wiley, p. 45.

21. Clement to Virginia, June 27–28, 1852.

22. Clement to Virginia, Sept. 30, 1852; and Virginia to Clement, Oct. 4, 1852.

23. Nuermberger, pp. 115–18; *Belle*, pp. 21–25; and Garrett, *Reminiscences of Public Men in Alabama for Thirty Years*, p. 582.

24. Virginia to Tom Tait Tunstall, Oct. 10, 1856. See also draft of entry for *Woman's Who's Who of America*, Oct. 1912; and Nuermberger, p. 120.

25. Virginia to Clement Claiborne, Sept. 16, 1856.

26. Undated clippings, Clay Papers, Duke, Box 56; James E. Saunders, *Early Settlers of Alabama by Col. James Edmund Saunders, Lawrence County, Ala., with Notes and Genealogies by his Granddaughter, Elizabeth Saunders Blake Stubbs* (New Orleans: L. Graham & Son, Ltd., 1899), 288; and undated newspaper clipping, Clay Scrapbook V, p. 5. Virginia long remembered success that night and devoted a whole chapter to the event in *Belle*, pp. 126–37. See also Mrs. D. Giraud Wright, *A Southern Girl in '61* (New York: Doubleday, Page & Company, 1905), 21; Mrs. Roger A. Pryor, *Reminiscences of Peace and War* (New York: Macmillan, 1905), 81; and Marian Gouverneur, *As I Remember: Recollections of American Society During the Nineteenth Century* (New York: D. Appleton & Co., 1911), 276–77.

27. Virginia to Tom Tunstall, Jan. 25, 1857. See also Virginia to Tom, Oct. 10, 1856; Tom to Virginia, May 23, 1859, Sept. 13, 1894, July 6, 1897, and Nov. 14, 1905. For biographical information on Tunstall, see Morris, *The First Tunstalls of*

Virginia, p. 86; and Owen, *History of Alabama*, 4: 1689–90. For Clement's lack of jealousy of Virginia's male friends, see his letters, 1853–61, passim.

28. M.A. Collier to Virginia, May 16, 1852; Virginia to Clement Claiborne, [Nov.] 19, 1854; Clement Claiborne to Clement Comer, Jan. 18, 1854; Clement Claiborne to Susanna, Dec. 15, 1854; "List of Notes & bonds due C.C. Clay, Jr., placed in the hands of J. Withers Clay by H.L. Clay—Jan'y 1858;" and Nuermberger, p. 296.

29. Virginia to Clement Comer, July 10, 1855, Nov. 17, 1857. For Clay's political views and stands, see Clement Claiborne to Clement Comer, Jan. 18, 1854, June 7, 1856; Nuermberger, pp. 123–74; and Levi S. Vanderford, "The Political Career of Clement Claiborne Clay," (M.A. thesis, Univ. of Alabama, 1935), 23–56. The Alabama legislature reelected Clay to the Senate over fifteen months before his term would expire in Mar. 1859 because no session was scheduled for 1858.

30. Virginia to Clement Comer, Dec. 25 [1855]. See also *Belle*, pp. 139–42, 220; Wiley, pp. 51–53.

31. Letters in the Clay Papers discuss his asthma and other details. See also Nuermberger, pp. 164, 176–84, 189–90. For the suggested causes of chronic asthma in adults, see Samuel I. Cohen, "Psychological Factors," in T.J.H. Clark and S. Godfrey, eds., *Asthma* (London: Chapman and Hall, 1979), 67–68, 84–87; Peter H. Knapp et al., "Psychosomatic Aspects of Bronchial Asthma," in Earle B. Weiss and Maurice S. Segal, eds., *Bronchial Asthma: Mechanisms and Therapeutics* (Boston: Little, Brown, 1976), 1055–80. David McCullough, *Mornings on Horseback* (New York: Simon and Schuster, 1981), 90–108, contains an absorbing account of the asthmatic attacks which Theodore Roosevelt suffered as a child and young adult. McCullough maintains that unresolved conflicts between Roosevelt and his parents caused the illness. Infections, as opposed to emotional causes, seem to play a greater role in adult than in childhood asthma. Milton B. Rosenblatt, "History of Bronchial Asthma," in Weiss and Segal, eds., *Bronchial Asthma*, pp. 10–12, provides a good summary of mid-nineteenth-century medical recommendations for the treatment of asthma. See also W.W. Gerhard, *The Diagnosis, Pathology and Treatment of the Diseases of the Chest*, 2d ed. (Philadelphia: Edward Barrington and George D. Haswell, 1846), 130–34.

32. The Clay collections at Duke and the Huntsville Public Library contain many letters describing conditions in wartime Huntsville. See also "Civil War Days in Huntsville; As Taken from the Diary of Mrs. W.D. Chadwick which Appeared in Regular Episodes of the *Huntsville Times*," pp. 3–14, Univ. of Alabama Library; and Nuermberger, pp. 191, 211–18.

33. Virginia to Clement, Feb. 14, 24, Mar. 2, 14, 19, 1863. See also Clement to Virginia, Feb. 13, Mar. 12, 19, 22, 25, 1863, and Wiley, pp. 58–59.

34. Clement to Virginia, Mar. 12, 1863; and Virginia to Clement, Mar. 19, 1863. See also Wiley, p. 59.

35. Woodward, ed., *Mary Chesnut's Civil War*, p. 553. See also Celeste to Virginia, Dec. 24, 1863; Wiley, pp. 54–56; and Constance C. Harrison, *Recollections, Grave and Gay* (New York: Charles Scribner's Sons, 1911), 176.

36. Clement to Virginia, Dec. 20, 1863; Withers to Clement, Aug. 17, Oct. 29, Nov. 29, 1863; Clement to Susanna, Nov. 11, 1863; Nuermberger, pp. 221–30, 233. Nuermberger's account, pp. 234–66, of the activities of Clement and the other commissioners in Canada is excellent. See also John W. Headley, *Confederate*

Operations in Canada and New York (New York: Neale Publishing Co., 1906), 256–73. The quotation on Clay's behavior in Canada is from the papers of Thomas H. Hines, quoted in James D. Horan, *Confederate Agent: A Discovery in History* (New York: Crown Publishers, 1954), 84–85.

37. Virginia to Clement, Nov. 18, 1864. Virginia Clay Diary, 1859–66, provides the data to reconstruct Virginia's movements and her sentiments during Clement's absence in Canada.

38. Celeste to Clement Claiborne, Feb. 16, 1865; also quoted in Nuermberger, p. 220. Celeste exaggerated. For Virginia's occasional nursing of wounded soldiers, see Virginia Clay Diary, 1859–66, entries for May 27 and Aug. 20 to Sept. 30, 1864.

39. Bible, Clement Clay Papers, Huntsville Public Library. See also "C.C. Clay memoranda *re.* return from Canada, 1865"; typescript of copy from Virginia Clay Diary, 1865–66; Lawson to Virginia, Jan. 7, 1865; Clement to Virginia, Mar. 30, 1865; Philip Phillips, "A Summary of the Principal Events of My Life Written between the 10th and 20th of June, 1870," pp. 54–58, Philip Phillips Family Papers, Library of Congress; and Nuermberger, pp. 262–69. The proclamation ordering Clay's arrest is in U.S. War Department, *War of the Rebellion: A Compilation of the Official Records of the Union and Confederate Armies*, 130 vols. (Washington: Government Printing Office, 1880–1901), ser. 1, vol. 49, 2:558–59, hereafter cited as *OR*. President Johnson's proclamation offered $25,000 for Clay's capture, but the newspaper which Virginia read gave the amount as $100,000.

40. The charges against Clay are summarized in Joseph Holt to Edwin M. Stanton, Dec. 6, 1865, *OR*, ser. 2, 8:859–61. See also in the same volume, Stanton to Andrew Johnson, Jan. 4, 1866, pp. 843–44; Joseph Holt to Stanton, Jan. 18, 1866, pp. 847–55. The dispositions accusing Clay are in ibid., pp. 867–69, 876–77, 878–80. See also *Report of the House Committee on the Judiciary*, 39th Cong., lst sess., no. 104. The perjury of most of those who accused him is admitted in Holt to Stanton, July 3, 1866, *OR*, ser. 2, 8:931–45.

41. Clement to Virginia, Aug. 11 and Sept. 18 to Oct. 1, 1865. See also Thomas Withers to Virginia, Sept. 16, 1865; Clement to Thomas Withers, Oct. 11, 1865; Nelson Miles to Virginia, June 20, July 29, Sept. 8, 1865; handwritten copy of "Comments in *Jay's Family Prayers* made by C.C. Clay, Jr., in prison." Reports of Clay's health by prison officials are published in *OR*, ser. 2, 8:570–892, passim. On the unpredictable impact of stress on asthma, see Donald J. Lane, *Asthma: The Facts* (New York: Oxford Univ. Press, 1979), 69.

42. Lawson to Virginia, Sept. 20, 1865. See also typescript of copy from Virginia Clay Diary, 1865–66; Virginia to Clement, Sept. 3, Nov. 3, 1865; and Nuermberger, pp. 269–71, 295.

43. Ben Green to Virginia, Oct. 21, 1865. See also Virginia to Clement, July 27, Nov. 3, 1865; Virginia to Ben Wood, Aug. 4, 1865; Virginia to Joseph Holt, May 23, 1865; J. Carlisle to Virginia, June 11, 1865; Ben Wood to Virginia, June 15, 1865; J.S. Black to Virginia, July 3, 1865; *Belle*, pp. 301–2; and Nuermberger, pp. 278–79.

44. Benjamin F. Perry to Elizabeth Perry, Feb. 18, 1866, Benjamin F. Perry Correspondence, South Caroliniana Library, Columbia, S.C.

45. Virginia may have moved the president by threatening to obtain a writ of habeas corpus, an idea suggested by Jeremiah Black. Virginia to Mary Clay, Apr. 14, 1866.

46. Will Book 1, pp. 357–58; Probate Record Books 28, pp. 258–60; 32, pp. 564–65; Deed Books JJ, pp. 104–5; BBB, p. 123; Minute Book 10, pp. 533–34; Madison County Courthouse; Clement C. Clay, "Executor's Book, 1866–1869"; and Clement to Jefferson Davis, Oct. 25, 1870, Jefferson Davis Papers, Confederate Museum, Richmond, Virginia.

47. The date of the Clays' move from Clay Lodge to Wildwood is not certain, but it probably was in late 1878. See Clement to Virginia, Dec. 15, 1878; Jefferson Davis to Virginia, Mar. 13, 1883. Although many of the numerous postwar manuscripts in the Clay Papers at Duke in one way or another deal with finances, many of the exact details remain unclear, such as how large their income was and how great their expenses were. Details concerning what crops and livestock they raised, how they sold them, and Clay's general dissatisfaction with his labor arrangements can be found in many of his letters. For the sale of their land, see Deed Books LL, pp. 368–70, CCC, pp. 108–9, Madison County Courthouse. Nuermberger provides, pp. 298–99, 301–11, 315–16, a useful general summary of their dismal financial situation. For Corcoran's loan, see William W. Corcoran to Virginia, Jan. 3, Oct. 12, 1880, Clay Papers, Duke; and Virginia to Corcoran, Oct. 16, 1880, William W. Corcoran Papers, Library of Congress.

48. Clay's disillusionment with selling life insurance can be followed in his letters to Virginia from July 1871 to Nov. 1872.

49. Virginia to Clement, Nov. 11, 1868.

50. Clement to Virginia, Aug. 27, 1871, July 5, Aug. 23, 1876, Dec. 15, 1878; and Thomas Withers to Virginia, Sept. 16, 1870. Clay's cousin Dr. Thomas Withers recommended that he abstain from using alcohol.

51. Virginia to Clement, Oct. 13, 1874. See also her other letters to Clement from 1870 to 1880 and Nuermberger, pp. 307–8.

52. Davis to Virginia, Aug. 8, 1870. Lamar's poem is in Lamar to Virginia, Dec. 20, 1874:

> My dearest, if beneath the sea,
> With all its waves above my head,
> I lay, and thou shoulds't call for me;
> Methinks that I would quit the dead
> And come to thee.

53. E.F. Brooks to Virginia, Nov. 17, 1876; Paul Hammond to Virginia, Jan. 13, 1877, A.C. Haskell to Virginia, Jan. 28, 1877; W.H. Forney to Virginia, May 9, 1877; Lionel W. Day to Virginia, Aug. 30, 1877; and Virginia to L.Q.C. Lamar, Aug. 30, 1877.

54. Clement to Virginia, July 5, 1876; Virginia to Clement, Dec. 19, 1874. See also many other letters exchanged between Clement and Virginia from 1871 to 1880.

55. Virginia to Clement, Jan. 6, 1877. See also Clement to Virginia, Sept. 27, 1872, July 5, 1873, Jan. 23, 1874; and Virginia to Clement, July 31, Oct. 1, Nov. 5, 1872, Oct. 15, 20, 1874.

56. *Huntsville Democrat*, Jan. 5, 1882. For information concerning Virginia's reaction to Clement's death, see Fannie Copon to Corrine Goodman, Jan. 27, 1882; Virginia to Jefferson Davis, Feb. 16, 1882; Virginia to Jeremiah Black, Feb. 28, 1882. Nuermberger, pp. 316–17, details Virginia's trips between her two marriages. Owen,

History of Alabama, 3:352–53, summarizes Judge Clopton's career. On his estate, see "Settlement of Estate of David Clopton," Mar. 8, 1892, and the many letters exchanged between Clifford A. Lanier and Virginia regarding the settlement.

57. See draft speeches in Box 48, Clay Papers, Duke. For Virginia's participation in the suffrage movement, see Virginia to Mrs. Neblett, Apr. 28, 1895; Virginia Clay Diary, 1893–96, entry for Jan. 21, 1895; Ruth Ketring Nuermberger, "Virginia Caroline Tunstall Clay-Clopton," in Edward T. James et al., eds., *Notable American Women, 1607–1950*, vol. 1 (Cambridge: Belknap Press of Harvard Univ., 1971), 348–49; Elizabeth Humes Chapman, *Changing Huntsville, 1890–1899* (Huntsville: privately published, 1972), 27–34; John Irvin Lumpkin, "The Equal Suffrage Movement in Alabama, 1912–1919," (M.A. thesis, Univ. of Alabama, 1949), 3–5; and Lee N. Allen, "The Woman Suffrage Movement in Alabama, 1910–1920," *The Alabama Review* 11 (Apr. 1958): 83–84. Virginia had literally made the transition described by Anne Scott in *The Southern Lady: From Pedestal to Politics, 1830–1930* (Chicago: Univ. of Chicago Press, 1970).

58. Virginia to Celeste, Jan. 25, 1902, Clay Papers, Huntsville Public Library.

59. Clipping from the *Houston Chronicle*, Jan. 31, 1915, Box 56, Clay Papers, Duke; and Octavia Zollicoffer Bond, "South of the Line: A Belle of the Fifties," *Southern Woman's Magazine* 5 (Sept. 1915):16–17, 33.

60. Clement to Virginia, Nov. 22, 1868.

61. The marriage of the Clays is one of eight to ten unions being explored by Carol Bleser in a book-length study on marriage in the mid-nineteenth-century South.

10. House and Home in the Victorian South: The Cookbook as Guide

1. Frances Trollope, *Domestic Manners of the Americans* (London: Bentley, 1839; reprint, Century Publishing Co., 1984), 50–51.

2. John Egerton, *Southern Food* (New York: Alfred A. Knopf, 1987), 2.

3. Martha McCulloch-Williams, *Dishes & Beverages of the Old South* (Knoxville: The Univ. of Tennessee Press, 1988), 9–10. This is a reprint of the 1913 volume.

4. Ibid., p. 10.

5. Egerton, *Southern Food*, p. 4.

6. Mrs. Thomas L. Rosser, *Housekeeper's and Mother's Manual* (Richmond: Everett Waddey Company, 1895), v–vi.

7. Egerton, *Southern Food*, p. 4.

8. *The Confederate Receipt Book. A Compilation of Over One Hundred Receipts, Adapted to the Times* (Richmond: West & Johnston, 1863). Facsimile edition (Athens: Univ. of Georgia Press, 1960), with an introduction by E. Merton Coulter.

9. *The Laurel Cook Book*, compiled by the Women of St. John's Guild, Laurel, Miss., was first published in 1900 and revised and reprinted in 1910 and 1914; *Housekeeping in Old Virginia*, edited by Marion Cabell Tyree (New York: G.W. Carleton & Co., 1879), enjoyed numerous editions between 1877 and 1890. Good (though perhaps inevitably incomplete) bibliographies of these books are James E. Gourley, *Regional American Cookery, 1884–1934* (New York: The New York Public Library, 1936); Eleanor and Bob Brown, *Culinary Americana* (New York: Roving

Eye Press, 1961); and Margaret Cook, *America's Charitable Cooks: A Bibliography of Fund-Raising Books Published in the United States (1861–1915)* (Kent, Oh.: published by the author, 1971).

10. *The State*, May 25, 1913.

11. Louis Szathmary, "Preface," *Mrs. Porter's New Southern Cookery Book or, Housekeeping Made Easy* (New York: Promotory Press, 1974). This is a facsimile reprint of the 1867 edition.

12. Ibid., pp. 245–46.

13. Annie E. Dennis, *The New Annie Dennis Cook Book. A Compendium of Popular Household Recipes for the Busy Housewife* (Atlanta: The Mutual Publishing Company, 1921), preface.

14. Estelle Woods Wilcox, *The Dixie Cook Book* (Atlanta: L.A. Clarkson & Co., 1882).

15. Elizabeth Robins Pennell, *My Cookery Books* (Boston: Houghton Mifflin, 1903), 103. Mrs. Pennell particularly liked 17th-century cookbooks because of their "self-expression," a quality she thought cookbooks lost (except for their title pages) in the 18th century with their greater emphasis on orderly presentation.

16. *How We Cook in Tennessee*, 3d edition, compiled by the Silver Thimble Society of the First Baptist Church, Jackson, Tenn. (Jackson, Tenn: n.p., 1906). Examples of the latter are too numerous to mention, but one in particular, *Columbia Cook Book*, published by the Ladies Aid Society of the First Baptist Church of Columbia, Tenn., illustrates how these books represent a kind of women's "network," the recipes representing (according to the preface) "the actual experiences and practical tests of the many grand old housekeepers of our town," and as is often the case, they are signed. *Columbia Cook Book*, 2d edition (Louisville: Press of the Bradley & Gilbert Co., 1902).

17. Mrs. Abby Fisher, *What Mrs. Fisher Knows About Old Southern Cooking* (San Francisco: Women's Cooperative Printing Office, 1881), i.

18. Ibid., p. 72.

19. E.T. Glover, *The Warm Springs Receipt Book* (Richmond: B.F. Johnson Publishing Co., 1897); Theresa C. Brown, *Modern Domestic Cookery* (Charleston, S.C.: Edward Perry Printer, 1871).

20. Jennie C. Benedict, *The Blue Ribbon Cook Book* (Louisville: John P. Morton & Company, 1904), 13.

21. Ibid.

22. Jessie Henderson Colville, *A Kentucky Woman's Handy Cook Book* (Louisville: printed for the Author by Jennings and Graham, 1912), 8.

23. Mrs. Henry Lumpkin Wilson, compiler, *Tested Recipe Cook Book* (Atlanta: The Foote & Davis Company, 1895).

24. Mrs. John G. Carlisle, *Kentucky Cook Book* (Chicago: F.T. Neely, 1893), 34.

25. Louis Szathmary, "Introduction," *Mrs. Porter's New Southern Cookery Book*, p. ix. This placement does not seem accidental, for it is repeated in another version of this cookbook published twenty years later, *The New World's Fair Cook Book and Housekeeping Companion* (n.p., John E. Porter & Company, 1891), 236–42, where they are followed by recipes for Silver Cake and Gold Cake.

26. E.W. Warren, "Introduction," *Mrs. Hill's Southern Cook-Book* (New York: G.W. Dollingham Co., 1898), 10. Introduction is the same as in *Mrs. Hill's Southern Cook-Book* of 1870.

27. McCulloch-Williams, *Dishes & Beverages of the Old South*, pp. 16–17.

28. Ibid., pp. 257–58 (the section is entitled "Upon Occasions").

29. Ibid., pp. 258–59.

30. Ibid., pp. 263–64.

31. Ibid., p. 39.

32. Ibid., pp. 279–83.

33. *Famous Old Recipes*, compiled by Jacqueline Harrison Smith (Philadelphia: The John C. Winston Co., 1908), 21–22.

34. *The Southern Lady: From Pedestal to Politics, 1830–1930* (Chicago: Univ. of Chicago Press, 1970), 4–21.

35. Brown, *Modern Domestic Cookery*, preface.

36. Ibid.

37. Mrs. A.P. Hill, *Mrs. Hill's New Family Receipt Book for the Kitchen* (New York: James O'Kane, 1867), 129–30.

38. Ibid., p. 247.

39. Wilcox, *The Dixie Cook Book*, pp. 422–23.

40. Mrs. W.H. Wilson and Mollie Huggins, *Good Things to Eat* (Nashville: Publishing House of the M.E. Church, South, 1909).

41. Lumpkin, *Tested Recipe Cook Book*, frontispage.

42. Kate Brew Vaughn, *Culinary Echoes from Dixie* (Cincinnati: the McDonald Press, 1914), preface.

43. Mrs. M.F. Armstrong, *On Habits and Manners*, revised edition (Hampton, Va.: Normal School Press, 1888), 110. The Hampton Institute published another cookbook twenty-five years later, S. Thomas Bivins' *The Southern Cookbook* (Hampton, Va.: Press of the Hampton Institute, 1912). This book was intended for use by cooks in major hotels.

44. Armstrong, *On Habits and Manners*, pp. 106–7.

45. Ibid.

46. Ibid., p. 125.

47. Ibid.

48. Ibid.

49. Ibid., pp. 163–64.

50. Warren, "Introduction," *Mrs. Hill's Southern Cook-Book*, p. 6.

51. Ibid.

52. Ibid.

53. Wilcox, *The Dixie Cook Book*, p. 499.

54. Marion Cabell Tyree, *Housekeeping in Old Virginia* (New York: G.W. Carleton & Co., 1879), 19.

55. Ibid. Another cookbook, Mrs. Clement Carrington McPhail's *"F.F.V." Receipt Book* (Richmond: West, Johnston & Co., 1894), contains, in fact, an advertisement that illustrates Mrs. Tyree's point for The Exchange for Woman's Work, an outlet for "Women, whose circumstances make it necessary for them to dispose of their handiwork."

56. Wilcox, *The Dixie Cook Book*, p. 3.

57. Ibid., p. 499.

58. Mary Stuart Smith, *The Virginia Cookery Book*, (New York: Harper & Bros., 1885), 198–99.

59. Hill, *Mrs. Hill's Southern Cook-Book*, p. 283.

60. Egerton, *Southern Food*, p. 16. The cover in question is for *Favorite Southern Recipes* (Atlanta: The Southern Ruralist Company, 1912).

61. Egerton, *Southern Food*, p. 16.

62. Smith, *The Virginia Cookery Book*, p. 4.

63. Wilcox, *The Dixie Cook Book*, p. 450.

64. Susan Strasser, *Never Done: A History of American Housework* (New York: Pantheon Books, 1982), 63.

65. Smith, *Virginia Cookery Book*, p. 7.

66. Wilcox, *The Dixie Cook Book*, p. 64.

67. Brew, *Culinary Echoes from Dixie*, p. 6.

11. A Family Tradition of Letters: The Female Percys and the Brontëan Mode

1. Seymour S. Kety, "Observations on Genetic and Environmental Influences in the Etiology of Mental Disorder from Studies on Adoptees and Their Relatives," in Seymour S. Kety, Lewis P. Rowland, et al., eds., *Genetics of Neurological and Psychiatric Disorders* (New York: Raven Press, 1983), 105–14; E. S. Paykel, "Life Events and Early Environment," in E. S. Paykel, ed., *Handbook of Affective Disorders* (New York: Guilford Press, 1982), 147–61; Felix Brown, "Bereavement and Lack of a Parent in Childhood," in E. Miller, ed., *Foundations of Child Psychiatry* (London: Pergamon, 1968), 435–55, an excellent review which suggests a connection between creativity and loss of a parent.

2. Walker Percy, *The Moviegoer* (New York: Alfred A. Knopf, 1961); id., *The Last Gentleman* (New York: Farrar, Straus and Giroux, 1966); id., *Love in the Ruins: The Adventures of a Bad Catholic at a Time Near the End of the World* (New York: Farrar, Straus and Giroux, 1971); id., *Lancelot* (New York: Farrar, Straus and Giroux, 1977); id., *The Second Coming* (New York: Farrar, Straus and Giroux, 1980); id., *The Thanatos Syndrome* (New York: Farrar, Straus and Giroux, 1987); William Alexander Percy, *Lanterns on the Levee: Recollections of a Planter's Son* (Baton Rouge: Louisiana State Univ. Press, 1973 [1941]).

3. See Bertram Wyatt-Brown, "Will, Walker, and Honor Dying: The Percys and Literary Creativity," in Winfred B. Moore, Jr., and John Tripp, Jr., eds., *Looking South: Chapters in the Story of an American Region* (Westport: Greenwood Press, 1990), 229–58.

4. Virginia Woolf to Ethel Smyth, June 22, 1930, in Nigel Nicolson, ed., *A Reflection of the Other Person: The Letters of Virginia Woolf*, Vol. IV, *1929–1931* (London: Hogarth Press, 1978), 180.

5. Michael Ignatieff, "Paradigm Lost," *Times Literary Supplement*, Sept. 4, 1987, p. 939. George H. Pollock, Department of Psychiatry, Northwestern Univ. Hospital, Chicago, has amassed this numerical data. See his unpublished paper, "The Mourning Liberation Process in the Older Patient," Univ. of South Florida Medical Center and Tampa Psychotherapy Study Group, annual conference, Feb. 17, 1989, Tampa, Florida.

6. G. Pickering, *Creative Malady* (New York: Oxford Univ. Press, 1974), 224.

7. Interview by the author with Walker Percy, Nov. 17, 1988, Covington, Louisiana.

8. See, especially, William Rodney Allen, *Walker Percy: A Southern Wayfarer*

(Jackson: Univ. Press of Mississippi, 1986). Allen's interpretation is based on Silvano Arieti and Jules Bemporad, *Severe and Mild Depression: The Psychotherapeutic Approach* (New York: Basic Books, 1978). I am inclined to give somewhat more credence to a genetic approach than he does. See for a brilliant but a perhaps overstated genetic interpretation, Thomas C. Caramagno, "Manic-depressive Psychosis and Critical Approaches to Virginia Woolf's Life and Work," *PMLA* 103 (Jan. 1988): 10–23.

9. Robert A. Prentky, *Creativity and Psycho-Pathology: A Neurocognitive Perspective* (New York: Praeger, 1980), 1–20. With Socrates probably in mind, Aristotle wrote, "Those who have become eminent in philosophy, politics, poetry, and the arts have all had tendencies toward melancholia." Ibid., p. 1. William Styron, "Why Primo Levi Need Not Have Died," *New York Times*, Dec. 19, 1988, p. 23.

10. George H. Pollock, "Mourning and Adaptation," *International Journal of Psycho-Analysis*, 43 (July–Oct. 1962): 341–61.

11. Walker Percy, "Mississippi: The Fallen Paradise," *Harper's*, (Apr. 1965), 170–71.

12. Margaret Percy, Oct. 23, 1785, burial book, archives, St. Giles-in-the-Fields Church, London; and John Hereford Percy, *The Percy Family of Mississippi and Louisiana, 1776–1943* (Baton Rouge: priv. pub., 1943), 3.

13. Master's Log Book, H.M.S. *Canceaux*, Nov. 8, 1770, Admiralty Papers, 36, no. 9661, Public Record Office, Kew.

14. Percy, *Percy Family of Mississippi and Louisiana*, pp. 1, 63, 64; William Diamond, "Nathaniel A. Ware, National Economist," *Journal of Southern History*, 5 (Nov. 1939): 501–26.

15. Entry no. 538, Sarah Ware, admitted June 22, 1819; disease: "Insanity"; "Discharged by her husband Mar. 7, 1820"; readmitted, Mar. 30, 1820, discharged Sept. 28, 1831, Admissions and Discharge Book; Nathaniel Ware to the Managers of the Asylum, Philadelphia, Mar. 16, 1824, in Sarah Ware, Patients' Papers, Pennsylvania Hospital Historic Library, Philadelphia. See also Nancy Tomes, *A Generous Confidence: Thomas Story Kirkbride and the Art of Asylum-Keeping, 1840–1883* (Cambridge: Cambridge Univ. Press, 1984).

16. Mary T. Tardy, [pseud. Ida Raymond], *Southland Writers: Biographical and Critical Sketches of the Living Female Writers of the South*, vol. 2 (Philadelphia: Claxton, Remsen & Haffelfinger, 1870), 30.

17. Tardy, *Southland Writers*, 2: 30–31, 217. On Sarah Ware's periods of violence, see Sarah A. Dorsey [pseud. Filia], *Agnes Graham: A Novel*, vol. 1 (Philadelphia: Claxton, Remsen and Haffelfinger, 1869), 51.

18. Sarah Percy's tombstone, dated 1835, Routh Cemetery, Homochitto Avenue, Natchez, Mississippi.

19. Tardy, *Southland Writers*, 2: 38.

20. William Beckford, *Vathek* in Peter Fairclough, ed., *Three Gothic Novels* (London: Penguin, 1986 [1968]). William Patrick Day, *In the Circles of Fear and Desire: A Study of Gothic Fantasy* (Chicago: Univ. of Chicago Press, 1985), 10; and Elizabeth McAndrew, *The Gothic Tradition in Fiction* (New York: Columbia Univ. Press, 1979), 71–73, 129–30.

21. Catherine A. Warfield, *Ferne Fleming: A Novel* (Philadelphia: T.B. Peterson and Bros., 1877), 74. See also, id., *Miriam Montfort: A Novel* (New York: D. Appleton & Co., 1873), 234.

22. Tardy, *Southland Writers*, 2: 28.

23. Eleanor Percy Lee, "Agatha," pp. 18–19, in Eleanor Percy Lee Papers, Hill Memorial Library, Louisiana State Univ. Library, Baton Rouge.

24. The Warfield family owned Darley, the progenitor of forty Derby winners, including Man o' War, the only horse ever given an honorary degree. The most famous family member was Wallis Warfield, later Duchess of Windsor. See Elizabeth M. Simpson, *Bluegrass Houses and Their Traditions* (Lexington, Ky.: Transylvania Press, 1932), 105–13; Evelyn Ballenger, *Warfield Records* (Annapolis, Md.: Thomas Ord Warfield, 1970), 335, 466–67.

25. See various undated notes (c. 1840) between Eleanor Percy Ware and Henry William Lee, in Ware (Eleanor and Catherine Ann) Papers, Lower Mississippi Valley Historical Collection, Hill Memorial Library, Louisiana State Univ., Baton Rouge. Nathaniel Ware, Indenture, December 20, 1838, Deed Book G, p. 415, Circuit Court Clerk's Office, Washington County Courthouse, Greenville, Mississippi. Nathaniel A. Ware, indenture, with Thomas George Percy Ellis and Thomas George Percy, May 13, 1836, Book Y, p. 107, Circuit Court Clerk's Office, Adams County Courthouse, Natchez, Mississippi.

26. J.S. Hartin, "Eliza Ann DuPuy," in James E. Lloyd, ed., *Lives of Mississippi Authors* (Jackson: Univ. Press of Mississippi, 1981), 147.

27. Nathaniel A. Ware, *Henry Belden: Or, a True Narrative of Strange Adventures. By the Author of "Notes on Political Economy" and "A Treatise on the Natural Method of Education"* (Cincinnati: priv. pub., 1848). Ware was not, however, the author but only copyright holder of *Notes on Political Economy*. Cf. Diamond, "Nathaniel A. Ware," pp. 502–26, as refuted by Douglas R. Egerton in his forthcoming biography of Charles Fenton Mercer, the actual author. Copy kindly lent to the author.

28. Edgar Legare Pennington, "The Ministry of Joseph Holt Ingraham in Mobile, Alabama," *Historical Magazine of the Protestant Episcopal Church*, 26 (Dec. 1957): 344–60. Robert W. Weathersby, II, "Joseph Holt Ingraham," in Lloyd, *Lives of Mississippi Authors*, pp. 247–52. Ingraham authored *The Prince of the House of David* (1855), first of the biblical romances, which sold 4 to 5 million copies. Author of the *Buffalo Bill* series, his son Prentiss Ingraham published 600 novels and 400 novellas. See Richard Robertson and Joseph Rosenblum, "Prentiss Ingraham," in *Lives of Mississippi Authors,* pp. 252–67.

29. See, for instance, Catherine Ann Warfield and Eleanor Percy Lee, "The Lake of Coeur Creve," in *The Indian Chamber, and Other Poems* (New York: priv. pub., 1846), 46–53, and "The Mammoth Legend," ibid., pp. 54–59.

30. See Richard H. King, *A Southern Renaissance: The Cultural Awakening of the American South, 1930–1955* (New York: Oxford Univ. Press, 1980), 85–98; David L. Cohn, "Eighteenth-Century Chevalier," *Virginia Quarterly Review* 31 (Autumn 1955): 561–75.

31. Walker Percy, "Introduction," in William Alexander Percy, *Lanterns on the Levee*, p. x.

32. Lewis A. Lawson, "William Alexander Percy, Walker Percy, and the Apocalypse," *Modern Age* 24 (Fall 1980): 396–406; id., "Walker Percy's Southern Stoic," *Southern Literary Journal*, 3 (Fall 1970): 5–31.

33. Carolyn G. Heilbrun, *Writing a Woman's Life* (New York: W.W. Norton, 1988), 15.

34. Warfield and Lee, "Remorse," in *Indian Chamber*, p. 65.

35. William Alexander Percy, *Collected Poems* (New York: Alfred A. Knopf, 1944), 357. For the location and dating, see William Alexander Percy typescript, Box 43, Percy Family MSS, Mississippi State Department of Archives and History, Jackson.

36. William Alexander Percy, *Sappho in Levkas and Other Poems* (New Haven: Yale Univ. Press, 1915), 13.

37. "The Forsaken," in Catherine Ann Warfield and Eleanor Percy Lee, *The Wife of Leon and Other Poems* (Cincinnati: E. Morgan & Co., 1844), 23–25.

38. Eleanor Percy Lee, "The Deserted House," in Julia Dean Freeman [pseud. Mary Forrest], *Women of the South Distinguished in Literature* (New York: Derby & Jackson, 1861), 151–54; see also Catherine Ann Warfield and Eleanor Percy Lee, *The Indian Chamber, and Other Poems* (New York: priv. pub., 1846), 237–40.

39. Mark Twain, *The Adventures of Huckleberry Finn*, Henry Nash Smith, ed. (Boston: Houghton Mifflin [c. 1958]), 87–88.

40. Quoted in Tardy, *Southland Writers*, 2: 42–43.

41. Catherine Ann Warfield, undated MSS poems, "written for Mrs. Stephens' Magazine," Cincinnati Historical Society.

42. Catherine A. Warfield, "Madeline," in Freeman, *Women of the South*, p. 147.

43. Broadus Mitchell, "Nathaniel A. Ware," in *Dictionary of American Biography*, 20 vols. (New York: Charles Scribner's Sons, 1928–37), 19:451.

44. Sandra M. Gilbert and Susan Gubar, *The Madwoman in the Attic: The Woman Writer and the Nineteenth-Century Literary Imagination* (New Haven: Yale Univ. Press, 1979).

45. Adrienne Rich, *Of Women Born: Motherhood as Experience and Institution* (New York: W.W. Norton, 1976), 245.

46. Warfield, *Miriam Montfort*, pp. 241–42; Norman N. Holland, *The I* (New Haven: Yale Univ. Press, 1985), 35; N. Holland, "Literary Interpretation and Three Phases of Psychoanalysis," in Alan Roland, ed., *Psychoanalysis, Creativity, and Literature: A French-American Inquiry* (New York: Columbia Univ. Press, 1978), 233–47; and Alan Roland, "Toward a Reorientation of Psychoanalytic Literary Criticism," in *Psychoanalysis, Creativity, and Literature*, pp. 254–58, (quotation, p. 257).

47. Henry James, quoted in Henry Nash Smith, "The Scribbling Women and the Cosmic Success Story," *Critical Inquiry*, 1 (Sept. 1974): 50.

48. Charlotte Brontë, *Jane Eyre*, (New York: Crowell, [c 1890]), 242.

49. Quoted in Leavis, "Introduction," *Jane Eyre*, pp. 7–8.

50. Quotation from Lucy M. Freibert, review of Susan Warner, *The Wide, Wide World* (1850; New York Feminist Press, 1987), in *Legacy* 4 (Fall 1987): 67.

51. Diana Hume George, "Who Is the Double Ghost Whose Head is Smoke? Women Poets on Aging," in Kathleen Woodward and Murray M. Schwartz, eds., *Memory and Desire: Aging-Literature-Psychoanalysis* (Bloomington: Indiana Univ. Press, 1986), 134–53.

52. Tardy, *Southland Writers*, 2:38.

53. Unpublished poem quoted in Tardy, *Southland Writers*, 2:38.

54. John Maynard, *Charlotte Brontë and Sexuality* (Cambridge: Cambridge Univ. Press, 1984), 31–39, 55.

55. William Patrick Day, *In the Circles of Fear and Desire: A Study of Gothic Fantasy* (Chicago: Univ. of Chicago Press, 1985), 84–85. The parallels between Walker Percy's *Lancelot* and Warfield's *The Household of Bouverie* receives extended treatment in the author's paper for the Walker Percy: Faith, Philosophy and Fiction conference, Univ. of Århus, Jutland, Denmark, Aug. 5, 1989, to be edited by Jan Gretlund and published by the Univ. of Mississippi Press.

56. Catherine Ann Warfield [A Southern Lady], *The Household of Bouverie; Or, the Elixir of Gold*, vol. 1 (New York: Derby & Jackson, 1860), 74.

57. Ibid., pp. 75–76.

58. Sigmund Freud, "Some Psychical Consequences of the Anatomical Distinction Between the Sexes," in *The Standard Edition of the Complete Psychological Works of Sigmund Freud,* trans. and ed. by James Strachey, vol. 19 (London: The Hogarth Press, 1961), 257–58.

59. Carol Gilligan, *In a Different Voice: Psychological Theory and Women's Development* (Cambridge: Harvard Univ. Press, 1982), 12.

60. Ibid., p. 17.

61. Day, *In the Circles of Fear and Desire*, p. 108.

62. Gilligan, *In a Different Voice*, pp. 24–51.

63. Catherine Ann Warfield, *The Romance of Beauseincourt: An Episode Extracted from the Retrospect of Miriam Montfort* (New York: G.W. Carleton, 1867).

64. Tardy, *Southland Writers*, 2:36.

65. Ibid., pp. 36, 109.

66. Ibid., p. 210.

67. Ibid., p. 130.

68. Ibid., p. 133.

69. Catherine Ann Warfield, *The Cardinal's Daughter: A Sequel to Ferne Fleming* (Philadelphia: T.B. Peterson & Bros., 1877), 148.

70. The novel was apparently written much earlier. See Tardy, *Southland Writers*, 2:36.

71. Catherine Ann Warfield, *Hester Howard's Temptation: A Soul's Story* (Philadelphia: T.B. Peterson & Bros., 1875), 107.

72. Walker Percy, *The Last Gentleman* (1966; New York: New American Library, 1968), 210.

73. Dorsey, *Agnes Graham*, pp. 77–78.

74. Percy, *Lanterns on the Levee*, p. 345.

75. Wyatt-Brown, "Will, Walker and Honor Dying," pp. 229–58.

76. William Styron, "Why Primo Levi Need Not Have Died," p. 23. See also Charles Salter, Jr., "In the World Again," interview with Styron, in Raleigh *News and Observer*, Oct. 3, 1989, pp. 8A, 9A.

77. See Charlotte Elizabeth Lewis, "Sarah Anne Dorsey: A Critical Estimate" (unpublished M.A. thesis, Louisiana State Univ., 1940), 1–5; this thesis, now outdated, offers the only critical evaluation of her work; J.B. Smallwood, "Dorsey, Sarah Anne Ellis (Mrs. Samuel W.): 1829–1879," in Lloyd, *Lives of Mississippi Authors*, pp. 137–40; "Warfield, Catherine Ann Ware," in *The Dictionary of American Biography*, vol. 10 (New York: Charles Scribner's Sons, 1936), 454–55; Tardy, *Southland Writers*, 2:21; Freeman, *Women of the South*, pp. 150–57.

78. See Robert H. Brinkmeyer, Jr., *Three Catholic Writers of the Modern South* (Jackson: Univ. Press of Mississippi, 1985), 119–68. Mr. Percy died of cancer in May 1990 while this manuscript was in preparation.

79. Charlotte Brontë, *Villette* (1853; New York: Bantam Books, 1986), 154.

80. Ibid., p. 220.

12. The Political Economy of Sharecropping Families: Blacks and Poor Whites in the Rural South, 1865–1915

1. William H. Holtzclaw, *The Black Man's Burden* (New York: Neale Publishing Company, 1915), 17.

2. Ibid., pp. 18, 20, 25, 27, 31.

3. Ibid., pp. 32–36. For an account of another black family (in Arkansas) about the same time, see William Pickens, *Bursting Bonds* (Boston: The Jordan and More Press, 1923). Pickens estimated that his family moved at least twenty times before he was eighteen years old (1881–1899).

4. United States Department of Commerce, Bureau of the Census, *Historical Statistics of the United States, Colonial Times to 1970*, pt. 1 (Washington, D.C.: GPO, 1975), 465.

5. Theodore Rosengarten, *All God's Dangers: The Life of Nate Shaw* (New York: Alfred A. Knopf, 1974), 119.

6. *Meriweather [Georgia] Vindicator* (1874) quoted in Lewis N. Wynne, "The Role of Freedmen in the Postbellum Cotton Economy of Georgia," *Phylon* 42 (Dec. 1981):320; Edward L. Ayers, *Vengeance and Justice: Crime and Punishment in the 19th-Century American South* (New York: Oxford Univ. Press, 1984), 185–222.

7. Planter quoted in Francis W. Loring and C.F. Atkinson, *Cotton Culture and the South Considered with Reference to Emigration* (Boston: A. Williams, 1869), 5.

8. Winnsboro, South Carolina, *Tri-Weekly News*, Jan. 9, 1866, quoted in Francis Butler Simkins and Robert H. Woody, *South Carolina During Reconstruction* (Chapel Hill: Univ. of North Carolina Press, 1932), 233.

9. Loring and Atkinson, *Cotton Culture*, p. 5.

10. Joseph Daniel Pope in Ira Berlin et al., eds., "The Terrain of Freedom: The Struggle Over the Meaning of Free Labor in the U.S. South," *History Workshop* 22 (Autumn 1986): 112. See also George Campbell, *White and Black: The Outcome of a Visit to the United States* (London: Chatto and Windus, Piccadilly, 1879), 143.

11. Report of Carl Schurz on the States of South Carolina, Georgia, Alabama, Mississippi, and Louisiana, 39 Cong., 1st sess., ex. doc. no. 2 (1865), reprinted in Carl Schurz, *Report on the Condition of the South* (New York: Arno Press and the New York Times, 1969), 25.

12. See, for example, Laurence Shore, *Southern Capitalists: The Ideological Leadership of an Elite, 1832–1885* (Chapel Hill: Univ. of North Carolina Press, 1986), 116; Jonathan M. Wiener, *Social Origins of the New South: Alabama, 1860–1885* (Baton Rouge: Louisiana State Univ. Press, 1978), 192–93.

13. See, for example, Steven Hahn, *The Roots of Southern Populism: Yeoman Farmers and the Transformation of the Georgia Upcountry, 1850–1890* (New York: Oxford Univ. Press, 1983).

14. Ted Ownby, "The Defeated Generation at Work: White Farmers in the Deep South," *Southern Studies* (Winter 1984): 325–47.

15. Forrest McDonald and Grady McWhiney, "The South from Self-Sufficiency to Peonage: An Interpretation," *American Historical Review* 85 (Dec. 1980): 1095–

1118; W.O. Atwater and Charles D. Woods, "Dietary Studies with Reference to the Food of the Negro in Alabama in 1895 and 1896," United States Department of Agriculture Office of Experiment Stations *Bulletin* No. 38 (Washington: GPO, 1897). See also Dolores E. Janiewski, *Sisterhood Denied: Race, Gender and Class in a New South Community* (Philadelphia: Temple Univ. Press, 1985), 8–54.

16. Testimony of Prof. R.J. Redding, *Report of the Industrial Commission on Agriculture and on Taxation in Various States*, vol. 11 (Washington: GPO, 1901), 94. See also United States Department of Commerce, Bureau of the Census, *Plantation Farming in the United States* (Washington: GPO, 1916).

17. Testimony of W.L. Peek, Conyers, Georgia, *Report of the Industrial Commission on Agriculture and Agricultural Labor*, vol. 10 (Washington: GPO, 1901), 459.

18. Alfred H. Stone, *Studies in the American Race Problem* (New York: Doubleday, 1908), 112; C.O. Brannen, "Relation of Land Tenure to Plantation Organization," United States Department of Agriculture *Bulletin* No. 1269 (Washington: GPO, 1924); Carl Kelsey, *The Negro Farmer* (Chicago: Jennings and Pye, 1903), 50; Jacquelyn Dowd Hall et al., *Like a Family: The Making of a Southern Cotton Mill World* (Chapel Hill: Univ. of North Carolina Press, 1988), 14.

19. Testimony of Robert Ransom Poole, Agricultural Commissioner of Alabama, *Industrial Commission*, vol. 10: 919.

20. Kelsey, *Negro Farmer*, p. 39. See also Clyde Vernon Kiser, *Sea Island to City: A Study of St. Helena Islanders in Harlem and Other Urban Centers* (New York: Columbia Univ. Press, 1932).

21. Peter Gottlieb, *Making Their Own Way: Southern Blacks' Migration to Pittsburgh, 1916–30* (Urbana: Univ. of Illinois Press, 1987).

22. Harriet A. Byrne, "Child Labor in Representative Tobacco-Growing Areas," United States Department of Labor, Children's Bureau Publication No. 155 (Washington: GPO, 1926). See also John M. Gillette, "Rural Child Labor," *Child Labor Bulletin* 1 (June 1912); Lewis W. Hine, "Children or Cotton? Raising the Question of Cotton Picking in Texas," *Survey* 31 (Feb. 7, 1914): 589–92.

23. Report of H.A. Turner on Bledsoe Plantation, Leflore County, Mississippi, 1915, File No. 0221, Entry 133, Bureau of Agricultural Economics, Record Group 83, National Archives, Washington, D.C. (reel 22, "Black Workers in the Era of the Great Migration, 1916–1929," Univ. Publications of America; available on microfilm); hereafter, BAE.

24. These small enterprises offered seasonal work to plantation workers throughout the South. Information on individual businesses is provided by the R.G. Dun Collection, Baker Library, Harvard Univ. Graduate School of Business Administration, Cambridge, Mass., and the 1880 Manufacturing Manuscript Census for Louisiana, South Carolina, Texas, Virginia, and Tennessee (on microfilm), National Archives, Washington, D.C.

25. Mamie Garvin Fields with Karen Fields, *Lemon Swamp and Other Places: A Carolina Memoir* (New York: Free Press, 1983), 106.

26. *Industrial Commission*, vol. 10: 819. See also Steven Hahn, "Hunting, Fishing, and Foraging: Common Rights and Class Relations in the Postbellum South," *Radical History Review* 26 (1982): 37–64.

27. Fields, *Lemon Swamp*, p. 106.

28. See, for example, the interview with John Belcher in George P. Rawick, ed., *The American Slave: A Composite Autobiography*, 41 vols., series 1, supp. series 1

and 2 (Westport, Conn.: Greenwood Press, 1972, 1978, 1979), supplementary series 1, vol. 6, (Mississippi Narrs.), pt. 1, pp. 109–12 (hereafter FWP *Slave Narratives*).

29. Jane Maguire, *On Shares: Ed Brown's Story*, (New York: W.W. Norton, 1975), 22 (" . . . it seem like I would sleep some walkin' home").

30. Edwin DeLeon, "Ruin and Reconstruction of the Southern States. A Record of Two Tours in 1868 and 1873," *Southern Magazine* 14 (Jan., Mar. 1874): 23, 301.

31. Testimony of William C. Stubbs, director of the Louisiana Experiment Station, *Industrial Commission*, vol. 10:109, 770.

32. John Lee Coulter, "The Rural Life Problem of the South," *South Atlantic Quarterly* 12 (1913): 64.

33. Helen M. Dart, "Maternity and Child Care in Selected Rural Areas of Mississippi," Rural Child Welfare Series No. 5, Children's Bureau Publication No. 88 (Washington: GPO, 1921): 14.

34. Ibid., p. 37.

35. In the Cotton Belt, annual plantation turnover rates were 30–40 percent among sharecroppers. See L.C. Gray et al., "Farm Ownership and Tenancy," United States Department of Agriculture *Yearbook for 1923* (Washington: GPO, 1924), 590. See the data summarized in Charles Orser, *Material Basis of the Postbellum Tenant Plantation: Historical Archaeology in the South Carolina Piedmont* (Athens: Univ. of Georgia Press, 1988); and Robin M. Williams and Olaf Wakefield, "Farm Tenancy in North Carolina, 1880–1935," North Carolina Agricultural Experiment Station, Raleigh (Sept. 1937).

36. Testimony of O.B. Stevens, *Industrial Commission*, vol. 10: 908–09.

37. Stone, *Studies in the American Race Problem*, chapter 4, "A Plantation Experiment," pp. 125–47.

38. *Historical Statistics of the United States*, pt. I, p. 465; Frederick A. Bode and Donald E. Ginter, *Farm Tenancy and the Census in Antebellum Georgia* (Athens: Univ. of Georgia Press, 1986).

39. See, for example, descriptions of various forms of plantation management in *Report on Cotton Production in the United States* (Washington: GPO, 1884); H.M. Dixon, "An Economic Study of Farming in Sumter County, Georgia," United States Department of Agriculture *Bulletin* No. 492 (Washington: GPO, 1917).

40. Brannen, "Relation of Land Tenure to Plantation Organization." See also E.A. Boeger and E.A. Goldenweiser, "A Study of the Tenant Systems of Farming in the Yazoo-Mississippi Delta," United States Department of Agriculture *Bulletin* No. 337 (Washington: GPO, 1916).

41. Georgia planter quoted in Robert Preston Brooks, *The Agrarian Revolution in Georgia, 1865–1912* (Madison: The Univ. of Wisconsin Press, 1914), 64.

42. LaWanda Fenlason Cox, "Tenancy in the United States, 1865–1900: A Consideration of the Validity of the Agricultural Ladder Hypothesis," *Agricultural History* 18 (July 1944): 97–105.

43. *Report on Cotton Production in the United States*, pt. I, p. 173.

44. Testimony of Prof. R.J. Redding, *Industrial Commission*, vol. 10: 804; James R. Green, "Tenant Farmer Discontent and Socialist Protest in Texas, 1902–1917," *Southwestern Historical Quarterly* 81 (1977): 133–54; Charles L. Flynn, *White Land, Black Labor: Caste and Class in Late Nineteenth-Century Georgia* (Baton Rouge: Louisiana State Univ. Press, 1983).

45. Testimony of Harry Hammond, planter, of Beech Island, South Carolina, *Industrial Commission*, vol. 10: 819.

46. Ulrich B. Phillips, "Plantations With Slave Labor and Free," *American Historical Review* 30 (July 1925): 750. On Smithsonia, see also William F. Holmes, "Labor Agents and the Georgia Exodus, 1899–1900," *South Atlantic Quarterly* 69 (1980): 444; Harry Hodgson, "A Great Farmer at Work," *World's Work* 9 (Jan. 1905): 5723–33.

47. Lewis Cecil Gray, "Southern Agriculture, Plantation System, and the Negro Problem," American Academy of Political and Social Science *Annals* 40 (Mar. 1912): 97.

48. Rosengarten, *All God's Dangers*, p. 162; Holtzclaw, *Black Man's Burden*, p. 138. See also Harold Woodman, "Post-Civil War Southern Agriculture and the Law," *Agricultural History* 53 (Jan. 1979): 319–37; Pete Daniel, *In the Shadow of Slavery: Peonage in the South, 1901–1969* (Urbana: Univ. of Illinois Press, 1972).

49. Interview with Ollie Smith conducted by Colette Blount in Toledo, Ohio, Dec., 1987 (transcript in author's possession).

50. Gavin Wright, "Postbellum Southern Labor Markets," in *Quantity and Quiddity: Essays in United States Economic History*, ed. by Peter Kilby (Middletown, Conn.: Wesleyan Univ. Press, 1987), 133; Gavin Wright, *Old South, New South: Revolutions in the Southern Economy Since the Civil War* (New York: Basic Books, 1986).

51. On labor contracts in the tobacco region, for example, see Rick Gregory, "Robertson County and the Black Patch War, 1904–1909," *Tennessee Historical Quarterly* 39 (1980): 341–58.

52. Brannen, "Relations of Land Tenure to Plantation Organization," p. 50. See also W.J. Spillman and E.A. Goldenweiser, "Farm Tenantry in the United States," United States Department of Agriculture *Agricultural Yearbook for 1916* (Washington: GPO, 1917), 345.

53. Testimony of Rep. George Henry White, *Industrial Commission*, vol. 10: 419.

54. FWP *Slave Narratives*, Supplementary Series 2, vol. 1 (Ark. Narrs.): 71. For other similar case histories, see Charles Johnson, *Shadow of the Plantation* (Chicago: Univ. of Chicago Press, 1934), and Arthur F. Raper, *Preface to Peasantry: A Tale of Two Black Belt Counties* (Chapel Hill: Univ. of North Carolina Press, 1936).

55. Stone, *Studies in the American Race Problem*, p. 13.

56. Interview with Ollie Smith, p. 6.

57. See, for example, correspondence in file 50–326 documenting the case of Joe Daniels's family held on the Bledsoe Plantation in Leflore County, Mississippi, after he (Daniels) was forced to leave the plantation. Box 10804, primary class 50, Department of Justice Classified Subject Files Correspondence, Record Group 60, National Archives, Washington, D.C.

58. "Farm Family Living Among White Owner and Tenant Operators in Wake County," *Bulletin* #269, Agricultural Experiment Station of the North Carolina State College of Agriculture and Engineering and the North Carolina Department of Agriculture (Raleigh, Sept. 1929), 13.

59. Howard A. Turner, "An Account of Runnymeade Plantation," Leflore County, Mississippi, Jan., 1916, File No. 0179, Entry 133, Reel 22, BAE.

60. Rosengarten, *All God's Dangers*, p. 117.

61. Shepard Krech, III, "Black Family Organization in the Nineteenth Century: An Ethnographic Perspective," *Journal of Interdisciplinary History* 12 (Winter 1982): 429–52.

62. J.A. Dickey and E.C. Branson, "How Farm Tenants Live," University of North Carolina Extension *Bulletin*, vol. 2, no. 6 (Nov. 16, 1922): 20–21.

63. Interview with Ollie Smith, p. 21.

64. Thordis Simonsen, ed., *You May Plow Here: The Narrative of Sara Brooks* (New York: W.W. Norton, 1986), 58, 144, 105.

65. Rosengarten, *All God's Dangers*, pp. 61–62.

66. W.E.B. Du Bois, "The Negro American Family," Atlanta Univ. Study No. 13 (Atlanta: Atlanta Univ. Press, 1908), 125.

67. Johnson, *Shadow of the Plantation*, p. 143.

68. FWP *Slave Narratives*, Supplementary Series 2, vol. 5, (Tex. Narratives), pt. 4, pp. 1469–71. See also Janice L. Reiff, Michel R. Dahlin, and Daniel Scott Smith, "Rural Push and Urban Pull: Work and Family Experiences of Older Black Women in Southern Cities, 1880–1900," *Journal of Social History* 16 (Summer 1983): 39–48.

69. Hall et al., *Like a Family*, pp. 38–39.

70. Margaret J. Hagood, *Mothers of the South: Portraiture of the White Tenant Farm Woman* (New York: W.W. Norton, 1977; orig. pub. in 1939). See also Gilbert C. Fite, "The Agricultural Trap in the South," *Agricultural History* 60 (Fall 1986): 38–50.

71. On the political significance of black landowners in the South, see Sydney Nathans, "Gotta Mind to Move, a Mind to Settle Down: Afro-Americans and the Plantation Frontier," in *A Master's Due: Essays in Honor of David Herbert Donald*, ed. by William J. Cooper et al. (Baton Rouge: Louisiana State Univ. Press, 1985): 204–22; Manning Marable, "The Politics of Black Land Tenure, 1877–1915," *Agricultural History* 53 (1979): 142, 147–48.

72. Report of Thomas L. Beville, Forest Home, Alabama, Apr. 27, 1866, M809 (Alabama), Reel 18, Bureau of Refugees, Freedmen, and Abandoned Lands, RG 105, National Archives, Washington, D.C. (available on microfilm).

73. Brannen, "Relation of Land Tenure to Plantation Organization," p. 44.

74. Maguire, *On Shares*, p. 27.

13. A Woman Made to Suffer and Be Strong:
Ella Gertrude Clanton Thomas, 1834–1907

1. Journal of Ella Gertrude Clanton Thomas, 13 volumes, approximately 430,000 words. (Duke Univ. Library, Durham, N.C.), hereafter cited as Journal; Journal, vol. 3, January 1, 1859. The bulk of this paper is drawn from the 13 volumes of the Thomas journal plus the 10 volumes of Gertrude Thomas's scrapbooks.

2. Journal, vol. 8, Aug. 27, 1864.

3. Scrapbooks of Ella Gertrude Clanton Thomas, 10 volumes, in the possession of Mrs. Gertrude T. Despeaux of Atlanta, Georgia. The clippings are seldom dated and the sources rarely given. In many cases, the approximate date and source can be determined from the content of the article.

4. Anne Firor Scott, *The Southern Lady: From Pedestal to Politics, 1830–1930* (Chicago: Univ. of Chicago Press, 1970).

5. H.R. Casey, "Reminiscences: Columbia County Then and Now," *Our Heritage: Personalities 1754–1983 Columbia County Georgia*, compiled by Janette S. Kelly Thomson (Ga.: Lucky Printing Co., 1983), 13. Also family sources and the Will of Turner Clanton, Richmond County, Georgia, Richmond County Courthouse, Augusta, Georgia.

6. Florence Corley, *Augusta: A Confederate City* (Columbia: Univ. of South Carolina Press, 1960), 19; and interview with Robert Rood, great-nephew of Gertrude Clanton Thomas, Augusta, Georgia, 1983.

7. Stowe, "The Not-So-Cloistered Academy: Elite Women's Education and Family Feeling in the Old South," *The Web of Southern Social Relations: Women, Family and Education*, Walter J. Fraser, F. Frank Saunders, Jr., Jon L. Wakelyn, eds. (Athens: The Univ. of Georgia Press, 1985), 92–93.

8. Helen Glenn, "And So It Began . . . ," *Bulletin of Wesleyan College*, vol. 38, no. 3 (Apr., 1958).

9. Journal, vol. 3, Mar. 18, 19, July 9, 1852. The Clanton and Thomas families were doubly united in 1860, when Gertrude's sister Mary Clanton married J. Pinckney Thomas, Jefferson's brother.

10. Ibid., vol. 6, Apr. 5, 8, 1855.

11. Ibid., Sept. 20, 1855.

12. Jefferson Thomas's interest in medicine was sincere and a reflection of a family interest in that field. It is interesting to note that one of his sons, Julian Pinckney; one nephew, one great-nephew, and three great-great-nephews practiced medicine—the latter three are still practicing (1989). Another great-nephew was an optometrist and another was a pharmacist.

13. Journal, vol. 6, Jan. 1, 1856.

14. Ibid., vol. 7, Aug. 18, 1856, Feb. 7, 1858.

15. Ibid., vol. 7, Feb. 20, 1857.

16. Ibid., vol. 6, June 2, 1855.

17. Ibid., vol. 6, June 13, 1855; vol. 7, Feb. 9, 1858. Gertrude wrote lengthy comments on *Christine: Or, Woman's Trials and Triumphs* by Laura J. Bullard (New York: DeWitt and Davenport, c. 1856).

18. Journal, vol. 7, Jan. 2, 1859.

19. Ibid., vol. 8, Oct. 12, 1861, Sept. 6, Sept. (n.d.), 1862; vol. 9, Oct. 9, 22, 1864.

20. Ibid., vol. 9, Dec. 31, 1863.

21. Ibid., vol. 9, Nov. 21, Dec. 12, 1864.

22. Ibid., July 4, Aug. 27, 1864.

23. Ibid., Oct. 8, 1864. Gertrude mentioned reading Harriet Beecher Stowe's *Uncle Tom's Cabin*, Mary Hayden Pike's *Caste*, E.W. Warren's *Nellie Norton*, and a wide selection of magazines and newspapers.

24. Journal, vol. 9, Sept. 23, Nov. 22, 1864.

25. Ibid., May 1, 1865.

26. Ibid., May 8, 1865.

27. Ibid., Oct. 8, 14, 1865.

28. Ibid., July 9, 1866; Mary Elizabeth Massey, "The Making of a Feminist," *Journal of Southern History*, vol. 39, no. 1 (Feb. 1973): 1; Scott, *The Southern Lady*, pp. 98–99. See also in this book the essay, "The Clays of Alabama: The Impact of the Civil War on a Southern Marriage," by Carol Bleser and Frederick Heath.

29. A volume of the journal for the period Oct. 1866 to Oct. 1868 is missing.

30. Journal, vol. 10, Nov. 30, 1870.

31. Ibid., Nov. 1, 1868.

32. Ibid., Nov. 29, 1868, May 3, 1869.

33. Will of Turner Clanton, Richmond County Courthouse, Augusta, Georgia.

34. Journal, vol. 10, June 19, 1869.

35. Ibid., vol. 6, July 4, 1864; vol. 10, Feb. 7, 1869; vol. 12, Nov. 26, 1880.

36. Ibid., vol. 10, June 19, 1869, Jan. 10, 1870.

37. Ibid., Jan. 27, Aug. 1, 1870; vol. ll, Dec. 14, 19, 1870.

38. Ibid., vol. 10, May 3, 4, 1869, Jan. 10, 1870; vol. 11, Nov. 29, Dec. 12, 30, 1870, Mar. 9, May 28, 1871.

39. Ibid., vol. 11, Dec. 5, 19, 1870.

40. Ibid., Dec. 5, 1870, Mar. 9, 1871.

41. The Georgia Homestead Act of 1868 allowed Mr. Thomas to select one of his properties as a homestead not liable to seizure for debt within certain limits.

42. Journal, vol. 9, May 29, 1865; vol. 10, May 7, June 1, 1869; vol. 11, May 4, 1871.

43. Ibid., vol. 11, Nov. 30, 1870, May 28, 1871.

44. Ibid., vol. 12, Dec. 31, 1878.

45. Turner Clanton (1853–1917), Joseph (1855, died in infancy), Annie Lou (1857, lived six months), Mary Belle (1858–1929), Jefferson Davis (1861–1920), Cora Lou (1863–1956), Charley (1865, premature birth and died within hours), Julian Pinckney (1868–1929), James Clanton (1872–1879), Kathleen Maureen (1875–1968).

46. Journal, vol. 12, Jan. 1, 1879.

47. Ibid., Dec. 16, 1880; vol. 13, Jan. 5, 1881.

48. Journal, vol. 12, Feb. 8, May 7, 1879.

49. Ibid., Nov. 24, 1880.

50. Ibid., Feb. 9, 1879. Also, *The Secret Eye: The Journal of Ella Gertrude Clanton Thomas 1848–1889*, ed. by Virginia I. Burr, with an introduction by Nell Irvin Painter (Chapel Hill: The Univ. of North Carolina Press, 1990).

51. Journal, vol. 12, Dec. 18, 1879.

52. Ibid., Mar. 25, May 15, 1880.

53. Ibid., Aug. 10, 1879, Feb. 3, 1880.

54. Ibid., May 15, Sept. 2, Dec. 16, 1880.

55. Ibid., vol. 13, Sept. 10, 14, 15, 1886, Apr. 3, 1888.

56. Gertrude's reference to owning so much land after twenty years of foreclosures calls for explanation. The Thomases could mortgage her lifetime interest only. Turner Clanton's will was upheld in court so that the land remained in her name to be passed on to her children at her death. In the end, however, nothing was left of the once vast estate; nothing for Gertrude, nothing for the children.

57. Journal, vol. 13, Jan. 5, 1887, Apr. 3, 1888, Aug. 30, 1889.

58. Mary Elizabeth Massey, "The Making of a Feminist," *Journal of Southern History,* vol. 39, no. 1 (Feb. 1973): 16; and Carol K. Bleser, "The Perrys of Greenville," *The Web of Southern Social Relations: Women, Family and Education,* ed. by Walter J. Fraser, R. Frank Saunders, Jr., and Jon L. Wakelyn (Athens: The Univ. of Georgia Press, 1985), 75, 85.

59. Scrapbooks, Augusta *Chronicle* and Thomas, "As to Temperance," 1889.

60. Scrapbook, source unidentified. Written from Atlanta, 1894.

61. Atlanta *Journal,* Nov. 28, 1899.

62. Journal, vol. 12, May 15, 1880.

63. Mary Belle married Frederick Laurens Ingraham of South Carolina, son of Captain Duncan Nathaniel Ingraham of the United States and Confederate navies and great-grandson of Henry Laurens, South Carolina patriot, president of the Continental Congress, and member of the Paris Peace Commission. Mary Belle Thomas and Frederick Laurens Ingraham had three children, one of whom was my father, Henry, "Harry" Laurens Ingraham, who married Myrtle F. Sims, of whom I was the only issue.

14. A Victorian Father:
Josiah Gorgas and His Family

The author acknowledges support of the Univ. of Alabama Research Grants Committee and the National Endowment for the Humanities for a larger research project from which this essay developed. An earlier version of this article appeared as "Josiah Gorgas, A Victorian Father," in Civil War History, *32 (Sept. 1986): 229–46. The author appreciates the cooperation of the editor of that journal and the Kent State Univ. Press in granting permission for revisions and reprinting of the essay.*

1. Journal of Josiah Gorgas, 1857–1878, Jan. 27, 1867, original and typescript in Gorgas Family Papers (Univ. of Alabama Library, Tuscaloosa). Copies of the reasonably accurate typescript are also located in the Bayne-Gayle Family Papers (Southern Historical Collection, Univ. of North Carolina, Chapel Hill) and William Crawford Gorgas Papers (Manuscript Division, Library of Congress, Washington, D.C.). The Civil War portion of the Gorgas Journal was published in Frank E. Vandiver, ed., *The Civil War Diary of General Josiah Gorgas* (University: Univ. of Alabama Press, 1947).

2. Philip Greven, *The Protestant Temperament: Patterns of Child-Rearing, Religious Experience, and the Self in Early America* (New York: Alfred A. Knopf, 1977), 151–260, and in his earlier work *Child-Rearing Concepts, 1628–1861* (Itasca, Ill.: F.E. Peacock Publishers, 1973), 4–5, further develops this theme. For useful insight into a sample of Victorian British fathers, see David Roberts, "The Paterfamilias of the Victorian Governing Classes," in *The Victorian Family: Structure and Stresses*, ed. by Anthony S. Wohl (New York: St. Martin's Press, 1978), 59–81. Lorna McKee and Margaret O'Brien, "The Father Figure: Some Current Orientations and Historical Perspectives," in *The Father Figure*, ed. by Lorna McKee and Margaret O'Brien (London: Tavistock Publications, 1982), 3–25, and Marshall L. Hamilton, *Father's Influence on Children* (Chicago: Nelson-Hall, 1977), 1–18, trace research since 1960 on the topic of fathers.

3. Michael P. Johnson, "Planters and Patriarchy: Charleston, 1800–1860," *Journal of Southern History*, 46 (Feb. 1980): 48. Gorgas family correspondence may also be found in Gorgas Family Papers; Bayne-Gayle Papers, UNC; WCG Papers, LC; William Crawford Gorgas Papers (Univ. of Alabama Library, Tuscaloosa); Stanhope Bayne-Jones Papers (Manuscripts Collection, History of Medicine Division, National Library of Medicine, Bethesda, Md.).

4. Frank E. Vandiver, *Ploughshares into Swords: Josiah Gorgas and Confederate Ordnance* (Austin: Univ. of Texas Press, 1952), 3–5, 9, 15, 35–37.

5. Amelia Gayle (AG) to [Sarah Gayle Crawford], Mar. 29, 1848, Folder 79, no. 2; AG to [Matthew Gayle], Apr. 23, 1848, F79, no. 3; Amelia Gorgas, "Sketch of John Gayle" (manuscript), F97, no. 4, Gorgas Family Papers. Mary Tabb Johnston, *Amelia Gayle Gorgas: A Biography* (University: Univ. of Alabama Press, 1978), 1–2, 12–16; Carol Bleser, ed., *Secret and Sacred: The Diaries of James Henry Hammond* (New York: Oxford Univ. Press, 1988), 3–4.

6. Unidentified typescript in Gayle Family Papers (Alabama Department of Archives and History, Montgomery); Thomas L. Bayne to My Dear Children, Oct. 6, 1870 (typescript), pp. 15–16, Stanhope Bayne-Jones Papers; Sarah Haynsworth Gayle Diary, original and typescript, Gorgas Family Papers (Univ. of Alabama Library, Tuscaloosa); copies of this poor typescript are also located in Bayne-Gayle Papers, UNC, and in Thomas Bayne Denégre Papers (Tulane Univ. Library, New Orleans). Confusion exists on the spelling of Haynsworth. Sarah Gayle and her grandmother, Sarah Haynsworth, spelled the name differently than have their descendants, who consistently spell the name Haynesworth. See Gayle Family Bible, Box 726, Gorgas Family Papers.

7. Johnston, *Amelia Gayle Gorgas*, pp. 12–14, 28; Vandiver, *Ploughshares into Swords*, pp. 37–38.

8. AG to Josiah Gorgas (JG), June 2, [1869?], F65, no. 2; AG to Sarah Crawford, [Dec.] 4, [1864], F79, no. 6; AG to WCG, [Fall 1875], F70 unnumbered, Gorgas Family Papers. Josiah and Amelia do not reflect the image of nineteenth-century child rearing expressed in Bertram Wyatt-Brown, *Southern Honor: Ethics and Behavior in the Old South* (New York: Oxford Univ. Press, 1982), 126. The impact of Amelia on Willie's life is discussed in Sarah Woolfolk Wiggins, "Introduction" to John M. Gibson, *Physician to the World: The Life of General William C. Gorgas* (Tuscaloosa: Univ. of Alabama Press, 1989; orig. pub. Durham, N.C.: Duke Univ. Press, 1950).

9. Johnston, *Amelia Gayle Gorgas*, pp. 38, 45, 51, 55, 106. AG to JG, May 30, 1858, F61, no. 1; June 2, 1858, F61, no. 2; June 11, 1858, F61, no. 4; June 18, 1858, F61, no. 5; and July 15, 1858, F61, no. 10; JG to AG, June 8, [1858], F8, no. 2; [1858], F8, no. 9; and [1858], F9, no. 1; AG to Sarah Crawford, [Dec.] 4, [1864], F79, no. 6; AG to Jessie Gorgas, [1872], F79, no. 11, Gorgas Family Papers. Jessie Gorgas to WCG, Feb. 29, [1916?], WCG Papers, UA. Gorgas Journal, Jan. 19, 1859.

10. Gorgas Journal, Sept. 20, 1857, Apr. 1, 1864. JG to AG, [1858], F8, no. 8; AG to Sarah [Crawford], May 17, 1883, F88, no. 6, Gorgas Family Papers.

11. Gorgas Journal, Apr. 1, 1864, Aug. 26, 1865. Johnston, *Amelia Gayle Gorgas*, pp. 40, 41, 55, 66, 71.

12. Gorgas Journal, Oct. 10, 1867, Oct. 18, 1872. AG to WCG, July 1, 1900 [1901], Sept. 25, [1898]; AG to Aileen Gorgas, July 5, 1898; WCG to AG, May 28, July 2, 1913; Jessie Gorgas to WCG, Sept. 30, 1916; WCG to Richard Gorgas, Aug. 22, 1881; WCG to Jessie Gorgas, Sept. 3, 1919, WCG Papers, UA. AG to Jessie Gorgas, [1872], F79, no. 11; AG to [Jessie and Mamie Gorgas], June 8, [1872], F79, no. 10; M[ary Gayle Aiken] to Maria [Gayle Bayne], Mar. 19, [1879], F89, no. 5; AG to Thomas L. Bayne, Aug. 9, 1883, F79, no. 14; AG to WCG, Oct. 7, 1886, F75, no. 1, and Aug. 27, 1901, F56, no. 3; AG to Marie Gorgas, July 4, 1900, F76,

no. 1, Gorgas Family Papers. Johnston, *Amelia Gayle Gorgas*, p. 78. This attitude endures among Gorgas descendants. The first letter to the author from one descendant proudly opened with "I was born in the Gorgas House." George Tait to Sarah W. Wiggins, May 14, 1989, Gorgas Family Papers.

13. Gorgas Journal, Jan. 12, June 8, Feb. 11, Mar. 17, 1857.

14. Ibid., Feb. 9, 1858, Jan. 19, Feb. 13, 1859.

15. Ibid., June 1, 16, 1858. AG to JG, June 2, 1858, F61, no. 2; and June 11, 1858, F61, no. 4; JG to AG, [July] 10, [1858], F7, no. 2; Aug. 1, [1858], F7, no. 1; [1858], F7, no. 7; June 8, 1858, F8, no. 2; [1858], F8, no. 7; July 1, [1858], F8, no. 3; [1858], F8, no. 4; and [1858], F8, no. 8, Gorgas Family Papers.

16. JG to AG, June 8, [1858], F8, no. 2; [1858], F7, no. 5; [1858], F8, no. 4; and [1858], F10, no. 6, Gorgas Family Papers. See JG to AG Dec. 15, [1854], F5, no. 4, for similar pain during separation when Amelia was visiting in Mobile while Josiah remained at Mount Vernon.

17. JG to AG, Aug. 1, [1858], F7, no. 1. See F8, 9, 10, Gorgas Family Papers, for numerous other examples.

18. JG to AG, [June] 11, [1858], F8, no. 5; [June 1858], F8, no. 4; July 1, [1858], F8, no. 3; [July 1858], F9, no. 1; and [1858], F8, no. 7, Gorgas Family Papers. Gorgas Journal, June 3, 1858.

19. Gorgas Journal, June 8, 27, July 1, 1858.

20. JG to AG, Aug. 3, [1862], F10, no. 1; [1862], F10, no. 10; [1862], F10, no. 13; [1862], F10, no. 16; [1862], F10, no. 17; [1862], F10, no. 20; [1862], F10, no. 21; [1862], F10, no. 19; and Oct. 11, 1862, F10, no. 4, Gorgas Family Papers.

21. JG to Jessie Gorgas, May 27, 1872, F23, no. 17; AG to [Jessie and Mamie Gorgas], June 8, [1872], F79, no. 10; AG to JG, Aug. 23, 1865, F62, no. 4, Gorgas Family Papers.

22. JG to AG, Sept. 16, 1862, F10, no. 3, Gorgas Family Papers. Gorgas Journal, Apr. 24, Dec. 13, 1857, Feb. 26, Apr. 12, June 16, 1858, Jan. 19, Mar. 20, 1859, Mar. 28, 1860.

23. Gorgas Journal, Jan. 28, 1857, Apr. 29, 30, 1858. See also entries for Mar. 16, 1858, Feb. 9, 1859.

24. Ibid., Dec. 20, 1863, Mar. 13, Aug. 10, 1864.

25. Ibid., May 13, Sept. 3, 1863.

26. AG to JG, Sept. 22, 1865, F62, no. 7; AG to Amelia Crawford, Sept. 24, [1864], F79, no. 5, Gorgas Family Papers.

27. Gorgas Journal, Aug. 26, 1865. Vandiver, *Ploughshares into Swords*, pp. 267–73. Johnston, *Amelia Gayle Gorgas*, pp. 76, 103. [Thomas L. Bayne], *A Sketch of the Life of General Josiah Gorgas, Chief of Ordnance of the Confederate States* (Richmond, Va.: Wm. Ellis Jones, Book and Job Printer, 1885), p. 10. [Christine Gorgas Zerbe to Mary Gayle Gorgas], Sept. 2, 1884, F25, no. 18a, Gorgas Family Papers. Hugh A. Bayne Memoirs (microfilm), Bayne-Gayle Papers.

Josiah's estrangement from his own family is noticeable in the voluminous Gorgas Family Papers. For example, after Josiah's death in 1883, condolence letters poured in from members of Amelia's family and from friends—from the United States and Confederate armies, Mobile, Sewanee, and the Univ. of Alabama. Even one of her mother's former slaves wrote Amelia. Members of Amelia's family and the Univ. of Alabama offered money if the family needed assistance. In contrast, the only letter in the collection from a member of Josiah's family is one from

Josiah's sister in 1884. See Mary Ann Gayle to AG, June 5, 1883, F88, no. 30, and other letters in F88, Gorgas Family Papers.

28. JG to AG, July 7, 1865, F11, no. 8, Gorgas Family Papers. Gorgas Journal, Dec. 27, 1865.

29. AG to JG, [Jan.] 21, [1866], F63, no. 14; Feb. 18, 1866, F63, no. 6; Jan. 28, 1866, F63, no. 3; and Apr. 2, 1866, F63, no. 12, Gorgas Family Papers.

30. [JG to AG], [1865], F62, no. 2; [1865], F62, no. 10; and Sept. 22, 1865, F62, no. 7, Gorgas Family Papers.

31. See Daniel Blake Smith, *Inside the Great House: Planter Family Life in Eighteenth-Century Chesapeake Society* (Ithaca: Cornell Univ. Press, 1980), 87, for an excellent discussion of the use of the power of paternal approval by eighteenth-century southern planter-fathers in shaping their sons. Wyatt-Brown, *Southern Honor*, pp. 128–29, believes that discipline through withholding affection was peculiar to northern child-rearing concepts. For an excellent summary of different theories about father-son relationships, see Henry Biller, "The Father and Sex Role Development," in *The Role of the Father in Child Development*, ed. by Michael E. Lamb (New York: John Wiley & Sons, 1981), 320–23. See also John Munder Ross, "The Roots of Fatherhood: Excursions into a Lost Literature," in *Father and Child Development and Clinical Perspectives*, ed. by Stanley H. Cath et al. (Boston: Little, Brown, 1982), 3–20; and Ross D. Parke, *Fathers* (Cambridge: Harvard Univ. Press, 1981), 4–11. Among the biographers of members of the Gorgas family, only William Crawford's wife, Marie, appreciated that "the one way in which the elder man [Josiah] could control the younger [William Crawford] was through the affections." Unfortunately, the biography does not pursue this important father-son relationship. Marie D. Gorgas and Burton J. Hendrick, *William Crawford Gorgas: His Life and Work* (Garden City, N.Y.: Doubleday, Page and Co., 1924), 45.

32. Johnson, "Planters and Patriarchy," pp. 57, 58.

33. JG to WCG, Feb. 25, 1868, F28, no. 2, Gorgas Family Papers. Josiah kept such accounts himself. See Josiah Gorgas Account Books, 1857–1873, 1877–1878, F56, Gorgas Family Papers.

34. AG to JG, Aug. 23, 1865, F62, no. 4, Gorgas Family Papers.

35. Ibid., Sept. 11, 1865, F11, no. 14; Feb. 12, 1866, F63, no. 5; JG to AG, Jan. 28, 1866, F12, no. 4; and Feb. 11, 1866, F12, no. 6, Gorgas Family Papers. Gorgas Journal, Mar. 20, 1866.

36. AG to JG, Mar. 10, 1866, F63, no. 8, Gorgas Family Papers.

37. Gorgas Journal, Feb. 24, Oct. 10, 1867.

38. Ibid., Nov. 28, 1867, Feb. 2, June 7, 1868. AG to WCG, [Jan. 1868], F67, no. 1; JG to WCG, Jan. 30, 1868, F28, no. 1, Gorgas Family Papers.

39. JG to AG, Aug. 30, 1869, F15, no. 7; July 31, 1869, F15, no. 3; [Aug.] 1869, F15, no. 24; and Sept. 17, 1869, F15, no. 10, Gorgas Family Papers.

40. Ibid., Oct. 6, 1869, F15, no. 14; Oct. 22, [1869], F15, no. 16; and [Sept. 1869], F16, no. 26, Gorgas Family Papers.

41. JG to AG, enclosed as P.S. on letters of WCG to AG, Nov. 4, 1869, Feb. 1870, WCG Papers, UA. JG to AG, Feb. 28, 1870, F16, no. 2a, Gorgas Family Papers.

42. JG to WCG, Nov. 5, 1875, F28, no. 4; July 22, 1878, F28, no. 14; and Feb. 10, 1876, F28, no. 6, Gorgas Family Papers.

43. JG to AG, Apr. 8, 1870, F16, no. 10a, Gorgas Family Papers. Gorgas Journal, Aug. 20, 1871.

44. JG to AG, June 4, 1865, F11, no. 3, Gorgas Family Papers. Gorgas Journal, Jan. 7, July 10, 1867.

45. JG to AG, 1869, F15, no. 25; and Oct. 24, 1869, F16, no. 14, Gorgas Family Papers; WCG to Jessie Gorgas, Oct. 1, 1871, WCG Papers, UA. Gorgas Journal, Nov. 14, 1871.

46. Gorgas Journal, June 3, 1860.

47. WCG to Frank Polk, June 26, 1918, WCG Papers, UA.

48. See [AG to JG], [1865], F62, no. 10, Gorgas Family Papers.

49. Gibson, *Physician to the World*, pp. 21–22.

50. WCG to AG, Oct. 8, 1884, WCG Papers, UA. Gorgas Journal, Oct. 13, 1875.

51. AG to JG, [1869], F65, no. 7, Gorgas Family Papers.

52. JG to AG, Aug. 9, 1869, F15, no. 4; Aug. 11, 1869, F15, no. 5; [Sept. 1869], F16, no. 26; 1869, F15, no. 24; Mar. 23, 1870, F16, no. 6; and Oct. 2, 1869, F15, no. 13, Gorgas Family Papers.

53. For example, see AG to WCG, Feb. 15, 1876, F68, no. 4, Gorgas Family Papers.

54. AG to JG, June 2, [1869?], F65, no. 2; AG to WCG, [Fall 1875], F70, unnumbered, Gorgas Family Papers.

55. JG to AG, Feb. 7, 1876, F19, no. 11, Gorgas Family Papers. Years later Mamie's brother bluntly recalled the relationship as one that began during the siege of Richmond when Willie was nine and Mamie eight. "As the years went on he became more and more in love with her, while she, in love with life, tortured him by showing her preference for one rival after another." Willie's study of law with Bayne was to be near Mamie, and "he gave up the law only when he gave up trying to make her reciprocate his passion. She was a terrible flirt." Hugh A. Bayne Memoirs. Mamie married George Behn in Nov. 1877 in New Orleans.

56. AG to JG [Jan. 24, 1876], F19, no. 12; and [Jan. 24, 1876], F19, no. 13; AG to WCG, Feb. 9, 1876, F68, no. 1; and Feb. 13, 1876, F68, no. 3; JG to WCG, Feb. 10, 1876, F28, no. 6, Gorgas Family Papers.

57. Gorgas Journal, Oct. 13, 1875. JG to AG, Jan. 18, 1876, F19, no. 4; Jan. 22, 1876, F19, no. 6; Feb. 4, 1876, F19, no. 9; and Feb. 5, 1876, F19, no. 10; AG to WCG, n.d., F70, no. 8; n.d., F70, no. 9; and n.d., F69, no. 3, JG to WCG, Jan. 19, 1876, F28, no. 5, Gorgas Family Papers. WCG to AG, Oct. 8, 1884; John A. Campbell to U.S. Grant, n.d.; P.G.T. Beauregard to JG, Jan. 28, 1876, WCG Papers, UA.

58. JG to WCG, Feb. 10, 1876, F28, no. 6, Gorgas Family Papers.

59. AG to WCG, Feb. 9, 1876, F68, no. 1; and [1876], F68, no. 5; JG to AG, Feb. 4, 1876, F19, no. 9, Gorgas Family Papers.

60. JG to AG, Jan. 18, 1876, F19, no. 4; JG to WCG, Nov. 5, 1875, F28, no. 4; and Jan. 19, 1876, F28, no. 5, Gorgas Family Papers.

61. JG to AG, Jan. 22, 1876, F19, no. 6; and Feb. 4, 1876, F19, no. 9, Gorgas Family Papers.

62. Gorgas Journal, Oct. 29, 1876.

63. JG to WCG, Aug. 8, 1877, F28, no. 9; AG to WCG, [1877], F69, no. 1, Gorgas Family Papers.

64. JG to AG, Sept. 8, 1878, F20, no. 8; and [Nov. 14, 1878], F20, no. 60, Gorgas Family Papers.

65. JG to WCG, Dec. 8, 1878, F28, no. 19, Gorgas Family Papers.

66. Ibid., Jan. 16, 1879, F28, no. 20; and Mar. 9, 1877, F28, no. 8, Gorgas Family Papers.

67. Gorgas Journal, July 16, 1878, July 1, 1877 (located at end of journal out of order). Mary [Gayle Aiken] to My Dear Sister, July 22, 1878, Josiah Gorgas Papers, Archives, Univ. of the South, Sewanee, Tennessee. See Vandiver, *Ploughshares into Swords*, pp. 302–7, for a discussion of Josiah's problems at Sewanee and his move to Tuscaloosa.

68. AG to WCG, Mar. 8, 1879, F71, no. 4; and Feb. 27, 1879, F71, no. 3, Gorgas Family Papers.

69. Gorgas Journal, July 16, 1878.

70. JG to WCG, Dec. 8, 1878, F28, no. 19, Gorgas Family Papers. For a discussion of the image of the superfather and the role of the father in encouraging self-confidence and a desire for achievement in children, see Henry Biller and Dennis Meredith, *Father Power* (New York: David McKay Company, 1974), 110–16.

71. AG to WCG, Mar. 12, [1879], F72, no. 1; and Mar. 16, 1879, F72, no. 2, Gorgas Family Papers.

72. Ibid., Oct. 3, 1879, continuation of a letter of Richard H. Gorgas to WCG, Oct. 2, 1879, F71, no. 7; Apr. 4, 1880, F72, no. 3, Gorgas Family Papers.

73. Ibid., June 20, 1879, F71, no. 6, Gorgas Family Papers.

74. William Crawford Gorgas Account Books, 1880–1910 (4 vols.), Box 31, WCG Papers, LC. William Crawford Gorgas Account Books, 1877–1879, 1915–1919 (5 vols.), WCG Papers, UA. Amelia's household account books, 1883–1891, 1895–1902 (2 vols.), reflecting Willie's regular contributions to his mother's household are located in WCG Papers, UA. For examples of his support to his sisters, see WCG to Jessie Gorgas, June 3, 1893-May 26, 1920; WCG to Maria Gorgas, Oct. 3, 1919; WCG to Mary Gorgas, Aug. 27, 1913–Apr. 22, 1920, WCG Papers, UA.

75. WCG to Richard H. Gorgas, Aug. 31 and Dec. 7, 1879, WCG Papers, UA.

76. AG to WCG, Dec. 3, 1884, F73, no. 4, Gorgas Family Papers.

77. For studies of William Crawford Gorgas, see Gibson, *Physician to the World*; Gorgas and Hendrick, *William Crawford Gorgas*; David McCullough, "The Imperturbable Dr. Gorgas," in *The Path Between the Seas: The Creation of the Panama Canal 1870–1914* (New York: Simon and Schuster, 1977), 405–26.

78. JG to WCG, May 10, 1880, F28, no. 24, Gorgas Family Papers. Josiah Gorgas died on May 15, 1883.

Epilogue

1. Walter E. Houghton, *The Victorian Frame of Mind, 1830–1870* (New Haven: Yale Univ. Press, 1957), 341.

2. Elizabeth Fox-Genovese, *Within the Plantation Household: Black and White Women of the Old South* (Chapel Hill: Univ. of North Carolina Press, 1988), 38.

3. William Faulkner, *Absalom, Absalom!* (New York: Random House, 1936), 20.

Contributors

PETER W. BARDAGLIO is a professor of history at Goucher College. He has written several articles on Southern history and the history of American family law, the most recent of which is "Challenging Parental Custody Rights: The Legal Reconstruction of Parenthood in the Nineteenth-Century South," *Continuity and Change: A Journal of Social Structure, Law, and Demography in Past Societies*, vol. 4, no. 2 (1989). At present, he is working on a book-length study of families, sex, and the law in the nineteenth-century South for the Univ. of North Carolina Press.

CAROL BLESER is the Kathryn and Calhoun Lemon Distinguished Professor of History at Clemson University and was the initiator and organizer of the Fort Hill Conference on Southern Culture. A specialist in Southern history, Professor Bleser has published *Secret and Sacred: The Diaries of James Henry Hammond, a Southern Slaveholder* (Oxford Univ. Press, 1988), *The Hammonds of Redcliffe* (Oxford Univ. Press, 1981), and *The Promised Land: The History of the South Carolina Land Commission, 1869–1890* (Univ. of South Carolina Press, 1969). Carol Bleser is both a contributor of an essay and the editor of this volume. She is currently working on a book-length study of marriages in the mid-nineteenth-century South.

VIRGINIA I. BURR is an independent scholar with a particular interest in Southern history. She is focusing on her own family, including her great-grandmother Ella Gertrude Clanton Thomas, a nineteenth-century diarist and active feminist. Mrs. Burr has edited the Ella Gertrude Clanton Thomas journals, *The Secret Eye,* which was published by the Univ. of North Carolina Press in the spring of 1990.

CATHERINE CLINTON is a visiting professor of African-American studies at Harvard University. She is the author of *The Other Civil War: American Women in the Nineteenth Century* (Hill & Wang, 1984) and *The Plantation Mistress: Woman's World in the Old South* (Pantheon, 1982). Professor Clinton and G. J. Barker-Benfield are the general editors of a new work published in 1990 by St. Martin's Press, *Portraits of American Women*. She is at work on a biographical study based on Fanny Kemble's journals to be published by Harvard Univ. Press.

327

DREW GILPIN FAUST is the Stanley Sheerr Professor of History at the University of Pennsylvania. She is the author of *The Creation of Confederate Nationalism* (Louisiana State Univ. Press, 1988), *James Henry Hammond and the Old South: A Design for Mastery* (Louisiana State Univ. Press, 1982), and *A Sacred Circle: The Dilemma of the Intellectual in the Old South* (Johns Hopkins Univ. Press, 1977). Professor Faust is presently at work on a study of Confederate women.

ELIZABETH FOX-GENOVESE is the Eleonore Raoul Professor of the Humanities and director of women's studies at Emory University. Her publications include: *Within the Plantation Household: Black and White Women of the Old South* (Univ. of North Carolina Press, 1988); with Eugene D. Genovese, *Fruits of Merchant Capital: Slavery and Bourgeois Property in the Rise and Expansion of Capitalism* (Oxford Univ. Press, 1983); and *The Origins of Physiocracy: Economic Revolution and Social Order in Eighteenth-Century France* (Cornell Univ. Press, 1976). She is currently working on a collection of essays, *Feminism Without Illusion* (Univ. of North Carolina Press), and with Eugene D. Genovese on *The Mind of the Master Class* (under contract with W.W. Norton).

EUGENE D. GENOVESE is a Distinguished Scholar in Residence at the University Center in Georgia. He is a specialist in the history of the Old South and the author of six books: *Fruits of Merchant Capital: Slavery and Bourgeois Property in the Rise and Expansion of Capitalism*, with Elizabeth Fox-Genovese (Oxford Univ. Press, 1983); *From Rebellion to Revolution: Afro-American Slave Revolts in the Making of the Modern World* (Louisiana State Univ. Press, 1979); *Roll, Jordan, Roll: The World the Slaves Made* (Pantheon, 1974); *In Red and Black: Marxian Explorations in Southern and Afro-American History* (Pantheon, 1971); *The World the Slaveholders Made: Two Essays in Interpretation* (Pantheon, 1969); and *The Political Economy of Slavery: Studies in the Economy and Society of the Slave South* (Pantheon, 1965). He is currently working on a book, *The Mind of the Master Class* (under contract with W.W. Norton), with Elizabeth Fox-Genovese.

ALAN GRUBB is a professor of history at Clemson University, and has received two W.K. Kellogg Foundation grants (1985 and 1986) for a study to utilize cookbooks as social historical documents. He also organized a symposium at Clemson University, "Food and Society." He is currently completing a study of Mrs. Isabella Beeton, the popular nineteenth-century British cookbook author.

FREDERICK M. HEATH is a professor of history at Winthrop College. A former chairman of the Department of History at Winthrop, the South Carolina Department of Archives and History Commission, and the South Carolina Board of Review of Historic Places, he has published on the history of Progressivism in Connecticut, the era of Prohibition in South Carolina, and other topics. His research in recent years has been concentrated on gender roles in the Old South.

JACQUELINE JONES is a professor and department chair of history at Wellesley College. She is the author of *Labor of Love, Labor of Sorrow: Black Women, Work, and the Family from Slavery to the Present* (Basic Books, 1985) and *Soldiers of Light and Love: Northern Teachers and Georgia Blacks, 1865–1873* (Univ. of North Carolina Press, 1980). Professor Jones is working currently on a book to be entitled, *Families in Search of Work: Southern Sharecroppers and Seasonal and Migratory Laborers, 1865 to the Present.*

MICHAEL P. JOHNSON is a professor of history at the University of California, Irvine. He is the co-author with James L. Roark of *Black Masters: A Free Family of Color in the Old South* (W.W. Norton, 1984) and *No Chariot Let Down: Charleston's Free People of Color on the Eve of the Civil War* (Univ. of North Carolina Press, 1984). Professor Johnson published *Toward a Patriarchal Republic: The Secession of Georgia* (Louisiana State Univ. Press) in 1977. He is currently working with co-authors Patricia Cohen, James Roark, Sarah Stage, and Alan Lawson on *The American Experience: A History of the United States* (Houghton Mifflin) and *White Hands: White Workers in Southern Cities, 1780–1880*, and with co-author David Rankin on *The Master Class: Slaveholders in the United States, 1790–1860.*

JAMES L. ROARK is the Samuel Candler Dobbs Professor of American History at Emory University. He is the co-author with Michael P. Johnson of *Black Masters: A Free Family of Color in the Old South* (W.W. Norton, 1984) and *No Chariot Let Down: Charleston's Free People of Color on the Eve of the Civil War* (Univ. of North Carolina Press, 1984), and author of *Masters Without Slaves: Southern Planters in the Civil War and Reconstruction* (W.W. Norton, 1977). Professor Roark is presently working with co-authors Patricia Cohen, Michael Johnson, Sarah Stage, and Alan Lawson on *The American Experience: A History of the United States* (Houghton Mifflin) and *White Hands: White Workers in Southern Cities, 1780–1880.*

ANNE FIROR SCOTT is the William K. Boyd Professor of History at Duke University. She is the author of *Making the Invisible Woman Visible* (Univ. of Illinois Press, 1984); editor of *Women in American Life* (Houghton Mifflin, 1979); co-author with Libby A. Cater of *Women and Men* (Praeger, 1977); and co-author with Andrew McKay Scott of *One Half the People* (Lippincott, 1975; Harper & Row, 1979; reissued by Univ. of Illinois Press, 1983). She also authored *The American Woman: Who Was She* (Prentice-Hall, 1970), and *The Southern Lady: From Pedestal to Politics, 1830–1930* (Univ. of Chicago Press, 1970).

BRENDA STEVENSON is a professor of history at the University of California, Los Angeles. She is the editor and annotator of *The Journals of Charlotte Forten Grimké* (Oxford Univ. Press, 1988) and is currently working on a comparative study of black and white families in antebellum Virginia, and on a history of slavery in Virginia from the colonial to the antebellum period.

WYLMA WATES is senior archivist at the South Carolina Department of Archives and History, where she has guided a generation of scholars through sources in South Carolina history. For the Archives, she edited three volumes: *Stub Entries to Indents Issued in Payment of Claims Growing out of the Revolution*; (with others) *Extracts from the Journals of the Provincial Congresses, 1775–1776*; and *Journals of the General Assembly and House of Representatives, 1776–1780.* Her articles in the field of women's and family history include "Charleston Orphans 1790–1795" and

"James L. Petigru and the Revolutionary War Widow: The Petition of Christiana Teulon." She retired in June 1990.

SARAH WOOLFOLK WIGGINS is a professor of history at the University of Alabama and is editor of *The Alabama Review*. She compiled *From Civil War to Civil Rights: Alabama, 1860–1960* (Univ. of Alabama Press, 1987) and edited "As I Saw It: One Woman's Account of the Fall of Richmond," by Amelia Gorgas. She is the author of *The Scalawag in Alabama Politics, 1865–1881* (Univ. of Alabama Press, 1977) and the "Introduction" to John M. Gibson, *Physician to the World: The Life of General William C. Gorgas* (Univ. of Alabama Press, 1989; orig. pub. by Duke Univ. Press, 1950). Professor Wiggins is currently editing the diaries of Josiah Gorgas, 1857–1878, and is writing an essay that focuses on Amelia Gorgas and her children.

C. VANN WOODWARD is Sterling Professor of History Emeritus at Yale University. He is one of the foremost historians of the United States and has written six books on the South: *Tom Watson: Agrarian Rebel* (Rinehart and Company, 1938), *Reunion and Reaction: The Compromise of 1877 and the End of Reconstruction* (Little, Brown, 1966), *Origins of the New South, 1877–1913* (Louisiana State Univ. Press, 1951), *The Strange Career of Jim Crow* (Oxford Univ. Press, 1955), *The Burden of Southern History* (Louisiana State Univ. Press, 1960), and *American Counterpoint: Slavery and Racism in the North-South Dialogue* (Little, Brown, 1971). Among the books he has edited is *Mary Chesnut's Civil War* (Yale Univ. Press, 1981), for which he received a Pulitzer Prize. His most recent publication is *The Future of the Past*, published in 1989 by Oxford Univ. Press.

BERTRAM WYATT-BROWN is the Richard J. Milbauer Professor of History at the University of Florida. He is the author of *Yankee Saints and Southern Sinners* (Louisiana State Univ. Press, 1985) and *Southern Honor: Ethics and Behavior in the Old South* (Oxford Univ. Press, 1982); editor of *The American People in the Antebellum South* (Pendulum Press, 1973); and author of *Lewis Tappan and the Evangelical War Against Slavery* (Case Western Reserve Univ. Press, 1969). Professor Wyatt-Brown has two books in preparation, *Slavery, Race and Honor* (to be published by Alfred Knopf) and *Lost Innocence: Ethics and Behavior in the Modern South*.